FEMALE HUSBANDS

Long before people identified as transgender or lesbian, there were female husbands and the women who loved them. Female husbands – people assigned female who transed gender, lived as men, and married women – were true queer pioneers. Moving deftly from the colonial era to just before World War I, Jen Manion uncovers the riveting and very personal stories of ordinary people who lived as men despite tremendous risk, danger, and threat of violence. *Female Husbands* weaves the story of their lives in relation to broader social, economic, and political developments in the United States and the United Kingdom while also exploring how attitudes toward female husbands shifted in relation to transformations in gender politics and women's rights, ultimately leading to the demise of the category of "female husband" in the early twentieth century. Groundbreaking and influential, *Female Husbands* offers a dynamic, varied, and complex history of the LGBTQ past.

Jen Manion is Associate Professor of History at Amherst College, the author of *Liberty's Prisoners: Carceral Culture in Early America* (2015), and a lifelong LGBTQ rights advocate.

FEMALE HUSBANDS

A Trans History

Jen Manion

Amherst College, Massachusetts

CAMBRIDGE
UNIVERSITY PRESS

CAMBRIDGE
UNIVERSITY PRESS

University Printing House, Cambridge CB2 8BS, United Kingdom

One Liberty Plaza, 20th Floor, New York, NY 10006, USA

477 Williamstown Road, Port Melbourne, VIC 3207, Australia

314–321, 3rd Floor, Plot 3, Splendor Forum, Jasola District Centre,
New Delhi – 110025, India

79 Anson Road, #06–04/06, Singapore 079906

Cambridge University Press is part of the University of Cambridge.

It furthers the University's mission by disseminating knowledge in the pursuit of
education, learning, and research at the highest international levels of excellence.

www.cambridge.org
Information on this title: www.cambridge.org/9781108483803
DOI: 10.1017/9781108652834

First published 2020

First paperback edition 2021

A catalogue record for this publication is available from the British Library.

Library of Congress Cataloging-in-Publication Data
Names: Manion, Jen, 1974– author.
Title: Female husbands : a trans history / Jen Manion.
Description: Cambridge, United Kingdom ; New York, NY : Cambridge University
Press, 2020. | Includes index.
Identifiers: LCCN 2019038186 (print) | LCCN 2019038187 (ebook) |
ISBN 9781108483803 (hardback) | ISBN 9781108718271 (paperback) |
ISBN 9781108652834 (epub)
Subjects: LCSH: Female-to-male transsexuals–History. | Transgender men–History. |
Husbands–History. | Gender nonconformity–History.
Classification: LCC HQ77.9 .M26 2020 (print) | LCC HQ77.9 (ebook) |
DDC 306.76/809–dc23
LC record available at https://lccn.loc.gov/2019038186
LC ebook record available at https://lccn.loc.gov/2019038187

ISBN 978-1-108-48380-3 Hardback
ISBN 978-1-10871827-1 Paperback

For Leslie Feinberg
(1949 – 2014)

CONTENTS

ACKNOWLEDGMENTS

I AM SO GRATEFUL TO THOSE FRIENDS AND COLLEAGUES who have been excited about this project from the beginning.

A generous grant from the National Endowment for the Humanities allowed me to spend a semester at the American Antiquarian Society (AAS). AAS staff and curators went above and beyond in helping me identify a usable archive of newspapers, books, magazines, and children's literature including Ashley Cataldo, Vincent Golden, Lauren Hewes, Elizabeth Watts Pope, Kimberly Tony, and Laura Wasowicz. Then Director of Academic Programs Paul Erickson ensured every scholarly gathering was both generative and fun with his humor, smarts, and savvy. An Andrew Mellon Foundation Fellowship from the Massachusetts Historical Society enabled early research on women's rights, education, and abolition with great support from then Director of Research Conrad Wright.

Several Research Matters Grants from Connecticut College funded exploratory research trips to New York Public Library, San Francisco State University Archives, and the Library Company of Philadelphia (LCP). I am continually grateful to Connie King from LCP for her thoughtful engagement with the project and ongoing support for bringing LGBTQ history to life. A New England Regional Fellowship Consortium Research Grant gave me the opportunity to travel to numerous state archives including Maine Historical Society, Rhode Island Historical Society, and Vermont Historical Society, allowing me to survey a variety of nineteenth-century organizational and carceral records from these wonderful places. Andrew Lott at London Metropolitan Archives helped me find sources I never would have found on my own.

An Amherst College Trustee Faculty Fellowship supported a sabbatical year in which I completed most of the research and some of the writing. Jane Kamensky generously invited me to be a Research Associate in the Department of History at Harvard University during my sabbatical year to facilitate my research. The Research Grant at the Schlesinger Library on the History of Women in America allowed me to examine writings by key feminist writers on a variety of subjects including medicine, education, labor, and women's rights activism. The Slavery, Abolition, and Resistance Fellowship from the Gilder Lehrman Center at Yale University helped me think through connections between slavery, abolition, carceral practices, and transing gender.

I am still amazed and grateful that these organizations have funded this unconventional project in transgender, queer, and feminist history. Many people who have done important dissertations in LGBTQ history have not gotten the institutional support (in the form of fellowships or jobs) needed to finish their books.

This project benefited from generous engagement by colleagues across the country from the earliest stages until the bitter end. I am grateful for the opportunity to present the findings at the Nineteenth Century US History Workshop at Brown, the McNeil Center for Early American Studies at Penn, the Yale Research Initiative on the History of Sexualities, the Humanities Action Lab and Department of History at the New School, the Alice Paul Center for Research on Gender, Sexuality, and Women at Penn, the Department of African American Studies at Wesleyan University, the Francis A. Countway Library of Medicine at Harvard, the Stanford Humanities Center, the Rothermere American Institute at Oxford, and the Five Colleges History Seminar. Each of these talks gave me a chance to test arguments and receive so much amazing, thoughtful feedback.

It has been an honor to join the history department at Amherst College, especially during Biddy Martin's presidency. Amherst has generously supported my work in countless ways, including funding research trips to nearly a dozen archives. Thank you to Dean Catherine Epstein and Austin Sarat for often saying "yes." Amherst students Daniel Lee, Sydney Tate, Isabel Tessier, and Elliot Van provided research assistance and important insights. Thank you to Amrita Basu, Nellie Boucher, Nicola Courtright, Frank Couvares, Judy Frank, Tariq Jaffer, Sheila Jaswal, Rick Lopez, Ted Melilo, Monica Ringer, Sean Redding, Karen Sanchez-Eppler, Adam Sitze, and Martha Umphery for being friends and colleagues in all the best ways.

Several colleagues read parts of the book at various stages. This is the invisible labor of academic life and friendship which makes all of our scholarship better. Thanks to Kathy Brown, Brian Connolly, Bruce Dorsey, Richard Godbeer, Nancy Hewitt, Sarah Knott, Joanne Meyerowitz, Claire Potter, Lizzie Reis, Dan Richter, and Nick Syrett. I have learned so much in talking this project through with Jessica Halem, Kathy Brown, and Ann Fabian. I still can't believe that Jan Lewis is no longer with us but I thought of her often as I debated whether I needed to keep doing research for this book. Jan once told me if the new findings affirm what you already know and don't change your argument, then are you done. She said it much more eloquently than that.

I can't thank Cecelia Cancellaro of Word Literary enough for helping me get the book into shape, clarifying its argument, and finding it a great home at Cambridge University Press. It has already been a pleasure getting to know the team at Cambridge who will bring this book into the world. Debbie Gershenowitz gave this manuscript the best read an author could ask for in balancing critique, curiosity, and encouragement. It has meant the world to me throughout this process that Cecelia and Debbie get that this is a work of love for and about the LGBTQ community as much as it is a conventional history book.

One day, Jessica Halem declared that I was her female husband. Why hadn't we thought of that sooner? It was the perfect category for me as someone assigned female who happily took on many of the responsibilities typically expected of husbands. Being her female husband is my greatest joy, as I aspire to be worthy of all the love and laughter she has brought into my life.

INTRODUCTION: EXTRAORDINARY LIVES

I N 1746, CHARLES HAMILTON OF GLASTONBURY, England found what they were looking for – Mary, a curious young woman who was taken by their charms. With the approval of the girl's aunt, the pair were joined in marriage and set off on a honeymoon. Hamilton had little money and no family. But they were resourceful, determined, and charismatic. They offered Mary companionship and adventure. As someone who was assigned female at birth, Hamilton became known as a female husband. Nearly one hundred years later and across the Atlantic, the *Journal of Commerce* ran a story called, "Extraordinary Case of a Female Husband." Scottish immigrant George Wilson was found passed out on the streets of New York's Lower East Side. A policeman took them into the station. Wilson was just another poor laborer who drank too much after a long day of work. But as someone who was raised as a girl and now lived as a man, they were incredibly vulnerable to harassment, violence, and punishment at the hands of the authorities.

Hamilton, Wilson, and dozens of others like them were designated "female husbands" – a term that persistently circulated throughout Anglo-American culture for nearly 200 years to describe people who defied categorization. Though assigned female at birth, female husbands assumed a legal, social, and economic position reserved for men: that of husband. Female husbands were presented as shocking and controversial figures, often with headlines featuring the word "extraordinary." By their very existence, they challenged essentialist understandings of sexual difference. They demonstrated by their actions every day that gender was malleable and not a result of one's sex. In their ability to flirt, charm, and attract female wives, they threatened the stability of the

1

institution of heterosexual marriage. They lived lives that in contemporary terms might be described as transgender, nonbinary, butch, lesbian, bisexual, or asexual. They were often said to have assumed the "character of a man."

Female Husbands: A Trans History follows the category of the "female husband" from its origin in 1746 through its demise just before World War I. The book highlights the very fact that people assigned female at birth chose to trans gender and live fully as men, in small towns and big cities, in the UK and the US. They found joy and love in intimate partnerships with women, often entering into legal marriages recognized by the state. These relationships set them apart from the numerous other groups who transed genders for work, war, and adventure. Female husbands were defined by both their marriages to women and their chosen occupations. People persisted in living as men despite tremendous risk, danger, violence, and punishment. Punishment often involved the forced surrender of one's gender expression – even if just momentarily until they were in a new town, outside of the gaze of local authorities. When husbands were outed as being assigned female at birth, newspapers were often the first to spread the word throughout the community. The press reported such accounts enthusiastically and frequently, exposing dynamic, contested, and varied stories of love, courage, risk, loss, and sadness. I utilize these accounts to offer a rigorous social history of the lives lived by female husbands as well as a cultural history of the category of the "female husband."[1]

Female Husbands shows how the meaning of what seemed like a self-evident category changed over time. Beginning in England in the mid-eighteenth century, female husbands lived full time as men and entered legal, seemingly heterosexual marriages with women. One of the most celebrated and stable relationships was that of James and Mary Howe who together ran the White Horse Tavern in the Poplar neighborhood of London's East End for decades. While the couple were held in great esteem by the community and acquired significant wealth for working people, even James shared the same fate of every female husband featured in this book: none were permitted to continue going about their lives in their chosen gender expression once the community determined they were assigned female at birth. Gender conformity itself was the punishment required by authorities and neighbors alike.

While much was made about why and how people assigned female at birth transformed themselves into men, the female lovers who married them are equally intriguing. Female wives were sometimes portrayed as innocent victims of deception, though they were often active participants who knowingly and happily chose to enter these unconventional partnerships. Sometimes female wives disavowed their husbands, declaring ignorance about their lovers' sex. Female wives of female husbands are often overlooked and neglected as queer figures of the past. The newspaper record of such relationships has shaped this sexism, as accounts often don't even include the wives' names. Despite this public erasure, female wives held a tremendous amount of power in their marriages (especially for the time) because they could publicly denounce their husband's gender at any time. Wives were known to do this under two circumstances: when they were surprised to find out their husband was female or when their husband denied them a divorce on favorable terms. There is no denying that female wives gave legitimacy and stability to the gender of female husbands in the eyes of co-workers, friends, and society.

Female husbands were primarily viewed through the lens of gender – given their claim to manhood – until the middle decades of the nineteenth century. Around mid-century, views and representations of female husbands began to change. The UK press largely lost interest in such stories, possibly because they occurred less frequently but probably because the concept had run its course as an attention-grabbing headline that sold papers. The US press grew by leaps and bounds during this era and adopted this longstanding British custom as its own. In US newspapers in the 1840s and 1850s, female husbands were seen as a part of the growing women's rights movement. In the 1870s, they were associated with poverty and vagrancy. By the 1880s, they were cast as precursors to and legitimizers of same-sex relationships. Accounts of female husbands in the news increasingly emphasized sex over gender – arguing that those assigned female were really women and therefore could not be husbands.

Authorities remained uncertain about how to react to those who transed gender and often struggled to determine if any laws were broken. Countless people who were arrested for transing gender later explained that they were released because they had not broken any law. Female husbands presented a particular conundrum for authorities charged with determining the basis of their wrongdoing. Was it because someone assigned female lived as a man? Or because the marriage legitimized sexual relations between the two? Or because two women were not allowed to marry? Even when authorities weren't clear about the exact wrong committed by a female husband and their wife, they knew it was up to them to get to the bottom of a situation and decide. In this process, they reveal to us how they understood sexual difference and why the social conventions of gender were important to them.

In the 1880s and 1890s, accounts of female husbands exploded in the US, as those assigned female at birth who lived as men and married women were increasingly visible. The press still found these stories newsworthy. The catchy "female husband" headline, however, was used in reference to a wider range of people and circumstances, diluting its meaning. For instance, someone assigned male at birth who lived as a man was accused by their wife of being a "female husband" in an attempt to secure a divorce. Another writer wondered, given the rise of heterosexual married women in the workforce, if in fact "females" made good husbands and could be entrusted with such duties. One-half of a couple who lived openly as women in a same-sex relationship also earned the designation, as the concept lost its association with female masculinity, conflict, and duality. By the turn of the twentieth century, female husband was no longer a clear signifier of manhood and transing.

*****

I came out as a lesbian in 1994. It was something I had recently figured out and felt excited about sharing with others. To my surprise, several people said they "had suspected" as much or had "always known." How could they have known it when I didn't? It quickly became clear that the basis for their remarks had nothing to do with my sexuality, per se, and everything to do with gender. When I came out as a lesbian, it *seemed* to explain my lifelong refusal to conform to expectations for people raised

4

as girls. For as long as I can remember, I was interested in the activities and clothes that were generally reserved for boys. I was largely met with judgment, shame, and punishment for these tendencies, yet I persisted. But in 1994, my gender nonconformity was seen as proof or evidence of my homosexuality; I made sense.

The association between gender nonconformity and homosexuality was argued by numerous sexologists around the turn of the twentieth century. They used the phrase "sexual invert" to describe people who were attracted to members of the same sex while also exhibiting gender characteristics of the other sex. It was anchored in a heteronormative framework, presuming that for someone to have same-sex desire, they had to shift (or invert) their gender identification. In this model, as I often tell my students, people like me were seen as "true" homosexuals while those who conformed to gender norms were not seen as homosexuals. Feminine and/or femme women were thought to be victims of circumstance, deception, or seduction.

My students generally find all of this shocking, hilarious, and/or upsetting, for a variety of reasons. When I offer open acknowledgment of my gender in this way, it gives students permission to laugh and sigh; *to know what they see, but have been taught not to see.* Somewhere along the way, most of them determined that anyone could be gay (regardless of gender expression) and that it was stereotyping and homophobic to equate female masculinity with homosexuality. There is a view that homosexuality transcends – rather than incorporates – gender. Gender conversations are increasingly relegated to self-disclosing transgender and nonbinary subjects.

In the one hundred and some odd years since sexologists fused gender nonconformity with homosexuality, we have learned the limits and bias of this view. LGBTQ organizations now argue that gender is distinct from sexual orientation, one having no bearing on the other. This allows that transgender people might be straight – or gay, bi, pan, or queer. It allows that people who *seem to conform* to gender norms can still be queer – or lesbian, gay, bi, or pan. This logic fights against centuries of stereotyping that conflates male effeminacy or female masculinity with homosexuality. It resists the privileging of trans people who identify as straight after transitioning over those who identify as gay. Scholars and activists have challenged and shown the flaws in this early research by sexologists. How does this book speak to these questions?

Anyone reading old newspapers with some frequency will eventually run into one or more accounts of people transing gender. For years, friends and colleagues sent me such clippings, knowing of my interest in learning more about gender nonconformity and same-sex desire in the past. I knew there were many such accounts in nineteenth-century newspapers that are filled with contradictions. At the very least, I suspected they would offer ample evidence of a wide variety of gender variant experiences and expressions. I was not sure how sexuality would figure in such accounts, but I knew there was a "pre" story to be told about the argument that gender nonconformity was the sign of same-sex desire in women.

Because most people assigned female at birth had so little access to economic advancement, educational achievement, or legal autonomy, no one was surprised when they claimed the rights and privileges reserved for men – especially white men. This idea was logical to men who believed themselves to be superior to women; they could easily reconcile why – in their eyes – a woman would want to be a man.[2] In this equation, being a man meant social, economic, and political power. Some men accepted this, others mocked it, and still others rejected it, but they had a clear framework for understanding why someone assigned female at birth might want to live as a man. This explanation, however, is too simple.

As we shall see, by centering the lives of female husbands and contextualizing them in relation to accounts of others who transed genders, new patterns emerge. In the case of female husbands in particular, it is impossible to isolate economic and social power from gender and sexual freedom. Sexual freedom – including the freedom to have sex with women, to not have sex with men, or to not have sex at all – was at the heart of the vast range of social powers that accompanied manhood. And, tragically, it was a key practice for which female husbands were punished.

Female husband accounts offer us a window into the historic construction of sexual difference as well as precious evidence about what it meant for someone assigned female at birth to live as a husband.[3] Female husbands invite us to grapple with what exactly gender is.[4] Female

6

Figure I.1 B. Cole, "A True Representation of a Printing House with the Men at Work," 1752. The expansion of the popular press facilitated the spread of stories of female husbands.
Image courtesy of the Lewis Walpole Library, Yale University

husbands challenged notions of sexual difference, refusing total coherence and stability for both heterosexuality and the categories of "male" and "female." They exposed what was to remain hidden and revealed the incoherence of something that was supposed to be clear. For this, they were deemed social outliers and marginalized historic subjects.

It turns out that newspapers played a crucial role in the circulation of information about female husbands (Figure I.1). In the eighteenth century, they reported a wide variety of local, regional, and even international news. In choosing the tone, length, and section for any given story, editors crafted narratives that gave meaning to events. The newspaper became even more influential than books or theater in the nineteenth century with the rise of the daily paper. The public life of print culture was expansive, as people shared copies of papers and read stories aloud in pubs, coffee houses, reading circles, boarding houses, boarding schools, shop floors, and lending libraries. There is no reason to believe that cost presented a barrier to working and poor people's access to the news, given this very public and collective nature of news consumption.[5]

By printing news of female husbands, the press asserted the inclusion of this group in civil society. All types of British newspapers reported on female husbands, from late eighteenth-century dailies devoted to advertising, such as *Public Advertiser* and *General Advertiser*, to the established papers aimed at middle-class interests, including the *Morning Post*, the *Morning Chronicle*, and the *Standard*, to cheap late nineteenth-century weeklies, such as *Tit-Bits*. The North American press was no more discriminate. Features about female husbands can be found in eighteenth-century stalwarts the *Pennsylvania Gazette* and the *Pennsylvania Packet* and in every imaginable local and regional paper amid the mid-nineteenth-century press explosion. The *New York Times* ran stories in the 1870s that included more fiction and were less reliable than small-town upstate papers. Though the widely popular men's sporting tabloid the *National Police Gazette* began to regularly feature such accounts in the 1880s, they were no more detailed or scandalous than accounts published in mainstream dailies for over a hundred years. The nearly indiscriminate and continuous reprinting of accounts across colonial and national borders signaled both fascination and concern about sexual difference, gender roles, and marriage.[6]

Beyond newspapers, a variety of print sources made transing gender even more visible and normalized for eighteenth- and nineteenth-century readers. Books, pamphlets, and dime novels seldom referenced female husbands in particular, but these publications established context for gender transing generally. Political magazines and religious sermons expanded the conversation about acceptable gender by invoking the adjective "masculine" as a slur to criticize women involved in any number of activist endeavors, especially concerning the abolition of slavery and women's rights generally. Police reports featured those arrested for transing gender, raising broad public awareness of such practices while criminalizing them in the process. Together, these print sources both captured and further advanced a robust public debate about what kinds of gender expressions and rights were desirable, possible, or tolerable.[7]

For better and for worse, the history of gender and sexuality has been shaped by modern concepts and categories. This has led to an abundance of powerful and important books documenting contemporary LGBTQ communities, especially when the subjects of study concern the post-1950s era. Histories of earlier periods are less legible as explicitly "queer" histories. Our contemporary belief that gender and sexuality are identities that individuals articulate has dramatically skewed our view of the long-ago past. We are less interested in the significance of rebellion against systemic gender norms in the absence of a declaration of selfhood. We are less able to even see such expressions when the words used to describe them do not line up with our current vocabularies.

For this reason, the origins of modern lesbian identities have long been debated. European historians generally point to the late eighteenth century, focusing on women who were sexually attracted exclusively to other women and adopted some "masculine behaviors" so that they might be noticed (think Anne Lister of the BBC/HBO show *Gentleman Jack*). This "sapphist" paradigm excluded feminine women who also had sexual involvement with men, as well as those who lived as men and were referred to as "passing women."[8] There is no place for female husbands and female wives as queer ancestors in this sapphic paradigm. An important body of work in both British and US history charts intimate friendships between gender-conforming women throughout the nineteenth century as historic antecedents to modern lesbianism.[9] Somewhere along the line, it became common practice for scholars to *minimize* gender differences and to *elevate* same-sex attraction as the driving force behind such partnerships. If one person was masculine or seemed to embrace men's clothing and character, this gender expression was seen as a means to an end – a relationship with a woman. The scholarship on female husbands follows this same logic, emphasizing sex and minimizing gender.[10] Just where female husbands stand on a lesbian to transgender continuum is unclear and in many ways depends on the particular case. Jack Halberstam wrote, "While it is true that transgender and transsexual men have been wrongly folded into lesbian history, it is also true that the distinctions between some transsexuals and lesbians may at times become quite blurry."[11] In other words, it can be impossible to make accurate generalizations about the border between gender and sexuality or the border between genders.

Until relatively recently, judges willfully refused to speak of same-sex intimacies, denying us legal verification in cases that were public; diarists and letter-writers self-censored and wrote in euphemisms and analogies, offering us suggestions easily disputed by historians; family guardians and archivists would further purge evidence that might scandalize a reputation when offering papers to a historical society. Records were never meant to provide information about illicit non-procreative sexualities. The fact that historians continue to argue that the absence of such evidence constitutes its nonexistence reveals the limits of historical method and the lie of objectivity. Maybe it is time that we embrace – rather than continue to fight – the ephemeral nature of sex, especially the way that illicit, non-normative, non-procreative sex eludes the archives' reach, refusing any notion of certainty or permanence.

Female Husbands attempts to do just that, exploring the complex role played by the female husband in the changing understanding of sexual difference as well as the emergence of heterosexuality as an ideal relationship form. It principally explores the relationship between sex and gender, while examining sexuality secondarily. Throughout, I show that female husbands belonged to a category that was never simply woman or man. It was effectively a trans position, in one way or another, affirmed through accounts that move back and forth between masculine and feminine descriptors and male and female pronouns. Female husbands were put into a political category when they were outed; they did not control the narratives that were crafted about them. Gender is relational, external, and often out of our control. Female husband narratives attest to the importance of external recognition in defining and stabilizing gender.

Accounts of the past nakedly demonstrate this dynamic of external recognition. With each passing sentence about the men of this town or the women of that city, the categories are rendered natural and a simple gender binary is reproduced. Though often qualified by racial, class, occupation, and family status descriptors, man and woman still stand as the solid nouns, further obscuring the multiplicities and instabilities of the past.[12] This book aspires to grapple with the challenge of documenting the pasts of those subjects who are beyond categorical recognition and language, embracing the role of gendered language – from names to pronouns to social groupings – which has taken front and center stage as a critical practice of transgender recognition and affirmation.[13]

Transgender studies and community practice have revolutionized our understanding and usage of gendered language, offering us a powerful new intellectual toolkit for examining gender in the past.[14] Rather than privilege any notion of the sex assigned at birth as a benchmark of gender truth, this book engages the gender that people embraced, negotiated, and became during their lives. Susan Stryker pioneered the notion that transgender refers to "people who move away from the gender they were assigned at birth," offering an expansive and nonidentitarian view that has paved the way for historical research.[15] As such I use the concept of "trans" as a verb, a practice most notably brought to life by Clare Sears in their work to redirect the reader "away from the recognizable cross-dressing *figure* to multiple forms of cross-dressing *practices*."[16] To say someone "transed" or was "transing" gender signifies a process or practice without claiming to understand what it meant to that person or asserting any kind of fixed identity on them. In this way, we might view the subjects of this book as traveling through life, establishing an ongoing and ever-unfolding relationship with gender, rather than viewing them as simply shifting between two unchanging binaries. Examining lives unfolding over time, we can consider how circumstance, age, and prior experiences with gender influenced their present and future decisions – as well as how others perceived these changes.

What motivated someone assigned female at birth to decide to live as a man remains one of the most elusive dimensions of the stories that fill this book. It is easy for a modern reader to ascribe a transgender subjectivity to the female husbands, given our contemporary notions of gender identity. It might be that simple – that some or even all of the female husbands had a sense of themselves as male and decided to live as men in order to bring their external lives into alignment with their spirits. This is one explanation. But as a historian, it is my mission to try to understand how female husbands understood themselves and were perceived by others in the terms defining gender and sexual difference that were available to them during their own lifetimes. Fellow historian

Joanne Meyerowitz offers the following insight about terminology and self-determination: "Like everyone else, they articulated their sense of self with language and cultural forms available to them."[17] This approach allows for expansive and compassionate inquiry and understanding, something every subject deserves.

* * *

The book is divided into two parts. In Part I, we see the introduction of the concept of the female husband in Great Britain and the definition of two principal tropes: one that focuses on sexual desire and intimacy, another on respectable manhood and patriarchy. Accounts of husbands were read in relation to narratives of sailors and soldiers published at the same time. Together, these texts explained how someone assigned female could live as a man as well as some of the barriers that made this challenging and led to their outing. In the 1820s and 1830s, such accounts shed particular light on the female wives, interrogating these relationships. This recognition of wives was threatening, as seemingly any woman might be drawn to a female husband of their own. While the US press widely circulated these accounts, the husbands featured all lived in the UK. After 1840, there are far fewer instances of female husbands in the British press.

In Part II, we mark the appearance of female husbands in the United States in the 1830s. The issue of work and geographic mobility features prominently in all of these cases, as industrialization transformed home and work for people of all genders on both sides of the Atlantic. Both the British and North American press recirculated modified accounts of earlier female husbands while reporting on accounts of new husbands in the antebellum US. One husband – Albert Guelph – created a bridge across time and place. They were first designated a female husband in 1853 for their marriage in Westminster, England and again for their 1856 marriage in Syracuse, New York. Both US and UK papers were taken with news of Guelph's first marriage, reprinting it dozens of times, but UK papers showed little interest in Guelph's second marriage (of which US papers could not get enough). Guelph's case and others in this era became a focal point for debates over women's rights and laws regulating dress.

In the 1880s and 1890s, husbands peaked in the US press. In this period, there were more female husbands noted in the US than ever before. Simultaneously, however, the category lost its meaning as it was used to describe a wide variety of people and relationships.[18]

Accounts of female husbands in eighteenth- and nineteenth-century newspapers, magazines, and pamphlets were haphazard, contradictory, and unpredictable. They raised questions about everything from sexual difference and intersex conditions to gender identity and women's rights to marriage and same-sex intimacy. They recognized the legitimacy of husbands and then challenged their manhood. They judged female wives on the basis of their own reputations in the community along with whether or not they claimed to have known that their husbands were female. They provided a critique of women for stepping out of line but also offered instruction for men to be better workers, citizens, and husbands. They reveal important truths about the dominant norms of marital manhood in Anglo-American culture for nearly two centuries. They asserted the idea that gender was malleable and not linked entirely to sex; just as people assigned female at birth could learn how to be husbands, even people assigned male at birth needed repeated instruction and social reinforcement in their efforts to be men. In trying to narrate the complicated, dynamic, and sometimes surprising accounts of love, adventure, and death involving female husbands, news reports raised all of these possibilities and more. A close reading of these deviations from socially sanctioned gender reveals a great deal about unspoken norms.

Female Husbands is a window into the lives of people in the past who defied simple categorization of gender and sexuality, but also a call for privileging the gender expression and identity asserted by a person over the sex or gender they were assigned at birth. For instance, all of the principal subjects of study in this book are described as being "assigned female at birth" rather than by the category this group was socialized into being: "women." Gendered language and pronouns are a tremendously powerful force that dramatically influence how we see and understand a person.[19] When writing about a female husband in the third person, I use gender neutral pronouns they/their/themself.[20] None of the subjects of this book were known to have requested people use "they" to describe them in the third person. But "they" is a powerful, gender neutral way to refer to someone whose gender is unknown, irrelevant, or beyond classification. By using gender neutral language in writing about their lives, I am acknowledging that gender is "a set of practices" that contains and defines what is possible for any given individual or group of people.[21] I aim to minimize my own assertion of this power, recognizing that our gendered language manipulates and limits our view of the past. Using "they" also allows me to minimize disruption and avoid a false sense of stability when writing about a person over a long period of time, marked by varied gender expressions. In so doing I offer a model for people reading, writing, and thinking about the past and present in a more expansive manner, freeing stories and experiences from a telling that has been for far too long reduced to and contained by the gender binary.

It is my fervent hope that *Female Husbands* will offer a necessary alternative to traditional approaches to the past that render LGBTQ history invisible while nonetheless claiming to be objective and politically neutral. The pages before you do not tell a feel-good story. The lives I reconstruct are based on sources that usually mock and trivialize those who transed gender, and in that way it captures a very painful past. But by reading against the grain and approaching the material and above all the subjects with compassion, we can see the full humanity and vulnerability of those who have gone before us. And in their struggle, courage, and resilience, may we find hope for a better future.

PART ONE

UK HUSBANDS, 1740–1840

CHAPTER 1

THE FIRST FEMALE HUSBAND

CHARLES HAMILTON

Charles Hamilton married Mary Price on July 16, 1746 in Wells, England. The ceremony was administered by Mr. Kingston, the curate of St. Cuthbert.[1] Hamilton was born nearby in Somerset but lived most of their childhood in Scotland with their parents William and Mary Hamilton. At the age of fourteen and without a stated reason that has survived, Hamilton put on clothes belonging to their brother and presented themself as male.[2] Hamilton secured apprenticeships with two different doctors over the years, gaining knowledge and confidence in both their gender expression and their trade, then set off on their own, traveling to southwest England and offering pills, ointments, and advice to anyone who would have them along the way. Hamilton rented a room in the house of Mary Creed, where Creed's niece, Mary Price, also resided. The two became involved and were wed, traveling the country as husband and wife while Hamilton worked selling treatments for common ailments. Just shy of two months of marriage, Mary Price resolved that she was done with Charles. She reported her husband to the authorities and claimed that she had just figured out that Hamilton was not actually a man, triggering an investigation into the person who would become famously known as the "female husband."

Hamilton's case is compelling for many reasons. Not only do we catch a glimpse of the life lived, decisions made, and obstacles faced by someone who refused to neatly contain their life within the categories of "woman" or "man," but we also learn about the very definition of gender in mid-eighteenth-century England. The trial, newspaper coverage, and later fabricated adaptation of the relationship between Mary Price and Charles Hamilton expose prevailing views of sex, sexual difference, and sexual knowledge. ~~The case shows the significant role the community played in determining the legal response. It reveals how the courts – despite uncertainty and the lack of clearly applicable laws – assumed responsibility for stabilizing sexual difference and punishing non-reproductive sexual intimacies.~~ In many regards, Hamilton became the first publicly noted, scrutinized, and debated "female husband."

Hamilton successfully lived and passed as a boy from the moment they put on their brother's clothes at the age of fourteen. When Hamilton traveled south from Scotland to Northumberland, the northernmost county in England, and entered the service of a noted mountebank named Dr. Edward Green for two to three years, they likely offered themself in exchange for small compensation or room and board.[3] Hamilton could help Green collect supplies, mix compounds, and sell the treatments in the community.[4] Hamilton would make some money, learn the trade, and eventually envision a way to support themself when they set out on their own.

Edward Green advertised himself as an "Operator and Oculist" who could cure a long list of illnesses, from cancer and dropsy to leprosy, fistulas, and scurvy.[5] Dr. Green was the first notable mountebank to travel from England to Dublin offering cures for eye diseases and various other ailments. Being characterized as a mountebank – "an itinerant charlatan who sold supposed medicines and remedies" – was not exactly a ringing endorsement of one's knowledge or trustworthiness (Figure 1.1).[6] But many people flocked to mountebanks for cures and trusted their advice. While they may not have had the same training or skills as university-trained surgeons and practitioners, they still knew more than most people about human ailments. For much of the early modern period, many people did not actually think much more highly of university-trained medical faculty than of itinerant quack doctors anyway.[7] Dr. Green was well-regarded enough to be hired by Poor Law administrators to treat the ailments of the poor, receiving two guineas for treating various distempers, including fistula.[8]

Hamilton left Dr. Edward Green and continued in the service of a Dr. Finley Green for another year to finish training. Then they set out on their own. While training and later traveling the country working as a quack

Figure 1.1 "The Infallible Mountebank, or Quack Doctor," 1670 (cropped). Charles Hamilton apprenticed for years in the art and science of the mountebank before setting out to make a living on their own.
Image courtesy of the Lewis Walpole Library, Yale University

doctor, Hamilton enjoyed a freedom and mobility that would have been difficult for them to envision during their childhood as a girl. Sure, women worked as caregivers and nurses in their own families and villages. Respected midwives might travel a small radius to care for expecting mothers nearby. Working as a laundress could offer mobility but this freedom, combined with the intimacy of the work involved, led to their association with sex work.[9] None of these women's occupations would grant the freedom from supervision and stigma to travel alone, from one part of the country to the other, hawking their wares and drinking in public houses along the way. Manhood made independent travel easy and dramatically increased one's options for economic opportunity and social mobility.

Hamilton traveled around England for a bit before settling in Wells, Somersetshire in the boarding house of widow Mary Creed.[10] Mary Creed rented out rooms to earn extra income, in part to help care for her niece, Mary Price, who lived with her.[11] Creed was in a unique situation to offer insights into the two central figures involved in the suit that Price filed against Hamilton. While the bar might be rather low for a potential lodger – often simply the ability to pay – Creed had a duty to at least nominally vet her niece's future husband. She must have felt good enough about Hamilton's character and financial prospects to consent to her niece's marriage. Had Creed been a man, such as the bride's uncle or father, the court would have turned to them for testimony during the trial. But no such record exists.

By the time of their arrest, Hamilton was living the dream – a confident, extroverted, social, and self-sufficient man with a new wife. Hamilton was dressed in "Man's Apparel" which consisted of breeches, ruffles, and a periwig. Hamilton was reportedly "very gay" in their affect, as well as "bold" and "impudent."[12] Such traits would serve Hamilton well given their chosen profession. They would interact with many different people on a daily basis, appeal to them, earn their trust, and finally, convince them to pay for medical assistance. This suit of clothing so described – breeches, ruffles, and a periwig – was also notable in that it signaled conventional English styles. Hamilton was said to have lived in Scotland as a young child before leaving for England in their brother's clothes at the age of fourteen. At the time of Hamilton's arrest, tensions between England and Scotland over the Crown raged on. The latest Jacobite uprising of resistance by Scottish highlanders inspired King George II to pass a law disarming the Highlands and banning the so-called "Highland Dress" of the Scottish men. This law aimed to weaken their shared sense of culture and identity in order to thwart future invasions. This particular dress was most defined by "the plaid, philibeg, or little kilt, trowse, shoulder belts" as well as "tartan, or partly-coloured plaid" on overcoats.[13] Hamilton offered no such affiliation or identification with the Scottish Highlands or Jacobitism. In this respect, their transformation in expression as a teenager seeking to build a life for themself may have been political and cultural as well as gendered.

It was noted in the formal charge that Hamilton "follow'd the Profession of a Quack Doctor."[14] Hamilton's occupation already lent itself to suspicions about who they were, what was real, and whether they could be trusted – especially in the eyes of those who viewed "quack" doctors as charlatans. But such a view was by no means universal in the eighteenth century. Many such people had years of training as apprentices to reputable doctors. While some known quacks lied, exaggerated their abilities, or profited from the sale of "cures" that were useless, others were skilled in the treatment of common ailments.[15] Like their mentor, Hamilton could envision making a decent living for themselves. The constant travel and frequent interaction with new people would have presented both challenges and opportunities for someone who transed genders. On the one hand, no one would ever have a chance to get too close to them. And if anyone did suspect their gender did not reflect their sex, Hamilton could quickly move on to the next place. On the other hand, they had to constantly assess new people, places, and situations and hope for the best. Perhaps the loneliness and exhaustion of life on the road inspired Hamilton to look for a companion.

Mary Price may have been charmed by this well-dressed, buoyant, traveling man. Or maybe her aunt pressured her into the marriage, eager to find a suitor for her niece to conform to social expectations of marriage and improve her economic future. While it was not entirely unheard of for women to remain single, the rate of women who never married was at an all-time low in England in the 1740s, at 5 percent. The average age for women at marriage was the mid-twenties.[16] In most regards, Mary Price remains a mystery. We only know her through her testimony before the court against her husband. In the record, she is both fierce and weak, determined and ignorant. Though vulnerable as a legally married woman who wanted to end her marriage, Price believed the legal system would be on her side in this case. She didn't wait to return to Wells or go running home to her aunt for support. While still in Glastonbury with Hamilton, Price determined to end her marriage once and for all, marching over to the authorities to file a report.

Price's claim was fascinating. She said she didn't know her husband was not a man until after two months of marriage and numerous sexual intimacies. This left Price vulnerable to potential negative criticism on two counts. First, who could be sure that she wasn't lying and had actually known Hamilton was assigned female all along? Surely some people in Price's own time would have presumed that it was impossible *not to know* the sex of a lover. This would have left her subject to prosecution for fraud herself. The second possibility is that she was telling the truth – and was entirely ignorant about sexual matters. The strength of this explanation depends upon several other conditions: chiefly, that Price was young, presumably a virgin, and sheltered from the reputed sexually experienced poor underclass. The fact that Price was believed and defended by the local governing authorities speaks volumes about Price's place in English society.

Her goal of having her marriage voided was more important than the risk presented by either of these possible scenarios in going public. Price would go on to testify that she believed at first that Hamilton was "a real Man" before something changed and she came to believe otherwise. Even though Hamilton "entered her Body several times" without raising suspicions, Price came to believe and testified that Charles "was not a Man but a Woman."[17] The discussion of Hamilton's manhood – or lack thereof – rested solely on Price's accounts of sexual intimacies between the two.

Mary Price was a wife who did not choose to marry a female husband. When she realized her husband was different than other men, she panicked and rejected Hamilton. Or so she says. Price denies us access to further insights into the desires and motives of the female wives of female husbands. But her case does reveal important matters of sex and sexual intimacy. We know they engaged in penetrative sex numerous times before she suspected her husband was different. How could that be? One explanation is that their intimacies were extremely pleasurable, transporting Price to another dimension of feeling and being. She would have no reason to wonder what was happening – just a feeling of happiness that it did. Hamilton could have made use of one of the variety of dildos available at the time or may have penetrated Mary with their hand. Historians often get bogged down in these details, assuming that nothing other than conventional heterosexual intercourse involving a penis and vagina could constitute sex – or be as pleasurable. We must not indulge this distraction. Hamilton did something that made Mary feel so good that she did not question Hamilton's manhood for *two entire months*. The court officers, however, felt differently.

In the case against Charles Hamilton, who would become the most noted so-called "female husband," proof of manhood lay in one distinct area: sexual intimacy. Hamilton stood accused of being "the woman imposter" who pursued a fraudulent marriage.[18] In the court testimony of Hamilton's wife Mary Price, sexual intimacy played a dual role – both seemingly affirming Hamilton was a man and then later negating their manhood. Such exclusive emphasis on the issue of penetrative sex, however, was not a forgone conclusion. Eighteenth-century sexual practices focused considerably on touching, petting, kissing, mutual masturbation, and cuddling with minimal emphasis on penetrative sex.[19] Any of these intimacies could have been up for discussion. It was not until the century's end that references to sex became phallocentric, and increasingly defined as penetrative sex between a penis and vagina.[20] Did legal marriage, unlike courtship intimacies, emphasize penetrative sex for consummation? That was not even the case. Consent, not consummation, was the most important variable in validating a marriage in the eyes of the Protestant church.[21] Mary Price testified on October 7, 1746 that "the pretended Charles Hamilton / who had married her as aforesaid / entered her Body several times, which made this Examin.t believe, at first, that the said Hamilton was a real Man, but soon had reason to Judge that the said Hamilton was not a Man but a Woman."[22] The lack of precision about what constituted sex between the two suggests that Price herself wasn't sure what was happening. She ignored her own ignorance at first, because she genuinely liked Hamilton.

In the eighteenth century, dominant tropes of women of the lower sort promoted the view that they were sexually knowledgeable, experienced, and insatiable.[23] Mary Price was none of these things. She presented herself as someone who didn't really understand sex and couldn't determine how Hamilton was penetrating her. Mary's testimony established the fact of penetrative sex between husband and wife. The real question is why did the jury believe Mary? There may have been some subjective truth not captured by the court documents. Mary may have been truly distraught, surprised, shaken, and vulnerable – a seemingly reliable witness worthy of protection. It is also likely that no one really wanted to hear any more details in open court, as detailed accounts of illicit sex might give other people ideas.[24]

There was nothing inevitable about the fact that Price's complaint would be taken seriously and result in a trial. Trials cost money – and Price had none. She lodged her complaint during a period when court procedures were undergoing a shift from victim-led to state-led prosecutions. Judging the many variables about the history of the courts, the relative youth of the corporation of Glastonbury where the case took place, and the extensive number of elite men involved, legal scholar Carolyn Derry concludes that prosecution of the case – including the use of professional lawyers – was rather remarkable.[25] From this, we can determine that Hamilton's actions posed a significant threat, not only to one woman wronged in love and to one small village alerted to the details, but really to the entire principal of sexual difference and the social order which rested upon it. This was typical of the early modern period, as Kathleen Brown has shown, where "law, religion, and custom" together defended gender roles in the absence of "a stable biological concept of sexual difference."[26]

Hamilton sat in jail awaiting trial for nearly a month. Life in England's jails was deplorable by all accounts. A report and estimate for much needed repairs to Shepton Mallet Gaol was submitted one year earlier, but it is unclear if the repairs were made before Hamilton's arrival.[27] Prisoners could expect to experience cruel neglect – minimal servings of the lowest quality of food sometimes containing maggots, cold drafty cells with no heat source, dirty floors covered in filth, an old worn and torn blanket if one was lucky. It was thirty-one years before John Howard would visit hundreds of British prisons and publish a critique of the inhumane conditions that would serve as the basis for the prison reform movement throughout Europe and the United States.[28]

The community of Glastonbury found Hamilton's deception unforgivable and wanted them severely punished. They went so far as to submit a letter to the Clerk of the Peace requesting that Hamilton be "punished in the severest manner."[29] This could have been personally motivated by negative encounters people had with Hamilton in the previous weeks, though there is nothing to substantiate that. It is also possible that the community felt a duty to protect and defend Mary Price, a young woman raised in a nearby town who was placed in a situation no one would want their own nieces, daughters, or sisters to find themselves in. One thing was clear from the vantage point of the community: they wanted Hamilton to suffer terribly for what they had done and they wanted to make an example out of them.

The court deliberations expose what was really at stake in the case. It was not so much concern about the fact that Hamilton presented themself as a man and worked as a man in an occupation typically reserved for men as a quack doctor. If Hamilton had kept to themself and not entered into a legal marriage with Mary Price, they may have escaped punishment entirely or merely been subject to a short imprisonment under vagrancy laws. People could imagine, hope, or assume Hamilton was celibate or asexual. But Hamilton seduced a woman, married her, and had penetrative sex. The court openly discussed the peculiarity of the case, debating the nature of Hamilton's crime and what to call it. What seemed of greatest concern was Hamilton's sexual savvy in pleasuring a woman in such a manner that she could not distinguish it from penetrative sex with a man who was assigned male at birth. The court declared these sex acts to be "vile and deceitful" and one wonders what the punishment would have been if such intimacies were reported outside the bonds of marriage. This suppression of sexual discourses was neither politically neutral nor accidental but rather served to sustain social hierarchies.[30] The lack of detail or clarity about what constituted sex preserved an air of mystery, casting Hamilton as an immoral trickster.

It is remarkable that despite the uniqueness of this case – the threat to marriage, the vivid recounting of sexual intimacies, and challenge to sexual difference itself – Hamilton was charged under something as mundane and ubiquitous as the Vagrancy Act. The Vagrancy Act of 1744 focused principally on employment – or lack thereof – and deception in one form or another, especially the use of deception as a means of acquiring money. But the formal criteria for a vagrancy charge were only a guide for the authorities. People were arrested under charge of vagrancy for a wide range of activities. William Blackstone articulated a justification for the broadest possible application of vagrancy laws as a way to not only punish disorder but also maintain order – preemptively. Restrictions on mobility of the poor were always also embedded with values regarding gender and sexual norms, even when they were not explicitly named.[31] We have yet to reckon with how extensively and pervasively laws alleged to protect local communities from the financial dependency of women, children, and strangers were used to punish people who acted against gender and sexual norms.

That is precisely the group of people with whom Hamilton shared the jail, serving their sentence under the custody of William Hodges with a group of men charged predominantly with crimes pertaining to settlement and bastardy. John Bartlett, Thomas Andrews, and J. Brock were all held on bastardy charges. Alfred Andersey was a "loose, idle, and disorderly person" who got Elizabeth Bawler pregnant. John Watts was similarly "loose, idle, and disorderly" for refusing to submit to examination about his legal settlement. William Rogers was not legally settled and was suspected of running away with a widow, leaving behind "her bastard child there chargeable." William Weeks was the father of Ruth Savage's bastard child. Thomas Reynolds abandoned his family, leaving them "chargeable." Within this context, it is possible to see that the local authorities were heavily invested in monitoring the comings and goings of strangers and the intimate sex lives of strangers and neighbors alike. At the heart of these concerns is financial responsibility and the risk of local authorities and taxpayers being charged with the care of women and children. Hamilton shared the prison cells with other men involved principally in disputes pertaining to wives, lovers, and children – just like they were. But Hamilton's case was about sexual difference and sexual intimacy. With no question of paternity, bastardy, or money on the table, it stands out.[32]

Hamilton's punishment was harsh, suggesting the charges involving evidence of "vile" sex acts, a fraudulent marriage, and an aggrieved wife were deemed even greater violations to the community than those of the other men mentioned (Figure 1.2). The court took the community's wishes to heart and went even further. First, they wanted to ensure Hamilton in particular could never get away with living as a man in their community again. Second, they set out to publicly humiliate Hamilton through public whipping over a period of time throughout the four towns they were known to have visited within the county. Third, they sent a loud and clear message to others who might trans gender that entering into legal marriage with a woman was one step too far and would not be tolerated. Hamilton's punishment was cruel – six months of hard labor under vagrancy laws and public whipping in the towns of

Figure 1.2 "Mary Hamilton," 1810–15 (cropped). Illustration of Charles Hamilton's public punishment in a later edition of *The Female Husband*.
Image courtesy of the Carl H. Pforzheimer Collection of Shelley and His Circle, The New York Public Library

Taunton, Glastonbury, Wells, and Shepton Mallett.[33] Hamilton was a grave threat – and their ability to engage in sex with a woman *as a man* was at the heart of this threat. By their very existence, they exposed the instability of sexual difference and the imitability of heterosexual sex.

The case itself was no more newsworthy than other types of criminal cases commonly reported in the press. It took a few months, but the story eventually made its way across the Atlantic to the British North American colonies, into papers far from Wells, England.[34] In February 1747, the *Boston Weekly Post Boy* reported on numerous political issues, including executions at Kennington Common, an update on the Manchester rebels, and a reassurance of the Crown's friendship with Prussia. Amid these stories appeared the case from the quarter sessions of Somerset-shire about Hamilton's life, trial, and punishment. The account, adopted from an article that circulated in several British newspapers in November 1746, stated:

At a quarter sessions of the peace, held at Taunton, Somersetshire, Mary Hamilton, was try'd for pretending herself a man, and marrying 14 Wives, the last of which, Mary Price, deposed in court that she was marry'd to the prisoner, and bedded and lived as man and wife for a quarter of a year, during which Time she thought the prisoner a man, owing to the prisoner's vile and deceitful practices. After a debate of the nature of the Crime, and what to call it, it was agreed that she was an uncommon, notorious cheat, and sentenc'd to be publickly whipt in Taunton, Glastenbury, Wells, and Shipton Mallet, to be imprison'd for 6 months, and to find security for her good behavior for as long time as the justices at the next quarter sessions shall think fit.[35]

Just like that – the account of the court's effort to comprehend, define, and address allegations against a quack doctor who transed gender circulated in the great and growing colonial cities of Boston and New York. The gaps and fractures in the British criminal code were revealed, as the court admitted that it struggled to determine the "nature of the crime." Readers might use their imaginations in determining what "vile and deceitful practices" Hamilton used when they "bedded" their wife Mary. Hamilton was no longer an ordinary charlatan, but became extraordinary by the suggestion they had fourteen wives, which was not substantiated.[36] Such an account rendered the life of one female husband visible – and offered inspiration for others who might want to follow suit.

The policing of most kinds of sexual offenses generally went down as the century progressed. While the Hamilton case raised a specific kind of quandary for officials who struggled to determine what the exact nature of the offense was, the broader context for this was a legal transformation that made it harder to prosecute people involved in adultery or sex work. In 1750, Henry Fielding criticized the fact that it was no longer possible to charge known sex workers with disorderly conduct, as had long been the practice. In this respect, we can see the original punishment of Hamilton – the harshness of the sentence and the intense involvement of the local community – as a legacy of the past, centuries-old traditions of policing sexual misconduct with impunity in small towns throughout England because of the potential for broader social and moral corruption.[37] Such a view was strongly challenged by the end of the century.

HENRY FIELDING

Hamilton was not the first person assigned female to marry a woman, nor were they the first person described as a "female husband." But they were the first person for whom both of those things were joined together – by the writer Henry Fielding – creating an archetype that lived on for 175 years. But what came before this? The first known use of the phrase female husband in English is the title of a broadside about a person thought to be intersex, *The Male and Female Husband*, 1682.[38] In this account, a midwife from St. Albans was presented with a child of ambiguous genitalia who she took as her own and raised as a girl, named Mary Jewit. The midwife sought to disguise the child's condition through clothing, the song stating, "which she in female habit dress, that it might not be known." Jewit worked side by side with the midwife for many years, learning the profession and being known to all as a woman. Jewit – unexpectedly for those who knew them socially – got a woman pregnant. A judge ruled that the fact of the pregnancy sealed Jewit's fate: they were to live as a man and marry their pregnant lover, "For since the wench was got with child they both must married be. To which our hermaphrodite did give his free consent: And changing habit for a man he to the Church straight went."[39] The title of this broadside, *The Male and Female Husband*, points to the duality of one who is both male and female who then becomes a husband. The particulars of this fictionalized case are unique but the broad strokes that would later shape representations of female husbands are sketched out here: their parents aren't actively involved in their life, they get romantically involved with a woman, and they present themself as male to help stabilize both the relationship and their gender.

In the same era as the 1682 broadside, a person who presented themself as a man named James Howard was married to a woman, Arabella Hunt, in London on September 12, 1680. After about six months of marriage, Arabella tired of her husband and filed for divorce on several grounds, including that Howard was still legally married to a man as a woman and that Howard was "'of a double gender' or an hermaphrodite." Howard did not put up a fight, instead suggesting that their gender expression and the marriage were both "a mere frolicsome prank." Furthermore, they were determined to clear their name of suspicion that they were intersex, something that could have led to untold harassment. Subjecting themself to examination by a group of midwives, it was determined that Howard was "a perfect woman in all her parts." It is interesting to note here that being thought of as intersex was the worst thing in Howard's mind – worse than being known as someone assigned female who lived as a man.

Howard's wealth shaped the outcome of the case. Howard was considered gentry, a status that protected them from harsh punishment and the application of vagrancy laws. Furthermore, Howard was willing to walk away from their chosen gender, seemingly with frivolity and ease, something authorities would have both expected and rewarded. While Howard's status shaped their punishment, it did not protect them from investigation in the first place, including what could be an invasive and humiliating physical exam by a group of midwives. Only once their gender threat was seemingly resolved – by verification they were not intersex, by their willingness to have the marriage annulled and embrace a gender expression expected of a woman – did their class status serve as a buffer.[40]

Charles Hamilton followed in the footsteps of many people who came before them. It was neither common nor rare for someone assigned female at birth to present themself as male and legally marry a woman. Henry Fielding, however, coined a catchy new way for people to conceptualize these people – as female husbands – and crafted an identity category in the process. Hamilton's story might seem familiar to some readers since the lives of Hamilton and Price were the basis for Henry Fielding's 1746 fictionalized narrative, *The Female Husband*.[41] Fielding enjoyed local popularity as an irreverent, satirical playwright for years until Parliament passed the Licensing Act of 1737 which authorized censorship and drove Fielding from the theater to the novel.[42] Fielding was no stranger to courtrooms or the law as the child of a judge. He trained in the law himself and helped to establish the London police force while serving as a magistrate, all the while becoming an acclaimed novelist, earning the most regard for his 1749 book *The History of Tom Jones, a Foundling.*

Fielding wrote of female husbands at a time when dozens of other creative works also used "female" as a descriptive modifier. A surge in titles about "female" actors and subjects was one of many ways that Enlightenment ideas shaped public culture and literature by embracing accounts of women as worthy historical subjects, allowing for a version of womanhood that was varied, dynamic, and changing.[43] Women's education and culture was encouraged during this period.[44] Women themselves wrote serious social commentaries and historical studies on the great women of yore. The sudden appearance of hundreds of accounts of the lives of women doing unusual and heroic things left a transformative mark on the public discourse, expanding the vision of what was possible for women.

Provocative writings that interrogated and provoked social debate about sexual and gender difference were printed as plays, broadsides, cheap pamphlets, or in magazines and newspapers. They might be serious political polemics, romantic stories, irreverent and farcical comedies, or some combination of the above. They belonged to "everybody's culture" because of their accessibility, affordability, and familiarity to a wide range of people.[45] Popular culture was more visible but less important than elite cultural forms. This characterization made it easier for prominent male writers and critics to dismiss the political and social critiques featured in such work.[46]

The world around Fielding in 1740s London embraced a variety of practices where individuals blurred gender conventions, experimented with gender expressions, and embraced gender customs typically expected of people of a different sex. Transvestitism had an important place in early modern English culture. "Transvest," meant "to clothe in other garments, e.g. those of the opposite sex; to disguise."[47] Annual festivals and carnivals were acceptable places for temporary, playful expressions of both male and female transvestitism.[48] Masquerades were popular and might run all night long, offering people a legal and socially respectable environment to express themselves in ways that were deemed immoral or inappropriate in other contexts. Here people transed all sorts of boundaries when mixing with each other, including class, age, gender, and culture. The power and importance of these gatherings for women is evident from one important tradition: women of any age or rank could attend the gatherings without a male escort.[49] And yet those who embraced transvestitism more fully as a way of life were scorned, making it unlikely that a subculture of people who transed genders in London was knowingly tolerated.[50]

Simultaneous to these seemingly expansive attitudes, however, was increased rhetoric among conservatives that female inferiority was "natural." Doctors and scientists developed new theories of natural sexual difference that seemed to prove just that.[51] By increasingly privileging biological differences as the basis for categorizing human behavior, those who did not conform to gender and sexual norms were marginalized and stigmatized.[52] People who transed boundaries – especially female husbands – stood as test cases for these competing theories. And so, Henry Fielding took the real life criminal case against Charles Hamilton and interwove it with a variety of views about sexual difference and sexual intimacy that were both serious and absurd.

* * *

The first advertisement for Fielding's take on the Hamilton/Price case appeared in November 1746 in *The Gentleman's Magazine* promoting, "The female husband; or, the surprising history of Mrs. *Mary,* alias Mr. *George Hamilton,* convicted for marrying a young woman" (Figure 1.3).[53] Later ads expanded the description, offering their place of residence and promising a firsthand account from Hamilton, "of Wells, and liv'd with her as her Husband, &c. Taken from her own Mouth since her Confinement."[54] *The Gentleman's Magazine* was known for publishing provocative pieces that debated women's place in society.

The advertisements for the sale of Fielding's pamphlet put the category of the "female husband" into wide and frequent circulation. It is not far-fetched to attribute the creation and later widespread adoption of the category to such newspaper advertisements.[55] Furthermore, as was common at the time, magazines printed excerpts from the book, ensuring even more widespread knowledge of its existence.[56] The actual pamphlet itself was a hit, selling out two runs of 1,000 copies each in

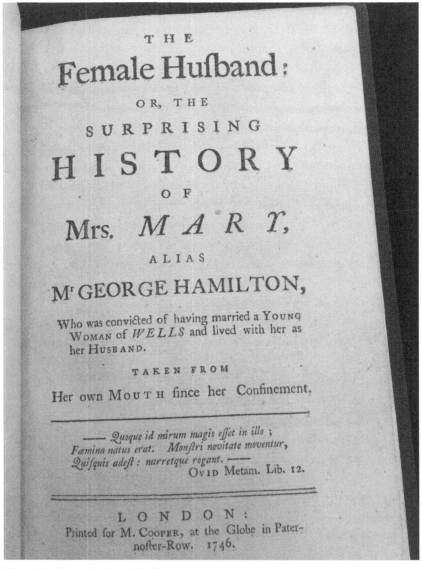

THE

Female Husband:

OR, THE

SURPRISING

HISTORY

OF

Mrs. *MARY*,

ALIAS

Mr GEORGE HAMILTON,

Who was convicted of having married a YOUNG WOMAN of *WELLS* and lived with her as her HUSBAND.

TAKEN FROM

Her own MOUTH since her Confinement,

_____

—— *Quoque id mirum magis effet in illo;*
Fæmina natus erat. Monftri novitate moventur,
Quifquis adeft: narretque rogant. ——
OVID Metam. Lib. 12.

_____

LONDON:

Printed for M. COOPER, at the Globe in Pater-nofter-Row. 1746.

Figure 1.3 Henry Fielding, *The Female Husband. Or, the surprising History of Mrs. Mary, alias Mr. George Hamilton, Who was convicted of having married a Young Woman of Wells and lived with her as her Husband. Taken from Her own Mouth since her Confinement* (London, 1746). Cover of the first edition of Henry Fielding's fictionalized account of Hamilton's life.
Image courtesy of The Huntington Library, San Marino, California

November 1746 alone.[57] Priced at six pence, it would have been accessible to nearly all but the poorest of London's inhabitants.

In fictionalizing Hamilton's story, Fielding emphasized different aspects of Hamilton's transgression from those that appeared in either the court records or the press coverage. In Fielding's hands, we see an approach to defining manhood through two traits in particular: feelings of possession and the sexed body.[58] First, consider the role of emotion. Fielding emphasized emotions – not the calm, rational man of the Enlightenment but the hot, possessive, jealous husband who was betrayed. Fielding portrayed Hamilton living as a woman earlier in life who discovered their female lover was cheating on them with a man, stating, "But she was no sooner informed of it, than she became almost frantic, she tore her hair, beat her breast, and behaved in as outrageous a manner as the fondest husband cou'd, who had unexpectedly discovered the infidelity of a beloved wife."[59] In Fielding's text, this incident led Hamilton to resolve to present themself as male, something they had not done prior to this moment.

The implications here are numerous. On the one hand, it presumes that women will only ever be satisfied by male lovers, and thereby Hamilton must trans gender if they hope to compete with men for the love of women. This view suggests that sexual desire is fixed by presuming that Hamilton was and forever would be sexually attracted to women. In Fielding's formulation, the only way for Hamilton to have their desires for the love of a woman satisfied is to become a man. This renders gender expression and identity secondary to sexuality. Further, it naturalizes heterosexuality as the only viable way to pursue or satisfy desire. Fielding's text promotes the idea that gender is easily mutable and that in doing so, one can successfully live and present oneself as a sex different from what one was assigned at birth. Adding another layer, Fielding asserted that emotions were an important site of gender transition because passion and jealousy – long deemed negative emotions belonging to women – could also be repurposed for manhood and reinterpreted as the rightful prerogative of a husband.[60] For Fielding, intense emotion was also an appropriate dimension of manhood.

Fielding persisted in the use of female pronouns at this stage in the narrative and offered a brief test of the limits of Hamilton's new gender by asserting that secondary sex characteristics – in this instance, breasts – could undo Hamilton in the earliest moments of their journey as a man. Fielding writes that a fellow shipmate "thrust one of his hands into" their bosom, which caught them by surprise and led them to give "so effeminate a squawl" that the Captain of the ship declared "we have a woman in the ship."[61] This crisis was abated and soon Hamilton, who Fielding took to calling "our adventurer" was on their way to living as a man and pursuing the love of women. In these passages, Fielding used male pronouns as a means of affirming Hamilton's male identity for the reader. But Fielding would not let the reader become comfortable with this perspective and occasionally used female pronouns, refusing to let us fully see or embrace Hamilton as a man.

Hamilton was exposed as not really being a man on several occasions in Fielding's text. In one scene, Hamilton's wife exclaimed, "I am married to one who is no man. My husband? a woman, a woman, a woman." Fielding supported the wife's viewpoint and outrage by using female pronouns throughout this portion of the narrative. Hamilton was quickly off on another adventure and posed as a doctor in a new town. Here, Fielding again enabled Hamilton's transition by using male pronouns in describing their work as a doctor and courtship of yet another young woman, whom they also married. Hamilton's new wife again discovered they were not who they presented themself to be because they did not have a penis. "Done, says she, have you not married me a poor young girl, when you know, you have not – you have not – what you ought to have. I have always thought indeed your shape was something odd, and have often wondered that you had not the least bit of beard; but I thought you had been a man for all that, or I am sure I would not have been so wicked to marry you for the world."[62] Here Fielding asserts the centrality of anatomical sex in establishing the legitimacy of a gendered embodiment. Further, he emphasizes the absence of a beard, which would distinguish youth from adults.

Though the trial record included Mary Price quite clearly declaring Hamilton entered her several times during their sexual intimacies, Fielding obsessed over and privileged Hamilton's physical differences, which he presented as weaknesses, rather than Hamilton's ability to engage in what seemed like penetrative heterosexual sex. While the real

Hamilton succeeded sexually through desire, practice, and skill, Fielding's Hamilton would never overcome the limits of their sexed body.

The claim that distinct anatomical sex gave legitimacy to a gendered embodiment was just emerging at the time. Many scholars view this as a conservative response to broader social challenges. Science was only beginning to embrace the idea that men and women were anatomically distinct.[63] The fact remains that all of these systems of meaning making – from humoral theory to anatomical distinctions to women's unique capacity to give birth to secondary sex characteristics to social roles – were at play to some degree during the period. Fielding asserted his theory: men and women have distinct anatomical and sexual capacities and gender reflects these differences. While the real Hamilton proved time and again that they were fully capable of assuming all of the typical rights, privileges, and responsibilities of manhood, Fielding's Hamilton would never overcome this alleged lack.

Fielding scholars ignored the gendered themes in his well-known work for centuries. Once feminist literary critics raised these issues, however, it was hard not to see broader social and political debates about sexual difference and the place of women in society as a constant theme in many of Fielding's writings.[64] Still, Fielding's *Female Husband* remained marginal. It was never deemed a critical success or a vital part of the Fielding canon. It is crass, pornographic, and principally about one person claiming male privilege, seemingly at the expense of a young woman. It is not the message of women's liberation that feminist scholars were looking for and never fit neatly into literary debates over women's status in the early modern period.

The case of Hamilton in the news provided Fielding with a scandalous event to draw from as he developed these ideas in his writings. Yet he also drew on other experiences: Fielding was friends with a well-known actor, Charlotte Charke, who was assigned female at birth, lived in male attire, and regularly performed the breeches parts in the local theater.[65] His knowledge of Charke's life as someone known to be a woman who presented themself as a masculine woman on a daily basis may have clouded his ability to see Hamilton more clearly for who they were: someone who had more completely transed gender and was only known by others as a man. Hamilton never embraced the identity or expression of a woman in any way, while Charke was known as a masculine woman.

Ultimately, many scholars accepted Fielding's view by framing Hamilton as a woman who wanted to be with other women, using the account as evidence of public perceptions of same-sex desire and a testament to the lengths to which women would go in order to be together.[66] But Hamilton was never simply, only, or actually a woman. Assigned female at birth, Hamilton describes their decision to present themself as male at the young age of fourteen. They did not qualify what motivated this decision or explain it away to earn sympathy from a judge. It was a fact of their life, one that remained unchanged throughout and seemingly after their prosecution.

HAMILTON AFTER FIELDING

The story of Hamilton does not end with their co-option by Fielding, however, but picks up a few years later on the other side of the Atlantic. In 1752, Hamilton was detained by authorities on suspicion that they were not the man they presented themself to be. How on earth did Hamilton end up in Chester, Pennsylvania?

The public whipping and publicity surrounding the punishment in 1746 would have made life untenable in Somerset. But Hamilton apparently didn't move very far, simply relocating to the adjoining county of Devon, England. It is from there that Hamilton set sail for Philadelphia on a ship commandeered by a Mr. Robinson out of Topsham in the fall of 1751.[67] Hamilton was no stranger to travel or hardship, but this experience may have been the most extensive and challenging to date. The ship hit rough weather, landing far south of its target in North Carolina in January 1752. From there, Hamilton made the journey north. Encounters with authorities in Virginia, Maryland, and Delaware did not raise suspicions about Hamilton's gender. Hamilton eventually landed in Chester, a suburb of Philadelphia that had grown exponentially in population and riches in the previous decades.[68]

Chester County officials brought a closer level of scrutiny to their visitor than had other North American municipalities, perhaps because Hamilton went door to door selling medicines for a range of medical disorders.[69] It afforded them flexibility, mobility, and money. They could earn a living anywhere with little oversight or long-term commitment. The newspaper article in the *Pennsylvania Gazette* reporting on Hamilton's detention alleged that they weren't trained or qualified to offer treatments. Chester residents enjoyed a proximity to Pennsylvania Hospital, which had recently opened its doors in Philadelphia, making it the first hospital in the British North American colonies.[70] But most people in the period would not have recognized the need for medical expertise, instead entrusting nurses, midwives, and traveling doctors for a great deal of their care.

Is there a chance that this Hamilton was an imposter, lifting the details of Charles Hamilton's life from newspaper accounts of the 1746 trial and Fielding's pamphlet? That is highly unlikely. The level of detail recounted in the 1752 article from Chester, Pennsylvania includes information that was not publicly reported in the press but that is verifiable in the court manuscripts. The article states that Hamilton, "pretending he was brought up to the Business of a Doctor and Surgeon, under one Doctor Green, a noted Mountebank in England." This is exactly what Hamilton told the magistrates during their interrogation in 1746 but this detail was not reported in surviving newspapers from the time. In the various newspaper articles about the trial, most made no mention of Hamilton's background or livelihood. The first article in the *Bath Journal* on September 22, 1746, referenced their work as a "quack doctor" but never mentioned Dr. Green, reporting that Hamilton, "has for some Time follow'd the Profession of a Quack Doctor, up and down the Country."[71] Similarly, Fielding portrays Hamilton as a doctor but provides no detail or reference to training with a mountebank, Dr. Green.

This crucial account confirms the resilience, determination, and mobility of those who transed gender. Despite scandal, public shaming, and brutal corporal punishment, Hamilton did not change the course of their life or reject their male gender but simply moved to another location to start again. They seem to have done so with conviction and in good spirits, as the local papers in both Philadelphia and Bath described Hamilton as "bold." The 1752 report of their detention in Chester County refers to Hamilton with male pronouns for the first part of the story, for instance, "pretending he was brought up. . .he embarked on board a Brigatine. . .he had travelled from thence," all speak of Hamilton as a man. When the account outs Hamilton as being "a Woman in Mens Cloths" it switches to female pronouns, such as, "she had used that disguise. . .she is very bold. . .she is about twenty-eight. . .she wears. . .she is detained. . .she will be discharged. . .she says." It is easy to focus on the narrator's adoption of feminine pronouns, effectively refusing to respect Hamilton's gender. But it is just as important to note the recognition of Hamilton's manhood through the use of masculine pronouns prior to their encounter with Chester authorities. Perhaps most significant is the ongoing instability of the gender binary that is raised when accounts use *both* sets of pronouns to refer to one person's life.

Once again, Hamilton had broken no law. This created distress for authorities who felt they should detain and punish Hamilton but lacked an appropriate criminal code to support them in doing so. Hamilton, simply by being themself, had done no wrong, forcing authorities to hope and wait that someone would read the notice and step forward with a claim against them. They wrote, "She is detained in Prison here, till we see whether any Body appears against her, if not she will be discharged." Without a follow-up to the story reporting otherwise, Hamilton was likely let go to resume their travel and work. There was also no mention made of an attempt to remove Hamilton's clothes, punish them, or to force them into wearing women's attire. This was unusual and it is possible the story only captured a fraction of what happened. In the nineteenth century, prison officials, police, and reporters alike enjoyed speaking of physical harassment, inspection, and regendering of people like Hamilton. This silence can mean a few possible things. First, perhaps this treatment occurred but was not recorded because of lingering eighteenth-century hesitation to outline in detail sexual and gender transgressions for public consumption. Second, perhaps Hamilton was not punished because they were seen as a simple laboring person – not as a potential sexual actor or suitor of women.

When David Currie of Lancaster County, Virginia responded to the account two months later, Hamilton was probably already on their way to Philadelphia. Currie claimed that the detained Hamilton was not who they claimed to be but instead was their own servant who ran away.[72]

Could that be true? Highly unlikely. It seems only possible if in fact Currie's servant, Sarah Knox, actually knew and associated with both Charles Hamilton and Edward Green in England. Currie alleges that his former servant Knox (who ran away in May 1752) had mentioned being "sometime with the above Dr. Green."[73] They could then use the alias of Charles Hamilton and the reference to Dr. Green as a way to completely throw off the trail that they were Sarah Knox, a runaway servant from Virginia. But the Hamilton who was detained in Chester was confident, knowledgeable, and assertive in both their gender and their profession. It took many years for Hamilton to achieve confidence and skill in both areas – making it highly unlikely that Knox, however desperate she may have been, would have been able to pull off the cover.

While news traveled far and wide – even in the eighteenth century – it also had its limits. News did not even reach all readers, not to mention all inhabitants; even readers might not necessarily connect the dots between accounts of one person in the news over a period of years. Digital technologies have transformed the relationships that modern researchers have to old newspapers, making them very accessible. Most notably, we can see connections between stories about particular individuals or incidents over time or across place in ways that never would have been available to target readers of the original papers, in their own time.

Hamilton made one more appearance in the local papers near Philadelphia a decade later in 1764. It is likely that the Charles Hamilton wanted for stealing a Mare from a town just outside of Philadelphia was the very same person who wed Mary Price in Wells, England in 1746. The complainant, Robert Iredell of Horsham Township, described the thief as "a Person who called himself Charles Hamilton, but perhaps may change his Name, a small built Person, long visage, and very full Eyes, wears his own Hair; he pretends to be a Doctor, and says he has been Captain of a Vessel for some Years past."[74] This description lacks a clear verifying detail but is filled with strong indicators from the consistent usage of the name Charles Hamilton to the reference of the questionable profession. But physical cues help as well – Hamilton was "small built" with "very full eyes." It's also not surprising that people would be suspicious of Hamilton, at least once in a while, given the role of deception in their life; while some viewed quack doctors as people who were deceitful and not to be trusted, Hamilton knew that the ethics of their professional life were the least of their worries. Even if they believed they were living the truth – their truth – in embodying the gender norms reserved for men, Hamilton risked serious punishment if others found out. It is likely that Hamilton persisted to make a life for themself in the region as a man and picked up other work as needed and available. If Hamilton did indeed steal the horse, it signals desperation – perhaps an attempt to get away from someone who suspected their sex was different from their gender. Horse stealing was a capital crime in 1763 – one to be undertaken in only the direst of circumstances. But it was also widely known as a man's crime, making Hamilton true to their gender to the end.[75]

* * *

Charles Hamilton was the original female husband. While not the first person assigned female to live as a man and marry a woman, Hamilton was the first person to do so who was characterized as a "female husband." This designation took on a life of its own in the ensuing decades, creating a catchy, memorable, and succinct way to describe transing gender and same-sex love all at once. The glimpses we have of Hamilton's life could not have been more different from the one manufactured and sensationalized by Henry Fielding in their name. Hamilton was bold, brave, outgoing, confident, and solicitous. They adopted a protective defense of selective "truth telling" when in the hands of the authorities, confirming for the authorities what they needed to hear (that Hamilton was a woman) though that category failed to adequately or accurately describe Hamilton for much of their life. Once freed from state authorities, whether in Wells, England or Chester, Pennsylvania, Hamilton resumed living their life as a man. Hamilton had numerous lovers and at least one wife, refusing a life of solitude that might protect their gender but deny their longings for love and intimacy. Even in later years, they were described as someone who was "very talkative, and apt to frequent Taverns," signaling a desire for connection and community that always outweighed the risk of being outed.[76]

Accounts of Hamilton's life lived on in a variety of print media, from crime literature to newspapers looking to fill space. Some were featured in sensational accounts of unusual characters throughout history. They provided anecdotes of the quirky long-ago past as the historical memory-making industry of the late nineteenth century took off. Such accounts often added their own editorial flare, reflecting the views and values of the times more so than the lives of the subjects. A short excerpt from an account of Hamilton's life in a central Pennsylvania newspaper, the *Carlisle Republican*, in 1820 added nothing to the story but kept it alive in the press long after the last traces of Hamilton were recorded.[77]

The historical memory of Hamilton lived on in a series of popular "true crime" books entitled the *Newgate Calendar*.[78] The interesting part of this remembering is the emphasis placed on the idea that Hamilton had fourteen wives. This claim is not substantiated by the surviving court documents. There is only one named aggrieved wife as plaintiff: Mary Price. The court found Hamilton guilty of vagrancy, not polygamy. But the facts of Hamilton's crime of living as a man and marrying a woman *were not sensational enough* for an early nineteenth-century readership that was reassessing its views of marriage, incest, polygamy, and interracial relationships. Hamilton's case was one of many examples used to support the contention that lenient marriage laws led to illicit sex and social disorder. In 1682 British common law had previously established that two people of the same sex could not legally enter a marriage contract.[79] That was old news.

But the report circulated by the *Bath Chronicle*, "That the said *Mary, & c.* pretending herself a Man, had married fourteen Wives," became the most enticing part of the story for nineteenth-century readers.[80] This emphasis on the most outrageous part of the story (who had time for fourteen wives?) illustrates the way exaggeration was used in reference to female husbands, rendering them less believable or realistic than they already were. The *Newgate Calendar* accounts present Hamilton's principal crime not as transing gender or same-sex love but rather as polygamy. The story begins, "Poligamy, or a man marrying two or more wives; and, vice versa, a woman marrying two or more husbands, is a crime frequently committed; but a woman, according to the rites of the established church, marrying a woman, is something strange and unnatural. Yet, did this woman, under the outward garb of a man, marry FOURTEEN of her own sex!!!"[81] It was unbelievable because it probably wasn't true.

In exaggerating the nature of Hamilton's transgression by the sheer numbers of wives, authors of the account tried to fit Hamilton's case into an existing legal paradigm which stood against heterosexual bigamy. This was necessary because there was no explicit law against transing gender (though vagrancy laws were usually invoked); there was no explicit law against sex between two people assigned female at birth (though sodomy laws could have been invoked); to legislate against transing gender or same-sex sex would be to recognize and legitimize their existence. Rather, a conversation about polygamy and bigamy opened the door to older, less rational forces: nature and religion. "According to the rites of the established church," the argument went, "marrying a woman, is something strange and unnatural."[82] By invoking religion, the question shifted from one of laws to one of morals. Everyone knew fourteen wives was unnatural! Who could dispute that? Sex between men was typically cast as "unnatural" in the legal code of this era. Writers and editors in the early nineteenth century cast same-sex love between women as "strange and unnatural" by invoking religion, not law. Hamilton was denied their claim to manhood (via female names and pronouns) but they were offered a debased version of manhood through their association with the worst kind of men – those who used, abused, married, and abandoned women – time and time again.

The fragments of evidence about the life of Charles Hamilton have long been superseded in popular culture by fantastic accounts that would cause any reasonable person to question the veracity of the story. For decades, an abundance of robust scholarship on Hamilton has poured over every word of Fielding's construction of Hamilton, making Fielding's Hamilton the basis for the trope of the "female husband." There is no doubt that Fielding's treatment of Hamilton's life was important because of its timing and circulation; it helped to establish the lens through which one might judge and make meaning of someone assigned female who lived as a man and loved women. But as this book shows, Hamilton's life, punishment, and resilience are just the beginning of this dynamic, long-lived concept. It is no more the "definitive" female husband account than any of those who would come later. Hamilton was merely the first in a long line of people whose creative, subversive, and unusual lives inspired curiosity, anger, love, and instability for those around them.

CHAPTER 2

THE PILLAR OF THE COMMUNITY

JAMES HOWE

When someone using the legal name Mary East signed their will before John Salter, public notary of Poplar, England in 1779, they were declared a "spinster" – the legal designation for an unmarried woman. But none of these categories – spinster, woman, or unmarried – completely or even accurately described the person to whom they were assigned. The will revealed several things about the life and values of its author: a desire to reward dedicated employees and their families, concern for the poor of the community, respect for the local church and its minister, and a lack of relationship with relatives. But nothing in the will points to the life that inspired news coverage by dozens of publications throughout England and the North American colonies from 1766 to 1902.[1] That life belonged to James Howe, who transformed themself into a man and husband at the age of sixteen in 1732. Howe lived as a man for over thirty years undetected, achieving wealth and the esteem of the local community of Poplar, England, as the owner of the popular White Horse Tavern in London's East End (Figure 2.1).

Howe's life was going far better than they probably ever imagined possible. Their family was poor. As a young person, they worked as a servant in the house of another family. The fact that they worked their way up to become a prosperous and respected business owner was enabled in part by their transition. Few boys of their class standing would have expected such successes. Howe was raised and socialized as a girl, yet managed to find love, community, friendship, and financial security as a man and a husband.

Howe's life of contentment and stability was challenged by a woman named Mrs. Bentley who recognized them from their childhood and threatened to "out" them as female. The extortions began in 1750.

Figure 2.1 "The White Horse Poplar High Street," 1930s. The Howes successfully ran the White Horse Tavern for decades in the eighteenth century.
Image courtesy of the Tower Hamlets Local Studies and Archives

Howe agreed to a pay-off of ten pounds so that their life might continue its course. Bentley was satisfied and seems to have left Howe alone for a long stretch of time – fifteen years – before returning to demand another sum. Howe again complied, offering her ten pounds, hoping their life might peaceably resume as before. But Mrs. Bentley got greedy and quickly returned for more, at which time James only had enough money on hand to offer her five pounds.[2] After the third extortion, Howe probably came to expect that Mrs. Bentley would return again someday, demanding more money in exchange for silence. But when the next time came, it was altogether different and absolutely terrifying for Howe. Mrs. Bentley sent two men – William Barrick and John Charles – to impersonate a constable and policeman and threaten to charge Howe with "going in disguise in mans apparel being a woman" and committing highway robbery decades earlier unless Howe gave them one hundred pounds.[3] Howe was fed up. One can only imagine the rush of fear and outrage that coursed through their body when faced with two authority figures, a false robbery charge, and the threat of undoing their gender.

Living outside of conventional gender norms made life precarious, no matter how stable or successful one's life was otherwise. James Howe and their wife Mary Howe lived together and worked hard for years, "in good credit and esteem."[4] They were in the business of keeping public houses, which they did to great success by evidence of their ability to upgrade their situation numerous times over the years before settling in at the White Horse Tavern for roughly two decades. No matter how completely or convincingly Howe embodied the positions of man and husband, they were never safe or secure. Even though Howe lived an extraordinary life marked by success and admiration, the exposure of their difference could have destroyed them. The extortion to date – twenty-five pounds in exchange for keeping Howe's secret over the course of about fifteen years – was a small price to pay for the joy and acceptance James had found. But in purely financial terms, it was analogous to a penalty of nearly two pounds per year, considerably more than the one pound four shillings Howe paid in taxes annually throughout the 1760s.[5] This is an early powerful example of the myriad ways that transgender, gender nonconforming, and people with same-sex desires throughout history have been informally financially penalized for their choices.[6]

Two developments fueled Howe's decision to undo their own public gender. First, Howe's beloved wife Mary of thirty-two years died, leaving Howe alone, despondent, and without another person intimately impli-cated in the secret of their past. With their wife gone, Howe's status as a widower did less to reinforce their gender than their previous role as a husband. Second, Mrs. Bentley went too far, raising the demand to one hundred pounds and enlisting people to impersonate officers of the court who roughed Howe up physically and suggested they would be executed for their crimes. Howe was terrified and furious. They knew the only way to clear their name of the false robbery charge was to remove the power of the extortionist and address the issue of their gender. It was not a freely chosen assertion. It was not an identitarian claim of social location. It was a qualified expression born of fear, sadness, frustration, and acceptance. "I am really a woman but innocent of their charge," Howe shared with Mr. Williams, a pawnbroker and close acquaintance who immediately came to their aid to fight off Howe's harassers and help press charges against them for extortion.[7] Howe realized the only way to save themself – quite possibly their life, freedom, property, and reputation – was to speak of their past and to reassociate with the category of woman.[8] They claimed the category for themself, dressed in women's clothing for court, and began to use the name Mary East in legal documents.

~~Female husband tales only had room for one central political drama – the usurpation of male identity and privilege.~~ The Howes' lives seemed untouched by slavery, for example, even though they lived merely yards away from the docks where ships weighted with the bodies of the enslaved and/or the fruits of their labor – sugar, cotton – were tied up. There was no mention that the laborers, sailors, servants, travelers, and others who frequented the White Horse Tavern to eat, drink, and relax also worked in industries that fueled and were in turn fueled by slave labor (Figure 2.2). There is no mention that the rum Howe served in the tavern originated in the sugar plantations of the West Indies.[9] There are only the briefest hints of Howe's life's proximity to Atlantic slavery and racism, such as the reference to one of Howe's extortionists not by name, but rather by race, "the mulatto."[10]

We learn later in the news record of the trial proceedings that the male defendant was William Barwick. This account reads, "Yesterday came on, at Hick's-Hall, a most remarkable trial, the Mistress of the White Horse at Poplar (who for many years kept the said house, dressed in man's cloaths, and served all parish offices with reputation) was Plaintiff; and one William Barwick, Defendant."[11] Barwick was sentenced to stand on the pillory three times and serve four years in Newgate Prison.[12] This account is even more compelling because there is no mention of Mrs. Bentley, who led the extortion of James Howe for sixteen years. Barwick was a pawn in her larger scheme but in this story of his trial, he was at the center. Barwick was named in all three indictments.[13] Bentley was only named in one. John Charles was named but never appeared before the court. Mrs. Bentley and William Barwick both

Figure 2.2 Francis Harvey, "Soldier and Audience in Tavern," n.d. The White Horse Tavern catered to sailors passing through as well as locals.
Image courtesy of the Uncat Auchincloss Rowlandson Collection, Beinecke Rare Book and Manuscript Library

served the same amount of time in prison – four years – and were released December 1770.[14]

This perfect storm of death, greed, fear, and the law became entangled in a remarkable trial that was covered in the local, regional, and international press. When the trial wrapped up, Howe retired as tavern-keeper of the White Horse Inn and lived the final fourteen years of their life out of the public eye, signing legal documents under their first legal name, Mary East, rather than their chosen legal name, James Howe.[15] Though technically declared a spinster, for all intents and purposes James Howe was a widower – a husband whose wife had died. Ultimately, they were portrayed as a person of integrity – despite their gender ambiguity – due to their hard work, active participation in the community, ability to maintain a stable relationship, and successful business. The widely circulated account of the trial concludes with a characterization of Howe as a wise, accomplished, and respected soul – as a woman. It states,

"She intends retiring into another part to enjoy with quiet and pleasure that fortune she has acquired by fair and honest means, and an unblemished character."[16] By transing gender again and assuming the gender expression of a woman, Howe (as Mary) was able to clear their name and protect their status as an esteemed member of the community – on the community's terms.

* * *

It is only through the public records generated by this trial that the community learned more details of Howe's remarkable life. James Howe quickly replaced Henry Fielding's account of Charles Hamilton as the most famous female husband of the eighteenth century. This paper trail enables us, some hundreds of years later, to piece together the incredible story of the eighteenth century's most popular female husband. The main account of James Howe's life that was widely reprinted points to several different dimensions of manhood. It showed that dedication to and comfort in one's roles as husband, businessman, and civic leader were more significant than physical embodiment. Howe was portrayed as a person of integrity due to their hard work, active participation in the community, ability to maintain a stable relationship with a woman, and successful business. At the end of the story, near the end of their life, special note was made that they retired in peace to enjoy the fortune "acquired by fair and honest means, and with an unblemished character." The fact that "fair and honest" were key descriptors is remarkable because they were known to have gone "in disguise in man's apparel."[17]

Howe served the town in various public offices and was an active churchgoer. They did everything and more that was expected of a model man, all of which stood to quiet most criticism during the trial.[18] Successful management of the household economy was also a key factor in the story. The concept of oeconomy, known as "the practice of managing the economic and moral resources of the household for the maintenance of good order," was particularly prized during this period.[19] While Howe's wife would have been the target of books on household oeconomy and may have played a key role in the successful management of their finances, Howe received all the credit and was heralded as a model for other men in managing both household and business resources.

The story of James Howe took on a life of its own in the press for well over a hundred years. English papers during this era were dynamic sites of information and debate about international and national politics and local events such as crime and entertainment. They encouraged broader engagement in political life.[20] While Charles Hamilton's story was the first widely circulating female husband account (characterized by betrayal and overtly sexualized), Howe's life would become the most dominant and widely reprinted one, marked by an emphasis on hard work, respectability, and acceptance. One reason for the longevity of Howe's story was its powerful depiction of a husband who embraced civic duty and recognized "the social good of the polity among their own responsibilities."[21] Howe's commitment to the community earned them respect, which later provided a buffer against their critics. A lifetime of responsible management of household resources, a successful business, beloved friendships, and self-less community service all served to minimize the likelihood that Howe would ever be charged with being an imposter or a fraud. Most original stories about Howe were only secondarily and minimally concerned with questions of gender in relation to physical embodiment. None even hinted at the question of sexual desire or relations between the two.

We are told that Howe's wife adopted the typical role and work expected of a wife in eighteenth-century England. A married woman would have been expected "to fetch water, produce and prepare food, bear and care for children, mend and provide clothing."[22] The Howes did not have children, which would have enabled Mary to prepare food for the tavern as well as the household without additional employees or servants. Women engaged in nearly every aspect of food provisioning, making or preparing baked goods, alcohol, meats, fruits, and vegetables.[23] This conventional division of labor would have left Mary with plenty to do behind the scenes while Howe "served the customers and went on errands."[24] James assumed tasks more commonly reserved for men while Mary did everything else that would have been expected of a wife.

Their tavern was a respectable establishment, evidenced by the great esteem in which Howe was held in the community by religious and state officials alike. In the 1760s, London's Sir John Fielding all but declared war on public houses, attacking especially "low, and common bawdy-houses, where vice is rendered cheap, and consequently within the reach of the common people, who are the very stamina of the constitution."[25] We have no reason to believe that the White Horse Tavern fell into this category.

The Howes were private people. They did not have any servants or hired help in their home, which was unusual for people with their resources. Most accounts noted explicitly, "They never kept either maid or boy, but Mary East, the late James Howe, always used to draw beer, serve, fetch in and carry out pots herself."[26] This would have required both James and Mary do a considerable amount of labor that they could have afforded to hire others to do. It was also noted that they didn't entertain in their house. They chose privacy over domestic help and intimate socializing for any number of reasons. The most obvious, of course, is that they did not want people to get too close to them. They sought to avoid unnecessary scrutiny of their domestic habits and belongings. After working in the public eye for long hours, James needed a place to relax and unwind in their undergarments without worry. They were frugal, driven by poor childhoods and fear that their special marriage might be discovered someday and leave them without future means of support. They saved a considerable sum of money by not hiring help. When Mary died, they reportedly had between four and five thousand pounds between them, which made them better off than many laborers but not quite as secure as a middling family in England at that time.[27] James only took on a servant after Mary died.[28]

What motivated Howe to live as a man? The answer given in the press to this question must be read with skepticism. It may have been made up by the person writing the news story. It may have been manipulated strategically by Howe after they were outed. It may have been the truth. The story of James Howe was reprinted dozens of times from 1766 through 1902 in both the British and North American press, often including the following origin story.[29] As the account goes, James Howe and their childhood friend from the neighborhood decided to build a life together "as man and wife" because each had "met with many crosses in love" and they gave up on men. Because they were "intimate," however, they decided that rather than settle for the lonely life of a spinster, they wanted "to live together ever after." They flipped a coin to determine who would be the man. In 1732, then, Mary East took the name of

A WEDDING IN THE FLEET. *(From a Print of the Early Part of the Eighteenth Century.)*

Figure 2.3 "Fleet Market, Farringdon Street." James Howe and Mary Snapes had a clandestine wedding outside of Fleet Prison like many others during this period. Image courtesy of the London Metropolitan Archives

James Howe and assumed a "man's habit."[30] There is no news record of the woman's name, leading the public to see her only relationally as Howe's wife, partner, friend, and lover. She became Mrs. Howe. Their marriage record, however, reveals her name was Mary Snapes (Figure 2.3).[31] This issue of motivation was addressed, settled, and dismissed. The fact of their life as husband and wife simply was.

Gender transgression was presented as something that was almost secondary to the larger aims of James' life and really a non-factor in Mary's life. Howe was presented as someone who did not consciously reject life as a woman and choose to be a man but rather one who lost the coin toss. This suggests that Howe was no more inclined than their wife to a transgender embodiment. This is a crucial point that neutralized the agency of both parties. It was chance that Howe would become a man, not desire; it was chance that the wife would have a female husband rather than become one herself; it was a response to structural heteronormativity, not a challenge to the gender roles that anchored it. Howe is neutered by this explanation. The homosocial world of men in London, anchored by gender play and people assigned male presenting as women and/or feminine was widely known of at the time.[32] But the same agency, creativity, and playfulness was not recognized or allowed for women who embraced masculine attributes and those assigned female who claimed a male identity. Jack Halberstam asserts, "Unlike male femininity, which fulfills a kind of ritual function in male homosocial cultures, female masculinity is generally received by hetero- and homo-normative cultures as a pathological sign of misidentification and maladjustment, as a longing to be and to have a power that is always just out of reach."[33] For the Howes, there was nothing playful or political about this decision. They were rejected by men and only then did they decide to reject men in turn. But it is unlikely James Howe was an accidental man for one reason: they were so good at it. Howe was a better man than most and became a powerful force in their community because of it.

When people were confronted as having transed gender, they were vulnerable to abuse, prosecution, and imprisonment. They had many reasons to provide an explanation that would garner them sympathy from those who literally held the power of life and death in their hands. Those reporters, publishers, and writers who stood to profit from printing the stories of female husbands were also motivated to spin a tale that would appeal to the broadest range of readers. The more reliable accounts are well situated within the historic and cultural context in which they appear, while less reliable sources are filled with exaggerations and hyperbole, often repurposing older tropes and simply filling in new details. The fact remains that it was – and still is – more important *that* someone assigned female at birth became both man and husband than *why* they did so.

Wives and lovers of female husbands were often portrayed as ignorant women who were duped into believing they married men, but this was never the case with Howe's wife. Mary and James came up with the idea that they live together as wife and husband. This was bold, unconventional, and a challenge to all laws and expectations governing women. The wife of James Howe – nameless as she long remained – was never given her due as a radical actor in the newspaper accounts or the scholarship. She chose to live without experiencing the "hot and dry" humors of sexual intimacy with a biological man. She did not need or want children. She enjoyed the care and company of her husband, the financial stability their shared business brought, and the respect of the local community. Mary Howe was by all counts living a good life. This is precisely why she was denied any agency or identity in the stories. She was the opposite of ignorant – she chose this life and as far as we can tell, was very glad that she did. In some respects, she was a greater threat to social order than James. What if other women recognized Mary as a bold and inspiring role model, rejecting motherhood and pursuing relationships with female husbands?

Gender as a physical attribute played a minor role in the accounts of Howe's life. Only one brief, vague reference even raised the issue that Howe may not have been perceived as entirely masculine or convincingly male. The story states that throughout their life, "her effeminacy was indeed remarked by most."[34] What exactly was the source of this alleged effeminacy? We are never told. Despite this alleged visible effeminacy, Howe was never denied a place in society as a man. Such assurances that Howe was feminine undermined their identity as male. But this was claimed retrospectively – after Howe transformed themself into someone who looked like a woman and appeared in court to testify in defense of themself. Such a claim served a very important function in allaying the fears of those who realized they might not be able to tell the difference between men and women. One female husband in the community was a thing to be dealt with, but what if there were others? People worried that they could be deceived by someone (an imposter? A thief? A lover?) known for using dress as a guise. A reference to some kind of effeminacy assured readers and community members alike that they need not worry. Surely, if they encountered a man who had not always lived in the world as such, they would be able to tell.

The questions raised by Howe's life are more concerned with the category of man than the category of woman. The question raised is, "What does it take to be a man?" and the answer is rooted in social roles, not body parts. Howe did everything and more that was expected of a respectable man in providing for a wife and serving their community in multiple ways.

The articles boldly asserted Howe's manhood. It was undeniable that thirty years of living as a man actually made Howe into more of a man. Howe had become so comfortable living as a man and wearing men's clothes that when they were forced to appear in court in women's clothing, everyone noted how awkward Howe looked, "The alteration of her dress from that of a man to that of a woman appeared so great, that together with her awkward behavior in her new assumed habit, it caused great diversion."[35] Everyone laughed at Howe in women's clothes, signaling a shift in their feelings about Howe from that of respect for an esteemed man to derision for a disgraced woman. Or, we might also read this passage as the community *laughing with Howe* at the absurdity that they were or ever could be a woman. While it was clear that Howe was at home in their life as a man, it seems like everyone else was comfortable with this as well. The affirmation of Howe's male embodiment reminds us that late eighteenth-century theories of gender have much in common with those of the twenty-first century. Gender was presented as something malleable that was shaped over time.

Marriage played a key role in stabilizing gender and sexuality. Deployment of gendered pronouns in the news reports provides a window into the power of both marriage and pronouns in defining one's gender. Howe was only granted manhood in the stories when described in reference to their wife. Consider the significance of this assertion that Howe was only a man because they were a husband. Early news accounts used female pronouns exclusively except when Howe was discussed in relation to their wife.[36] When Howe was understood as male, for example, "James lived with his supposed wife" and "he" didn't visit her on her deathbed, an allegation that may have been true.[37] Howe is only a man because of his relationship to a woman – at all other times in the story Howe is gendered female. Some editions of the story introduced edits that reduced the usage of male pronouns further, some even avoided them altogether.[38] By the nineteenth century, writers increasingly aimed to tell Howe's story without granting Howe male identity and pronouns at all.

James Howe died in June, 1780.[39] The official record says June 3, while a popular report in the *Gentleman's Magazine* cites June 8. The news was made public by way of an interested reader who wrote a letter to

Mr. Urban, appealing to the editor's stated interest in noting when people who have lived "remarkable" lives died. This reader, noted by their initials J.M., found the omission of Howe's obituary shocking given the magazine's prior reporting on their life. What was most notable was the fact that Howe did not live on the margins of society, did not cower in obscurity hoping to avoid being outed, and did not labor ceaselessly in anonymity in the bowels of a ship or on a factory floor – all fates shared by so many who transed gender in the long nineteenth century. Their social and economic standing made J.M. take the time to write a note so that all readers would be informed of the death of the female husband James Howe who "kept a public house, served all the offices of the parish, and attended Westminster-hall and the Old Bailey as a juryman." While they noted that the deceased "passed for a man 25 years" nowhere did they mention the name James Howe or use male pronouns. In death, Howe was transformed again into a woman named Mary East.[40]

When this letter was excerpted in North American publications such as the *Pennsylvania Evening Post* and the *Norwich Packet*, the editors added a queer twist by announcing the death of a so-called "Mrs. Mary East."[41] But Mary East, the female legal name of James Howe, was never legally married as a woman. Though their wife had long since died, when Howe assumed female attire and testified in court, they were designated a "spinster." The phrase Mrs. Mary East creates an impossible relationship whereby the female Mary East marries male James Howe – except they are the same person. Howe's death inspired new interest in their life, and a greatly shortened version of the story was published in 1790 and circulated.[42] This version was neutral and matter of fact, without pronouns or mockery and with all of the other disreputable elements erased.

FEMINIST ENTANGLEMENTS

James Howe's life – and the broad celebration of it for decades to follow – makes more sense if we consider its context, particularly the powerful struggle between individual liberty and government authority that marked the period.[43] Mid-eighteenth-century debates over personal freedom focused in part on its limits, especially as it related to the common good. This debate both fueled and was featured in political theory, philosophy, and laws concerning everything from religious affiliation to sexual morality to citizenship. In this climate, James Howe could be seen as a model citizen despite their gender transgression because they did not use their personal freedom to harm others but rather served the community at every turn. There was no immediate threat of sexual intimacies that were deemed unnatural because Howe's wife Mary had died.

Only a handful of women's rights advocates took note of the lives of James and Mary Howe. They did not see their story as something to celebrate or as evidence of social progress for an expansion in women's rights or a challenge to traditional gender norms. Those who did notice the Howes referenced their life briefly in passing, in a derogatory way. Even though feminists themselves used a great range of strategies in advocating for equal rights for women, they did not see any reason to pay close attention to the life or plight of the Howes.

Feminists disagreed over their broader aims as well as the best way to achieve them. Some emphasized women's similarities to men and sought to downplay arguments of sexual difference that were usually used to put women down. Others believed more rights could be gained if they granted assurances that women were fundamentally distinct from men and were not trying to assert otherwise. The notion that men and women in the nineteenth century existed in "separate spheres" is sometimes held up as evidence of sexual difference anchored in both society and biology.[44] But scholars have taken pains to demonstrate that this notion itself is a backlash against women's advances achieved in the late eighteenth and early nineteenth centuries.[45] The antebellum era's emphasis on difference was a reaction to women's successes in claiming a certain amount of equality with men.[46] Writings by feminists from this earlier generation reveal that the issue of sexual difference was still largely unsettled in their minds.

Take Hannah More. More took the audacious step of vowing not to marry and dedicating her life to girls' education. Advocating women's education was a comfortably liberal project, while refusing heterosexual marriage was quite dramatic. Both challenged key notions of conventional womanhood. But More was also one of the "great English domestic feminists," so characterized for their embrace of women's moral superiority that was demonstrated via "female sacrifice and obedience" and other "conventional gender values."[47] From this position, then, More was baffled by the idea that someone raised as a woman would ever want to live as a man. She was outright hostile toward those who transed genders. Hannah More urged women not to become "male imitators," writing, "is it not better to succeed as women, than to fail as men? To shine, by walking honorable in the road which nature, custom, and education seem to have marked out, rather than to counteract them all, by moving awkwardly in a path diametrically opposite? To be good originals, rather than bad imitators?"[48] More took a hard line against those who transed gender even though they demonstrated ambition and leadership – two qualities she valued. More was known for criticizing women for their frivolity and "pleasure-centered silliness."[49] The ideal for More was somewhere in-between, where women were serious, strong, and intelligent but never too strong or too ambitious so as to be seen as trying to be men.

Another feminist writer of the period, Pricilla Wakefield, was invested in the idea that there was a natural order and division between men and women. Wakefield complained, "The absurdity of an effeminate man or masculine woman, is too obvious to need observation." Wakefield was not herself conservative and believed staunchly in women's access to education as key to women's advancement and social progress more generally.[50] Wakefield was a Quaker feminist who authored seventeen books in her life. She wrote about the natural sciences, for children, and about women's place in society. An English writer based in London, her writings were widely reprinted in the United States.

Wakefield struggled to clarify her own views on what distinguished men from women, settling on both their "outward form" and their mental characteristics. Wakefield spilled little ink unpacking what she meant by outward form and instead outlined the most precious mental characteristics by which each sex could be known. Were a man's sex changed to that of a woman, she explained, he would be "an odious woman." Wakefield might have presumed the audience knew what she meant by this because she does not explain it. But she outlines far more clearly the limitations that would beset a woman who became a man, suggesting this was her chief concern with this reflection in the first place. A woman who became a man would be burdened by "exquisite feeling, delicacy, gentleness, and forbearance of female excellence." Such a "man" would make a terrible "citizen, husband, and father."[51] She suggests these traits were innate and not acquired through socialization.

Accounts of Howe published contemporaneously revealed the opposite to be true – Howe was deemed a model citizen by all who knew them. But Wakefield was ambivalent about the blurring of gender norms in other ways, especially when it seemed that women were excelling in arenas reserved for men. Sometimes, though, she thought this was impressive. She launched into a laudatory account of one such "masculine woman" whose life was exemplary. Margaret Rich Evans was born in Wales and "possessed a mind and body of masculine powers." She excelled at athletics and all manner of building and craft trades and was the subject of a poem that describes a place where women embody a physical strength equal to – if not greater than – that of men: "Robust are the females, hard labour attends them; With the fist they could knock down the man who offends them. Here liv'd Peggy Evans, who saw ninety-two; could wrestle, row, fiddle, and hunt a fox too."[52] Despite this celebration of one particular woman with masculine power, Wakefield did not think this was something other women should emulate.

Wakefield made a special point of acknowledging the difference between those women who "disguised" themselves as men to fight in battle and others who more completely "assume[d] the habit and character" of men and did so in secret for their entire lives. She detested the latter but did not approve of the former either, mocking those assigned female at birth who lived as men and served their countries in the military. She scoffed at the public commemoration of "the masculine courage of Ann Chamberlayne" who joined her brothers aboard a naval ship and fought the French. She criticized Christian Daries and Hannah Snell for misusing their "courage and fortitude" for worldly rather than domestic ends. Wakefield established a hierarchy for judgment of those assigned female who pushed the limits of gender that went something like this: (1) so-called "masculine women" like Evans were different but laudatory; (2) soldiers could be understood but should not be admired or followed because they abandoned the domestic sphere; (3) female husbands were disreputable and likely driven by some kind of broken inner sense of self rather than external considerations.

Wakefield held special condemnation for those who seemed motivated only by choice, not by circumstance or patriotism, to trans genders and live as men. Of those subjects, Wakefield speculates, "One would almost conclude, that the mind and body had been mismatched, and by some mishap had been discordantly united."[53] Without any obvious external motivating factors, such as war or a long-lost lover, Wakefield could see no other rational reason that someone assigned female would live as a man. She concluded there must be something innately different about such people, which she described as a mental mismatch.

Wakefield actually singled out James Howe, who she referred to as Mary East, for being "a very ignorant woman" and mocked them.[54] Wakefield basically articulated a distinction between sex and gender that would eventually be embraced by psychiatrists in the 1950s and 1960s. This idea, that there is a psychology of sex that is distinct from one's body, is a common foundation of twenty-first century transgender identity. Wakefield presents this view as something negative, that there is discord between one's mind and body.[55] From this, however, we might conclude that Wakefield and others recognized a range of transgressive gender expressions that were beyond the conventional category of woman.

Female husbands challenged a simple and direct correlation between sex and gender, but they were not alone. Those who transed genders, same-sex couples, and generally strong women of "masculine" power all challenged the notion of a clear binary between men and women and a simply hierarchy that declared men to be different from and better than women. The pages of newspapers and magazines created an important public space where those crafting the accounts as well as those reading them could grapple with the meaning of and differences between the groups. Just as feminist writers lumped a variety of people together in their reflections on what was an acceptable expansion of women's roles, so too did newspaper writers. Wakefield's classification and hierarchical assessment of such practices further legitimized trans subjects as active members of civil society, even though some people disapproved of their choices.

THE HOWES IN HISTORICAL MEMORY

In the early nineteenth century, people began seeking and embracing a wider range of heroes from the past. The focus of historical inquiry expanded beyond conventional political leaders and narratives to individuals of diverse backgrounds as well as broad cultural transformations. Studies of women and female heroism were increasingly popular, with some women deciding to write these histories themselves.[56] This expansive approach to the past included reproductions of stories of common people who were deemed extraordinary or eccentric. Historians have noted the wide range of people whose lives were suddenly of great interest to a general reading public, including those "previously regarded as disreputable."[57] This was the context in which accounts of James Howe's life were picked up, repackaged, and shared widely over many, many years.

Howe was a big enough deal in local lore to garner their own mention in urban history books about London. In the 1811 edition of *The Environs of London*, Howe was discussed under the town of Stepney. The book draws on a variety of accounts and sources, offering a largely factual and dry account. It correctly cites the date of death for both James, June 1780, and Mary, July 1766.[58]

Howe's extortionist, William Barwick, is named and is no longer "a mulatto" or "the mulatto" but is described as black. Here the argument is made that Barwick and others "had persuaded her that she was liable to be hanged for the imposture she had practiced." This framing of the situation is used to set up the idea that Howe was ignorant of the law and generally stupid and vulnerable. Mrs. Bentley was entirely absent from the story, leaving a black man, Mr. Barwick, to stand as the sole perpetrator of the extortion.

Though Howe lived the prime of their life in mid-eighteenth-century London, their message resonated in the early US republic as people looked for exceptional or heroic stories. In some ways, Howe's story was a perfect inspiration for both liberalism and republicanism — a tale of hard work and individual success in the context of a strong civic community that valued the whole of one's life and work over one simple act of deception. Stories of Howe that circulated in the early and mid-nineteenth-century United States told the same central narrative of their life but were tweaked and editorialized in ways that minimized Howe's claim to manhood and emphasized the feminine.

While eighteenth-century news reports were nearly copied verbatim from London editions into papers in New York, Massachusetts, Pennsylvania, and Connecticut, nineteenth-century accounts were more likely to include editorial commentary that was derisive of Howe's gender and the couple's relationship. This was done by combining references to Howe's male name with female pronouns. Usage of the male name – James Howe – and the female pronoun "she" invalidated Howe's chosen life.[59] Since Howe was recognized as a man precisely because of their relationship with a woman – one that the state, friends, and neighbors recognized for decades – another key to undoing their gender was to throw doubt on the legitimacy of their marriage. This was done by referencing Howe's "supposed wife" and never by name. References included, "James lived with his supposed wife in good credit," and "The supposed wife of James Howe now died," and "Before the supposed wife of James Howe died," and "She sent for her supposed husband."[60] By refusing to acknowledge their relationship as something that simply was and by emphasizing female pronouns when describing Howe, such reports perpetuated widespread knowledge of the couple but shifted dominant perceptions of readers away from the idea that someone assigned female could become a man and husband toward the idea that two women could try – unsuccessfully – to live together as man and wife. The language of qualification "supposed" worked to manage, mock, and erase the existence of nonnormative gender and marriage.

The story of Howe's life – presented as Mary East – was also included in the growing body of literature celebrating exceptional women from the past that compiled relevant nonfiction material for a growing female readership, such as the 1830 edition of *The Female's Encyclopedia of Useful and Entertaining Knowledge*.[61] These bibliographic documentarian publications anchor Howe's life in the early nineteenth-century book world, including an 1840 edition from Boston that published the classic story called, "Mary East, the Female Husband," in a book titled *The Life and Sketches of Curious and Odd Characters*.[62]

Antebellum accounts began to dabble with ideas vaguely related to transgenderism and early concepts of gender identity. In 1835, excerpts from the story of Howe's life were retold as the description of a "woman-man."[63] Accounts increasingly moved away from characterizations such as "female husband," in which someone assigned female adopted a role reserved for a man, and moved toward this language of merging dualities, of someone who was both man and woman.[64]

Howe was the lead feature in an article titled "Disguised Females" that focused on the legacy of female soldiers throughout history. The essay opens with a passage about women's delicacy and distinction, described as "two great principles of their nature," but quickly moves on to feature a number of people whose lives contradict that.[65] Howe was an odd choice for the story, never having been a soldier. This essay also undid Howe's life and identity as a man and husband, describing them as the "seeming husband" and using the name "Mary" and female pronouns. But this essay's author outlined a case for why some people assigned female simply could not conform to expectations of female delicacy. They wrote that "in most of [the] cases, a pure masculinity of character seems to lead females to take on the guise of men. Apparently feeling themselves misplaced and misrepresented by the female dress, they take up with that of men, simply that they may be allowed to employ themselves in those manly avocations for which their nature and taste are fitted."[66] Here we see a general shift in framing of female husbands away from an emphasis on a clear sex/gender distinction toward a challenge of the restrictions imbedded in the category of woman and attempt to make sense of people who pushed against those norms.

It was not the first time that reporting on female husbands contained analysis that would later feature in medical and psychological studies. It is quite possible, in fact, that the efforts among journalists and writers to understand and explain the motivation behind a range of trans gender expressions – including those of female husbands – actually became the basis for medical knowledge later in the nineteenth century. The language of interiority and inversion that would feature so prominently in the texts of late nineteenth-century sexology can be seen sprinkled throughout female husband and female sailor accounts as early as the mid-eighteenth century. Most importantly, as in this essay, the writer asserts the idea that the desire to present oneself in a gender different from one's sex stems from a combination of "nature and taste," what we might understand as being innate gender identity as well as preferences cultivated by socialization.

There are minor discrepancies throughout numerous accounts of Howe's life that have little bearing on the overall meaning of the story. One issue that requires reflection, however, is the portrayal of the circumstances surrounding the death of Howe's wife Mary. The original report and most variations of it for ninety years stated that Mary died in the company of friends in the countryside. These accounts also note that Mary "discovered the secret to her friend" on her deathbed. After Mary's death, this friend demanded Mary's share of the estate and then some. This passage has always struck me as odd because no one – not Mary, Mary's family, nor certainly an unrelated friend – would have any legal claim on Howe's property. Furthermore, why would Mary out her beloved to someone, knowing the harm they could cause James? Maybe it's not fair to judge Mary for wanting to share the truth about her life and relationship, especially on her deathbed. Maybe it is. She no longer had anything to lose. James still had everything to lose. Shortly after her death, James would decide that fighting for their gender expression and life as a man wasn't worth it anymore. Maybe for James, being a man and husband was less fulfilling without Mary.

One account says that Mary made a deposition that would ensure her portion of the wealth went to her relatives.[67] Mary still may have been in the company of friends when she initiated this paperwork. Or, as some accounts from later decades claimed, she may have been with her brother. These claim that she "told her brother all the circumstances: that she had lived, not with a man, but with a woman."[68] Upon learning this news, it was claimed that the brother "went to Poplar, and required Howe to give up the deceased's share of the property." What difference does it make if Mary was with friends or her brother? One privileges friends (i.e. families we choose) over legal definitions of kin. Mary and James were long separated from their families, even as teenagers. If anyone reconnected with family, however, it would have been Mary.

So, what if Mary did confide in her brother? Mary's brother had absolutely no legal or social claim to her property. The law of coverture forbids a married woman from owning property.[69] The fact that she was characterized as even having property, that the property was something the couple shared, was a fiction based on the hindsight knowledge that James was not legally male. The only thing that made it possible for Mary to lay claim to property was to deny the validity of their marriage on the basis of sex. In this case, for Mary to go ahead with such a move suggests one of two things. First, perhaps their marriage was not as happy as the story suggests. Why else would she risk danger for James? Or loss of wealth earned? Second, perhaps her relatives were impoverished and her desire to help them financially outweighed her concern for James. She knew James was resourceful and would find a way to carry on. Perhaps James and Mary even agreed to such an arrangement in advance of Mary's death. James was living as a man in every social and legal way when Mary's brother demanded more than half of the estate. Howe complied with the demand even though the property, business, and savings belonged to Howe as the husband.

Shortly after Mary's death, Howe gave someone – Mary's brother, other relations, or friends – half of their assets. This would have been anywhere from £1,500 to £2,500 – a fortune in 1766.[70] There are two ways to read this occurrence. We might see it as the culmination of a truly equal partnership where knowing Mary was sick, the couple decided to break from law and custom and offer Mary's portion of the wealth to her family. Perhaps the Howes were feminists after all. Perhaps they did truly reinvent the rules of marriage, even if it looked conventionally heterosexual to outside appearances. Or we might see it as the ultimate extortion, far more damaging than Mrs. Bentley's modest requests for ten pounds here and there. In this telling, Mary empowered someone to blackmail her lifelong partner James out of their wealth – an ultimate betrayal. This threat leveraged Howe's intimate relationship to deny Howe the right to their own property, to their own truth, to their own past. Why would Mary do that, knowing it would cause nothing but harm for her husband, partner, and friend of over thirty years? This version asserts that Howe was denied one of the most basic rights of manhood – control over the family's property upon the death of their wife.

* * *

By the late nineteenth century, the Howes were frauds, not heroes. As early as 1860, the term "woman-husband" was used to describe Howe instead of female husband.[71] By the 1880s, this was the go-to phrase. Harsh language was used in reference to Howe's wife Mary, characterizing her as "the actress who had for more than a generation enacted the part of wife and hostess."[72] Mary was portrayed as someone who was just as deceitful and duplicitous as James. There was a new certainty and authority about what was real. These accounts introduce the phrase "true sex" in the context of describing James, stating, "her true sex being never suspected, though a certain effeminacy in her appearance was the subject of frequent remark and comment."[73] The idea that there was such a thing as a "true sex" was a new assertion in the late nineteenth century.[74] This alleged "truth" of sex was something that was hidden or disguised by one's gender.

Historians of sexuality have long been challenged in writing about complicated and changing lives with language and terminology that is never quite flexible enough to do them justice. In pushing against the gross oversimplification of the origins of homosexual identities in the West, Anna Clark has argued, "It was not that sexualities were fluid at one moment and all of a sudden became rigid; rather, several different forms of same-sex desire could co-exist."[75] The same must be said of gender. It is not that transing gender was entirely free from any association with same-sex desire and then was instantly fused to it. Sexual difference and heterosexuality are so strongly linked by law, society, and custom that it is hard to see where one ends and the other begins. The dozens of accounts written about James and Mary Howe over the course of nearly 150 years reveal multiple, overlapping interpretive frameworks for making sense of their lives: gender was distinct from sex and something freely chosen; year after year of expressing a gender makes that gender seem more natural and stable; transing gender and living in a same-sex relationship did not necessarily raise questions or concerns about sex and sexuality; earning the esteem of the community by working on behalf of the greater good for decades goes a long way when one is discovered to have violated a major social norm; female wives faced an unpredictable jury when it came to interpreting the significance of their partnerships with female husbands.

Even with an abundance of records from the court and newspapers about a particular female husband and female wife pair, we still have virtually no access to their inner thoughts and feelings. What motivated them? Were they happy? Did they have friends who knew all of their truth? Were they lonely? Did they belong to a community of others like them? Did they despair over their difference? Did they feel a sense of triumph about the lives they carved out for themselves? Despite all that we have learned about the lives of James and Mary Howe, there is so much more that we cannot know. How would they have felt about the "female husband" moniker? Would they have chuckled, knowingly? Or felt offended? If offended, by which part – the "female" designation or the "husband" reference? What would Mary think about her near erasure from most of the stories about their relationship and business? Would she agree with the characterizations of her husband as such an amazing guy and community leader?

The story of James and Mary Howe is both exceptional and typical. The sheer number of things written about them over a great span of time is exceptional. In that respect, James Howe became "the" female husband for over a century, from 1766 when their story broke until the 1880s. No female husband's life was repackaged and repurposed in as many different ways as that of James Howe. Broadly speaking, they were the most typical and model female husband and wife pair. Their relationship was defined principally by their class status as laborers, the fact that they remained together as partners for decades, and their Anglo-American backgrounds. Most people designated female husbands shared these attributes. In this regard, histories of female husbands offer a window into one particular kind of transing gender. It was not universal, nor was it even legible as a category for people of other racial groups or classes. These limitations and erasures, however, provide further insight into the significance of gender as a concept shaped by so many other forces.

CHAPTER 3

THE SAILORS AND SOLDIERS

S TORIES OF PEOPLE ASSIGNED FEMALE AT BIRTH DONNING
men's apparel and joining the military or going to sea were
common in early modern Europe.[1] This phenomenon has been widely
written about, particularly in popular maritime lore. The most common
storylines involve a woman who followed a male lover to sea or went to
war for their nation. Many people knew transing gender was something
done successfully for generations and this knowledge was a strong
inducement for some to try it.[2] Poor people assigned female at birth
presented themselves as men to improve their opportunities to earn a
living and/or to resist the social restrictions placed on women's lives. Life
in eighteenth-century England for a working-class woman meant low
wages, political powerlessness, and the constant threat of violence,
including rape.[3] But we must remember that social and cultural expectations of gendered behavior were rather strong, preventing masses of
women from assuming a male identity.[4] To transform oneself and one's
life into something completely different than what one was taught, to
move among strangers seeking friendship and community, never knowing if or when they might turn on you, torture you, or turn your life
upside down – all of this was too much to expect of those who were
merely bored or simply poor.

A countless number of British and American people assigned female
at birth presented themselves as men and went to war or work as soldiers
and sailors. In the second half of the eighteenth century, a handful of
those were recognized by their governments with pensions for their
service and became respected minor celebrities. James Gray (aka
Hannah Snell), William Chandler (aka Mary Lacy), and Robert Shurtliff

(aka Deborah Sampson) were three people whose lives became the basis of published autobiographies, leading them to become widely known in their time.[5] Though partly fictionalized by their authors and editors, such accounts established the significance of these lives within the English laboring tradition, a transatlantic Anglo-American literary tradition, and eventually as an important thread of US nationalism. James Gray's life story, published as *The Female Soldier; or, the surprising Life and Adventures of Hannah Snell* in 1750, was roughly contemporaneous to the 1746 story of Chapter 1's Charles Hamilton, *The Female Husband.*[6] Chandler's autobiography, *The History of the Female Shipwright; To Whom the Government has granted a Superannuated Pension of Twenty Pounds per Annum, during her Life, Written by Herself,* first appeared in 1773 in England and was republished in New York in 1807 and 1809.[7] *The Female Review: Or, Memoirs of an American Young Lady: Whose Life and Character Are Peculiarly Distinguished – being a Continental Soldier, for Nearly Three Years, in the Late American War* enjoyed a long life as the partly biographical tale of Robert Shurtliff, first appearing in 1797.[8]

These early accounts of so-called "female sailors" and "female soldiers" established the model for how future generations of people could and would trans gender to enlist as men. The periodization of this was crucial to establishing its legitimacy. The British Navy – one of the most powerful and violent military fleets of the eighteenth century – gave us James Gray and William Chandler. Together, Gray and Chandler paved the way for the understanding and acceptance of Robert Shurtliff. Shurtliff's role in the Continental Army in the American War of Independence was celebrated and normalized to the point that it is part of the traditional US history canon. The press valorized Shurtliff (as Deborah Sampson) and characterized their actions as evidence of women's contribution to the nation's founding. Such accounts served a variety of contradictory meanings by both accepting that transing gender was vital to enable them to achieve their goals and then erasing this transition by attributing their accomplishments to women, as a seemingly natural and fixed category.

While religious, political, and popular discourse defined different ideals regarding sexual expression, most white men in the period exercised a great deal of freedom. Sexual desire was understood as something that was compelled by nature and contained by reason, but white men's lack of control was scarcely punished except in cases of sodomy, incest, or very particular kinds of rape.[9] Such was the world of soldiers, sailors, and travelers who moved from place to place and port to port, relatively freed from expectations of sexual modesty. A wild world of grog, women, and song awaited each sailor who survived the latest voyage – or so the legend of Jack Tar suggested.[10] In this world, the person who was socialized as a girl before transing gender might be naïve, shy, or uncomfortable at best, though surely some of them were elated by this new-found sexual freedom and enjoyed the opportunity to pursue women without reserve. Regardless of their own desires, however, most felt compelled to follow Jack Tar's well-worn path and pursue romantic or sexual encounters with women. Nothing could so convincingly shore up the gender identity of a man – especially a sailor – as cultivating one's reputation as a popular suitor and lover of women.

There was nothing natural about this seeming excess of heterosexual sex and desire but there were two powerful social forces driving it. First, dominant attitudes toward other forms of sexual expression became increasingly negative. In the early decades of the eighteenth century, there was an explosion of anti-masturbation writing and sentiment, starting with the publication of *Onania, or The Heinous Sin of Self-Pollution*.[11] Masturbation or mutual masturbation were no longer simply harmless sources of pleasure. Rather, they became associated with moral and social stigma as well as physical illness and harm. Sodomy and buggery had long been deemed immoral and illegal. As such, they were subject to harsh punishment.[12] The British Navy alone found twenty-three men guilty of buggery between 1756 and 1806, sentencing nineteen of them to death.[13] Second, sailors as a group were especially suspected of engaging in sexual activities outside of conventional heterosexuality – such as masturbation, mutual masturbation, or sodomy – given their long stretches of time at sea in single-sex social environments.[14] Many of them cultivated a boastful heterosexual sexual persona so as to detract from rumors that they might in fact prefer the company of other men.

The books and articles celebrating female soldiers were published within a broader social context that increasingly celebrated heterosexual liberty, premised on men being the initiators. While this tolerance had its limits as just mentioned (it did not include homosexuality or masturbation), it allowed for an expansive public to openly embrace a variety of extramarital sexual encounters and to celebrate the print culture that portrayed them.[15] The dramatic growth in the size of the British Navy over the course of the eighteenth century also fueled the expansion and acceptance of urban subcultures of bawdy and disorderly houses where sex workers received a steady stream of visitors. This assumed that it was perfectly natural for young men to be sexually ravenous and unable to control their desires. This somewhat new development fueled two seemingly contradictory narratives of female sexuality – that of the depraved insatiable prostitute and that of an innocent respectable young woman vulnerable to seduction and deception.[16]

An explicit and extensive engagement with ambiguous sexual relations between the female sailors and a whole host of women sets these narratives apart from most female husband accounts. These lives – especially those of James Gray (Snell) and Robert Shurtliff (Sampson) became much better known than most female husbands. Though the circumstances of their lives and the stakes associated with retelling their stories differed in substantive ways from the female husband, they offer many important insights about how sex, gender, and sexuality were given meaning, challenged, and fortified. These narratives feature numerous references to flirtation and sexual intimacies between the lead protagonist and a variety of women. This brought to the surface that which was often a silent subtext in female husband accounts – what exactly transpired sexually between the two parties, how the female soldier/sailor maintained their male identity during sexual encounters, and whether or not their women lovers at any time suspected their sailor lovers had transed genders. Only one person featured in this chapter – Samuel Bundy – was legally married as a man to a woman and described as a female husband. But these other accounts offer powerful examples of how sexual difference was conceptualized through the lives of others who embraced male identities and privileges without becoming female husbands.

JAMES GRAY

At the same time that the story of the life of Charles Hamilton was circulating in the print culture of England in the 1740s, another young person assigned female at birth pursued life as a man and went to sea. James Gray enlisted in the marines at Portsmouth, England in 1747 at the age of twenty-five, after first donning men's attire for a brief stint in the army two years prior (Figure 3.1). At sea, Gray engaged in a wide range of duties typical of a sailor and seems to have done a fine job working as a cabin boy, from going aloft and keeping watch to holding position in the after-guard at small arms to preparing food for officers.[17] They were assigned to serve aboard the sloop *Swallow* which sailed to Cuddalore, India.[18] There, the ship engaged in significant battles, leading Gray to fire many rounds before being shot in the groin themself. In order to avoid detection by a doctor, Gray took matters into their own hands. One account states, "she extracted herself the ball from her groin with her finger and thumb, after she had endured a most violent pain for two days, and always dressed it herself."[19] This scenario raises an issue that was always just below the surface in accounts of female sailors – the materiality of the sexed body *always almost* threatened to undo one's gender. This scene created tension for the reader.

There is no doubt that Gray was wounded in the battle. They were treated generously by the British military, which allowed them nearly a full year of rest and recovery in a hospital. They left India in August 1749 aboard the *Tartar* and two months later were transferred to the *Eltham* which headed back toward England. Their enlistment came to an end with a formal discharge and full pay.[20] In a period when the British military was widely known, condemned, and feared for its aggressive impressment practices and utter disregard for the health and well-being of enlisted men, Gray's experience stands as a testament to both the danger and hardship of military service as well as the opportunity to receive healthcare and social support.

News outlets reported Gray was awarded a pension of thirty pounds a year for life for their service after petitioning the king.[21] This was remarkable because Gray had already let the world know that James Gray was not their legal name. One account stated, "Sunday Hannah Snell, who served as a Marine in the late War, presented a Petition to his Majesty, she was dressed in her Regimentals."[22] According to law and custom of the day, Gray could have been arrested on fraud charges for deception. Typical punishments for deception and fraud in the period

HANNAH SNELL,
(Born at Worcester 1723.)

Figure 3.1 James Caulfield, "Hannah Snell," 1820. James Gray, more commonly identified by their birth name Snell, was a pioneer female soldier.
Image courtesy of the Library of Congress, Prints and Photographs Division

included standing on the pillory, public lashings, banishment, and even death. But when Gray outed themself as someone who was raised as a girl named Hannah Snell, they became a local hero rather than a criminal.[23] This was accepted because Gray was understood as abandoning their sex and transing gender in service of the greater good. Furthermore, they were not in a relationship with a woman. This rendered Snell's disclosure shocking but also safe and predictable – quite the opposite experience from that of Charles Hamilton. Absent a woman declaring that Gray deceived her into sex and/or marriage, the authorities simply did not care.

Gray managed the disclosure of their gender at the end of their term of enlistment and was not outed amid scandal at the hands of an enemy. They were so proud of their ability to live as a man and do the work of both solider and sailor that they wanted their fellow sailors to know that they were assigned female at birth. They shared this news on their own terms, after being paid for their service at the end of enlistment, stating, "In a Word, Gentlemen, I am as much a Woman as my Mother ever was, and my real Name is Hannah Snell."[24]

While they may have claimed the category of "woman" for themself, this moment does not mark the end of Gray's relationship with manhood or masculinity. Rather, they continued to live in a gender that was neither strictly that of a man or woman. Gray continued to wear men's clothes, along with "a laced hat and cockade, sword and ruffles."[25] This decision was explained by the fact that Gray would never tolerate two key aspects of a woman's identity: uncomfortable clothing and male authority. Gray is not presented as denying womanhood outright as a principled statement of self but rather as one who rejected the social trappings of womanhood, specifically: "the present fashionable Hoop" and the expectation of "having a husband to rule and govern her."[26] Gray was emboldened by their experience living as a man at sea and sought to carve out a social and cultural place for themself as a gender in-between.

Gray was born in April 1723 in Worcester, England, assigned female, and named Hannah Snell. Their mother and father raised them along with their three brothers and five sisters. The father earned a living as a hosier and dyer. Both parents were dead by the time Snell was seventeen, leading them to travel to London to live with their sister and her husband, a carpenter by trade.[27] They transformed their gender expression at the age of twenty-three in 1745 by taking their brother-in-law's clothes and name – James Gray.[28] After five years away, Gray returned to the home of their sister and brother-in-law to share the news of their adventures.

James Gray was the original so-called "female sailor" whose life became the basis of comparison for all who came after – especially in Great Britain. Sailor accounts focused on questions of embodiment, flirtation, and sexual intimacies. Gray's alleged autobiography was rushed to the presses, filled with fictitious flourish presumed to have been added by the publisher himself or a hired hand with a knack for infusing stories with dramatic, intimate tension regarding sexual desire and gender uncertainty, hoping to tap into the same market that devoured Fielding's *Female Husband*. Gray's memoir of their life at sea, *The Female Sailor*, was printed in 1750, just four years after *The Female Husband* first appeared. Their story was also a hit and took on a life of its own, chiefly marketed under their birth name – Hannah Snell. A close look at the life and representation of the life of Gray allows us another contemporaneous example of how manhood was assessed in the life of someone assigned female at birth.

Publisher Robert Walker first issued the autobiography in London in 1750 – the same year of Gray's discharge. The front piece of this 188-page edition included a picture and the caption "Hannah Snell, the female soldier, who went by the name of James Gray."[29] Excerpts of the account appeared immediately in magazines in both England and North America, and then sporadically for years and even decades after the original publication.[30] The hardship of life at sea, the intimate quarters, and the round-the-clock interaction with others created endless opportunities for someone to figure out that Gray was not like the other men. Finding out how they navigated one situation after another with their gender affirmed made for a page-turner.

The portrayal of James Gray's life in these various accounts offers further insights into views of what constituted sex and gender for the laboring classes, especially in the context of the British Empire and war. It is a story of white British masculinity and mobility moving with risk, yet still freely within spaces defined by colonialism, violence, exploitation, and racism, as the British fought the French to control parts of India. This life and this account became the foundational trope and historic antecedent for soldiers who transed gender in the British Empire and beyond, from 1750 through to the American Revolution.

While the story of Gray had a long life in print media, selective editing of their male name and masculine pronouns played a significant role in shaping the meaning of the narrative. For example, while the original autobiography from 1750 lists their chosen name of James Gray prominently on the title page, later edition reprints delete this up-front reference entirely, only mentioning the name James a few times in the body of the text. Most eighteenth-century newspaper excerpts printed to help promote the story omitted male and masculine references entirely, other than mentioning that they "put on a suit" that belonged to their brother-in-law. Newspaper excerpts never designate their men's name "James Gray" and never use masculine pronouns or referents in any way.[31] In trying to sell papers, they wanted to highlight the fact that a "woman" went to sea and did work reserved for "men."

The omission of their socially recognizable men's name along with persistent feminine gendering through naming, pronouns, and social groupings had a tremendous impact on the meaning generated by this autobiography. In these accounts, assigned sex was always the most important referent, while gender expression was secondary and fleeting. Authors and editors over the decades privileged assigned sex and legal name – female, Snell – over the desires, experiences, and identity of a sailor who embraced "man" as their gender and the name James Gray. The person who went to sea as a man named James Gray became instantly feminized as a woman named Hannah Snell who did things women were not thought to be able to do.

The sixteen-page narrative printed in Northampton, Massachusetts in 1809 points to their men's name a little bit more often than the short newspaper excerpts. For instance, it references the name James Gray several times: once when explaining the moment of transition, "she boldly put on a suit of her brother in law, Mr. James Gray's clothes, assumed his name, set out"; and later with a qualification, "During the siege our army suffered very considerably, from the enemy's incessant fire of bombs and shells. James Gray, (for that was the name she

assumed) was one of the party that was ordered under Lieutenant Campbell."[32] The last name of Gray is used in reference to the teasing they
endured, such as "Miss Molly Gray." Their fellow seamen and messmates
introduced a friendly nickname "hearty Jemmy."[33]

Other aspects of the account offered an even murkier picture about
dominant understandings of gender. Gender identity was shown to be
something internal and known at a young age, creating conflict for those
whose inner sense of themselves was different from their physical
embodiment. The concept of gender identity was raised as a key factor
that shaped Gray's life. In characterizing Gray's transition from Snell, the
narrative explains the importance of both gender expression and gender
identity, stating, "She boldly commenced a Man, at least in her Dress,
and no doubt she had a Right to do so, since she had the real Soul of
Man in her Brest."[34] Like so many transgender coming-of-age accounts,
we are offered a window into their youth that is a sign of things to come.
Not even ten years old, they declared they "would be a soldier" and went
on to organize role-playing games with the other children in which they
led the group, known in town as "young *Amazon Snell's* Company."[35]
There was something that set those who transed genders apart from
others – even at a young age.

Embracing certain personality traits, clothing, accessories, and affects
associated with manhood could effectively counteract the social meaning
of secondary sex characteristics. Gray was chiefly able to live as a man
because of strong personality traits that were commonly associated with
manhood and a convincing gender expression anchored in proper attire
and accessories. Yet all was not smooth sailing, so to speak. The narrative
of this particular part of their life threw everything at them to undermine
or undo their gender, including questions of facial hair, romantic
involvement with women, and the existence of breasts. Here we can see
that sexual difference is a very complex, multifaceted thing, anchored in
psychology, social practice, and secondary sex characteristics. It takes lots
of things to make gender, and no one single thing could undo it.

The fact that Gray was without facial hair raised suspicions regarding
their sex, but that was offset by excessive expressions of heterosexual
desire, such as the flirtation or objectification of women. Though a
significant number of people working at sea during this period would

have been young boys without facial hair, this issue is constantly raised in such accounts. While Gray was teased in the narrative "for want of having a rough Beard as they had" they used flirtation and romance to bolster their gender expression. Gray joined the crew "in parties of pleasure" promoting "every species of joviality" to fit in as one of the guys. While they claimed to be repulsed by their own behavior – still anchored emotionally in a modest woman's sensibility toward sex – they achieved their goal of securing a "title to manhood."[36] From that time on, Gray was affirmed in the eyes of other men. What might be perceived as a lack of masculinity in one area could be made up for in excessive demonstrations of masculinity in other ways.

Female sailor narratives stood apart from female husband narratives most dramatically in their presentation of sexual desire and intimacy. The women involved with Gray and other sailors were assertive women who found a way to get their lovers to spend all of their money on them. "Jemmy" had their pockets emptied by the widow from Winchester in one of several love affairs.[37] Sex was a staple, celebrated dimension of sailor narratives. Sex seems to have played the same role for sailors as marriage did for husbands: shoring up one's manhood. Once secure in marriage, sex was secondary and irrelevant between female husbands and female wives, as it was never mentioned. For sailors and soldiers, however, sexual intimacies were key but also dangerous. A lover provided intimacy and affirmation of one's manhood but was always in a position to find out and then tell others that the sailor's gender was different from their sex. As a result, Gray kept people at arm's length and sometimes lied in order to protect themself.

While heterosexual virility was used to offset a perceived lack of masculinity, Gray was still rendered vulnerable by their embodiment. One physical trait that held tremendous weight in defining sexual difference during the period were breasts. Visible breasts were an important signifier of womanhood in art and literature for decades. Just a generation earlier, the author of the 1724 *A General History of the Pyrates* used the revelation of the pirate Anne Bonny's breasts as a way for someone assigned female who had transed gender to signal their womanhood. The existence of breasts – a widely variable secondary sex characteristic – offset a life lived in flagrant violation of expectations for a woman of their race and class. One flash of a breast rendered a life lived as a man, marked by expressions of manhood day in and day out for years, moot. These events – recorded and/or fabricated by men – reveal one way that men perceived sexual difference during the period.

The original longform narrative from 1750 offers two scenarios where Gray was ordered stripped for a public whipping. This would generally mean to the waist, only exposing the chest and back. The text stated, "At that Time her Breasts were but very small; and her Arms being extended and fix'd to the City-Gates, her Breasts were towards the Wall, so that then there was little or no Danger of her Comrades finding out the important Secret, which she took such uncommon Pains to conceal."[38] At another instance of whipping, the text states, "She stood as upright as possible, and tied a large silk Handkerchief round her Neck, the Ends whereof entirely cover'd her Breasts, inso much that she went through the martial Discipline with great Resolution, without being in the least suspected."[39] A short excerpt of the account printed in the *Boston Weekly Newsletter* merged both of these incidents into one modified account, "She prevented a discovery of her sex, by tying an handkerchief round her neck, and spreading it over her breasts. When she was whipped at Carlisle, she was not to run, and her arms being drawn the proturberance of the breasts was inconsiderable, and they were hid by her standing so close to the gate."[40] Neither situation can be verified, leading scholars to believe they were made up to create tension in the text about Gray's sex as well as to encourage the reader to reflect on the idea of their breasts.[41] The key point is still important because the text made a gigantic fuss about the presence of breasts and their power in signaling womanhood. But this threat was never realized in Gray's life because their gender identity as a man was entirely intact when they ended their military service.

Narratives about those who transed genders commonly feature discussion of incidents or moments when someone noticed something peculiar about them that signaled discord between sex and gender. This was crucial in allaying readers' fears that their own lovers, friends, or neighbors might embody a gender that was different from their sex without their even knowing it. For instance, the original account concludes its discussion of breasts by pointing out that a boatswain did in fact notice Gray's breasts, stating, "they were the most like a Woman's he ever saw." He didn't pursue this issue because he had no reason to believe that Gray or any other sailor could actually be a woman. The passage concluded, "but as no Person on board ever had the least Suspicion of her Sex, the whole dropped without any farther Notice being taken."[42] Some readers would assure themselves that they would be more observant and less trusting than the boatswain, ensuring that they would never be deceived.

There is a significant body of scholarship in fields of history, literature, and maritime studies on the military service of James Gray, written in reference to Hannah Snell. Much of the common language and paradigms used in this scholarship – both descriptive and illuminating – privileged a notion that Gray's true sex was female and that this was ultimately of greater significance than their gender. This scholarship emphasized a fleeting and casual relationship to the category of man, often reducing gender simply to dress by centering the language of cross-dressing, masquerade, and disguise in the analysis. Few scholars challenged the assumption that female warriors, female sailors, or female soldiers were really women. Most of this work in fact bolsters Gray's relationship to the category of woman by celebrating their achievements doing things that women were not supposed to be able to do.

Transgender studies asks us to consider more fully the concept of gender identity in relation to gender expression and theories of performativity. A new study on James Gray argues that Gray is presented having both masculine and feminine virtues that are "innate and natural."[43] Here, masculine and feminine traits coexist within one person. This complexity helps explain why the pamphlet was well received by the reading public. Anyone could relate to some part of Gray's character. This duality rendered them less threatening, which explains why they were not punished. But there is no denying the account explicitly asserts that Gray's gender identity was that of a man and that it was traceable to their childhood. The potential social and political threat of this claim is offset by Gray's alleged and unsubstantiated heterosexual relationships and desires with men that bracket the narrative: compelled to sea in search of a husband and in receipt of a marriage proposal from a former shipmate at the end.

The account of Gray's life, written in reference to Snell, was chiefly promoted as a celebration of one person's ability to temporarily transcend the boundaries of sexual difference under extremely trying circumstances. The fleeting temporality and extreme scenarios made the publication of this information not only enticing to a thrill-seeking readership but also rendered it seemingly less of a threat to the gender binary and the social hierarchy it upheld. In this regard, news of Gray's adventure could be read as a form of fantasy fiction – extreme, fantastic, and nearly out of this world, except for the fact that it really happened and they lived to tell about it. The account blends common everyday experiences – men working at sea – with Gray's somewhat superhuman ability to survive multiple gunshots and not die of infection in the aftermath.

Gray's legacy as Hannah Snell lived on in the press in reference to other sailors and soldiers. The popular meaning attributed to their life also changed over time. In 1756, when another person assigned female and "dress'd like Sailor" was found sitting aboard a ship at port, the captain kicked them off. The writer suggested this was futile, that they would just find another ship with a less attentive captain. This writer concluded, "it is generally thought she will go to some other ship, or enter herself for a marine, as did the late famous Hannah Snell, not for Love of Man, but Love of Fame."[44] James Gray's experience and ability to earn income as a performer and storyteller introduced another explanation into popular equations about what motivated some to trans gender: attention. But life was never easy for Gray despite this brief notoriety. They died in 1779 impoverished and seemingly alone at Mousehold Heath, near Norwich, in the East Anglian region of England. The death notice declared that "this unfortunate woman, who constantly went about in man's apparel, had long subsisted on *charity*" and was declared dead of natural causes.[45] Here it suggests that Gray was a source of pity and scorn more because of their poverty than their gender, though it would be foolish to think the two unrelated.

SAMUEL BUNDY

Samuel Bundy liked to dress as a sailor. They were eleven years old when the first edition of *The Female Soldier; or, the surprising Life and Adventures of*

Hannah Snell was published in London in 1750. Maybe someone read excerpts from the story to them as a child and they too decided to pursue a sailor's life when they were a bit older. Sailors were everywhere in the streets of London in the 1750s and 1760s. It would have been easy to acquire the articles of clothing typical of a common seaman and certainly would have helped Bundy in their plan to live as a man and pursue the love of and marriage to a woman. One late day in March 1760, however, they sat on the floor of a jail house on a charge of "defraud" for their marriage to a young woman. Now, they had countless hours of emptiness to fill with thoughts about where everything went wrong. Trial was set for the next quarter sessions.[46] Newspapers described Bundy as a female husband who was also known as Sarah Paul.

Shocking both observers and legal authorities, Samuel Bundy's wife did not want charges brought against her husband and refused to prosecute. This allegiance led to Bundy's release. Maybe their life was not such a wreck after all? The dismissal of the case was significant because the crime was seen as one against the individual – Bundy's wife – rather than against the community. In a brief blurb, the point was made that Bundy received countless visitors in prison, including twelve women who allegedly knew Bundy as a potential suitor, "to whom she paid her respects as a man for marriage."[47] If it was true that Bundy pursued countless women in search of a bride, it was also true that Bundy made a great choice since Mrs. Bundy did not want to pursue legal action against her husband. Though not listed by name in the news reports, Bundy's wife had a name: Mary Parlour. Church records show that Samuel Bundy entered into a legal marriage as a man with Mary Parlour at St. Saviour Parish in Southwark, England, on October 22, 1759.[48]

Bundy did not present themself entirely as a man at all times but rather they dressed "occasionally in Women's Apparel, and some Times in a neat Sailor's Habit."[49] In contemporary terms, we might see their gender as nonbinary. Bundy's arrest was featured in several news reports, leading to what was beginning to seem inevitable: yet another largely fictionalized but partly accurate account of the life of someone assigned female at birth who lived for a time as a man. This book was quickly and cheaply produced, available for two shillings under the title, *The Female Husband; or, The Life and Imaginations of Sally Paul.*[50] A longer announcement in the *Monthly Review* warned and enticed potential readers with this characterization of the text, "A very silly, lying story cooked up from the few particulars, true or false, commonly related of one Sarah Paul, said to have been committed to Bridewell, about half a year ago, for assuming the dress of a *man*, and the character of a *husband.*"[51] Printers used the lives of real people as a hook to gain interest in their stories but they also explicitly claimed to fictionalize the accounts. The volume asserts as much in the opening pages, claiming that though the book is "enlivened with flights, elucidations, and wonderings," it remains the story of its author who stands as "living evidence of my own migrations, transformations, &c."[52] Why fictionalize the account when there was so much demand for history and gossip about unique people? This gesture offered creative license and freedom from liability. More than that, however, readers were enticed by the promise of half-truths and half-lies. This caveat freed readers from the burden of complicity in the transgressions of the subject. Many were happy to have the freedom to choose which parts of a story to believe actually happened.

The 1760 account of Bundy's life addresses sexual inversion, same-sex marriage, and gender malleability. Just what exactly these concepts meant and how they related to each other were still up for grabs. Bundy was outed, detained, inspected, and arrested. In their narrative, they suggest that a team of people – the justice prosecuting the case, the people who inspected them, and the man midwife who is expert on the subject of anatomy – together will help the reader understand their gender. Bundy writes: "a certain neighboring justice…is well instructed by the civilians in the true construction of the doubtful gender, and I doubt not, with the aid of a neighbor man midwife, will be able to give you a full and clear discussion of the nature and distinction of sexes, and by what means they may, from time to time, by art or accident, become inverted."[53] Here they situate their motivation to trans gender as a result of a natural inversion, something internal to them. This foreshadows ideas of sexual inversion that anchor early sexology over a hundred years later. The invocation of the "man midwife" further raises the dynamic that gender is far from stable or settled. Male midwives were, unexpectedly, able to successfully tend to women's reproductive needs. Their success demonstrated that ideas about manhood, masculinity, and sexual difference more generally were far from settled.[54] They were part of a new gender system that emphasized commonalities rather than differences between the sexes.[55] In this respect, male midwives and female husbands were part of a development that both minimized notions of sexual difference and exposed the distinctions between sex and gender.

Bundy grappled with an issue raised in several female husband accounts – the fact that the law had nothing to say about marriage between two women, or two people assigned female at birth, even when one lived as a man. Bundy wrote, "The truth is, the law could not say anything to the matter, consonant with its own maxims, which are grounded in reason; but as there is no reason for two women marrying, there could not be any law consonant with reason to prevent it, consequently no law about the matter."[56] Bundy distinguishes themself from other female husbands in that Bundy accepts their own membership in the category of woman. This was contradicted earlier in the text, however, when they described their marriage as two people who "lived together as happy as two angels, that know not the distinction of sexes."[57] They were willing to be seen as a woman but also saw the categories of man and woman as not fixed. As a result, they grappled with the same idea the justices did in determining the basis for their violation.

The news coverage of Bundy's release from prison suggests that Bundy's primary violation was against their wife Mary. Once Mrs. Mary Bundy decided not to press charges, Bundy was released. But the narrative of this period supposes a graver violation and a stronger investment on the part of the community in seeing that Bundy was punished. It was not enough that Mrs. Bundy did not want to charge her husband. To satisfy legal authorities, their marriage needed to be undone and Bundy was expected to assume the gender expression typical of a woman. Bundy wrote, "The committing matrimony was the principal crime; and when that knot was untied, the breeches immediately dropt off, petticoats resumed their proper station, and all matters in *status quo* again."[58] In shorthand, Bundy described this punishment as a process that required they "be fairly unmanned and divorced," driven by the demands of both "public justice" and "public satisfaction."[59] Gender was itself a punishment. Mr. and Mrs. Bundy assumed a privilege that was not theirs for the taking – a legal marriage. But it was not enough to deny them that. This further affirms the idea that they were not simply seen and judged as a same-sex couple but rather their threat also resided in the fact of their different genders. Forcing Bundy to be "unmanned" by both taking off their breeches and putting on a petticoat was key to re-establishing normalcy and asserting dominant social expectations.

The published narrative is a convoluted tale of adventure leading up to the time where they became a sailor and then married a woman. It fused together themes common in other sailor narratives as well as more serious philosophical writings on the differences between the sexes and the question of women's rights. The protagonist emphasizes on several occasions that they made new friends with people of "both sexes" because they learned "that it was the fashion of the times to have some intimate connexion with women."[60] While at sea, they worked hard to prove they could handle all of the tasks required, while noting the ways they did not fit in, including the smooth skin on their face and the refined manners that they simply could not help.[61] Bundy's sex was ultimately thrown into doubt because of their voice. Someone who heard them singing raised the issue, as Bundy recounted, "[It] struck him that my pipes were much too fine for the masculine gender."[62]

This question of what made a man or a woman was raised throughout the text. There was very literal commentary on the role that clothes play in shaping gender. They write, "This was to change my sex, or what is the same thing, the appearance of it…the essential difference between breeches and petticoats was meerly in the imagination, it being no uncommon thing to see effeminate men in breeches, or masculine women in petticoats."[63] It turns out that clothes did make the man. "There is no difficulty in this town of readily procuring the requisites; so I was stript and measured with great accuracy, one circled my neck, another my wrists, a third my waste, and so on. They complained that it gave them much unnecessary trouble, for that a man might have been measured at once by the common rules of proportion."[64] Bundy points out the challenge the shape of their body posed but then also the ease with which they passed into manhood.

But their position was always tenuous. Once suspicion of one's sex was spoken aloud, a storm was unleashed. They first realized there was trouble from their landlord, who offered a warning about the state of gender: "You are taken to be of a different sex from what you appear, and you know how prophane a thing it is for a woman to be a man; for if you are a woman, you must be a woman, there is no help for it."[65] Bundy thought the landlord might be sympathetic or open to persuasion. The landlord then disappoints, telling Bundy that she has basically told her friends that Bundy might not be a man. In a twist of comedic farce, Bundy implies that it is true, they are "by accident neither the one, nor the other," basically because a shark ate their penis. To put it in their words, "I owe this to a shark in the West-Indies."[66] Bundy quickly realized they had lost this argument and shortly thereafter was arrested.

Just nine months after Bundy was first imprisoned on a fraud charge for marrying a woman, they were married again, this time *as a woman to a man*. Those who read the narrative would not have been surprised because they previously announced their acceptance of the category of woman, writing, "I shall put it out of doubt, by declaring, not only that I am female, but that I intend for the future to continue so."[67] The news announcement reported a marriage at St. Sepulchie's Church of Sally Paul, a person "whose extraordinary Adventures have lately been published." The story of the new wedding does not name the new lover or offer any details about their family. Rather, it dwells on how remarkable it was that some time back Bundy's first spouse – a woman – did not turn against them when they were determined to be a woman. Bundy's wife remained fond of her "she husband" and "cheerfully maintained" said husband in prison.[68] Their mutual affection is reflected in the narrative as Bundy explicitly advocates on behalf of their wife, stating she "should be reinstated in her virginity, and her purity and innocence proclaimed at the market-cross."[69] Who would have guessed that it was Bundy, not Mary, who would so soon be rushing back to the altar.

What bearing this had on the new marriage is unclear. Samuel Bundy had previously married Mary Parlour. Now Bundy (going by the name of Sally Paul) was set to marry a man – William Kitchen – on December 29, 1760. In the news coverage, however, writers found the fact of Bundy's marriage *as a man* more compelling than their latest marriage *to a man*.[70] More to the point, however, is that Bundy, presenting as a woman named Paul, was a special kind of person who inspired great love and devotion of those close to them.[71] Bundy was a nonbinary female husband who embraced both male and female gender expressions in their adult life. Like typical sailor/soldier accounts, they pursued marriage to a man after their marriage to a woman was negated. They don't fit neatly into either group – that of husbands or that of soldier/sailors. Their 1760 narrative followed the groundbreaking tales of Charles Hamilton (1746) and James Gray (1750) with key threads drawn from both. Like Hamilton, Bundy wound up in jail after a short-lived marriage. They were alleged to have pursued over a dozen wives in their lifetime and received many visitors in jail. They were punished by having their marriage voided and their gender violated. They earned local notoriety through short news stories on their activities and a fictionalized biography of their life published shortly after their outing. Bundy never enjoyed the attention or longevity of James Gray, either in the press or the hands of scholars. The same can be said for the next account, a pathbreaking tale of the so-called "female shipwright" – William Chandler.

WILLIAM CHANDLER

William Chandler was born in January 1740 to poor parents in the town of Wickham, England.[72] Chandler learned a great range of useful skills at a young age, from how to fix things to horseback riding "without saddle or bridle."[73] There is no doubt that Chandler was a free spirit as a child who would never be happy with a life confined to domesticity. "I never liked to be within doors; and if I could get out with the young child, I thought myself happy; for if I staid within doors, I was idle, and studying what mischief I should do; so that my thoughts were never inclined to any good for myself."[74] Like James Gray, they articulated a sense of themself as different: unable and unwilling to conform to the life expected of young girls. They determined to leave home, dress "in mens apparel" and set off to make a life for themself.

While Chandler seemed well suited to life as man given such descriptions, no one event clearly sparked their decision to give it a go. They wrote, "A thought came into my head to dress myself in mens apparel, and set off by myself; but where to go, I did not know, nor what I was to do when I was gone."[75] This casual thought, however, was soon transformed into tangible, life-altering action. "On the first day of May, 1759, about six o'clock in the morning, I set off; and when I had got out of town into the fields, I pulled off my cloaths, and put on mens, leaving my own in a hedge, some in one place and some in another."[76] And so began the adventures of William Chandler, yet another poor Brit who left home as a teenager in search of new opportunities and found themself in the British Navy.

William Chandler shared James Gray's desire for adventure and a different kind of life than what was socially sanctioned for women in eighteenth-century England. Nearly a decade passed between the publication of Gray's autobiography in 1750 and Chandler's pursuit of life as a man in 1759. Maybe they read Gray's story or heard of it from others who read it in a coffee house or at a neighborhood gathering. Chandler set off in 1759 at the age of nineteen, leaving the remnants of their women's clothing in a hedge.[77] With no money, nowhere to stay, and no plan, Chandler determined they would make it, stating that "to go home again, was death to me."[78] After surviving their first night sleeping in a barn with pigs, they wandered down to town where they met a group of men who offered them food, drink, and an invitation to work at sea. There is no doubt the vast empire and rapid growth of maritime culture for political and economic enterprises opened this door to Chandler. Once aboard ship, they declared themself to be William Chandler – William was their father's name, Chandler was their mother's maiden name.[79]

Most who knew of Chandler's extraordinary life learned about it through their autobiography, *The History of The Female Shipwright*, published in London in 1773. This text and the life of its author were largely neglected by scholars for over 200 years. In 1996, Suzanne Stark verified many of Chandler's claims in the naval records, generating new interest among scholars.[80] Chandler was never the target of a criminal investigation. They were neither arrested nor detained by authorities because of their gender. Newspapers which documented the minor and anecdotal comings and goings of ordinary people took no notice of them. All of the ways we learn about female husbands, for example, are not applicable here. If it weren't for the publication of the memoir, we might not ever have learned about their gender-transing experiences.

The advertisement for the memoir in the local press, however, was filled with information. It stated:

The Female Shipwright, being the History of Miss Lacy, who disguised herself in the Year 1773, and entered on board of his Majesty's Ship the Sandwich, and was four Years in the Service at Sea during the last War, in which she continued till the Peace; after which Time she put herself an Apprentice to a Shipwright in his Majesty's Yard near Portsmouth, where she worked eight Years and an Half; with the Account of the Manner by which she was discovered and betrayed.[81]

The year was obviously wrong – it was 1759, not 1773 – but the general outline of events was accurate. Now anyone who read the daily *Public Advertiser* in the fall of 1773 could easily know about Chandler. The text of *The Female Shipwright* characterized manhood through numerous lenses including physical strength, sexual prowess, and gendered clothing. The account made a big deal about how important gendered clothing was and the challenge of acquiring enough proper items that a seaman of this age and rank would be expected to have. Chandler sourced clothing from a number of different people, including "an old frock, an old pair of breeches, an old pair of pumps and an old pair of stockings" from their master's brother and a hat belonging to their father.[82] Chandler was "presented with a clean shirt" and an entire new suit of clothes including stockings, shoes, a coat, waistcoat, handkerchief, and a night-cap.[83] They still worried, however, because they had to be prepared to show their freshly laundered and folded clothes to the captain for inspection upon request. They still owned a "shift" – a woman's undergarment – and convinced a sailor to sell them an extra man's undershirt so they could get rid of the shift and with it, any trace of womanhood.

William Chandler's narrative features extensive, if slightly ambiguous accounts of flirtation and romance. There is a lot of lying in bed with women and bunking with men, allowing the reader to impose practically any sexual desire or identity on Chandler that they wish. Chandler had a number of suitors but none more intimately flirtatious and aggressive as their shipmaster's wife. Chandler claims the mistress was too "familiar" with them but there was nothing they could do because they needed to maintain their cover and not anger their master. The wife's intimate touches aroused Chandler, if ever so slightly. While preparing dinner for the master, Chandler wrote, "While I was laying the cloth, my mistress would stroke me down the face, and call me a clever fellow, which behaviour often put me to the blush."[84] Chandler pursued other women in part to get away from the mistress but also to squash rumors they were sleeping together. But the mistress herself was always one step ahead of Chandler, taking them out to meet another woman and planning for the three of them to share the same bed. Chandler had no choice, "To have refused would be hazarding a discovery of my sex."[85] They entered the bed wearing their "breeches" and endured a night of abuse and frolicking, claiming, "They pinched me black and blue."[86] Such suggestive pornographic scenes put the Chandler account on the margins of related sailor stories which generally left more to the imagination of the reader. This may be one reason why Chandler's autobiography did not enjoy the popularity or longevity of others.

Surviving records of Chandler's actual life provide an important window into the way these fictionalized autobiographies popularized lies that changed the meaning of their lives and minimized their transgressive threat to social norms, including sexual difference. The narrative characterized Chandler as a physically weak person who found working at sea too taxing. This was presented as a focal point of concern for Chandler, who feared their lack of strength would raise suspicions about their sex, stating, "the first work I was put to being to bore holes in the bottom of a ship, proved so very laborious, that I feared I should never be able to conceal my sex until the expiration of my time."[87] Nothing could have been further from the truth. The real Chandler worked in the most taxing manual labor positions for over thirteen years. First, Chandler served in the British Navy aboard numerous ships from 1759 to 1763. After resuming land-based work, they became an apprentice to a shipwright in Portsmouth Naval Dockyard (Figure 3.2). Such labor was the most physically demanding kind. An apprenticeship required a balance of both skilled and manual labor, including the frequent lifting of huge beams. This position took seven years to complete and came with certification.[88] Chandler was strong, skilled, and successful in this pursuit.

Figure 3.2 Thomas Tegg, "Portsmouth Point," 1814. Portsmouth, England was a major maritime port where Chandler sailed from and later trained in the art of shipbuilding. Image courtesy of the Lewis Walpole Library, Yale University

Though famous for their time at sea in the British Navy, Chandler, like most sailors, spent the majority of their life ashore. Seafaring was just a stage in life for most sailors.[89] Most accounts of female sailors claim that upon returning from sea they enthusiastically gave up the privileges that society offered them as men to reclaim the role of woman.[90] Chandler, however, lived on land for many years as a man while apprenticing to a shipwright in Portsmouth. The autobiography ends with Chandler petitioning the Crown for a pension, which they received to the tune of twenty pounds a year. Chandler had become ill and was unable to continue their work at the shipyard. This initiated the appeal for the pension and resulted in Chandler transforming their gender again, presenting themself in women's clothing.

Chandler's life reveals the contradictions in popular views of the seriousness of transing gender – was it simply a matter of changing clothing or was it a dramatic metamorphosis? Chandler became reacquainted with another shipwright, Mr. Slade, who they had known previously while living as a man. Of Mr. Slade, Chandler noted that he "had not seen me before in women's apparel; yet having heard of my metamorphosis, he enquired kindly after my health."[91] A later edition of the book notes that Mr. Slade had "heard much talk of" Chandler's metamorphosis. This encounter raised questions of both gender and marriage. Despite their many years of living as a man, Chandler resumed "the dress proper for my sex" which instantly made them both eligible and desirable for marriage.[92] Chandler initially resisted Slade's advances, claiming they really intended to remain single. But once "a real and mutual affection" formed between the two, they changed their mind.[93] There is no resolution to the seemingly opposing theories – that changing clothes was a simple, minor act and that transing gender was akin to a "metamorphosis."

Scholars have long believed the courtship of a Mr. Slade was fabricated by the publisher. Most female sailor/soldier narratives include a marriage proposal from a man at the end, wrapping up every story of gender transing and illicit sexual and homoerotic liaisons into a neat and tidy heteronormative package, with a marital bow on top. This was a popular trope in fictitious ballads and newspaper accounts of sailors. But it was not always true. Those who have researched Chandler found it hard to believe that Chandler would voluntarily accept the restrictions of married life as a woman after decades of freedom.[94] This suspicion has been bolstered by research findings suggesting that Chandler later lived with a woman and may have been involved in a same-sex relationship.[95]

Advances in archival technologies, however, now lead us down a different path. William Chandler assumed women's attire, reclaimed their birth name – Mary Lacy – and did in fact marry shipwright Josias Slade in October 1772 in Deptford, Kent, England.[96] This information is also verified in a bond which lists Mr. Slade's occupation: shipwright. The pair, who had known each other from their work in Portsmouth, would live together at King Street in Deptford. They had several children who did not live beyond infancy. A boy was baptized Josias on May 14, 1775 at St. Nicholas in Deptford, followed by another baptism under the same name three years later.[97] In 1781, the second son died as well.[98] The couple found each other but never had easy lives – even in marriage. The loss of children would have been devastating, though common. Chandler, now living as Mary Slade, outlived both of their children and died in

1801 at the age of fifty-four.[99] Despite this hardship, there is every reason to believe that life together on land, with pensions and each other and without the most arduous and dangerous manual labor possible, made this period of their lives peaceful by comparison.

Chandler was not a female husband. They did not marry a woman as a man. They were not declared as such by others. They ceased living and presenting themself as a man, motivated by numerous mounting circumstances, including injury, age, and illness. They began presenting as a woman and married a man who shared a similar life trajectory and occupation. But this does not mean that they suddenly embraced femininity or felt fully comfortable with the expectations outlined for women. Perhaps they embraced conventional women's attire and roles after so many years living socially as a man and enjoyed it. Perhaps they tolerated women's attire and roles, resisting as many parts as they possibly could without causing problems in their marriage or community. These important questions of feeling, preference, and desire simply elude our grasp. Chandler lived a life across and in-between gender roles in a space we simply don't have adequate language for. To call them a woman is to deny the numerous ways they rejected that category. We know they transed gender for many years. We do not know if they continued to understand themself as someone who was transing gender even after their marriage or if they believed their marriage to a man marked yet another phase in their relationship to gender – one that was legible to those around them as "woman." Chandler's life and story challenged their friends and readers of their story to recognize that sexual difference was not rooted in sex but rather was given meaning by gender, which was mutable. Even their husband, Mr. Slade, recognized they had gone through a metamorphosis in becoming someone recognizable to him *as a woman*.

ROBERT SHURTLIFF

Robert Shurtliff enlisted in the Continental Army to fight against the British in the American War of Independence. They served from May 20, 1782 to October 25, 1783, nearly a year and a half. Shurtliff was twenty-one years old when they enlisted. Much has already been written about

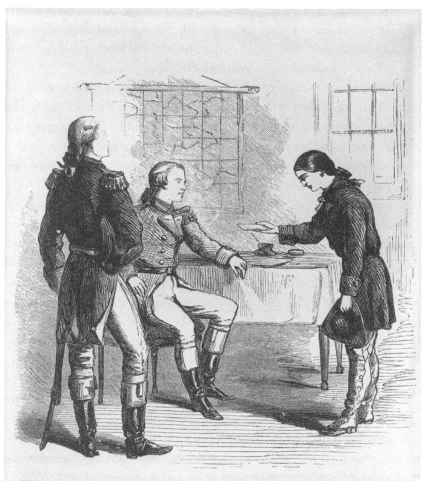

DEBORAH SIMPSON PRESENTING THE LETTER TO GENERAL WASHINGTON.

Figure 3.3 "Deborah Simpson [i.e., Sampson] Presenting the Letter to General Washington," n.d. Robert Shurtliff, more commonly referred to as Sampson, in a rare image portraying them in male attire just as their military service came to an end. Image courtesy of the Library of Congress, Prints and Photographs Division

the life and legacy of Robert Shurtliff, as Deborah Sampson (Figure 3.3). What is compelling for us, however, is to consider how sexual difference and sexual intimacies were portrayed in the accounts of their life. While it may present a challenge to the reader who is already familiar with this story, I will maintain a consistent writing method using gender neutral pronouns and the name adopted by those who transed gender. In this case, my attempt to minimize the intrusiveness of normative gendered language presents an altogether different kind of intrusion, forcing the reader to distance themself from a historic figure seemingly well known, that of Deborah Sampson, in exchange for a relative stranger, Robert Shurtliff. Allow me to remind you that this transition and this name was their choice, and of their own doing.

The legacy of Shurtliff bridges together old world and new, leveraging the British tradition of celebrated gender transing in the service of empire and a new American tradition of transing gender for revolution. While British sailors, husbands, and soldiers were compelled to trans gender by economics, love, and desperation, the first major American story was seemingly simple: patriotism. Shurtliff was part of a legacy established long before their time. Accounts of their experiences regularly invoked those who came before, especially James Gray (as Hannah Snell) and Joan of Arc.[100] Such historical precedents helped to legitimize Shurtliff's actions, minimize concerns about violations of gender norms and sexual improprieties, and allow the narrative that was ultimately crafted about their life to be patriotic, celebratory, and wholesome.

When news of the soon to be legendary "female soldier" broke in the US press in 1784, the account described someone who combined the best mental, emotional, and moral traits expected of men and women. Notably, this solder was only referred to as Robert Shurtliff – no women's name was given.[101] Robert Shurtliff was said to have displayed all of the following and more: virtue, activity, alertness, chastity, and valor. They were admired by superiors, sober at all times, and surrounded themselves with others of similar values. This joining of traits painted a picture of Shurtliff that was not threatening. It made soldiers as a group look good by emphasizing sobriety, respect, and order. It preserved the character of Shurtliff, removing from consideration the idea that they engaged in sexual relations with others.[102] The fact that one person could embody the traits mostly highly regarded for both men *and* women presented a new model for a new nation. Love of country was even more important than marriage, as Shurtliff was said to have joined the military in part to escape an unwanted marriage. Underlying this desire, however, were feelings of patriotism, as they were "warmly attached to the cause" of their country. In this way, American independence is about independence from the burdens of womanhood generally, and marriage in particular.

Many years later, Shurtliff was living in Sharon, Massachusetts under the name Deborah Sampson Gannett, married to Benjamin Gannett, and parent of three children. Their farming family of five lived on the edge of poverty. When writer Herman Mann approached them with an offer to write their biography, the profits were too enticing for Shurtliff to ignore. The biography turned out to be heavily fictionalized and somewhat pornographic. But the publicity generated raised Shurtliff's national profile and created opportunities for them to go on a speaking tour about their experiences in 1802. It played a role in the government's decision in 1805 to finally award them a pension.[103] Writer Herman Mann followed a well-worn path in filling *The Female Review* with suggestive references to romantic and sexual intimacies between their gender-transing protagonist and countless women who they encountered. It offers a window into not only how someone might trans gender, but also how sexual difference itself was understood in the early republic.

With the publication of *The Female Review*, Robert Shurtliff took a back seat in the public eye to their other persona, Deborah Sampson. The full color front piece featured the protagonist as we might expect them to appear on the farm in Sharon, with long hair, rosy cheeks, wearing a dress with some frills – not as the male-presenting soldier who enlisted. The title and subtitle both signal "female" without contradiction or tension, *The Female Review: or Memoirs of an American Young Lady*. The entire account is written with female pronouns, instructing the reader to only envisage them as a woman, even in the midst of their intense soldiering and romantic dalliances with women.[104] It is no mistake that Mann's *Female Review* mimics numerous themes found in Walker's *Female Soldier*.[105] In a close reading of the two texts, Judith Hiltner argues that Herman Mann used Walker's successful formula "for transforming the suspect woman of the army into a paragon of republican womanhood."[106] Indeed, the parallels are striking.

Clothes play a minor but important role in the account. Shurtliff was said to have made themselves "a genteel coat, waistcoat and breeches without any other assistance, then the uncouth patterns belonging to her former master's family. The other articles, hat, shoes & c. were purchased under invented pretexts."[107] This was somewhat of a departure from other narratives which feature people borrowing or stealing clothes from a male relative. In a fictionalized scene where the general who supervised Shurtliff suspects they are not a man, clothing plays a key role in that their clothes were soaked wet and clung to their body. The general asks, "Does that *martial attire*, which now glitters on your body, conceal a *female's form!*" Mann answers on behalf of Shurtliff in the third person, describing the scene: "Her heart could no longer harbor deception. Banishing all subterfuge, with as much resolution, as possible, she confessed herself – *a female.*"[108] Clothes often make the man in these accounts – rarely do they unmake them.

True to late eighteenth-century writing conventions, Mann uses the terms "female" and "sex" – not the word "woman." In reaching out to assuage the readers who might be shocked or uncomfortable by the scenes of desire between Shurtliff and women, Mann calls out directly to his readers, "REMEMBER, females, I am your advocate; and, like you, would pay my devoirs to the Goddess of love. Admit that you conceived an attachment for a *female soldier*. What is the harm? She acted in the department of that sex, whose embraces you naturally seek."[109] Here he seeks to minimize any suggested impropriety and repackage the experiences into something akin to heterosexuality by naturalizing the attraction of a "female" to a "soldier" who presented themself as "that sex, whose embraces you naturally seek." Mann's aim at upholding heteronormativity inadvertently fortified Shurtliff's manhood.

After the war, Shurtliff returned to Massachusetts but continued living as a man, once again assuming their brother's name and working as a farmer for an uncle.[110] Shurtliff was popular with the girls of the village, inviting a reprimand from their uncle for their flirtations.[111] But as soon as springtime came, ushering in yet another transformation, Shurtliff was inspired to assume female attire and present themself as a woman who had lived as a man – a third gender. In Mann's words, "Spring having once more wafted its fragrance from the South, our Heroine leaped from the masculine, to the feminine sphere." Shurtliff would forever be known as a person who transed gender for several very formative years of their life in the service of rebellion and nation building.

Stories of Shurtliff's life, often taken in part or wholly from *The Female Review*, were printed in national magazines for decades.[112] The glory of these early years of revelation waxed and waned. In 1812, an editor reprinted an early account of their life, adding a disapproving editorial which characterized Shurtliff as "repugnant to the laws of nature" and called on all men to feel similarly.[113] Many excerpts were somewhat dry, factual accounts of varying length. A long article from 1851 compared Shurtliff to Joan of Arc, stating, "Like Joan d'Arc, we find an humble girl of seventeen inspired with an ardent patriotism and resolution to stand forth in the defense of her injured country."[114] The *Historical Magazine* published a mini biography in 1858.[115] The outbreak of Civil War generated new interest in the topic of Shurtliff, as *Working Farmer and United States Journal* published a celebratory essay in 1862 entitled, "Deborah Sampson, the Woman Soldier."[116] As time went on, such mainstream publications normalized Shurtliff's life and story by minimizing reflection on the very questions of sexual difference.

One exception to this development was in the treatment of Shurtliff as Sampson by Elizabeth F. Ellet in her biographical book, *The Women of the American Revolution*, which also ran as a special feature in *Godey's Lady's Book* in 1848, titled, "Heroic Women of the Revolution." Ellet's account encouraged her readers to think through just exactly how someone assigned female could live as a man. Specifically, the essay suggests that experience with manual labor and *lack of training* in the ways of middle-class womanhood were key factors that enabled Shurtliff's transition. Ellet promised to correct the historic record with her profile given that Shurtliff, then living as Deborah Gannett, was greatly dissatisfied with the many fictions written about them in *The Female Review*. Shurtliff allegedly claimed the book was "a production, half talk, half biography," while the writer of the essay for *Godey's* stated, "the heroine had repeatedly expressed her displeasure at the representation of herself, which she did not at all recognize."[117] The authors of this piece were happy to provide a more factual, literal account that removed the flirtations with other women, but did not shy away from offering their own reflections on their motives or their gendered embodiment.

By the time this essay was printed in 1848, readers would have been familiar with dozens of stories of people assigned female at birth who lived as men to get more lucrative employment, to escape restrictions on women's mobility, or to get away from controlling or abusive fathers, boyfriends, or husbands. It was important for *Godey's* to point out that none of these things were motivating factors here, putting Shurtliff in a league of their own – they were exceptional. The author claims, "We have no reason to believe that any selfish motives, or considerations foreign to the purest patriotism, impelled her to the resolution of assuming male attire, and enlisting in the army."[118] Patriotism as a motivating force left them without peers and beyond reproach.

The question of physical strength and gendered embodiment was raised in a non-sensationalized way. It was noted that Shurtliff was "tall for a woman" and someone who "might have been called handsome" as a man. They carried themself in a "manner calculated to inspire confidence," an intangible and not necessarily gendered trait that would go far in leading others to trust them.[119] But where did this stature and confidence come from? It was nurture, not nature. The author notes that someone who was "delicately nurtured" as a typical woman at the time (i.e. white middle class) would never have had the physical or mental strength to endure the life of a soldier. Rather, it was through a childhood spent working on a farm that Shurtliff "acquired unusual vigor of constitution." It helped them develop a body that was not only "robust" but also "of masculine strength."[120] The gendered conventions of elite society that rendered so many women physically weak were a result of socialization. As a poor laboring person, Shurtliff developed a physicality on a par with any man – at least that of an average soldier at the time.

While this class-based experience of labor and gender may have gone far in helping to explain Shurtliff's accomplishments, the author of the piece was also careful to avoid seeming to encourage others to pursue a similar course. "The career to which her patriotism urged her, cannot be commended as an example to any of her sex; but her exemplary conduct after the first step had been taken will go far to plead her excuse." In other words, Shurtliff still did something reprehensible in pursuing life as a man. If we ignore the fact of that terrible initial judgment, however, we must recognize their excellence.[121] This argument echoed that of *The Female Review* and is a double bind that often accompanies popular takes on those who did respectable, laudable things after transing gender.

GENDER IDENTITY AND MALE EFFEMINACY

The longstanding maritime tradition of celebrating female warriors and sailors propelled these accounts to broader popular acceptance than husbands ever enjoyed. None of the ballads or chanties about legendary female sailors featured someone who *both* asserted their male identity and then married a woman. Neither Bundy nor Chandler – who were both sailors – ever enjoyed the powerful place in nineteenth-century historic memory that was reserved for the famed soldiers, James Gray (as Hannah Snell) and Robert Shurtliff (as Deborah Sampson). These soldiers' tales were central in defining the parameters, tone, and expectations for countless others who transed genders in the ensuing centuries. James Gray was the most often noted soldier whose journey anchored the meaning-making efforts of those who came after them, especially in British North America where the press cited Gray repeatedly to justify and celebrate the actions of Robert Shurtliff. Gray also occupied a larger-than-life space in late eighteenth- and early nineteenth-century reflections by women writers seeking to carve out a place of importance for women in history and letters. In these accounts, Gray was alternately celebrated for courage and bravery and berated for going too far against the boundaries of conventional womanhood.

These accounts point to something akin to a gender identity that set these people apart from their assigned female peers who were by and large content to live lives within the confines of girlhood and womanhood. The language used in accounts of Gray ("she had the real Soul of Man in her Brest") and Bundy ("the nature and distinction of sexes…become inverted") explicitly invoked such concepts. Shurtliff is also implicated in this indirectly. *The Female Review* is filled with references to new challenges, feelings, and experiences triggered by the war. Early battles, especially, "are well known to have affected the minds, even of both sexes, throughout the Colonies, with sensations and emotions different from whatever they had before experienced."[122] This passage is less explicit than the others but suggests an explanation for transing gender as a reaction to new experiences. Collectively, two different theories of gender identity are represented: first, that gender identity is something innate that people are born with, that for some is at odds with

100

their sex; second, that gender identity and expression is shaped by external experiences.

While historians have long debated the relevance of female sailors to histories of feminism and lesbianism, two other threads run more prominently through many of the accounts: the question of male homosexuality and gender nonconformity. Many female sailors are portrayed as appearing to be effeminate men. The weight of this suspicion was said to rest on one singular secondary sex characteristic: the absence of a beard. The absence of facial hair as a distinguishing factor was noted in nearly all accounts of female husbands, soldiers, and sailors at one point or another. In the two most widely celebrated eighteenth-century soldier narratives, that of Gray in 1750 and Shurtliff 1797, this noted lack of a beard was used to suggest a femininity indicative of male homosexuality. For instance, Gray was said to have been teased with the nickname "Miss *Molly Gray*," by the other sailors "for want of having a rough Beard as they had."[123] Shurtliff was also referred to as "Molly" by their fellow soldiers "in playful allusion to her want of a beard."[124] Bundy's account also notes that fellow sailors thought of them as a "Molly" which made them less of a man. Bundy writes, "I was rather esteem'd amongst them as a molly than a man; that which makes us pleasing in other places, such as civility, good manners, a decent demeanor, is the aversion of these people; and as I was not naturally turned for the nonsense of the place, I was pointed out for abuse, and sufficiently felt the effects."[125] Bundy emphasized how their good manners and respectful deportment contributed to the assessment that they were effeminate.

The "Molly" reference was loaded. Molly was not simply a nickname for a woman or a way to suggest the sailors were women, not men. Rather, in the mid-eighteenth century, "Molly" was widely known throughout the British Empire as a slang reference for "An effeminate or homosexual man or boy."[126] It is easy to conclude that the authors inserted such slang for homophobic effect, which may have been the case. But it would be shortsighted on our part to overlook another explanation: Molly, as several early historians of sexuality demonstrated, was not simply a reference to sexuality but was in many ways a claim to a third gender.[127] The category of the "Molly" was created by those assigned male at birth who embraced feminine personas in part as a way to signal their sexual desires for men of more masculine genders. It circulated in casual conversation and print media. The adoption of the term in reference to female soldiers suggests not only broad recognition of gender nonconformity but also perhaps the idea that female soldiers might inspire or engage in same-sex intimacies with other male sailors *as men*. Sex between men during this period was somewhat acceptable though also harshly punished in particular circumstances.[128]

It is still up for debate whether there was a correlation between gender nonconformity and illicit same-sex sexual desires during this period. Susan Lanser argues that they were linked as early as the mid-eighteenth century, more than a century before the findings of most historians of sexuality who have situated this connection in late nineteenth-century sexology. One basis for this argument is her claim that "sexual innocence begins to disappear, that gender and sexuality begin to form their modern linkage, and that the cross-dressed woman becomes more than circumstantially associated with the courtship of other women rather than with such adventurous projects as seafaring and soldiering."[129] The argument is very convincing in many regards but requires us to consider the question of "sexual innocence" in the lives of husbands and others in the ensuing chapters. It presumes that sexuality, rather than gender, was the truly transgressive category. But these encounters between two people assigned female at birth who occupy different genders are not simply same-sex encounters.

Scholars have indiscriminately used the descriptor "cross-dressed woman" to describe two distinct relationships to gender: first, a gender nonconforming person who was still perceived by others as a woman; second, a person assigned female who lived and passed as a man in their society. People could move between these two expressions, but they were perceived differently. Female soldiers and sailors fundamentally destabilized notions of sexual difference. Their lives demonstrated the kind of sexual, social, and relational chaos that could result from a gender transition. Accounts that link transing gender with an end to sexual innocence are still the exception, not the norm.

In most cases, mere gender transing by people assigned female at birth without evidence of sexual transgressions or claims of legal marriage to women were of minimal interest to the state. When such people were turned over to the authorities, they were detained under charges of vagrancy. Most policing of gender transgressions happened at the level of the family and the community – often inspired by religious teachings and social norms, not legal ones. This is not to claim gender transing was accepted or that people were allowed to continue transing gender once noticed. It was quite the opposite in fact. We must never forget that *no one* who was found out to be assigned female and living as a man in these eighteenth- and nineteenth-century accounts was allowed to continue doing so. Even in the absence of formal legal punishment, at the very least they were all expected and generally forced to give up their male identities, personas, and clothing. Gender itself was the punishment. This was as true for sailors and soldiers as it was for husbands. No amount of government service, patriotism, or hard work would ever generate enough respect, tolerance, flexibility, or gratitude to decide to let the person live as they wished.

CHAPTER 4

THE WIVES

JAMES ALLEN

Abigail Naylor and James Allen met while working in the service of Mr. Wood, Abigail as a housemaid, James as a groomsman.[1] James enjoyed an excellent reputation as someone who was good-looking, intelligent, and skilled in their job. For work, James would dress neatly in a uniform consisting of a waistcoat, collared shirt, cockade hat, buckskin breeches, and boots.[2] James did not offer upward mobility for their bride but would have been a safe and familiar choice for a woman of similarly limited economic prospects. James and Abigail married in 1807 at St. Giles' Church, Camberwell in the Southwark borough of London.[3] Life was never easy for the couple, but they were hardworking, resourceful, and had each other. After numerous jobs, several relocations, and twenty-one years of marriage, things came crashing to a halt. James Allen was bashed in the head and killed by a falling piece of timber while working as a "bottom sawyer" for shipwright and builder Mr. Crisp in Mill Street, Dockhead, England in 1829.[4] James was declared dead en route to St. Thomas' Hospital. The end of James' life was the beginning of Abigail's nightmare.[5] Not only had she just lost her husband of twenty-one years and the primary earner for the family, but everyone learned that her husband was assigned female at birth.

Allen's death was a public affair with nearly a dozen people witness to the final moments of their life and the immediate aftermath. Co-workers witnessed the accident and rushed James to the hospital. Doctors and nurses received the now lifeless body, which was turned over to medical students, the coroner, and a jury to determine cause of death and rule out any foul play. Allen's wife was summoned and she brought a friend with her. The owner of the shipyard where the incident took place came too, hoping he would not be found liable for the incident. Over two dozen news stories ran within the first week in London and nearby cities. Within two months of Allen's death, another two dozen articles ran in the United States. Several editions of "Narratives" of Allen's life were printed and sold in book form and several broadsides circulated as well (Figure 4.1). The death of a so-called "female husband" was news because people wanted to know how someone assigned female at birth managed to go through life as a man. This fact challenged views that gender was directly correlated to one's sex, casting doubt on dominant social assumptions that sexual difference was natural and obvious. The parties assembled had different stakes in these issues.

First, consider Mr. Crisp, owner of the shipyard. Just a few years later, given the rise of workplace accidents and deaths involving railroads, coroners became increasingly aggressive in trying to assign blame on employers for negligent and unsafe working conditions. Juries in such cases held business owners liable when workplace conditions could be shown to endanger workers. Coroners courts used fines known as "deodands" to signal misconduct.[6] In medieval times, the deodand was understood as an appeasement gift to the gods in cases of violent death.[7] Mr. Crisp was not held liable, an outcome that would have been far less likely had Allen died just three or four years later. It is possible that the focus on Allen's gender distracted from concerns over workplace safety. Instead, Mr. Crisp was largely an aftermath in this story that featured a much more compelling question for those assembled. He was presented somewhat minimally and neutrally in the press. No accounts raised concerns of his culpability. Some noted that the small amount of money he offered to the widow Abigail was a pittance, not even enough to pay for the funeral.[8]

The coroner overseeing the inquest was Thomas Shelton. Every death did not merit an inquest, which was an expensive and time-consuming process. The local justices of the peace oversaw the coroners, ordering them only to undertake an inquest "when there were signs of violence or a real mystery about the cause of death."[9] Shelton was trained as a lawyer who held numerous government appointments throughout his career.

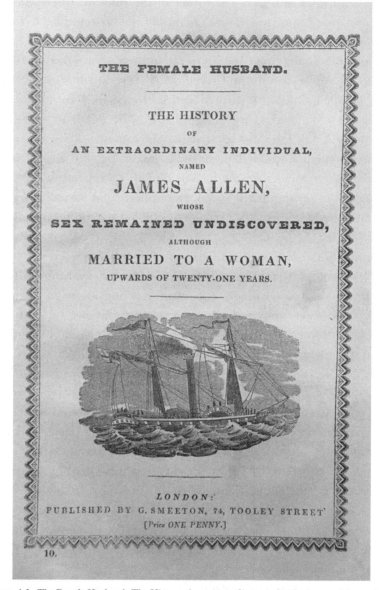

Figure 4.1 *The Female Husband. The History of an extraordinary individual, named James Allen, whose sex remained undiscovered, although married to a woman, upwards of twenty-one years* (London, 1829). Once the story of James Allen hit the papers, printers moved quickly to package it in pamphlet form, offering both cheap and expensive editions in anticipation of broad interest.

Image courtesy of the Center for the History of Medicine in the Francis A. Countway Library of Medicine

He was the assistant coroner to Thomas Beach throughout the 1780s and succeeded Beach as coroner for the City of London and Borough of Southwark upon Beach's death in the summer of 1788. While there was a push from some quarters to appoint a medical doctor in the position, the coroner was principally charged with protecting the financial interests of the Crown and ensuring justice was done.[10] Shelton argued that the responsibilities of the coroner had more to do with enforcing criminal law than it did with medical concerns. This was not uncontested. Some doctors believed the coroner's office took a lazy, unskilled approach in determining cause of death, allowing countless homicides to go uncharged. Fifty years passed, however, before this argument prevailed with the appointment of Dr. Thomas Wakely in 1840.[11] Thomas Shelton worked as the coroner from 1788 until his death in July 1829 and oversaw the jury inquest into the cause of James Allen's death, just seven months before his own. Shelton was nothing if not skilled and experienced.[12] And yet he had never encountered a situation quite like this one. He expressed "astonishment" particularly about "so extraordinary a circumstance as two females living together as man and wife" for over twenty-one years.[13]

The work of the autopsy itself, however, was completed by someone with medical training. In the eighteenth century, this was principally the task of a surgeon. But as the numbers of people frequenting hospitals increased, the bodies of the dead were left in the hands of those less experienced at healing – senior medical students referred to as "dressers."[14] In the case of James Allen, the dresser was Mr. John Martin, who worked under the supervision of a surgeon, Dr. William Green.[15] Martin declared that Allen was dead upon arrival at the hospital, about 3 p.m. on a Monday. The cause of death was very clear: "the whole of the bones of the skull were fractured." This was not an injury anyone was expected to survive.[16] Studies of coroners' reports from surrounding areas during the same period show that those who died as a result of a falling object were predominantly men.[17] Inadvertently, however, Martin discovered that this hardworking man and beloved husband was anatomically female. One reporter characterized this by stating, "on subsequent examination witness discovered the deceased to be a female, perfect in all respects."[18] The inquest itself cites John Martin plainly stating, "the dead is a woman."[19] Word spread quickly throughout the hospital that there was something much more interesting at play in this case than a simple workplace accident. By the time the coroner arrived to oversee the trial, medical students from throughout the hospital packed into the jury room.[20] The relationship between the coroner and medical students wasn't always smooth. One of Shelton's predecessors later complained in the press that medical students disrupted his inquisition. The students responded with a letter of their own claiming, "I think the coroner has acted with scant courtesy to the authorities of St. Thomas's Hospital, through whose kindness he is permitted to use the room in which he holds his court, and to which he has no manner of right."[21] The medical students believed the work of the coroner was secondary to the aims of the hospital.

This coroner, however, had no such challenges to his authority, as eager students piled into the room, joining those who knew James Allen personally and would attest to their life, character, skill, and gender. But the coroner struggled with the challenge that Allen's life posed to conventions of gender and language. Coroner Shelton repeatedly referenced Allen using male pronouns and offered a rational for why he did this. Shelton declared, "I call the deceased 'he,' because I considered it impossible for him to be a woman, as he had a wife."[22] Shelton felt the need to substantiate this decision with further information – the fact that he saw the actual marriage certificate.[23] He used his position to put an end to further inquiries into Allen's life, asserting the sole purpose of such an inquest was to determine cause of death and not to investigate the lives of the dead. He wouldn't let the jury question Abigail formally, though later she did field some questions from the students.[24] Shelton was the most powerful person to officially weigh in on Allen's life and gender. He represented the Crown in various capacities throughout his professional life and was highly regarded throughout his career. Shelton respected law, custom, and institutions. He refused to refer to Allen with female pronouns because Allen was married to a woman; he refused to question the legitimacy of this marriage because he saw the legal document that made it so. Allen's social gender – evident to co-workers, employers, and himself – was more important to Shelton than anatomical sex. The state of Allen's legal sex remained in limbo – suspended between competing claims from medical students asserting female anatomy and a lifetime of relationships, paperwork, and legal documents stating otherwise.

Perhaps most remarkable in this era of grave digging, body snatching, and general desperation on the part of doctors and medical students to gain access to dead bodies for dissection and training, Shelton declared Allen's body off limits. News stories reported on "rumors" that "several well-known 'resurrection men' were lurking about, in the hope of procuring the corpse of so remarkable a subject for dissection."[25] Neither Dr. Green nor the dresser John Martin sought further access to the corpse for their own research. Perhaps Martin was satisfied there was really nothing so remarkable about Allen, having already declared them a woman.[26] Still, Shelton took no chances, ordering the body of this impoverished laborer not to Potter's field where it may easily have landed for Abigail's lack of money but into a vault, safe and secure. The news report characterized the vault as "belonging to a private burial-ground, in the parish of St. John's Bermondsey, access to which is impossible it being well secured and guarded against the attack of body-snatchers."[27] No one was permitted additional examination of the naked body of James Allen. This was a remarkable dignity rarely allowed for people of indiscriminate sex or gender.[28] For this, we have Coroner Thomas Shelton to thank. He was in charge of the proceedings and made two things clear: he recognized Allen's legal manhood and he would not tolerate the abuse of his office. As a law man, he respected the authority of the state (and the marriage certificate it issued) over the knowledge and interests of doctors – and doctors in training.

This tension between legal manhood and anatomical femaleness played out in the hearing as other people expressed their views of Allen. Clues that would help them make sense of Allen's gender were believed to be contained in their choice of clothing, social relations, physical attributes, and emotional disposition. It is important to notice here the range and variety of things that were thought to constitute one's gender. Allen was described as "a sober, steady, strong, and active man" and "a smart and handsome young man, and an excellent groom." These characterizations were positive assessments of a laboring man, emphasizing both physical traits – strong and handsome – as well as mental ones – steady and smart.

Co-workers of Allen explained their impressions of Allen's gender over the years. Only two issues raised any suspicion at all that Allen was not like the other men. Co-workers from the shipyard asserted that the pitch of Allen's voice was strange and that they teased them because of it. Newspapers characterized this testimony several ways, stating, "There was rather a peculiarity in the tone of voice, which subjected the deceased to raillery amongst the men with whom she was employed, but they never for a moment doubted of her being of the male sex."[29] Other accounts noted not only their voice but also a lack of facial hair, "His fellow-workmen, from the weakness in the voice, and his not having a beard, considered him an hermaphrodite, but always thought he was 'most of a man' from his having been married so many years."[30] These statements suggest that when they thought about it, the co-workers believed Allen was not a typical man and was different from them in a few physical ways. Co-workers did not think Allen was a woman or accuse Allen of as much in any way, but they turned to "hermaphroditism" as a way to try to explain certain secondary sex characteristics that gave them pause.

But Allen was clearly a man in other respects: from their masculine hands to their sailor's attire to their twenty-one-year marriage to a woman. Several different sources noted that James had masculine hands, including the doctor and their wife Abigail. When pressed on how it was possible that she did not realize that her husband was not a man, Abigail said she was not suspicious of her husband's sex because Allen was uncannily strong, with hands of a "masculine character."[31] A news story that spoke of Allen with feminine pronouns conceded as much, stating, "The deceased appears to have been an interesting looking girl; her limbs were well proportioned; and the only thing of a masculine character that we observed about her was her hands, which were large, and the flesh extremely hard, owing to the work she performed for so many years."[32] There was no disputing that working as a servant and laborer for decades, in jobs usually reserved for men, gave one exceptionally strong, muscular hands. Living as a certain kind of man – in this case, as a laborer – led one's body to a physical transformation.

Clothing was a crucial indicator of gender and really the starting point for many people who thought about transing gender. Allen embraced a range of styles of men's clothes depending on their occupation. They wore the uniform of a groomsman for years at service and then later turned to sailor's clothes. For the last two years of their life, Allen worked in a shipyard and would have easily blended in with their described "thick flannel waistcoats, which extended from the neck down to the hips."[33] Not only did this outfit allow Allen to blend in among co-workers, but it also supported Allen's attempt to minimize their chest by binding, for which Allen wrapped a linen bandage around their upper torso.[34] Abigail reported she didn't think twice about this practice because Allen claimed the bandage was to protect their lungs, something perfectly reasonable to assert for someone who worked outside, often in cold, rainy, or snowy conditions.

When people grappled with Allen's life and gender, it is evident that one thing was more important than the others: marriage. The fact that they were married to a woman made Allen into more of a man than any job, jacket, or beard ever would. In short, being married to a woman affirmed one's manhood. Marriage was crucial to Allen's ability to live as a man in the eyes of co-workers who felt that Allen must be "most of a man" because they were "married so many years" despite their suspicions that Allen was a "hermaphrodite."[35] While physical embodiment was one aspect of gender, it stood in contention with – and was overridden by – marital status as the most meaningful signifier of manhood.

Allen actually lived and worked as a man for years before proposing marriage to Abigail. It is unlikely the marriage was one of exploitation or convenience. The two worked in the same home of Mr. Wood for nearly three years before getting involved. After their marriage, Abigail stayed in service with Wood while Allen went to work for Mr. Lonsdale of Mayshill, Blackheath.[36] Eight months into their marriage, they scarcely saw each other and so resolved to find a way to be together more often. They decided to try to go into business together. The stability of marriage, the combined incomes, the vision for a future all led them to an opportunity. They combined their savings and took over a public house at Baldock in Hertfordshire called The Sun. Perhaps they heard of the success of the Howes in running a public house decades earlier. In a freak incident of bad luck, however, they were robbed of everything. The couple abandoned the business and relocated to Dockhead, where each labored in various capacities.

Abigail's friend Mary Daly asserted that Abigail had no idea Allen was assigned female and swore to this effect on the life of her granddaughter. She also claimed that Allen "had left his wife several times on account of jealousy" and that Mary advised Abigail "to leave her husband" because of this. But Abigail stayed.[37] News reports picked up on this theme and emphasized that Allen was someone who was frequently jealous when Abigail paid attention to other men. Abigail neither confirmed nor denied this claim herself. It can be read in several different ways. On the one hand, it suggests that Allen was insecure in their manhood and fearful that Abigail would leave them for someone else. One report stated, "The deceased was described as of rather an ill temper and expressed strong resentment against the poor woman to whom she was married whenever the latter noticed a man particularly. Upon those occasions the deceased never failed to act the part of the jealous husband, and has often inflicted corporal chastisement on the wife when she considered that she was not conducting herself as she ought to."[38] On the other hand, possessiveness of one's wife fit well within the confines of a traditional model of manhood. Allen wasn't the first female husband to be portrayed in this way. Henry Fielding made his version of Hamilton jealous, suggesting that passion, possessiveness, and jealousy were core components of masculinity. Read in this light, it would be strange if Allen wasn't jealous when Abigail engaged other men, not because Allen wasn't man enough but because of the fact that Allen was a husband.

Were they compelled by love, money, or custom to remain together despite this source of conflict? It's not clear. They were poor but not destitute. Allen worked extra side jobs to earn more money, which they saved for fear of future hardship. Abigail had worked as a servant for many years and more recently turned to bonnet making while also managing their household. Women dominated the bonnet-making trade in England during this period (Figure 4.2).[39] Abigail labored in a largely hidden part of the workforce that was hard to document and quantify. This system of subcontract tailoring was known as "sweating" and characterized by long hours and low wages. Women working for piece wages

BONNETS AND HEAD-DRESSES OF THE TIME, 1806-1830.¹—From La Belle Assemblée and Ladies' Magazine.

Figure 4.2 "Bonnets and Head-dresses of the Time, 1806–1830," 1861–70. Bonnets were a staple accessory for women. Abigail Allen made bonnets in her home to try to make ends meet.
Image courtesy of the Miriam and Ira Wallach Division of Art, Prints, and Photographs: Art & Architecture Collection, The New York Public Library

were difficult to track.[40] Unfortunately, even this meager income was no longer available to Abigail who was unable to continue sewing with efficiency after she cut off a forefinger chopping wood.[41] None of this hardship was new to Abigail, who grew up in humble surroundings and was put out to service at a young age. Her father was a tradesman who made bedsteads and was notably still living when James died. But he labored in poverty himself and he was not able to offer Abigail financial support.[42] Labor and class marked their lives as ones of hardship. Like so many married couples, Abigail and James could find at least a modicum of financial stability by joining their lives, incomes, and expenses together under one roof. Now Abigail stood to lose everything.

Attitudes toward laboring people and the poor were undergoing significant changes in England during this period.[43] The idea of a "breadwinner wage" for laboring men with spouses and children was first viewed as a privilege that brought with it great responsibility when the New Poor Law was passed in 1834. In later decades this would shift; around the 1850s it was seen as a "reward for respectability" and at the turn of the century it became a form of unemployment insurance. Abigail Allen's claim for widow's benefits would not have been received with open arms because she didn't have any children and some felt such women should immediately return to work upon their husband's death. Only in 1837 were widows offered six months of out relief. The shift toward compulsory marriage as an economic imperative for women had unexpected consequences for poor relief policies, however. In the late 1840s and 1850s, single women were suddenly entitled to outdoor relief because they were viewed principally as dependents rather than workers.[44]

Abigail lost her husband and their family income – all that remained was her reputation. Doubts were immediately cast on the legitimacy of her marriage. Reporting on the story of Allen's life and death reveals the ambivalence writers felt in trying to accurately portray their marital status while also not undermining the gender binary. One of the first newspaper articles qualified their use of the language of marriage once it was revealed that Allen was assigned female, for instance: "The body was immediately conveyed to St. Thomas's Hospital, where, to the astonishment of all present, the husband (if the expression may be allowed) was discovered to be a female."[45] Furthermore, this story also qualified its use of the term widow, stating, "We have collected the following particulars from (to use a very common-place expression) the *disconsolate widow*."[46] While Abigail was in fact disconsolate, few treated her as a sympathetic figure or even recognized her as a widow.

While marriage served to uplift, legitimize, and verify the manhood of female husbands, it could lead to an incredible amount of harassment, judgment, and isolation for their wives. This is precisely what happened to Abigail when James died. People harassed her endlessly, raising doubts about her gender and alleging that she knowingly entered into a fraudulent marriage. Rumors that Abigail was herself "of the masculine gender" and passing herself off fraudulently as a woman circulated but were quickly repudiated.[47] Abigail lived in "great terror" of those neighbors who targeted her.[48] But she had also built up quite a bit of respect and goodwill over the years in her community. Most newspaper reports verified her good name and trustworthiness, asserting that "those who know her give her an excellent character" and that she had an outstanding work ethic, stating, "she is a most industrious creature."[49] Still, Abigail felt the only way people would leave her alone (and quite possibly not pursue legal claims against her) was if she swore that she did not know that her husband was assigned female.

A gentleman offered to help Abigail restore her good name.[50] He asked a magistrate to offer to swear an affidavit signed by her verifying that she did not know Allen was not a man. She swore, "I was entirely ignorant of the fact of the said James Allen being a female, until that circumstance was communicated to me by the woman who undressed the body after death."[51] Abigail was forced to disavow knowledge that James lived life in a gender that was different from their sex. Much has been written about "respectability" as a crucial aspiration for white women in the nineteenth century. For Abigail, the stakes were very high. This campaign to restore her reputation aimed to preserve the safety, dignity, and character of one poor widow who received no sympathy with the passing of her beloved. It is hard not to wonder if a woman of greater financial means would have been treated more or less harshly than Abigail was.

Abigail desperately needed the insurance money that James dutifully paid for over the years, though initially the group declined to honor the policy because of Allen's alleged deception, "by representing herself as a man, and always appearing in the character of one."[52] It was a mean-spirited move meant to signal disapproval of social disorder, to punish one suspected of violating basic norms like heterosexuality and sexual difference. This abusive rejection led Abigail to further despair. She couldn't even cover the costs of Allen's funeral, not to mention her own living expenses going forward. In this respect, however, the press coverage worked in her favor. Eventually, the private association reconsidered their decision and granted Abigail typical widow's benefits, deciding, "that Abigail Allen was duly entitled to all benefits arising from the club, as the widow of the deceased, and she was accordingly paid the arrears which she claimed, including the funeral expenses, &c. of the deceased."[53] It took some doing, but another group of people were willing to recognize the categories that defined their lives – as female husband and female wife – over Allen's assigned sex.

Abigail had very real legal, financial, and social reasons for asserting her own ignorance. The benefits of this – in her own life – clearly outweighed the downsides. But as a result, she was left standing as someone who was abused, manipulated, and duped. If Abigail had in fact chosen James knowing they were assigned female, who would ever believe her? Maybe she waited to meet someone who lived between genders and chose James precisely because of their difference. There was something intriguing about someone who blurred the line between sex and gender, embodying both masculine and feminine traits. Those who were raised and socialized as girls and then chose to live as men were special. Abigail herself – quite possibly uninterested in other men and so thrilled when James showed interest in her – was no ordinary heterosexual woman. When she married James, Abigail Naylor took the surname of Allen. This marked a legal and social transition of her own, even if others were ignorant and assumed they were a typical couple.

The general public seemed eager to dismiss the idea that Abigail knew James was different. This was the path of least resistance. It would establish Abigail as an ordinary woman. With James dead, it was Abigail's difference that remained an open question and threat. Not only did she know James was assigned female but did she love him because of it? This raised all sorts of questions. Rather, it would serve the status quo if she did not know and went back to life as an ordinary woman of typical heterosexual desire. The press certainly spent no time hypothesizing as to why she might have knowingly partnered with a man who had transed genders.

There was interest in getting to the bottom of what compelled Allen to this course of life. For unknown reasons, the coverage of Allen's life did not use a simple popular explanation: that Allen lived as a man to make more money. Rather, the unverified "conjecture" that was reprinted numerous times was that Allen lived as a man because they "had been violated when a child."[54] Those who examined Allen's body explicitly refuted this claim. It suggested that a life of gender transing was compelled by some terrible and/or extreme situation. Several dots remain unconnected in this theory. The only clue to the logic offered went like this: "the deceased had been violated when a child, which circumstance operating upon a mind of extraordinary strength, induced her to adopt the resolution which it appears she carried with her to the moment of her death."[55] What exactly was the resolution? To not marry a man? To not have sex with a man? To not move through the world as a woman? The first two would have been easily achieved by living as a single, chaste woman. Why go through all the trouble? It was more likely, then, the final option. Allen did not feel like or want to live as a woman – regardless of why that was the case.

In 1829, the mass market press had a field day using the story of James and Abigail to promote exaggerated portrayals in a way not seen since Fielding's 1746 *Female Husband*. Just eight days after the story broke, the publisher J.S. Thomas of 2 York Street advertised the sale of "A Correct Portrait" of James and Abigail, along with a forthcoming "authentic memoir."[56] The publisher took a different angle a few weeks later, modifying the ad to promote his book as an authority that would clear up the many "absurd stories" that were going around about the female husband.[57] Thomas' account was anchored in facts but also embellished with a vast array of details that only James or Abigail could verify. There was money to be made repackaging the story of James and Abigail Allen, especially when sold together with "A correct portrait of James Allen, the Female Husband; and also Abigail his wife" (Figure 4.3).[58] When presented with a case of two people that fundamentally denaturalized the categories of man and woman, this editor framed it with pages of gross generalizations about the nature of womanhood, such as women's inability to keep secrets. It presented the couple as hyper-sexual – very unusual for a female husband case – emphasizing Abigail's overwhelming sexual desire for James while exaggerating James's relationship to stereotypical laboring masculinity, via addiction to tobacco.[59]

A broadside was similarly irreverent but emphasized the opposite – their presumed lack of sexual intimacy: "This poor woman had a husband, That had nothing at all. Twenty years she liv'd a married life, Still a maid she may remain, But we trust she'll find a difference, If she ever weds again."[60] The contradictory representations of sexuality highlight the way female husband cases exposed the instability of marriage, heterosexuality, and sexual difference. The last of these, however, was probably closer to the truth – or at least that is what Abigail told the authorities. In her account of their wedding night, for instance, Abigail said that Allen "was taken ill, and continued, or pretended to be so, the remainder of the night."[61] Generally, she suggested that Allen did not pursue sexual intimacies with her. Writers could only conjecture, with James dead and Abigail

Figure 4.3 "Portrait of Abigail Allen; Portrait of James Allen," 1829. Full color companion portraits of James and Abigail Allen offered by T.S. Thomas in the more expensive edition of *The Female Husband*.
Image courtesy of the Lewis Walpole Library, Yale University

trying to re-establish her character among the neighbors. No good would come for anyone if Abigail revealed more details about their sex life. Her insistence that she did not know James was assigned female lent itself more readily to a view that their marriage was passionless. In the short run, it was not a bad conclusion for Abigail to be portrayed as an embodiment of middling nineteenth-century purity.[62]

In the long run, however, the social pressure on surviving wives to deny knowledge of their partners' bodies and distance themselves from questions of sexual intimacy served to minimize the connection between the two parties. This erasure undermined their credibility as evidence of queer, trans, or same-sex relationships in the past, all the while etching a partial truth in the historic record. Jack Halberstam has described this hostile view of female masculinity as one where the husband has "a longing to be and to have a power that is always just out of reach."[63] From the perspective of queer and trans history, acceptance of the notion that these relationships were asexual had a devastating function by erasing the significance of sexual intimacy and emphasizing a husband's inability to satisfy their wife. Even without sex, however, female husbands are deemed legitimate subjects of a queer past because of their gender. Female wives, however, are never granted this standing, largely because of how the accounts of their lives have been written. We can only imagine that Abigail may herself have been the instigator of sexual intimacies, the lover of female masculinity who lured James close to her. What if Abigail pursued James, persuading James that she could see them and would love them for who they were? What if their life and love together was her idea? In this case, the erasure of her role in shaping their relationship would be even more painful.

The local London press ran a wide range of stories in the ensuing weeks, ranging from brief overviews to long-form pieces that provided background and context on the parties involved. Those outside the city limits or less involved in original reporting incorporated subjective commentary with the facts of the case. Consider this account, which avoids gendered language and pronouns while still heightening feelings for a readership with words such as "extraordinary" and italics for the word female and exclamation points. It begins with the phrase, "Extraordinary Occurrence," and calls the couple "singular" while reporting, "The deceased died whilst being conveyed to the hospital, and on examining the body, to the astonishment of all, it proved to be that of a *female.*[64] The US press ran modified versions of the British stories, often including editorial notes at the beginning of the accounts. For instance, a reprint of a story several months later in the *Republican Advocate* from Batavia, New York emphasized Allen's femaleness. This article sought to correct the surgeon's claim that Allen was a man by changing the pronoun attributed to the surgeon, reporting, "The surgeon declared that the deceased and *her* wife had been regularly married."[65] In the US press, Allen was sometimes declared a woman while the British press privileged the claims of both Allen's wife and the coroner that Allen was both man and husband, albeit female. The US papers across the board were more likely to mock and belittle female husbands. The trend that began with James Howe is increasingly evident regarding husbands in this chapter, from James Allen to Henry Stoake.

HENRY STOAKE

Henry Stoake was not like the other laborers who worked long hours laying bricks for the new buildings going up all over the city of Manchester, England in the 1830s.[66] The other men could expect to earn about eighteen shillings per week for their labors, working especially long days in the summer.[67] But Stoake had greater aspirations. They served as an apprentice to a master builder in Yorkshire and eventually built their own successful business, employing eight men and one apprentice. Stoake had a reputation for being exceptionally skilled and would have been able to charge considerably more for their own time, especially when building the specialty ovens and flues they became somewhat of a local celebrity for making.[68] The business generated so much money in ten years, from 1829 to 1838, that Stoake claimed they could stop working and live off the earnings.[69] As a female husband, Stoake was not born with male privilege. But like most husbands in the nineteenth century, Stoake thought of the household wealth as belonging to them alone.

This is exactly what Stoake's wife Ann was afraid of when she sought the help of a lawyer in seeking a legal separation. Ann managed the books and accounts for the bricklaying business, playing a crucial role in their joint prosperity on top of all of the other homemaking duties expected of women.[70] News reports claimed this fact: "The wife had the entire management of the books and accounts in the business; and as far as we have heard, there was not the slightest imputation on her character."[71] Ann was widely noted as "a respectable female" who exhibited both responsibility and flexibility in her skillful management of home and business.[72]

Ann might be categorized as a "deputy husband" in relation to Stoake, her "female husband." While the role of husband is imbued with gendered connotations, it principally describes what is an administrative and caretaking position.[73] Laurel Thatcher Ulrich coined the phrase deputy husband to capture the many roles women adopted to support their families within otherwise conventional heterosexual marriages in colonial America. In clarifying her use of the phrase, Ulrich explained that, "Far from arguing for a general flexibility in role definition, I was attempting to resolve the paradoxical evidence concerning the economic behavior of colonial women by defining an unrecognized role, that of deputy husband."[74] But other historians have embraced it as a way to capture just that: flexibility. By the nineteenth century, flexibility was the name of the game for women who hoped to navigate the rapidly changing economic and domestic landscape. More often than not, women's roles and tasks expanded and contracted as need, duty, or desire required. As Jeanne Boydston explained, "But if eighteenth-century constructions of manhood proved problematic in the face of the market transition, female labor carried with it into the transition a long cultural assumption of flexibility in the form of the role of deputy husband. Under the rubric of household necessity and with the approbation of the household head, a free female could engage in virtually any form of labor without censure."[75] Many women neither sought nor wanted financial responsibilities, even when circumstances called for it.[76] The deputy husband category captures movement, flexibility, and change; it suggests the limitations of language in describing people's lives in a highly gendered society while recognizing that women's work was wide ranging.

Ann Stoake was nothing if not flexible and skilled in financial matters. Henry, however, did not appreciate how hard Ann worked. Henry manipulated and punished Ann by withholding her allowance "for housekeeping expenses."[77] This reveals the limitations of the power of Ann and other deputy husbands – their husbands ultimately were still in charge of finances. Ann also alleged that Henry "treated her very ill" when intoxicated.[78] No matter their financial success or the stability that twenty-two years of marriage brought to their lives, Ann had simply had enough. She wanted a divorce. She secured an attorney who immediately pressured Henry to give her the house and furnishings, for starters. Under typical circumstances, this hardly would have been newsworthy. But this divorce would not be typical because this marriage was not typical – a fact that Ann decided to use against Henry, to leverage the financial terms of their separation in her favor.

I wonder if Ann consented to her lawyer's strategy to take her case to the press? There were many downsides for her, not least of which was the fact that she would become socially stigmatized for her marriage to a man who had transed gender. Further, this could leave her liable for a fraud charge if the community was outraged and some prosecutor was interested in proving that she was in on the deception all along. It also could ruin her husband's business and leave Henry vulnerable to pros-ecution as well. Given all of these terrible outcomes that could result from involving a lawyer and outing her husband as being assigned female to the lawyer, it seems reasonable to conclude that Henry rejected Ann's private plea for a separation on reasonable terms. Only with no other recourse would someone subject herself to all of these risks. She felt she had nothing to lose and/or that the burden of public humiliation would fall on Henry, not her. She was right.

There were legal issues to be considered. At first, the lawyers were uncertain if Ann would even be eligible for "the maintenance of a wife" that the law allowed because they were not sure the marriage would be recognized as legitimate. This was one of the main ways that legal and social gender contradicted each other, forcing a reckoning. But the couple were in fact legally married as man, Henry Stoake, and woman, Ann Hants, in St. Peter and St. Paul's Parish Church of Sheffield, England, on January 14, 1817.[79] Henry occupied a legal standing as husband that was not allowed for women, leaving lawyers to wonder how this would factor into the undoing of their marriage. Wary that the law might not benefit their client, lawyers worked to persuade Henry of the value of their wife's labor, partly using the public papers to build their case. Several local and regional papers reported of Ann Stoake, "who, after having for 22 years filled the character of a wife, greatly benefitting the interests of her supposed husband, not only by her care of household concerns, but of the business books and accounts, had surely some claim to compensation as a servant, if she were unable by law to demand the maintenance of a wife."[80] The legitimacy of their marriage was further thrown into doubt by references to Ann as one who lived in "the character of a wife" and characterizations of Henry as "her supposed husband." This was a typical rhetorical style in such accounts. But they were legally married and Ann Stoake ultimately had a legal claim as spouse. The public opinion of co-workers, employees, neighbors, and the press was loud and clear: Stoake owed their wife the house and furnishings – and then some!

Female husbands and their wives believed that gender, not sex, was the feature that made their relationships possible. No matter that both were assigned female at birth, as long as one was happy, comfortable, and skilled at embracing a male gender identity and expression, there was no reason they could not have a successful relationship together within a heteronormative system. When someone – a boss, friend, neighbor, policeman – was uncomfortable and disapproving of people who transed gender to live, they generally argued that anatomical sex was the most important determining factor in defining the parameters of one's life. Gender deviations were still seen as negative violations of law, morality, and taste. A female husband was always more vulnerable in this regard than a female wife. Not only would a female husband have more "transgressions" to explain to hostile strangers, but their wives also had the power of the truth – and could hold it against them if they wanted to.

This fact made female wives of female husbands unlike any other wives in the UK or US in the nineteenth century. Ann Stoake could always turn on her husband and use gender against Henry. Ann must have been desperate. Who knows how many years passed since her first inkling that she might be safer, happier, or better off without her husband? How many times did Henry promise Ann that things would be different if she stayed? Women had little recourse but this issue gave Ann leverage. Did she threaten to out Henry's gender before or did this information just spill out of her when she was meeting with her lawyer for the first time? Did she finally feel free to share her circumstances with someone whose sole job was *to help her*?

Ann took an unusual tactic and used the issue of assigned sex to delegitimize *her own marriage*. Ann argued that their relationship was not real because her husband was a woman. Ann flipped the script that defined their twenty-one years of marriage and said that assigned sex was more important than acquired gender in making a relationship. She hoped to manipulate popular perceptions of the situation and get herself a divorce on favorable terms.

Wives seeking divorces from female husbands in the mid-nineteenth century fueled a shift in dominant attitudes of these relationships from that of a typical heterosexual marriage with an atypical husband toward that of a relationship between "two women." Other divorce cases from beyond the British Empire – France in 1858 and Chile in 1869 – demonstrate how wives could undo the gender of their female husbands. In both cases, wives came forward demanding their marriages be null and void on the basis of sex, asserting the marriages were not legitimate because they took place between two people of the "same sex."[81] These wives encouraged others to look beyond the gender of their husbands, instead emphasizing assigned sex to invalidate the legality of their marriages.

Ann received overwhelming support in her bid to receive a portion of the couple's property and wealth in divorce, but her very public appeal opened the couple to scrutiny. Ann was mocked alternately for her stupidity and ignorance – and for thinking the public was stupid and ignorant enough to believe her disavowal. Ann claimed she learned that her husband was assigned female and transed gender only in the past few years,[82] and alleged she found out by accident and kept it a secret.[83] An article in the US press (not surprisingly) mocked her, stating, "It is the first time, however, we have heard that married people find out the sex of each other by accident."[84] A St. Louis paper also jumped on this fact and declared "The parties had been married seventeen years, and thus she had been in a happy state of ignorance just fourteen out of that number."[85] These stories were mocking and irreverent but also had a normalizing effect by engaging their story in these short quippy takes that were typically reserved for the daily foibles of regular married couples.

Physical embodiment plays only a minor role in the coverage of the Stoake case. There was no evidence that anyone doubted or questioned Henry's manhood, not even the typical "after the fact" reflections where neighbors and co-workers say they suspected something different about this person. Stoake was born July 22, 1798 in Portsmouth, Hampshire, England to a Thomas and Sarah Stoake.[86] Stoake had been living as a man from the time they were sixteen or seventeen. Reports stated, "This female husband assumed the garb and character of a boy at an early age." The story suggests that Stoake's physique as a young person helped them secure an apprenticeship and attract girls, stating, "Being of good exterior, with prepossessing appearance and manners, and of features rather handsome, the supposed young man attracted the attention of many females in the same condition of life, and among others, was the one who afterwards became the wife."[87] Henry was eighteen years old when they married a seventeen-year-old Ann Hants in 1817.[88]

There is nothing to suggest any aspect of Henry's physical embodiment changed in such a way as to raise suspicions twenty years later. In fact, the opposite was true. Working at manual labor for so many years made one *into more of a man*. Newspaper reports noted as much, stating, "The habits of the latter, we believe, are much more in accordance with those of her assumed sex and occupation than a woman."[89] Here it is noted that Henry assumed not just the gender role of a husband, but also the sex of a man. This honors the idea that a female assigned person could successfully make this transition. One piece stated, "No one except perchance from her beardless cheeks, and a certain shrillness of voice, could for a moment suspect that the little broadset bricklayer was of the soft sex" (Figure 4.4).[90] This reference to two aspects of secondary sex were frequently raised as defining the limits of transing gender: facial hair and tonal voice.

Very little was actually revealed about Stoake's life in the coverage of their divorce, but the news inspired reporters to recollect previous examples of other people who lived lives beyond the gender binary. The earliest reports in the local press began with a dramatic disclaimer emphasizing how unusual and unlikely the story was. When news of Henry Stoake hit the papers in 1838, the stories called the report of a female husband not only "unfounded," "silly," "very improbable," and

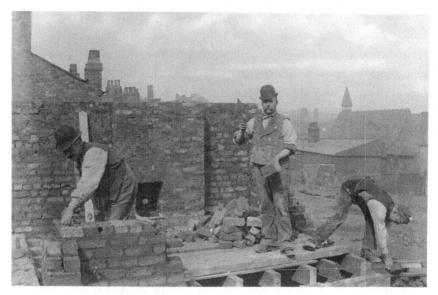

Figure 4.4 G. Wheeler, "Bricklayers at Work," 1900. Henry Stoake was a successful bricklayer in Manchester, England during an earlier era.
Image courtesy of the Manchester Archives and Local Studies

"remarkable" but also in fact true.[91] These accounts combined the "very improbable" but "not impossible" claims of the existence of a female husband with references to the numerous female husbands and other gender transers who were widely known.[92] James Allen is referenced at the end of the Stoake accounts, providing readers with context and comparison. News of James Allen may have been fresh in the mind of some readers, as it happened less than a decade earlier in London.

Allen and Stoake had a tremendous amount in common – they were both assigned female at birth, lived as men, married women, stayed in those marriages for a very long time, and did arduous manual labor for a living. Each was outed in the press as a "female husband." Both of their wives had complicated relationships with the public in the aftermath of their respective scandals, one as a victim of a tragedy, the other as an initiator of a divorce. Abigail was at first scrutinized and harassed and then later supported as an object of sympathy. For Ann, it was the opposite. The public was on her side against Henry in calling for reasonable division of their assets in divorce before turning on her and mocking her. References to James Allen in the accounts of Stoake would not have shocked readers.

INTERSEX BODIES AND THIRD GENDERS

Both James and Henry were referenced in terms of a "third gender" as a way to make meaning of their lives. Specifically, James was described as a likely "hermaphrodite" while Henry was called an "epicene creature." In both cases, this signaled an underlying view that gender and sex were strongly correlated. It suggests people believed – or wanted to believe – that for a female assigned person to live their life fully as a man, they must not really be female in the first place. This logic made perfect sense in a culture that advocated a clear distinction between the sexes, along with correlating and distinct gender customs. By blurring this distinction in their lives, female husbands threatened the clarity and rigidity of the categories "man" and "woman." It opened up the space for social recognition of great gender variability, that anyone might make the decision to trans gender. By invoking the idea of ambiguous sex, observers focused on the anatomical and sexed bodies of the female husbands, minimizing the significance of social gender. In advancing this claim, James and Henry were both treated as anomalous figures who because of their gender, must be of indeterminate sex. This seemingly physiological explanation for their social choices weakened the concept of their individual agency and further dehumanized them as those who were neither male nor female.[93]

Medieval and early modern views of intersex people (then referred to as hermaphrodites) were principally physiological, about bodies that were both male and female. The specificity of these views varied, with different weight given to visible anatomy, reproductive capacity, or secondary sex characteristics in determining if someone was truly intersex. As early as the seventeenth century, however, the concept of hermaphroditism was much less precisely understood than in the past. It was increasingly used as a way to reference "sexual ambiguity" broadly speaking, including cross-dressers, sodomites, and people who were anatomically neither or both male and female.[94] There was a marked shift away from references to hermaphroditism as a justification for same-sex intimacies between women in the mid to late eighteenth century. Rather, observers were more likely to point to external gender expressions of masculinity. Anatomical differences no longer stood as the basis for understanding same-sex desires, particularly in how authorities distinguished women with homoerotic desire from heterosexual women.[95]

Female husband accounts confound this periodization and logic, in part because the question is a different one. Employers, neighbors, observers, and writers in female husband cases were often trying to understand how and why someone assigned female was able to live successfully as a man and husband, first and foremost. Questions of sexuality were secondary and homoeroticism never entirely or adequately characterized what was happening. The meaning of the direction of one's sexual proclivities could not be determined unless the sex was designated first. Gender ambiguity was threatening on its own but also because it threw heterosexuality into chaos. Questions of physical embodiment, including references to hermaphroditism as a way to explain female husbands, persisted well into the nineteenth century.

The nineteenth century brought a change in dominant perceptions of intersex people from that of a monstrous creature to an actual person – though they were still judged harshly and denied humanity.[96] In several *Boston Medical and Surgical Journal* articles from this period, doctors described intersex people as "promiscuous and dishonest."[97] The technical medical understanding of what constituted hermaphroditism also changed, as doctors no longer believed one person could embody both male and female sets of perfect and complete organs. Rather, as Elizabeth Reis has shown, the term was thrown around in a wide range of scenarios, including, according to one doctor, "all those cases in which doubts exist concerning the real sex, in consequence of some aberration from the normal type of the genital organs."[98]

In order to better understand what people meant when they characterized James Allen and Henry Stoake as belonging to a third sex, we must examine a contemporaneous case involving someone who was shown to have ambiguous genitalia and declared intersex after medical investigation. In 1838, details of the life of James Carey were brought to light after their death. Carey lived in Philadelphia and held numerous laboring positions over the years in Pennsylvania and New Jersey, from work in manufacturing in Patterson, New Jersey to a foundry nearby, and then later in New Hope, Pennsylvania at both a farm and a factory.[99] All of these would have been arduous, physically demanding positions that required strength, dexterity, and attention to detail. It seems reasonable to suggest that Carey's health – already said to have been fragile in childhood and the reason Carey's uncle left Ireland with them – contributed to their decision to pursue less labor-intensive work. Carey worked for years, starting in 1831, as a stagecoach driver throughout Pennsylvania and New Jersey. Carey's boss in the business for three years, Mary Glenat, described them as "faithful, honest, and punctual."[100] Like most female husbands, Carey devoted themself to work.

On June 5, 1838, four days after Carey was put to rest, the coroner order their body exhumed for a post-mortem exam.[101] A woman, described as "the person employed to lay out his corpse," claimed that "all was not right" with Carey.[102] This woman, perhaps a nurse, assistant, or midwife, circulated gossip that heightened the curiosity of her co-workers. Still, a question of sex post-mortem was pointless and would not provide a legal basis to justify an exhumation. The coroner's job – as was so well illustrated by Thomas Shelton in the James Allen case – was to determine cause of death, period. So why on earth did this coroner in Philadelphia agree to make Carey's body subject to intrusive unnecessary examination? Did the swirl of gossip and innuendo about Carey's differently sexed body excite even the most professional medical men to push for another chance at a closer look? The official reason given for the inquisition was to determine foul play in their death. Dr. Goddard of the University of Pennsylvania led the team dissecting Carey's body.[103]

This unusual situation opened the door for artist James Akin to examine Carey along with a group of doctors and to illustrate his findings for them – and the world. Akin also interviewed eleven non-medical people who knew Carey, from former employers and landlords to local ministers. He printed brief statements by them, often verifications of basic facts of employment or residence, along with testimonies that they supported Akin's characterizations of Carey. Some people described Philadelphia's James Carey in ways that were not all that different from London's James Allen. Methodist minister Henry G. King concluded his assessment of Carey's physical and spiritual well-being with an assessment of their gender expression, stating, "His skin was smooth and sallow, and his chin destitute of beard: in a word, he neither resembled the masculine nor feminine gender – was abrupt in his manner – rather surly and eccentric."[104] Akin himself assessed Carey's physicality as a host of contradictions: "He was full made and bony, without bulkiness, having smooth polished and remarkably long limbs, of effeminate appearance, without muscular display, encased in a skin of delicate whiteness, evincing a capability to undergo much exertion. His voice partook of a faint boyish squeak; but his action betokened a firm and manly deportment, appertaining to *hard duties and business.*"[105] Both descriptions highlight a combination of masculine and feminine, male and female. Akin, however, used more judgmental and loaded language when describing the dead Carey than those who actually knew Carey when they were alive.

Carey's life signals a turning point in popular views of intersex people toward a slightly more humanizing characterization.[106] This can be seen in some of the testimonies at the end of Akin's book. Consider John J. Hickman, owner of the tavern where Carey was living when they fell ill. Hickman expressed a sorrowful apology that he was too busy tending to his business and family to offer Carey greater care and attention when they fell ill. Pastor Henry King stated that Carey grew to trust him slowly over time and that eventually, Carey "received me with some degree of warmth," a statement that pointed to Carey's humanity and offset Akin's harsh portrayal, if just a bit.[107] It was remarked by Pastor George Chandler that Carey had "no relative to soothe his passage to the grave, or follow his mortal remains to the narrow house."[108] Carey had much in common with female husbands, including separation from birth family and distrust of strangers, but was without the companionship of a female wife.

Allen and Stoake were not the only female husbands described in terms of a third gender. Other female husbands were characterized this way as well. In a lesser publicized account, a female husband named Captain Wright from Lambeth England was repeatedly referred to as a "creature" and referenced in the third person by "it." Wright confounded expectations for not only manhood, but also womanhood, when a report declared Wright's body was female *except* for the fact that they had a beard. "A few days ago, this individual died, when it was discovered that instead of being of the male sex, the body was *in every sense of the word* (a beard only excepted) that of *a woman!*" As was the case with James Allen, an explanation was given for how they used clothing to cover their body, stating, "Its garments were worn loose, with a view to conceal its shape, more particularly the upper part of the trowsers."[109] This dehumanizing gender neutral characterization stood in contradiction to other parts of the story which described Wright and their wife in positive terms as "respectable gentlefolks." In this way, the use of gendered pronouns that either affirm or negate the assumed gender of the subjects is not a definitive window for determining perceptions of female husbands. Rather, it captures a certain amount of recognition, ambivalence, and frustration at the limits of language to adequately characterize and report on these lives.

It was never suggested that anyone other than Abigail knew James Allen was assigned female at birth until their death. But several people who knew them suggested they had recently come to believe Allen was a third gender of sorts, either a "hermaphrodite" or "not a proper man." One article about Allen's death reported both claims together, "his wife expressed her opinion to a female friend that 'her Jemmy was not a proper man'; that *his* fellow-workmen, from the weakness in the voice, and his not having a beard, considered him an hermaphrodite, but always thought he was 'most of a man,' from this having been married so many years."[110] Several different threads from at least three people were exposed, threatening to unwind the community's perception of Allen's gender if anyone pulled too hard. They were subtle but important revelations made in a moment of crisis, things spoken out loud, maybe for the first time, only in death with the conviction that there was nothing to hide or no reason to remain silent any longer.

First, consider Abigail Allen, wife of James. Why did she decide after all these years to reveal to her friend Mary Daley that there was something different about her husband? Had they become exceptionally close friends, an earned confidant? Did Mary confide some equally powerful secret that made Abigail feel trusting enough for a swap? Did something happen, bringing Abigail to her wits end, desperate to get some fully informed advice about her relationship? One unverified account that circulated in narrative form after Allen's death claimed that James had a workplace scuffle at a prior place of employment where co-workers seemed to suspect something was different about them. If that did happen, one can see why Abigail may have grown nervous about the safety of her husband and wanted someone's advice and support.

Why did Mary Daley violate Abigail's confidence that Allen "was not a proper man" before the coroner's court? Poor people like Abigail and Mary would have been intimidated by the authority of Chief Coroner Thomas Shelton, his all-white male jury, and a room full of white male doctors and medical students. It is doubtful that she really thought through the implications of her testimony. One paper reported that the crowd assembled erupted in "great laughter" at the idea Abigail suspected her husband wasn't a proper man.[111] Poor Abigail! How painful this must have been for her. Her husband was killed and now her dear friend revealed her greatest secret before the world. Those people who should have been on her side – the jury, doctors, and students – were openly laughing at her and James. How could these mean-spirited people be the same ones who healed the sick and cared for the suffering? Abigail hoped she would never again return to St. Thomas' Hospital.

The third witness that made a point of Allen's third-gender status was the co-worker William Shrieve, who witnessed the accident that left Allen "bleeding from the mouth, nose, and ear." Shrieve explained that in his view Allen had a "very weakly voice" and that "the people who knew him considered him a hermaphrodite."[112] In this rendering, the voice was a clue that Allen was not male but there was not enough other evidence to make people think they were female. It is interesting, given the strong prevalence of a gender binary and the dominant view that there were two sexes – male and female – that Shrieve and his colleagues settled on a third alternative to explain Allen's differences. This diagnosis in the nineteenth century was, as scholars have shown, imprecise. Even doctors did not agree on what constituted hermaphroditism and ordinary people used it as a way to label those who were, in some way, neither clearly male or female.

The great difference between the case of Stoake and Allen is that Allen was characterized by three different people in their life as being a third gender, whereas Stoake was only designated as such by the press as a way to make fun of them. Allen was declared an anatomically perfect female during their autopsy. Stoake was spared physical examination and in no way stripped of their gender expression, as far as the records tell us. Even though Stoake was spared legal punishment and physical examination – two key responses to the outing of female husbands for most of history – they were not left unscarred by the situation.

Some resolved to have them run out of town, hoping to ensure they would have to abandon their successful business. One article concluded, "Nothing was done in the way of legal proceedings, but it is supposed that the epicene creature will be obliged to remove from the town."[113] The kind of hostile aggression featured in this account was often reserved for stories posted many years later and far away from the actual incident. Just because Stoake was no longer a target of the carceral authorities does not mean they were a welcome citizen in the community. The characterization of Stoake as "epicene" had several possible meanings. Epicene is an ambiguous category, defined as having characteristics of both sexes or neither sex. This was in some respects accurate and was broad enough to address sex, gender, or both. It marked Stoake as a third sex but did not commit to any one specific origin for sex itself. But given the usage of epicene as a qualifier for the term "creature," it was dehumanizing and hostile. In this regard, the association of Stoake with the non-human links them to much older perceptions of monstrous hermaphroditism.[114]

Stoake survived this scandal and lived to fight another day – and find another wife. They may have left their immediate neighborhood, but they remained in and around Manchester. Francis Collier says she got to know Stoake, who visited her beer house in Manchester with some frequency. Later she invited Stoake to live with her as a boarder in her new cottage in Salford, just northwest of the city. The pair grew closer and eventually got married. Collier assumed Stoake's name and her son from a previous marriage – Thomas Eaton – regarded Stoake as a stepfather. The pair opened a beer house back in Manchester, and later another one that was run by Thomas. Eventually they returned to Salford. All of this news about Stoake's second act was made known under terrible circumstances: their premature death.[115]

Stoake was found dead in a river in Salford, near the Mode Wheel Works. A worker found the body early in the morning. A local barkeeper, Mary Gorton, reported serving Stoake four beers the afternoon before their death. There is no public accounting for the thirteen hours after Stoake left Mary's bar and when Yates found them in the river. The coroner ruled the death a suicide, stating, "Found drowned. Supposed suicide."[116] It was 1859, twenty-one years since Henry first made the local papers in their divorce case. At least Henry got to live a full life. Most of the news coverage of this final chapter of Stoake's life addresses the coroner scene and the report of a juror who knew Stoake and said their "proper name was Harriet Stokes." This is remarkable in suggesting that friends and neighbors knew that Stoake transed gender and accepted them in their community anyway.

The additional paragraph of testimony by Francis Collier was not included in many stories. There we learn that Stoake had a rich and active family life with Francis and her son, Thomas. We are invited to follow the trail as this unconventional family moved out of the city and back again, leaving one business to take a break and then start another – and yet another. At the very least, this paints a picture of a couple that was hardworking, resourceful, and active. Stoake was both a female husband and a stepfather. They may have been run out of their neighborhood and publicly humiliated by their first wife, but they rebuilt a family and life once again.

* * *

Female husband cases routinely feature competing claims about legal and social gender against legal and anatomical sex. The central challenge in the cases of Allen and Stoake concerns the treatment of their wives as widow (Abigail) and divorcee (Ann). By virtue of their marriages, both were recognized as legally male and lived their lives as such for over twenty years. But their bodies contained another truth which would also serve as proof they were legally female. In Allen's case, the coroner recognized that Allen's legal and social manhood was more important than their anatomical sex after death. In Stoake's case there is less evidence as to what happened after Ann's divorce filing, but it seems as if there was a degree of tolerance and recognition of their legal manhood. Both Stoake and Allen were beneficiaries of dominant attitudes toward husbands under British marriage law. As Sharon Marcus argues, "law defined husbands as liberal citizens who had rights to protection from state interference, but conceived of wives as noncitizens, subject only to the protection and regulation of their spouses."[117] While Abigail and Ann had more leverage in their relationships than conventional female wives, the truth was that the state still regarded them as less important figures in this drama with few rights of their own. This willful neglect of married women by the state that deferred to husbands perpetuates a longstanding assumption that certain gender and sexual transgressions by women – especially those pertaining to transing gender, romantic friendship, or same-sex intimacies – were subject to less legal regulation than one might expect.

PART TWO

US HUSBANDS, 1830–1910

CHAPTER 5

THE WORKERS

THE LIVES OF PEOPLE PRESENTING THEMSELVES AS WHITE men to travel, work, and live in antebellum America were given meaning through several important national discourses, from the low wages paid to free working women to the extensive restrictions placed on African Americans – enslaved and free.[1] Much was made about the efforts of white people presenting themselves as men to secure work that only men were hired to do. They could be found anywhere from the most metropolitan cities to obscure rural outposts, on ships, in factories, or simply walking through town. The existence of this unique group sparked commentary on a host of issues large and small, from theories of economic transformation and the changing workforce to detailed descriptions of the clothing they wore. Each reported incident of a woman wearing male attire and working as a man affirmed what many already knew: when given the chance, those assigned female at birth could easily do the work that was reserved for men. But for the discerning reader, it said something far more significant: the distinction between male and female was not that great and could largely be overcome by those who wanted to embrace a social gender typically reserved for those assigned a different sex.[2]

News reports focus chiefly on labor and mobility as the motivating forces for transing gender, characterizing female assigned people as autonomous economic actors. Some of these enterprising workers reported that they were abandoned in love and chose to pursue men's work rather than accept what seemed like the only alternative: sex work. When caught, they declared it was easier to find work as a man, a claim few authorities bothered to dispute. One story offered a sympathetic portrayal of a young person arrested in New York City for wearing male attire by printing their explanation, "I put on male attire from necessity, but as I found afterward that it gave me advantages in obtaining an honest livelihood by securing a better remuneration, I concluded to keep it on as a matter of choice, and have since worn it entirely. I have worked constantly, except at such times as I have been out of employment, and have got a living almost unaided."[3] It was a logical argument – based in economic reality – that generated sympathy and understanding.

Stories of sailors, factory workers, and husbands shared the pages of newspapers with another group that was treated much more harshly by authorities when caught: African Americans who transed gender as a vehicle for freedom. This group was described in runaway ads when slaveholders suspected they used gender as a form of disguise to aid their escape. In other cases, they were celebrated in mainstream newspapers and abolitionist publications after escaping to freedom. African American mobility was already tremendously restrained, even for those who were born free. In the long, slow transition from slavery to freedom, African Americans were criminalized and heavily regulated through loosely defined policing categories such as "vagrancy" and "disorderly conduct." This issue was central in defining Southern cultures during Reconstruction and Jim Crow, but it also defined public life and policing in the North in the early republic and antebellum periods.[4]

Those who transed gender to escape enslavement were understood as doing so for singular reasons – freedom – and were not subject to scrutiny of motive. But this did not keep those who chronicled these experiences from offering detailed assessments of exactly how one assigned female at birth was able to successfully present as a man. Female husbands and others who transed gender for work, life, or a night on the town were also subject to increased scrutiny, interrogation, and arrest. While these groups – fugitive and free gender crossers – may not have shared a common cause with each other, policing authorities certainly viewed all of them as a threat to social order.[5] On the eve of war over the question of slavery, Northern elites, reformers, and the police who worked for them became even more punitive toward those they determined were not living up to their responsibilities as freed people.[6]

GEORGE WILSON

One summer night in 1836, a policeman walked his beat through the streets of the Lower East Side in New York City. He thought he stumbled upon a drunken sailor, sprawled across the sidewalk where Pearl Street intersects with Chatham, not far from city hall.[7] When they were not at sea on one of the countless merchant ships that plied the Atlantic, sailors were a visible presence on the streets of the major maritime cities from Charleston to Boston. This person, however, was not a sailor. They belonged to the rapidly expanding class of factory workers attracted by the promise of wage work and regular meals on dry land as the great industrial revolution transformed life, home, and work for everyone. New York City teemed with Irish, German, and English immigrants who were eager to take one of the many factory jobs. While sailors made up 20 to 25 percent of the adult male population of New York in the mid-eighteenth century, a hundred years later they were outnumbered by those working in manufacturing jobs by nearly four to one.[8]

American policing in the North grew exponentially during the antebellum period. This change reflected not only population growth in cities transformed by industrialization but also growing hostility toward the poor, homeless, and unemployed. African Americans were especially vulnerable. Police were principally charged with protecting private property – continuing their original mission – but many spent the bulk of their time patrolling for minor public disturbances, conflicts between people, and disorderly conduct. Anyone lying on the street and visibly intoxicated was subject to detainment by the police under very loosely defined vagrancy laws.[9] In a three-month period in 1845, for instance, New York City police officers charged 3,205 people with intoxication – more than any other crime.[10]

The New York police force grew by leaps and bounds, from 650 officers in 1844 to nearly triple that number twenty years later (Figure 5.1). This reflected both an investment in order and a recognition of the key role that police would play in civil society. The expansion also reflected a

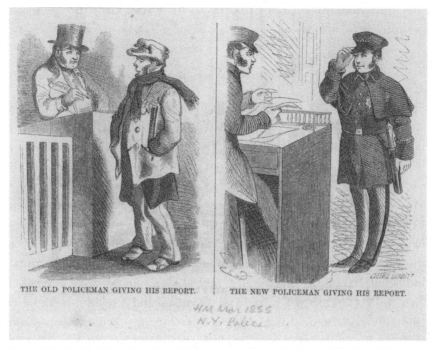

THE OLD POLICEMAN GIVING HIS REPORT.   THE NEW POLICEMAN GIVING HIS REPORT.

Figure 5.1 Carl Emil Doepler, "The Old Policeman Giving His Report; The New Policeman Giving His Report," 1855. The New York City police force was professionalized and greatly expanded during the antebellum era.
Image courtesy of the Wallach Division Picture Collection, the New York Public Library

rapidly growing population, from 312,710 people in 1840 to 900,000 in 1864.[11] The police arrested or detained countless people for a wide range of minor public nuisances. Drunkenness, disorderly conduct, and illegal housing topped the list in New York City in the 1840s. A wide range of sexual and gender transgressions would have been lumped into the category of "disorderly conduct" or "vagrancy."[12]

Officer Collins brought the fallen man to the station in a cart.[13] At some point Collins realized the person was not a sailor and suspected they were not a man, either. The various news accounts used gendered language in different ways to explain the situation. The earliest reports declared, "An intoxicated person, apparently a man"[14] or "A person in male attire"[15] was found in the street, inviting the reader to see the person as the policeman did – at first as a man. This possibility, however, does not even last for a complete sentence. The newspaper quickly made it clear that the subject of the article was female. Reporters used exclusively feminine pronouns and a woman's name in all of their stories. An article printed in the *Journal of Commerce* that was more widely reprinted than any other described the subject as, "a female who was found intoxicated in the street, on Friday night dressed in man's clothes." This simple descriptive sentence avoided the inflammatory language found in other accounts but it also put to rest any notion of gender ambiguity.[16] This account enjoyed extraordinary popularity among editors because it distinguished this person from other workers, designating them a 'female husband' with the following headline, "Extraordinary Case of a Female Husband." The newspaper that popularized the story, *The Journal of Commerce*, was founded in 1827 by abolitionist Arthur Tappan and inventor Samuel Morse.[17]

The reprinting of news stories – with and without attribution – was a common practice that encouraged wide circulation of female husband accounts. For much of the eighteenth and nineteenth centuries, there were no copyright laws governing the printing of news. Attribution of the original source was preferred though not always granted. In mid-eighteenth-century Britain, the rise of the commercial advertiser fueled this practice, as they combined advertisements with a variety of other content, both original and copied. Nearly all national and international news in both the US and UK was reprinted from other sources.[18] In 1841, the editor of the *Journal of Commerce* explicitly embraced the reproduction of news provided attribution was given. He wrote, "We hold that any paragraph or article, whether it be news or editorial remarks, or a communication, or review of the market, or any thing else, which originates in one paper, may be honorably copied into another, by giving credit for the same."[19]

Attempts to pass copyright laws in both the UK and US certainly threatened to change the mass reproduction of information, but they failed. In 1836 in the UK, prominent daily newspapers sought copyright protection because of the great expense that went into collecting the news – and the extra cost of distribution for those regulated by stamp taxes. The resulting bill lessened the burden of stamp taxation but did not impose copyright. Human interest stories – as most female husband accounts were – were simply not the kind of stories that editors sought to

Figure 5.2 "Hat-Making," 1845–7. George Wilson worked as a hat maker in the Lower East Side of New York City at the time of their arrest.
Image courtesy of the Miriam and Ira Wallach Division of Art, Prints, and Photographs: Art & Architecture Collection, the New York Public Library

protect in the first place. Key papers that argued for copyright protection, such as the *Morning Post* and the *Standard*, also circulated female husband accounts.[20] When the stamp tax was finally abolished in 1855, local newspapers proliferated throughout the UK.[21] Attempts to pass copyright laws on newspapers in the US began decades later than in the UK and failed just as miserably.[22]

The drunken laborer found lying on the streets of New York's Lower East Side was George Wilson. Wilson had had too much to drink after a long day of work and was found just blocks from the factory on Water Street where they worked making fur caps for Joseph Barron (Figure 5.2).[23] Barron was a furrier in the city at least since 1829 in several locations, both on his own and in partnership.[24] The company Rowland & Barron furs and caps operated out of 16 Maiden-lane in 1832.[25] Barron maintained the Maiden-lane address as his private residence, parted ways with Rowland, and set up the furrier on Water Street along the East River, at 171 Water St. in 1835 and then 185 Water St. in 1836.[26] The work involved dangerous chemicals, including mercury, but the industry was booming and Wilson was one among thousands of workers navigating dangerous work conditions in the city.[27] Wilson's arrest and ongoing detention after "confessing that she was a female" may have cost them their job, depending on how replaceable they were in the eyes of their employer and how long the police detained Wilson.[28]

Upon their initial detention, Wilson wove a great tale for the police, hoping to protect their life, wife, and job. They created an account of their life based on fabrications and partial truths, claiming they were from Ireland when they were from Scotland, stating they ventured to North America to meet a man who abandoned them rather than in the company of a woman to whom they were legally wed. They claimed to live with strangers in Brooklyn rather than with their wife in the Bowery. These false bits were immediately reported and may well have been accepted as truth.[29] The tale of a young woman promised the companionship of a man only to be abandoned had a long history that garnered the victim credence and sympathy. This story may have passed for the truth – at least until Wilson's wife showed up at the station.

Maybe this was the first time that Wilson didn't return home to their wife at the end of the night – or maybe Wilson drank too much so often that she knew exactly where to find them. Masculinity was increasingly contested in antebellum America, as the wave of evangelical reform sweeping the nation celebrated the idea that self-restraint and piety were central components of manhood.[30] But older notions also persisted, including ideas that aggression, drunkenness, sexual excess, and neglect of one's home life defined working-class manhood. Certainly, an argument can be made for the likelihood that this was not the first time Wilson drank too much on a Friday after work. But any question of how Wilson's drinking reflected or shaped their commitment to their wife and home became moot once the question of their sex was raised.

Elisabeth was looking for her husband and "applied to Mr. Lowndes, the magistrate, for permission to see a prisoner named George Wilson."[31] The widely circulated account from the *Journal of Commerce* described her as someone who was "decently dressed" upon arriving at the police station on a Saturday morning. Just who was this concerned wife? Elisabeth was the fourth child born to James and Margaret Cummin in June 1804 in Glasgow, Scotland.[32] Her father was a laborer who worked in the factories. James was a superintendent in one of the cotton factories in Glasgow where a young George Wilson happened to work.[33] Wilson made Elisabeth's acquaintance, possibly via her father James, leading to a courtship and eventually their marriage on April 6, 1821 at Barony Parish, Glasgow, Scotland.[34] They left Scotland immediately for North America and arrived in Quebec. Accounts of what happened next vary slightly. They purchased some land, settled down, and invited Elisabeth's father James Cummin to join them. One piece of evidence claims this happened in New Limerick, Canada.[35] Another, however, places the group in New Harmony, Indiana, the site where Robert Owen established his utopian community in 1825. As cotton factory workers from Glasgow, they would have been familiar with Owen's philosophy and projects. They may even have previously worked in New Lanark, Scotland where Owen began applying his values to the lives of mill workers – it was just twenty-five miles from Glasgow.[36]

After roughly six years in one or more of these locations, the family moved to Patterson, New Jersey where Elisabeth's husband George and father James went to work at the cotton mill of Clark & Robinson.[37] Elisha Clark and Robert O. Robinson operated their cotton manufactory on the Ivanhoe Mill Wheelhouse lots. In 1829, the company was near its peak. It tripled the number of spindles at work in just four years, from 480 in 1825 to 1416 in 1829. By this time, they had forty-nine employees who spun 130,000 pounds of yarn annually. Just six years later, however, they were in debt far beyond their means and surrendered their lease on the factory.[38] The textile industry was also in the midst of a labor war, as the predominantly Irish workers organized strikes in hope of improved working conditions and shorter hours. George and James may have been put out of work, leading to their move to New York's Lower East Side and George's new job making hats for a furrier.

Their lives were never easy. Elisabeth probably worked in the expanding manufacturing industry in the city as well. They all worked long hours at grueling jobs. If they left Glasgow to get away from that city's notorious tenement buildings, they may have come to regret this move entirely. New York's buildings were filled beyond capacity as the city's housing stock proved unable to keep up with the number of immigrants pouring into the city. Illegal housing was the second most common charge levied by the police against the community, pointing to both the crammed conditions and the reason why so many were not listed in city directories.[39] Elisabeth told the magistrate they lived at 47 Forsyth Street. The city directory offers a sampling of the occupations of those living on Forsyth Street in 1836: grocer, baker, tobacconist, tailor, shoemaker, carpenter, bookkeeper, painter, huckster, stonecutter, lamplighter, dentist, mason, shipjoiner, printer, binder, bootmaker, carter, combmaker, pilot, sailmaker, mariner, watchmaker. Though by no means in the majority, several people working in the same industry as Wilson called Forsyth Street home, including a fur cutter and four other hatters.[40] Whether they lived on Forsyth Street or nearby, they lived in a mixed neighborhood of laborers, characterized as the 'lower sort' along with others engaged in more secure or lucrative occupations.[41] If they ever hoped to move out, they needed George Wilson to get out of jail and continue working.

What might Elisabeth have felt when she found her husband at the police station that day, in this huge city very far from home? A combination of anger and fear must have raced through her as she set foot in the police station. She found herself face to face with the man who stood between her and her husband, between her husband and freedom – the magistrate, Mr. Lowndes. The magistrate told Elisabeth that he knew her husband was female. One account portrayed her as angry and disinterested, seeking to distance herself from the situation and leave her husband there.[42] In this way, she seemed like any wife who tired of her husband's reckless behavior. A different account that was less widely circulated, however, portrayed Elisabeth as concerned, reasonable, caring, and cooperative.[43]

Elisabeth sat with the magistrate and began answering the question that he was dying to know the answer to: when did she know her husband was female? The idea that wives of female husbands *might not know* their husbands were assigned female for years and years on end was rather absurd. This argument was only promoted in the most trying of circumstances by wives who were vulnerable themselves to prosecution and violence. Realistically, we have seen husbands trying to hide the truth of their difference for a short period of time during courtship in the hope of attracting women who will fall in love with them. Then, female husbands hope that upon revealing their difference, their wives will either love them more because of it or tolerate it because they already loved them anyway. The latter scenario appears to characterize the courtship of Elisabeth and George.

Wilson did not reveal themself to be assigned female prior to their wedding. When Elisabeth met and married Wilson in 1821 in Scotland, she did so "thinking him at the time to be a male." This is how Elisabeth explained the dynamic to the police under very trying, stressful, and possibly violent circumstances. Wilson waited to tell Elisabeth until they were legally married and making the voyage from Scotland to North America, in the middle of the Atlantic Ocean apart from family and friends. Elisabeth recounted, "She did not discover the prisoners real sex until some days after marriage, when they set sail for this country."[44] It was a selfish move, but no one could deny the strategy behind it. Elisabeth could not simply run home or report Wilson to authorities. She was vulnerable, at sea, and physically uncomfortable at best. She may also have been seasick and hungry. In these trying circumstances of transatlantic travel, with George as her lone companion and friend, the seventeen-year-old Elisabeth received the news and declared that this was fine with her. One report states, "The discovery, however, she says, did not in the least appear to disappoint her wife; and they have continued to live and labor together as man and wife, in harmony and love."[45] Inquiring minds might press further to explore the possibility that Elisabeth knew exactly what she was getting into, that even before the marriage she could have known her husband had transed genders – and this was precisely what attracted her to them. Or maybe she told the truth, that she didn't really know. If she was surprised, disappointed, or angry, what recourse did she even have? If she decided to fight the marriage on the grounds that George deceived her and was not legally male, she would have had both the law and popular opinion on her side. The public was still hotly against those who transed genders, especially when marriage and the possibility of sexual intimacies were on the table. But for

148

laboring people trying to make a life for themselves during times of tumultuous economic and social transformation, marriage was as much a financial relationship as it was an intimate one. Any combination of factors – love, convenience, fear, and financial stability – probably drove Elisabeth to stay in the marriage.

The other question most pressing for readers of Wilson's story was how, when, and why they took the first step in becoming a man. Newspapers reported several different versions of the particulars of their early years, but the broad contours were rather consistent. All agree that George Wilson was born in Liverpool to Scottish parents and that it was back in Scotland, around the age of twelve, that they assumed the attire and identity of a boy. For some reason – death, remarriage, disagreement, or bullying – George escaped the control and/or care of relatives and made themself into a boy. In the most widely circulated story, it simply states that their parents died while they were young, inspiring Wilson to move to Scotland, the land of their parents' birth, around the age of twelve.[46] In another telling, their father died and mother remarried, moving them to Ayrshire, Scotland while they were nine years old.[47] It was there, three years later, that Wilson "put on man's attire, assumed her father-in-law's name, George Moore Wilson, and proceeded to Glasgow."[48] In yet another version, both parents moved to Glasgow with their child, where they lived until both parents died. At this point, the child went to live with relatives before running away and assuming their new life as a man named George.[49] Regardless of the order and the specific family members involved, Wilson fled from family and moved to Glasgow, where they found opportunity, safety, and love.

By all accounts, George was convincingly male their entire life. James Cummins not only worked alongside George in the factories and blessed their marriage but also came to live with them. Wilson claimed they "slept with and worked among males" and had "never been suspected."[50] Even under this stressful situation at the police station, Wilson was described as "perfectly at ease" and "perpetually taking snuff." Living as a man for eighteen years made them into more of a man. They were dressed in "striped pantaloons, a plaid stock, and a grey roundabout."[51] There was really not that much discussion of the particulars of their gendered embodiment in these accounts at all, which makes it unusual.

There is one exception – an article printed in the *Columbian Register* out of New Haven, Connecticut that merges facts from multiple available accounts and adds some editorializing flare of its own. This essay suggests there was something about Wilson's embodied gender that made the officer suspect they were not male. It states, "From the softness of his voice the officer suspected that he had caught a female in man's attire, although she was sunburnt and appeared somewhat masculine."[52] While we must never entirely rule out such a possibility, such claims are often made in hindsight.

There were also competing claims as to who examined Wilson and what exactly was involved in such an examination. The New York City police handbook outlined the rules of examination as follows, "All prisoners, when arrested, shall be conveyed to the nearest Station-House, and confined until examined by a magistrate, and either committed or discharged, on bail or otherwise, according to law."[53] This suggests the examination was a routine verbal interrogation conducted by Magistrate Lowndes. One account suggests another inmate was charged with determining Wilson's sex, stating, "At the watch house the officer found a female brought in for the night, and requested her to examine the sailor. She spoke to the prisoner, and by some sort of freemasonry known only to the ladies, she pronounced the tar a member of the softer sex."[54] Leaving the physical examination to a random incarcerated woman rather than doing it himself not only suggested the officer was quite certain of his suspicion but it also invoked a centuries-old belief that women – not men – should be the judge of sex.[55] However, the snarky tone of this account renders it less reliable.

Another account claims that a surgeon was brought in to examine the prisoner. It doesn't go into detail as to what was involved but states, "She was examined by a surgeon, and it was found that the statement as regards her sex was correct, when she was removed for further examination."[56] Here we are told that Wilson was subjected to physical examination by a surgeon even after declaring they were female, which seems both excessive and abusive. It also points to an interest in determining if they were possibly intersex. One account adds a reference to the question of hermaphroditism, claiming that in captivity, Wilson "wished to persuade the magistrate that she was an hermaphrodite, but surgical examination proves her statement to be false. She is a perfect female."[57] Some editors played up this idea with provocative headlines such as, "A Man turned out to be a woman," or derogatory comments such as, "The wretched creature states that she is 30 years of age,"[58] or references to Wilson as a "she husband."[59] But perhaps the most important conclusion we can draw is that there was no universally agreed-upon authority in this issue. Who should be the judge? A random woman? A magistrate? A medical doctor? The person in question? Their wife? These competing accounts suggest that this issue remained up for dispute.

Wilson was the first designated female husband found living in the United States. By the 1830s, readers were familiar with many different kinds of gender-transing practices. Wilson's public outing was bracketed by the UK husbands Allen (1829) and Stoake (1838). Like Allen and Stoake, Wilson's wife featured prominently in the encounter with authorities and the newspaper's take on it. Female wives became just as important as female husbands. Female husbands were increasingly viewed in relation to a wider range of gender-transing practices. George Wilson's story inspired writers to reflect on the various people who in one way or another rejected the roles and expectations for women and embraced male identities and privilege. Beginning with news of the "female *husband* in New York," an account mentioned a person in Boston "wearing the uniform of a midshipman," another person in New York who wore "male attire," and another one in Greenfield, Massachusetts fined for "tramping the country at night in men's clothes." These stories referenced people assigned female who embraced male attire for different reasons in various contexts.[60] People saw connections between these acts of rebellion. And each time word of a female husband made the news, it inspired and challenged both readers and reporters to reflect on similarities with those who came before them as well as what this said about sexual difference.

Generally, newspapers offered those who transed gender a certain amount of sympathy and understanding. A minority of papers used the stories to make outrageously mean attacks on those involved. Without a female wife in the picture to raise a set of legal, social, and moral questions pertaining to violations of sexual norms, those caught working in "male attire" had an easier time explaining themselves to authorities.

But female husband accounts reminded readers that seemingly innocent workers in male attire might have female lovers of their own. The transgression of a gender norm always opened the door to the threat of a sexual transgression. By looking at female husbands within the broader context of antebellum laborers who transed genders, we can better unpack the significance of marital status and sexual intimacies in shaping dominant attitudes toward those who transed genders.

FEMALE SAILORS

While George Wilson turned out not to be a sailor, it was perfectly reasonable for the policeman to jump to that conclusion. The nineteenth century marked the heyday of maritime expansion in the United States, from whaling ships plying distant seas to Atlantic trade and transport routes to paddle boats on the inland waterways. Flocks of boys and young men from all walks of life were seduced, compelled, and lured to life at sea.[61] While there was a noticeable decline in the number of "female sailors" found among the ranks of the British Navy during this same period, accounts of "female sailors" from the United States working on a range of vessels became ordinary newspaper filler.[62] A story that was once predominantly British became a quintessentially American tale of perseverance, ingenuity, and adventure. Maritime labor provided an important workplace for African American men denied access to other jobs. Though the work was marked by danger, low pay, great hardship, and long stretches away from home, sailors were among those who formed the heart of early free black working- and middle-class communities.[63] There was more work available than workers to fill the positions, making it relatively easy for people assigned female to present themselves as "green hands" to work as cabin boys aboard a ship. One of the most popular publications in early nineteenth-century Boston was a fictionalized account of a female sailor referred to as Louisa Baker or Lucy Brewer. The enterprising publisher Nathaniel Coverly created an enticing lead character who experienced some of the most important events of the day, including fighting aboard the USS *Constitution* in the war of 1812.[64] With so many references to major local landmarks and political issues in the text, readers would not have known whether the person or events depicted were real. Many published accounts of female sailors and soldiers were highly fictionalized narrations of real people and events. Readers familiar with this genre would have every reason to believe that a significant part of the story was real. Whether history, fiction, or historical fiction, accounts of transing gender offered insight and guidance for their readers. The narrator of *The Female Marine* declared, "I had thoroughly studied the memoirs of Miss Sampson, and by a strict adherence to the precautionary means by which she was enabled to avoid an exposure of her sex, I was too enabled to conceal mine."[65] Passages like this one affirmed this point in a very literal way.

Newspapers played an important role in shaping how pamphlets such as *The Female Marine* and others like it, such as *The Surprising Adventures of Almira Paul*, were received.[66] Accounts of maritime adventures dominated the press. Readers came to expect headlines featuring "female sailors," and printers knew they were popular attention-grabbers. The story of one such person used the common headline "female sailor" but then opened the story with a declaration: "A black, named *Charles Williams*."[67] This both affirmed and confounded what readers already knew – that "female sailor" was fundamentally and implicitly a category bounded by whiteness, reserved for and used to describe the kinds of freedom that white people assigned female achieved when they passed as white men. Not every story used this designation, however. Other versions used the phrase "colored person" to describe Williams, such as, "A colored person, bearing the assumed name of Charles Williams,"[68] or "On Monday last, a colored person."[69] Racial labels such as "black" or "colored" signaled important distinctions in perceptions.[70] There was no mistaking the key importance of signaling a status that was not-white and therefore marked with even greater suspicion.

Charles Williams was born in Boston and raised in Providence. Williams was one of only a handful of known African Americans assigned female at birth who pursued life at sea as a man. Williams served in the US Navy and was later charged and convicted of stealing two hogs in New York City in 1834 when they were twenty-six years old. They were sentenced to four months imprisonment at Blackwell's Island (Figure 5.3).[71] They were forced to change their clothing from their sailor's uniform

Figure 5.3 Albert Berghas, "New York Police Courts – the Tombs, Early Morning – Discharge of the Watch," 1866. Many people picked up on minor disorderly conduct or vagrancy charges in antebellum New York passed through the Tombs.
Image courtesy of the Art and Picture Collection, the New York Public Library

into that of a prisoner. Through this process of undressing – a transition from the terms of freedom to the conditions of captivity – Williams was subjected to scrutiny that raised questions about their gender.

Williams' gender became an issue in their transition from free to unfree. There was no change in William's sex or gender, just a change in the perceptions of the prison guards who noticed something was different about Williams' body. This suggests guards watched and maybe even participated in stripping prisoners of their freedom clothes. This degree of objectification, observation, and even sexualization was openly practiced on women inmates from the penitentiaries' earliest days but has been less observed on the men's side. Without this invasive practice, Williams may have remained undetected, serving their four months at labor in the quarry as a black man before setting off to sea once more.

But the officers watched Williams closely, scrutinizing their body as they changed into prison attire. It was described in the news this way: "While undergoing a metamorphosis of clothing by the officers of the prison, it was discovered that the sailor was a female."[72] The term "metamorphosis" had three somewhat distinct connotations at the time, each offering a slightly different window for the reader to make sense of the revelation. The first describes a change "by supernatural means," which does not seem to be the case here. The second describes people, places, and circumstances as in "a complete change in the appearance, circumstances, condition, or character." This was the connotation invoked in earlier female sailor accounts.[73] The third definition was from the science of biology, signaling "change of one type of organ into another as an abnormal process."[74] Thus, the term "metamorphosis" signaled both a social and a physical transformation.

Chaos ensued as prison officials scrambled to figure out what to do. The prisoner had no say in this matter. While the sentence was clear – four months at moving and hauling stone – authorities would neither expect nor want a woman to do that because they were invested in a paternalistic vision of domesticity for female inmates. Though black women in Southern prisons were subject to brutal physical labor regimes, the North maintained greater deference to gendered labor distinctions.[75] Williams, now perceived by the guards as a black woman, would not receive the same kind of delicate care or protection reserved for select white women in prison. But they were still not expected or allowed to move stone.[76] By virtue of their race and gender, they stood between the two poles outlined by carceral authorities in policy and practice.

Now, what would Williams wear? Williams would have preferred the men's uniform but their desire didn't matter. If anything, guards would have known that forcing someone who lived as a man to wear women's clothing against their will was a violation, a further punishment. But this was standard protocol for all who transed gender – even those not convicted of any crime – and Williams was convicted of larceny. The keeper asserted his authority and re-established order, directing "that she should be habited as the rest of her sex, and put at the labour usually required of them in that institution."[77] While Williams confounded popular notions of who was a female sailor, racial prejudices about criminality were mapped on to them. Prison keepers had been known to give white people who transed gender the benefit of the doubt, sometimes lightening their sentences.[78] But Williams would not receive such treatment.

There were no African American female husbands designated as such in the press. There were a handful of black female sailors, such as Charles Williams or William Brown, who served in the Royal Navy from 1804 to 1816.[79] Even William Brown, heralded as smart and strong, was treated to racist objectification in an article that described their "features" as "rather handsome for a *Black*."[80] References to African Americans assuming male attire and personas to pass as men in nineteenth-century newspapers are anecdotal. An 1869 Philadelphia paper reported a brief story out of Georgia that stated, "A Negress called 'Big Jim,' has been sent to prison in August, Ga., for dressing like a man, and doing a man's work in loading and unloading vessels. The he negroes complained of her." It is notable that this account bears absolutely no resemblance to countless stories of white workers in similar circumstances who transed genders to do men's work and were heralded in the press.

When black people assigned female at birth presented themselves as men to get away from the violent exploitative system of slavery, they were also in search of the freedom to live and work on their own terms – a transing of gender for freedom. C. Riley Snorton describes this practice as an "ungendering of blackness" – a strategy to escape enslavement.[81] In this way, transing gender provided a source of power and possibility. African American men and women in transit were under serious scrutiny and suspicion. As resistance to slavery and support for its abolition grew, so too did hostility toward free black people. The Fugitive Slave Act of 1850 authorized federal officers to enforce the rights and authority of slaveholders in the North by kidnapping African Americans and punishing individuals who helped the enslaved escape in any way.[82] This legislation sent shockwaves of rage and terror throughout free black communities in the North, with around 20,000 African Americans moving to Canada as a result.[83]

While African Americans designated female at birth who aspired to live and pass as men navigated a complex terrain of race, gender, and mobility, accounts of their lives in the antebellum period are scarce. Narratives of people passing as men to escape enslavement all assert the category of woman as something only temporarily abandoned in pursuit of freedom, not as a desired embodiment or way of life. The privileging of whiteness as the primary identity and vehicle for transing gender both marginalizes African Americans who transed gender and links the experience of gender crossing to distinct aspirations of white manhood. While the longstanding Anglo-American tradition of quaintly celebrating the adventures of those who passed as men to work as sailors began to wane in the mid-nineteenth century, the whiteness of the accounts persisted.

Though the black American sailor Charles Williams was harassed and belittled by prison guards, the white American sailor George Johnson was treated like a delicate flower by a sea captain. George Johnson, who worked for seven months as a sea hand on the Nantucket whaling ship *Christopher Mitchell,* was reported to be female.[84] Reports of the incident appeared in August 1849, portraying the captain as a model of benevolent paternalism, deeply invested in an ideology that women were by nature distinct from men and in need of protection. Though Johnson was said to be dutiful, hardworking, cheerful, and skilled, the captain immediately demanded they change their clothing and retreat to the closest semblance of a domestic space, "into the cabin, a state room set apart," at which point they were no longer treated as a fellow worker but rather treated to "every attention shown which could be extended to a female on board ship."[85] There were so many reasons for the captain to allow Johnson to continue working on the voyage for which they were contracted, including the fact that whaling voyages were long, arduous, and required "all hands on deck" for the gruesome labor involved. Another great reason was Johnson's own wish to live and work as a man and the fact that they had proven themself capable of everything involved already, from "going aloft to take in sail in the heaviest weather" to taking "regular mastheads and helms all the voyage"[86] even on "the darkest night."[87] Johnson also participated in the most thrilling and terrifying task of whaling, having "pulled her oar twice in pursuit of whales," though without success.[88] But Johnson was also noted to be the most "green" of the boys, inexperience that was evident in the roughest weather and while behind an oar in the whaling boat.[89] Neither the wishes of the person involved, nor material labor concerns mattered. The overriding force was the captain's belief that women were to behave one specific way and in so doing, they earned the protection of men like him. Though Johnson had no interest in any of this, the captain forced them to assume such a role. The conflict between what people assigned female at birth could do and what they were allowed to do was again exposed.

The captain was primarily concerned with getting Johnson off his ship. He turned it around and went back to Paita, Peru, where Johnson would be able to find a ride back to the United States – eventually. Paita was a popular stopover for New England whaling ships and whalers often arranged to have mail sent there.[90] They left Johnson with the American Consul who sent word of the episode back to Nantucket. Brief excerpts circulated widely in the press, highlighting Johnson's backstory. "Upon her real sex being discovered, she gave her name as Ann Johnson, daughter of George Johnson, a shoemaker at Rochester, N.Y."[91] A similar account featured a twist, using the word "real" to qualify the name Ann but not the sex, stating, "who, upon her sex being discovered, gave her real name."[92] This story reveals as much about antebellum attitudes about white middle-class gender reforms as it does about the hardscrabble working life aboard a whaling ship. It is ripe with antebellum reform moralizing, from the benevolent captain to the precarious Johnson who was punished for deception. Some people assigned female who lived openly as women did go to sea – usually because they were married to the captain of a whaling ship. This became especially common after 1835, during the "golden age" of whaling, spawning a genre of diaries and books highlighting their experiences.[93]

Johnson was also pitied for being abandoned by a lover and celebrated on two counts: for their work aboard the ship and because they avoided falling into sex work at all costs. Johnson was characterized among the most pathetic of nineteenth-century figures: the fallen woman.[94] "She is a native of Rochester, N.Y., was seduced, like thousands of others, from her home, by a villain who promised to make her his lawful wife, but who abandoned her in a short time and absconded to parts unknown." Upon returning home after this event, their parents rejected them. At this point,

Johnson made a bad decision again. It states, "Too proud to ask assistance from strangers, and not so far lost to virtue as to think of subsisting by the only means which now seem left to her." At this point, Johnson donned male attire and assumed a variety of men's jobs, from driving a horse to working as a cabin boy to shipping out on the whaling voyage.[95] The backhanded compliments combined with punishment and occasional celebratory fascination served to maintain gender transing as a viable option only for people for whom the experience and rewards were well worth the risk. Johnson offers us a window into a life of someone who chose to live and work as a man so as to avoid sex work.

In a somewhat ironic twist to the typical tales that detail the many ways someone assigned female might fail at living as a man, this account emphasized the presence of a skill more typically associated with women – the ability to sew. The article states, "the quickness with which she plied her needle, being more than a match for other sailors in that respect," raised suspicions about their gender, which Johnson minimized "by suddenly working in a more bungling manner."[96] Of course, nineteenth-century sailors were among the most skilled sewers on the planet, required to repair torn sails and clothing under the most trying of circumstances. This anecdote was likely written by a landlubber for entertainment purposes but presents an interesting twist on public fascination with the relationship between sexual difference and gender in a variety of contexts, not to mention the dozens of attributes, characteristics, or skills that might make one into a man or woman.

This whaling voyage was merely one of many experiences Johnson would have working in male occupations in the antebellum era, both at sea and on land. Johnson briefly made the news again five months later on suspicion of larceny in the Five Points neighborhood of New York. Johnson was described as "a masculine looking woman" and at first claimed their name was "Shorty" or "Rough and Ready" before revealing details of the recent past adventures aboard the whaler. After an undisclosed period of detention, Johnson was cleared of the charges and discharged.[97] Johnson was no longer a sympathetic figure in the press given their entanglement with the legal authorities.

They left New York to start again, this time in Pittsburgh. Showing a forcefulness of spirit and a versatility of skills, Johnson went to work in a whip factory owned by Mr. Underwood. Johnson grew restless, missing the free-wheeling outdoor nature of maritime work and found a job working on the rivers as a cabin boy.[98] After a season working outdoors, Johnson returned to whip making, this time for Mr. John W. Tim for two years. In 1854, Johnson again grew restless and opened up a "fruit and confectionary" shop, but without much success. This setback seems to have inspired Johnson to move again, this time to Westfield, Massachusetts where they resumed working at whip making at the Westfield Whip Factory.

In summer 1856, Johnson made headlines because they were identified as female. The story stated, "A Male Girl – A young woman has been working in the factory of the American whip company, at Westfield, Massachusetts, during the last six months, attired in male clothes. She pretended to be a nice young man of 17, smoked strong cigars, was a successful beau among the young ladies, and acted her part as modern gentlemen very well to all outside appearances."[99] The sentiment of this early coverage in June 1856 was clearly on their side. While all of the details of their life were not yet pieced together in this account – including their time whaling – one writer wished Johnson nothing but peace and good will. "In all her wanderings up to this time, her secret was never suspected, and it is to be regretted she was not able to remain undiscovered and earn an honest living under the protection of male attire." This account, however, only refers to them as a woman and uses female pronouns, including the headline "A Woman Disguised as a Man," so there is no attempt to maintain respect for Johnson's chosen gender. Their version of masculinity, however, was presented favorably in that they held numerous jobs respectably and were noted for their kind treatment of women during the one or two years they worked in Pittsburgh for whip maker Mr. John W. Tim.[100] The account states, "she was noted for her gallantry to the fair sex, treating them to ices, confectionery, &c."[101] Johnson was no female husband but they were a very respectful and considerate date. This passage introduced the notion that some or even many people who followed this path in labor and life might also get romantically involved with women.

Johnson lived without notice during their years in Pittsburgh, only becoming the subject of news in Westfield. Something happened in

Westfield – an accident that was said to have "revealed her sex." This inspired the employer and minister from Westfield to seek references from their counterparts in Pittsburgh. The minister from Massachusetts did not turn to local legal authorities but rather to their own peers – fellow ministers with prior knowledge of Johnson. This reflects once again that there was no one way of handling this kind of situation and that the people involved basically improvised based on their own values and connections. It turns out that everyone in Pittsburgh had only glowing reports to offer of Johnson. Readers were presented with a sympathetic explanation for Johnson's life, based on a hypothetical scenario that widowhood drove Johnson to such a fate. One must think this response dramatically influenced how the Massachusetts minister would ultimately decide to treat Johnson.

Johnson's life straddled two central tropes of mid-nineteenth-century gender transing: the so-called female sailor and the common laborer. The sailor was long characterized in romantic terms, though few sailors fit this mold precisely and some didn't fit it at all. The sailor was one subcategory of laborer, a trope that dominated the genre in the eighteenth and early nineteenth centuries. But as the factory floor replaced the hold of a ship as the central workplace for young men, the accounts of female assigned laboring men diversified. When they weren't out at sea or on the riverboat, George Johnson made whips and sold confectionaries. George Wilson looked like a sailor but had only worked at manufacturing, whether spinning cotton or making fur caps. Johnson enjoyed smoking cigars while George Wilson was noted to be "perpetually taking snuff" while detained by police.[102] Hard work and tobacco were the hallmarks of life for trans laborers, whether at sea or on land.

ASEXUALITY

The most abundant and visible accounts of transing gender in the mid-nineteenth century concerned those of common laborers. Few of them were in intimate relationships with either men or women and the prevailing characterization was one of asexuality. Though some pursued transing gender after a failed heterosexual relationship (as was claimed in the case of George Johnson) their sexuality seemed to end once they began presenting as male. The dominant view was that economic desperation motivated many people assigned female at birth to trans gender and seek the much higher paying employment generally reserved for men. The fact that this group dominated in the press throughout the mid-nineteenth century is noteworthy. They represent a departure from eighteenth-century narratives that emphasized sexuality as a key dimension of life as a man. The ability to carry on a romance with a woman was no longer emphasized. That energy was instead put into finding work, succeeding at one's job, and earning opportunities for more skilled and/ or lucrative positions.

Not only was engaging in a seemingly heterosexual romance no longer a requisite to pulling off a gender transition, but now the entire question of sexuality was off the table. As industrialization forced changes to family economies, rendering the idea of a family living entirely off the earnings of a sole male breadwinner nearly obsolete, more and more women went to work, including those assigned female at birth who went on to work as men. News accounts reflecting favorably on these resourceful figures (when they were white) could be found everywhere – sometimes drowning out the female husbands in the process.

Female husband accounts offered an alternative vision of transing gender than those most visible. But even husbands could be and often were portrayed as asexual beings. Some writers juxtaposed the seemingly asexual laborers with female husbands. An article entitled "Transpositions" highlighted both of these experiences in one story: the case of a New York couple who "lived together as husband and wife some 15 years," before the husband was "accidentally discovered to be of the opposite sex from that [which they] assumed," and an account from Boston of "a young chap in midshipman's dress, soft-spoken, beardless, whiskerless," who hired a livery and never returned. The author characterized this situation as "a similar transformation, or rather transmigration."[103] These challenges to gender were presented together and a range of "trans" terms were used to try to make sense of what happened: transposition, transformation, and transmigration. The sailor could have been anyone but the married couple was most certainly George and Elisabeth Wilson. It is notable that the writer focused not on sexuality but rather on the issue of gender, bouncing around a range of terms to most adequately describe gender transing, settling on transposition – changing places – emphasizing the significance of external structures in establishing the parameters of transing gender for everyone.

Female husbands generally sparked greater outrage than others because they claimed the legal and social role of husband, including the right to sexual intimacies with women (even if that was left to the imagination of the reader). Intimate partnerships with women stabilized the gender of female husbands, making it more likely they were able to live in peace as men. Sailors and laborers who transed gender but did not have a visible or known female lover were often celebrated and respected. Regardless of this distinction, however, none of these people were expected or allowed to continue living openly as men. Gender conformity was *always* part of their punishment. Sometimes authorities required them to change their clothes on the spot and pledge to stop living as men. Absent another criminal charge, people were scarcely detained for an extended period of time. In big cities such as New York, people could disappear into the crowd and try to resume their lives anyway, especially if authorities failed to gather accurate information about their employers or residence.

Those who transed gender and labored while living seemingly alone in the world were figured as asexual in the press. There are several ways to make sense of this. On the one hand, it was a negative and conservative force that dehumanized laborers by stripping them of sexual desire. This practice worked to minimize the potential for same-sex intimacies and bury any evidence that could anchor the telling of a queer past. On the other hand, this forced asexuality may have been progressive and liberating for those long expected to be objects of sexual desire by men. In these accounts, they became independent autonomous subjects in the world. In this respect, accounts of female sailors and other laborers represented a powerful and empowering alternative to a life defined by sex with men, either as wives or sex workers.

* * *

Not everyone interpreted the cultural practices or formal laws regarding gender in the same way. Nor did every person with authority – including parents, teachers, police, and judges – impose their views about such things onto others. A young person might go through life receiving a tremendous number of mixed messages about their gender expression and other behaviors. For much of the nineteenth century, reactions to transing gender were wide ranging depending on the context and people involved. With the expansion of American policing and the professionalization of medicine in the 1840s, police routinely invited doctors to identify the sex of people suspected of transing genders. Explicit laws against cross-dressing further emboldened doctors to investigate the roots, causes, and consequences of transing gender and other expressions of gender nonconformity. A hostile and growing carceral state, combined with a professionalized medical establishment, ushered in a new era that stigmatized those who transed gender, especially those who refused to surrender their gender identity, no matter what the cost.

CHAPTER 6

THE ACTIVISTS

THE WOMEN'S RIGHTS MOVEMENT TOOK OFF IN THE
United States in the 1850s. Sparked by educational advances,
evangelical reform, and radical abolition, women wrote manifestos, organized conventions, and traveled the country garnering support for their
causes. Campaigns for legal rights in marriage, dress reform, better wages,
suffrage, and greater educational opportunities anchored the mainstream
movement while radical activists integrated racial justice with feminism,
working for peace, Indian rights, the abolition of slavery, and expanded
rights for free black women and men.[1] Debates about the similarities and
differences between the sexes were an important part of public discourse.[2]
Feminists had wide-ranging views themselves on the subject, though most
agreed that transing gender undermined their cause. Even the bloomers
caused a stir that made many uncomfortable.[3] Critics of women's political
advocacy, autonomy, and equality used the language of gender to undermine their efforts by calling them "masculine," "manly," or at the very
least, not "womanly." Such rhetoric was rooted in older arguments that
women who were too well read might develop masculine minds. But this
critique gained renewed potency as more women rejected conventional
expectations by wearing bloomers, refusing marriage, and standing as
political critics of slavery, war, and violence.

These collective movements of women advocating social change collided with the actions of individual female husbands. For nearly a hundred
years, female husbands in the news were not characterized as political
actors or activists. While their lives broke through some of these very same
barriers targeted by feminists, they were presented as individual eccentrics
who made peculiar choices for themselves. They never gave voice to a

critique of the institution of heterosexual marriage or women's lack of political power. They did not speak out against slavery. Female husbands did not become part of an organized movement seeking to convince others to support their lives or causes, at least that we know.

Female husband accounts, however, became a vehicle for others to address social change movements in the press. Growing numbers of people assigned female claimed freedom of dress, movement, and rights – *as women*. The bloomer dress, combining elements of both women's and men's clothing conventions, celebrated an androgynous attire which further blurred the lines between these groups. The two groups – female husbands and women's rights advocates – became linked in the press, shaping perceptions of each other in the process. Through all of these public debates about the rights of women and the distinctions between men and women, sexual difference was repeatedly exposed as unstable. Critics of husbands and feminists seemed to agree on one thing: women's rights activists were failures as women while female husbands were failures as men. This is a departure from the British press that repeatedly characterized female husbands as both convincing in their manhood and model workers, husbands, and leaders. While eighteenth-century British feminists noted their disdain for female husbands and those who transed genders, husbands were not associated with nineteenth-century women's rights activism in the UK in the same way as they were in the US.

JOHN SMITH

John Smith worked as a tinsmith and a tinker in Albany, New York for at least four years prior to 1842 (Figure 6.1).[4] Like the work of an eighteenth-century quack doctor, this required house calls and frequent interaction with all sorts of people in the community. They carried their tools with them and were skilled at repairing all sorts of metal objects, but especially pots and kettles.[5] This kind of work was independent, driven by need and demand that could be bottomless. It is easy to see the virtues in this kind of work for people passing as men – freedom from a boss and the collective work environment of other men that might be challenging or off-putting for those raised and socialized as girls. The portability of

Figure 6.1 John T. Smith, "Tinker," 1815. John Smith (no known relation to the artist) worked as a tinker in Albany, New York.
Image courtesy of the Miriam and Ira Wallach Division of Art, Prints, and Photographs: Art & Architecture Collection, the New York Public Library

the tools meant they could extend the geographic range of their services if demand dwindled – or pick up and go at a moment's notice to a new town. Smith's reputation in the community and familiarity among neighbors would offer some assurances to a potential wife despite the transient nature of their work.

Smith courted a widow named Mrs. Donnelly who was noted as both respectable and hard working.[6] Though the newspaper articles do not mention any children, the federal census of 1840 suggests that the widowed Mrs. Donnelly had two young children between the ages of ten and fifteen – a boy and a girl.[7] Accounts offer very few insights about the couple but the fact of their marriage was this: Reverend Stephen Lewis Stillman united Mr. John Smith and the widow Mrs. Donnelly in marriage at the North Methodist Church in 1842.[8] Stillman was a tireless minister for his faith, working to support believers and parishes all over the state of New York until his death in 1869.[9]

We do not know how the couple met, why they were drawn to each other, or what inspired them to marry. Maybe they met at the North Methodist Church, drawn together through and within a religious community they both shared. Maybe Mrs. Donnelly hired Smith to repair some of her pots and pans, welcoming Smith in her home as a contract worker. Maybe she was impressed with the quality of the work – or charmed by the conversation which ensued. Maybe Smith admired Donnelly from afar before working up the courage to ring her doorbell and offer their services as a tinker. It would be presumptuous for Smith to think the stable, respected Donnelly would show interest in an itinerant worker as a lover but perfectly reasonable for them to solicit business going door to door.

Donnelly was said to have saved a considerable sum of money. Smith was accused of pursuing their relationship to gain access to it.[10] If true, this was not the first time that someone married for money. Mrs. Donnelly was portrayed in the press as a pathetic figure for being used and duped. But Donnelly in fact held many cards in her hand. When wives of female husbands wanted to get rid of their husbands, they had numerous options at their disposal. Wives of female husbands had more rights and freedoms than wives with male husbands. Wives of female husbands were not able to protect their husbands from the state, but the state was eager to protect them from their husbands.

The central undoing of Smith's gender in this case had two sources that followed each other sequentially. The first had something to do with sexual intimacies, the second with physical embodiment. Donnelly's statement suggests something pertaining to sex that either didn't happen at all or didn't happen as she expected. After their marriage, Donnelly confided in a friend that she wasn't satisfied with her marriage because her husband "did'nt do the thing that was right." This was not the tearful confession of a young girl to a close female confidant. This was a carefully worded claim that preserved Donnelly's sense of respectability while providing enough information to inspire further action on her behalf. She shared this news with an adult male – Michael McGuire – who could and did challenge Smith to their face and report them to the authorities.

The second way that Smith's gender was undone was at the hands of McGuire. Smith was very successful in embodying and expressing their male gender. There was no prior suspicion that they were anything but a man. McGuire wanted to get to the bottom of Donnelly's claim on her behalf. Without obvious visible clues suggesting Smith was not a man, McGuire literally took matters – and Smith – into his own hands. He decided that Smith's body held the key to their sex and attacked Smith, first verbally calling Smith "Madam" and shouting "Yes, I will. . .and I'll know whether you are one or not." The physical assault was described as such, "Mike seized hold of John Smith, and tore his coat, vest, and – saw to his great surprise that Mr. Smith was indeed a woman!"[11] Together, Mrs. Donnelly's critique of their sexual intimacies and McGuire's forceful exposition of Smith's chest served as the criteria for determining their sex and invalidating their gender.

News accounts of this case did not circulate as far and wide as others. Many stories offered a bare-bones outline of the case, simply using the headline "female husband" to make the central point for readers.[12] The tone of these stories was hostile and the gendered language refused any recognition of the husband's manhood. Instead, it mocked them as "the faithless swain" and the "deceitful jade" and "her ladyship."[13] Writers used two main analogies to contextualize the husband's wrongdoing for their readers. One involved a maritime reference to flags, an old tradition that would have been familiar to all. It charged Smith the female husband "with hanging out false signals – being not exactly what outward appearances would lead honest and unsuspecting persons to believe – sailing under false colors."[14] The other invoked a reference that was of paramount concern to the public precisely in antebellum America – the issue of deception, describing Smith as a "counterfeit man."[15] Both suggested the violation of social norms and but not necessarily legal ones.

Smith was reported, arrested, and imprisoned with much fanfare and social righteousness. But the limits of using vagrancy laws to punish gender transgressions were tested by Smith's case. In this case, the magistrate was not willing to allow for Smith's longer-term detention under the vagrancy statute and he ordered Smith released. People learned from this case that there was no law explicitly against either cross-dressing or transing gender. Newspapers reported, "She has been discharged from custody, there being no law in the State against such a deception."[16] Another report added rhetorical flare to the same argument: "As there is no law in the state which covers the offence, the gay deceiver was released after the examination before the magistrate."[17] While many people personally believed that transing gender was immoral and reprehensible, the law was technically indifferent.

In 1842, New York did not yet have laws on the books specifically against cross-dressing. This did not keep police from arresting people for transing gender, however. But it did mean that such arrests generally resulted in short-term, temporary confinement unless other charges were also brought. When someone was arrested in Troy, New York the previous year, a writer questioned the basis for the arrest. The report states, "A woman was arrested and committed to prison in Troy, for appearing in male attire. They must have singular laws in Troy; in other places the women are allowed to wear the breeches and no body objects."[18] News of people transing gender in the press challenged the public to question not only the existing laws but also their own views on the matter.

The Albany case also marks the beginning of editorial associations between educated activist women and laboring female husbands by suggesting that any woman who challenges gender norms might be susceptible to the idea that they could/should live fully as a man and marry a woman. One author states, "This of course will serve as a warning to all ladies of a masculine turn of mind, not to carry the joke too far. If they get intimate with one of their sex, they will be sure to be found out."[19] In addition to linking those deemed "masculine" to the possibility of becoming a female husband, this brief passage emphasizes a notion of gender identity, suggesting those who transed gender had an internal masculinity of the mind which set them apart from those who were more comfortable being women. While the writer characterized this as a joke, there was nothing funny about it because most people saw female husbands as a very serious threat and literally ran straight to the authorities.

Why were female husbands such a threat? It is tempting in hindsight to view female husbands and their wives as the most conservative of figures. They took a great risk upon transing gender but if they were able to pass convincingly as men, they might settle into a seemingly conventional heterosexual married life. But this conformity was the greatest threat of all to neighbors and co-workers who felt betrayed and deceived upon learning that someone was assigned female. Their ability to blend in – for a time – is precisely what sparked passionate rage and retaliation against them. To that end, people wanted New York State to adopt a more explicit law against transing gender.

MASCULINE WOMEN

The emergence of an organized, visible movement for women's rights left individual acts of resistance subject to new interpretation. When someone assigned female donned male attire, such as John Smith, they were seen as exceptional or desperate figures who acted as individuals. But the line between individual and collective action was increasingly blurred during this era as more women spoke out about political matters, from abolition and temperance to peace and women's rights.[20] Women who organized and signed anti-slavery petitions in the 1830s drew the ire of political leaders who attacked the activists for being unwomanly or masculine. Southern defenders of slavery espoused traditional gender roles and a natural hierarchy of men over women while Northern abolitionists increasingly called for equality between the sexes. But what exactly was meant by equality? Even outspoken proponents of women's right to vote and hold public office worried the experience would change women and make them more like men.

The flurry of antebellum publications espousing the virtues of womanhood and heralding natural differences between men and women were a defensive reaction to women's expansive claim to education and public life. Lucia McMahon writes: "Indeed, the doctrine of separate spheres found its fullest expression in the prescriptive literature *after* women began to assert larger claims for political and economic equality."[21] This argument is extremely important because it signals a change in mainstream public opinion of women's capacity for reason, learning, and teaching – all things that were celebrated in the early republican period as long as women focused on running schools for children and did not demand political standing or power. Only after some women entered the political fray over slavery did their capabilities and standing as teachers come under attack.[22]

Women played a significant role in the early anti-slavery movement. Freethinker Frances Wright paved the way in the 1820s despite being lambasted in the press for even daring to speak to mixed crowds of men and women in public. Maria Stewart became the first black woman to deliver public lectures on abolition and women's rights, speaking in Boston in 1832.[23] Lucretia Mott helped found the Philadelphia Female Anti-Slavery Society in 1833 and also inspired the women's rights movement. These women defied a profound social taboo on women's political speech and inspired others to follow in their footsteps.[24] Angelina Grimke became the first Southern woman to publicly speak out against slavery, making her "the most notorious woman in America" in 1837 other than Fanny Wright.[25] Women who worked against slavery – circulating petitions, speaking in public, and organizing advocacy groups – drew public attacks from a wide range of sources.

Politicians, pro-slavery advocates, and ministers led the way in attacking not just their views but also their right to express those views in the first place. Critics turned to biblical teachings about women's submission to men, scientific theories of women's physical weakness, and the political role of the male head of household to justify their claims. The question of the morality or legality of slavery itself was suppressed. Instead, women were attacked for daring to assert themselves in political matters. Their own morality and even their womanhood challenged in the process.

Critics claimed that the particular things that made women and their sphere of influence different from that of men were ordained by God and nature. These ideas are illustrated in some remarks by Reverend Hubbard Winslow of Boston in response to the efforts of Wright, Grimke, and others who "assume the place of public teachers," which he frowned upon.[26] Winslow offered a litany of reasons for women's submission, citing Corinthians to claim that women are to maintain "silence in the churches, and act in subordination to the authority of man" and not "speak in public."[27] The epistle to Timothy states that women wear "modest apparel" and "learn in silence with all subjection" and embrace "shamefacedness and sobriety."[28] Women were to be learners, not teachers, according to both Timothy and the example set by Jesus.[29] Women who defied these teachings were "unnatured and repulsive" in Winslow's view, having "lost the characteristic graces of her sex." Because of this, such women were entirely undesired by men, which Winslow believed was rightly so.[30] The viciousness of these attacks suggests that abolitionist women struck a chord in their rousing speeches against slavery and in favor of expanded political rights for black men and all women.

Religious and conservative men like Winslow had profound investments in maintaining hierarchies of sexual and racial difference. In some cases, this amounted to explicit charges against abolitionist women by name, for not only their political views and actions but also their physical appearance. Winslow wrote, "The world has had enough of Fanny Wrights; whether they appear in the name of avowed infidelity, or of civil and human rights, or of political economy, or of morals and religion, their tendency is ultimately the same – the alienation of the sexes, the subversion of the distinguishing excellence and benign influence of women in society, the destruction of the domestic constitution, the prostration of all decency and order, the reign of wild anarchy and shameless vice."[31] Such exaggerated characterizations of the aim of activists suggested the power and righteousness of their message was getting through.

But if we turn our attention away from Winslow's attack on the activists and reading of scripture to consider his own reflections on the ambiguity of gender in society, the source of his and others' concerns emerges. Winslow admitted that gender was a force with unclear boundaries. He noted it could be difficult to clearly identify "the precise line of demarcation where the masculine character ends and where the feminine begins." He noted how social expectations shaped our perceptions of behavior, writing, "The same act which would be modest and delicate

173

in a man, would not always be so in a woman; while on the other hand what may be very bold and energetic in a woman, might be very tame in a man." Winslow plainly recognizes that feminine men and masculine women have a place in society. He continues, "It is on this principle that we are accustomed to say of the man, who partakes of the character appropriate to females, that he is *effeminate*; and also of the woman, who partakes of the character appropriate to males, that she is *masculine*."[32] Winslow characterizes such people and behavior as "out of place, something undesirable and unlovely"; to be tolerated, but neither celebrated nor condemned. This rather mild critique, however, is followed by an assertion that this group of people was going to grow and take over society. He warns that the threat is in the "not far distant" horizon that such people might "become universal."[33] As much as he and others might tout the biblical teachings on the "natural" differences between the sexes, these remarks suggest he believed otherwise.

Times were in fact changing. Winslow acknowledged that some women would reject marriage and motherhood in favor of their own intellectual advancement. Here Winslow found a model in Hannah More, someone whose feminism was not seen as diminishing her character. Winslow celebrated More as a model woman who demonstrated "the strictest female propriety and the highest excellence" despite the fact that she remained single and childless.[34] The key for Winslow – and for More – was the celebration of women's differences from men as an honor, not a burden.

While this elaborate reflection on one minister's views may seem excessive, historians of the period have shown how important the church was in shaping both "cultural and legal perceptions of women's civil status."[35] The black church was an important site for black women who were determined to speak openly in public forums about matters of both religious and political governance. African American ministers grappled with the significance of black women's political advocacy. Reverend James Forten of Philadelphia argued in favor of women's anti-slavery activism by couching it within an expanded notion of the domestic sphere. Forten tried to make public activism appropriately feminine rather than defend women's claim to a public sphere and concede that such a sphere was fundamentally masculine.[36] In this regard, Forten recognized that he too understood what female abolitionists were quickly learning: political representation was seen as a masculine endeavor, reserved for men.

Those who elevated the natural differences between men and women used it as a strategy for dismissing women's political advocacy. Northern women's use of petitions to challenge slavery sparked a public debate that focused less on the substance of the petitions and more on the gendered implications of the discourse. Specifically, Southerners accused these women of not behaving properly as women. In this respect, the challenge to slavery – including abuse of enslaved women by white Southern men and women – became associated with challenges to gender norms as well.[37] Some politicians used explicit language pertaining to embodied gender and sexuality in criticizing the women.[38] The politician Jesse Bynum called such women "mannish" and "old grannies" and "boarding-school misses." William Cost Johnson of Maryland said their political advocacy served to "unsex" them.[39] These attacks on abolitionist women throughout the 1830s and 1840s put the language and rules of gender at the heart of public debates over social change – even before these women turned their attention to the question of women's rights.

Southern politicians were by no means alone in their investment in sexual difference. Even progressive men who favored abolition and women's rights were opposed to what seemed like a dramatic step in minimizing the differences between the sexes. Though Ralph Waldo Emerson came to believe that women deserved equal rights, including the vote and the right to stand for office, he did not think they should pursue these activities because doing so would make them unfeminine/undesirable and more like men.[40] Emerson declined the invitation by Paulina Wright Davis to participate in the Women's Rights Convention in Worcester in 1850 with a note stating as much: "I imagine that a woman whom all men would feel to be the best, would decline such privileges if offered, & feel them to be obstacles to her legitimate influence."[41] A decade later, he gave a public lecture on women, remarking "that the 'masculine' woman is not so strong in influence as the lady."[42] Universalist Minister Edwin Hubbell Chapin preached women's equality as well but claimed public life had no place for women: "It is rather a fearful picture, to be sure, of a masculine woman, scheming in Wall Street, or shouting in Tammany Hall."[43] People might support women's rights in theory, but as the movement grew in visibility and strength so too did a backlash that invoked "masculine" women as the dreadful end result of any political advances.

"Masculine" became a shorthand way to reference and mock the growing number of women activists who spread across the country with their teachings. A critique of Reverend Antoinette Brown for trying to speak at the World Temperance Convention was framed as an example of the dramatic upheavals often led by "masculine women." The article starts, "The masculine women are always kicking up a row, generally. Their 'rights,' in defense of which they expend so much breath, seem to consist in the right of thrusting themselves in where they are not wanted."[44]

The attack on women's political activism could have taken many different forms, but it didn't. Northern ministers, Southern politicians, educators, reformers, and humanist writers *all* embraced the charge of "masculinity" as the ultimate way to slur, shame, and discredit women's political autonomy. Some self-identified feminists even used it to attack other feminists! Though female husbands were not active participants in these movements or debates, they were seen as a threat to feminism and women's rights. Female masculinity – in its many varieties – threatened sexual difference. Though activists who were characterized as "masculine women" wanted more rights *as women,* many of them went on the defensive in bending over backwards to claim that they did not want to *become men.* They did not want to be associated with those who *became men.* Establishing distance was not hard, as most people who publicly transed genders were of the uneducated, poor, laboring class.

Some women reformers and abolitionists criticized other women for being too masculine. Mary Grove Nichols was known as a free-love-advocating sex radical, but she still took a traditional, hard line on the question of sexual difference.[45] While she embraced reform dress for its health benefits, she celebrated feminine weakness and plainly stated, "Nor are bold, masculine women wanted in this work."[46] So too did Catherine Beecher, who attacked Fanny Wright for her gender, calling her a "great masculine person" whose style was too loud and bold.[47] With prominent women's rights advocates and writers taking such a position, it is no wonder that female husbands and their wives were never embraced as kindred spirits.

Upstate New York – where several female husbands lived during this era – was a hotbed of radical activism for the abolition of slavery, the rights of American Indians, the end to US military involvement in Mexico, and property rights for married women.[48] Women fought for standing and a voice within religious communities, reform organizations, and politically. Many of the early activists were radical Quaker Friends who championed an intersectional and expansive approach to human rights. There were colored conventions, anti-slavery conventions, and women's rights conventions.[49] Syracuse, New York hosted a Women's Rights Convention in 1852.[50] Samuel J. May, Unitarian minister of Syracuse, was an outspoken abolitionist and supporter of women's rights. His 1846 sermon on "The Rights and Condition of Women" took up the question of physical differences between men and women.[51] May noted that differences in strength were exacerbated by culture and tradition. Furthermore, he thought it was outrageous that physical weakness was seen as evidence of women's inferiority and then used to justify women's marginalization in political concerns. May wrote: "But allowing women generally to have less bodily power, why should this consign them to mental, moral or social dependence? Physical force is of special value only in a savage or barbarous community."[52] Here May pointed out the hypocrisy of Christian ministers who long celebrated Christian women's physical weakness as a sign of civilization in opposition to "savage and pagan tribes."[53] Furthermore, the whole point of the triumph of Western civilization was "the subordination of the physical in man to the mental and moral."[54] For May, physical embodiment was not important and was meant to be secondary to the inner life of the mind and spirit.

People increasingly accepted the idea that women probably had some right to participate in public, political, and professional life to a greater extent, but that did not mean they were qualified or that they should. This must be seen as progress for the movement. But opponents emphasized natural differences to justify why women should not exercise their rights. When the Reverend W.W. Gardner railed against women's medical education, he conceded, "she may have a *natural right* to practice physic or law" but she is "by nature and conformation unqualified for the professions," and the "harmony of society demands, that she occupy the proper sphere of action which nature has designed for her."[55] This author went on to charge that women's education was ruining the differences among the sexes, describing "masculine women and feminine men" as "monstrosities" who numbered "plenty about us," and whose presence "more clearly show the beauty of character belonging to each sex.[56] Reverend Horace Bushnell echoed similar sentiments in his book which deemed women's suffrage to be "a reform against nature."[57] It was significant that so many opponents of women's rights embraced "nature" as the basis for their claims. This is different than the way nature is used in contemporary claims of innate identity (as in, I was "born" gay). Rather, here "nature" is held up as a historic ideal for gender norms in the face of evidence everywhere that people are making new and different choices than they had before. Gender nonconformity, changing gender roles, and even transing gender were everywhere.

ALBERT GUELPH, PART ONE: LONDON, ENGLAND

Marriage rights were one of the many targets of the women's movement in both the US and the UK. Middling and rich white women in the US launched a campaign against both law and custom that rendered women legal non-entities after marriage and gave husbands total control over their wealth. Activists in the UK worked to shift the authority from church to state, thereby making divorce more accessible to women. They succeeded with passage of the 1857 Divorce and Matrimonial Causes Act.[58] Yet there was no denying that a key dimension of marriage for most women was the opportunity for financial security and stability. Certainly this was the case for Mary Ann Robins, a thirty-six-year-old widow with three teenage children.[59] The marriage of her oldest daughter, a seventeen-year-old also named Mary Ann Robins, offered her relief, pride, and hope for her family's future.[60] She celebrated her daughter's wedding on September 12, 1852 at St. Michael's in Highgate, Camden.[61] Her daughter's new husband was a well-dressed man who made a big fuss about her daughter and lived on familial largesse. The two got to know each other over a period of months, first as friends and later through courtship. There were so many stories of men promising future marriage as a means to gain trust, intimacy, or sometimes money before leaving their female lovers high and dry. With her daughter's wedding behind her, she could breathe a sigh of relief.

The ink on the marriage certificate was barely dry when daughter Mary Ann notified mother Mary Ann of upsetting news: her husband was female. Mrs. Robins reported that her daughter "went to York to spend the honey-moon" where she "discovered that she had been married to a woman in man's attire, and the mother of three children."[62] Some wives of female husbands were happy with their partnerships, but Mary Ann was not and made quite a plea to her mother for help. Mrs. Robins did the only thing she could think to do in that moment – she ran to the Westminster Police Station to get their assistance. The report she made was a convoluted one, revealing that neither she nor her daughter were particularly discerning. The police were confused though determined to assist this woman who they deemed upstanding and worthy of their support. With the marriage certificate on hand, it was hard to dispute a legal contract had been made. It said there in black and white – Albert Guelph was a thirty-two-year-old bachelor gentleman who was married to Mary Ann Robins, a seventeen-year-old spinster. There was nothing listed under "rank or profession" for Mary Ann but some sources suggest she may have worked in the theater. Newspapers ran sympathetic stories that portrayed Mrs. Robin as "quiet-looking" and "elderly."[63] Her daughter was characterized as someone who was duped – exactly the fate her mother hoped for her daughter to avoid.

Parents do not feature significantly in the history of female husbands.[64] Most female husbands were abandoned in childhood by death or poverty; others ran away in desperation, rebellion, or in search of a different kind of life.[65] None have documented ongoing relationships with parents that are captured by the newspaper stories reporting on their lives. While this could be a function of the coverage itself, it is not hard to believe that once they transitioned to boyhood or manhood, their parents were no longer in their lives. But wives of female husbands often followed a different course. In this case, the wife was close to her mother; in a case discussed later in the chapter, the wife was close to her father. Marriage to a female husband brought this female wife closer to her mother; later in the chapter we will see that marriage drove a wedge between a female wife and her father.

We still know very little about the feelings, motivations, and thoughts of female wives. We are left to read between the lines and draw conclusions from the shreds of evidence offered about them. In newspaper coverage of female husbands, the wives are never of equal interest. The women who married and built lives with female husbands were vital to the identity and happiness of the husband, yet the press generally portrayed them as mere accessories. We often don't even learn their complete names in the news, just a passing reference to a "Miss Robins" or "Miss Rubens."[66] I found the wife's given name – Mary Ann – through additional archival research.

There are some strange twists to this story. It was alleged that Mary Ann Robins first met her future husband under a female guise as a person who went by the name of Mrs. Panton. To outside observers, they were two women who became friendly. The age difference may have raised an eyebrow – Robins was only seventeen while Panton was thirty-two. Maybe Panton lied about their age at this juncture. Panton occasionally stayed the night with the Robins family when visiting.[67] Their friendship and intimacy lasted for several months. Then Mrs. Panton underwent a social transition from female to male and reintroduced themself to the family as Albert Guelph.

Guelph explained to both Miss Mary Ann and Mrs. Mary Ann Robins that they were a secret descendant of King George IV and Queen Caroline. Because of shame, they were hidden from the world and advised to live as a girl from a young age, even though they were assigned male at birth. A relative secretly supplied them with money and advice. Guelph assured Mrs. Robins that love for her daughter inspired this change of course, stating, "his love for her fair daughter had wrung it from his heart, and induced him to appear in the becoming habiliments of his own sex, in lieu of the female attire he had been disguised in for years."[68] Both Miss and Mrs. Robins accepted the truth of this claim and invited the newly transitioned Albert Guelph into their hearts and homes as a man.

If only Mrs. Robins' husband Bruton was still alive! Bruton Robins and Mary Ann Brooks were married in Hackney, England in 1834.[69] They had three children: Mary Ann, Bruton, and Louisa.[70] The young family lived with Bruton's parents, Fanny and William. Bruton had followed his father's occupational footsteps working as a brass founder. The large extended family made due and then Bruton died, leaving Mary Ann a widow with three children. Widows navigated the roles and tasks traditionally expected of both men and women. Mary Beth Norton once argued that widows embraced a gender identity that was both male and female, stating, "She was simultaneously both female and male: female, in that like other women she was excluded from certain political and military obligations; male, in that like men she had economic responsibilities and automatic rule over her own household."[71] Even for someone like Mrs. Robins, the category of "woman" never fully accurately described the range of skills and responsibilities she had.

Why would a woman marry off her daughter in such unusual circumstances, based on an original deception that introduced the possibility of gender instability? How did the bride feel about her girlfriend becoming her beau? There was one overriding factor that propelled this relationship forward even in the face of mysterious revelations and twists: *money.* Mrs. Robins reported to the police that Guelph "always had plenty of money."[72] This fact, concluded after months of socializing together, would have lent credence to the claim that Guelph was wealthy. Mrs. Robins would have every reason to believe that her daughter would not want for anything. Guelph was after all listed as a "gentleman" on the marriage certificate. In this regard, Guelph was exceptional and different from all other female husbands, who belonged to the laboring poor class.

Guelph left town and was never heard from again. Mrs. Robins was relieved to have her daughter back and the marriage void but the press coverage alone ensured the scandal lived on in their lives for years to come. Miss Mary Ann would never be able to hide or deny the fact of her failed marriage because of all the newspaper coverage. But eventually, life moved on. Both mother and daughter remarried. The thirty-nine-year-old widow Mary Ann Brooks (Mrs. Robins' maiden name) married a thirty-nine-year-old widower who worked as a tailor, Joseph Blewett, in February 1854.[73] Just one year later, the younger Miss Mary Ann Robins married a thirty-year-old artist, James Rogers, who was also a widower.[74] Mary Ann was two years older and a lifetime wiser.

The US press picked up the story in mid-November 1853, one month after it originated in England. It reappeared in one form or another for two solid months, in dozens of publications across every region of the country east of the Mississippi.[75] Major northeastern city papers always ran these kinds of stories from England but now papers from Louisiana, Tennessee, North Carolina, and Virginia carried them too. Even a small-town paper created to serve a growing mining community in rural east central Pennsylvania picked up the story. The *Miners' Journal* of Pottsville, Pennsylvania ran a brief summary and added their own editorial to the end: "We are not much of a lawyer, but we presume this case would fall under the head of 'obtaining goods under false pretenses.'"[76] This brief editorial raised the issue of legality while objectifying the wife by equating her to "goods." Such commentary was common practice as editors of small-town papers sought to put their own spin on news that was reprinted from elsewhere.

Editors sometimes ran stories verbatim but just as often they tweaked the lead, offered some catchy polemic, or made minor changes to make the story relevant to their readers. In the case of this account, two adjustments were made to pique the interest of the US readership. While the newly-weds took honeymoon in York, England, the US press inserted the word "New" suggesting they were on holiday in New York City. Further, they changed the date of the wedding from 1852 to 1853. These two adjustments made the story of more immediate relevance. Someone reading the paper on the streets of New York, or even in nearby towns, might imagine stumbling into the young couple. Regardless of these minor tweaks, a story featuring royal birth, mysterious packages of money, and someone who moved between gender expressions would have seemed both intriguing and unbelievable.

There are three key factors that made Alfred Guelph different from most other female husbands. First, Guelph received money from family and did not have to hold down a job. Second, ~~Guelph never lived full time or consistently as a man but rather seemed to go back and forth between a self-presentation as a man and as a woman~~. Like the sailor Samuel Bundy, they may have embraced a nonbinary gender. Third, Guelph was at the heart of two different marriages that were legally and socially contested by their wives' parents – one in London, England in 1853 and another in Syracuse, New York in 1856. In many ways, their life is a bridge not only between England and America but also between eighteenth- and twentieth-century understandings of female husbands.

ALBERT GUELPH, PART TWO: SYRACUSE, NEW YORK

Most female husbands disappear from the public eye shortly after they become the subject of public scrutiny. Albert Guelph was different. Two years after the US press coverage of their life in London, they reappeared in the headlines of Syracuse, New York in new, yet nearly identical circumstances. There were two key differences: Guelph was reported to the authorities by the *father* of their new bride and the father did this *against* the bride's wishes, who wanted to remain married to Guelph. The two – Miss Lewis and Albert Guelph – were married by Reverend Gregory in an Episcopal Church after a brief courtship. The bride's father became suspicious of Guelph and insisted on meeting with Guelph for a one-on-one confrontation. Mr. Lewis asserted his belief that Guelph "was not what she pretended to be." Guelph only put up a brief fight, at first asserting that they were a "man," then stating they were "female." It is interesting that the articles used the words "man" and "female" rather than "man" and "woman" or "male" and "female." It was true that Guelph was both a man and female, though Mr. Lewis and the officer on hand probably didn't notice that the two did not contradict each other. Together, Mr. Lewis and Officer Barnes conducted "a partial examination" and determined Guelph was "a woman disguised." What exactly constituted this "partial" exam is not revealed.[77] But it is a huge departure from tradition for two men to conduct a physical exam of someone suspected of being assigned female. History and custom would have called for a woman to do the search or, as was increasingly the case by the mid-nineteenth century, a medical doctor. Miss Lewis' father and the policeman fit neither of these criteria.

Guelph was arrested and imprisoned, quite possibly for the first time in their life. They evaded such treatment in London after their prior marriage. Guelph's young bride was horrified by this development and did not want Guelph arrested. But her father took over in an attempt to protect his daughter and assert order in his community. This was meddling his daughter did not want. She believed the arrest was a conspiracy against the couple. It was noted that Miss Lewis "still clings to her woman husband," and when granted visitation rights at the prison the two "embraced each other with the greatest marks of affection."[78] This story was rather ordinary: a young woman picked a lover who her father didn't like and thought was bad for her. The circumstances of Guelph's gender simply gave Mr. Lewis an extra tool with which to break the lovers apart, by leveraging the state in-between the newly-weds. One news outlet reported on the uniqueness of the situation involving the father of the bride, who was involved in "placing his female son-in-law in jail."[79]

The coverage of Albert Guelph in the Syracuse papers characterized them as feminine, female, and a woman at every turn. Headlines splashed the phrase "Man Woman" every chance they could, from "The Man Woman!"[80] to "It seems that the case of the 'Man Woman'."[81] These alternated with the more historically common "The Female in Disguise."[82] Questions of Guelph's sex featured prominently in the early news coverage. The writer of one story explained their use of female pronouns, stating, "There is now no doubt but the person is a woman, and although she is still attired in man's apparel, we will speak of her as one of the female sex."[83] Newspaper headlines continued to raise the issue of "The Question" that no one could seem to answer, "Is 'Albert Guelph' a Woman?" The *Warren Mail* mocked Guelph's gender and body, describing them as "An English woman, almost fat, fair and forty," while also playing with gendered pronouns, stating, "She (*or he*) lately made love to a young lady and married her."[84]

For their part, Guelph refused to answer a direct question from the judge about their sex. When Justice Durnford asked, "Are you a male or female?" Guelph answered, "your officers can tell you," or "have told you."[85] Guelph refused to offer the authorities clarity in any way. They rejected the common strategy of others in their situation who strategically admitted they were female before explaining why they began living as men. They also refused to double down and defend their manhood. Rather, Guelph put it back on the officers who interrogated them, knowing that their perspective – a third-party assessment – was really what mattered to the judge and the community. For his part, the arresting officer asserted with certainty that "he *knows* she is a woman."[86]

Guelph stood before the judge in their own clothes, a "blue frock coat, light pants, dark vest, and blue shirt."[87] The judge determined that Guelph's deception harmed the entire community as much as it had their wife, Miss Lewis. The community was said to be overwhelmed by excitement, astonishment, and prejudice toward Guelph. The presiding judge felt this sentiment was justification for a harsh sentence for Guelph, revealing the power of the community in shaping judicial practices. Justice Durnford decided that Guelph was "partially deranged," and sentenced them to a 90-day prison sentence on charge of vagrancy.[88] The judge did not forcibly require Guelph to wear women's attire in prison. This may have been a matter of convenience for authorities – vagrants generally didn't wear the prison uniform of convicts but rather served their time in their own clothes. But he did offer a wish and a warning that upon release from jail Guelph would resume the identity and expression of a woman in order "to win back the confidence and respect of community."[89] Guelph, however, did not make much of the judge's orders or opinion.

The most unusual dimension of Guelph's life in Syracuse throughout this controversy is that they lived with their sister, Sarah Edgars, and her family.[90] Guelph's wife, Miss Lewis, also moved in with Mrs. Edgars' family after the marriage and stayed there while Guelph was detained in prison.[91] More details about the Edgars family were revealed about six weeks after the original arrest when Guelph was again detained on charges of vagrancy. This time, Guelph's brother-in-law – Thomas Edgar – testified in the case. Thomas was born in England to a laboring household where he met and married Sarah, having five children before emigrating to the United States.[92] The forty-three-year-old white man was a laborer, husband, and father. His word would mean everything before the court.

Thomas testified that Guelph's name was really Nancy Stours, that Guelph had a son living at home with them who was about twenty years old. He confirmed that Guelph generally received money from England, though they had not recently.[93] Thomas claimed that Guelph was then living with a black woman named Diana Jackson and that Miss Lewis sometimes lived there as well. Diana Jackson was a fifty-seven-year-old black woman, head of household living at number 21 in Syracuse's seventh ward.[94] Mr. Edgars' family lived right next door, possibly in the same building, at number 22 with their five children.[95] The involvement of a sibling and their family in the life of a female husband was very unusual, suggesting that Guelph was known – in their nonbinary gender – by a network of family, friends, and neighbors long before their arrest for marrying Miss Lewis.

Guelph was not consistently living full time as a man but rather seems to have gone back and forth between gender expressions depending on circumstance. Guelph was reportedly "well known in town in the character of a female" and also went by the name Nancy.[96] It was said that Guelph first became acquainted with the Lewis family while presenting as a woman and then later changed into men's attire "with the knowledge of the family." The press reasoned that the family must have believed "her woman's dress was a disguise" and that by presenting as a man, Guelph was "assuming the proper habiliments of her sex." This was the same argument Guelph made to the family of their first wife, Mary Ann Robins. And this was the argument made for the father, Mr. Lewis, which inspired his distrust of Guelph in the first place.

What motivated Guelph to present as a man and propose marriage to Miss Lewis?[97] Was Guelph most comfortable presenting and living as a man or did they do so simply to achieve their goal of intimacy, love, and marriage to Miss Lewis? Unlike most female husbands who lived fully as men, Guelph's pattern suggests they were comfortable and enjoyed living as a woman as well. In this case Guelph likely transed gender as a means to satisfy their sexual desires. Furthermore, Miss Lewis seemed neither surprised nor hurt when Guelph was arrested for being female. Instead, she stood by Guelph's side, fought with her father, and continued to live in Guelph's residence even when Guelph was in prison. All of this points to the idea that Miss Lewis knew Guelph was assigned female and of nonbinary gender – and she liked it.[98]

The press was clearly divided in its assessment of Guelph's gender and their relationship. Did Guelph dupe their young bride into thinking they were biologically male or was this a same-sex relationship dressed up in disguise for others? A third alternative – that Miss Lewis knew Guelph was a female assigned person who transed gender and loved that about them – was not entertained. One local paper pressed the issue of Guelph as a threat because Guelph "has been making love to, gaining the affections of, and marrying a young lady."[99] People assigned female could become not only men but also lovers and husbands. Other accounts categorically declared Guelph a woman and saw this relationship as a same-sex marriage. A snippy one-liner titled "Hard Up" asserted, "Our Devil thinks the women must be hard up for husbands when they take to marrying each other" was repeated in widespread coverage of the story.[100] Stories about the incident qualified the news with the phrase "This is leap year" so as to signify irregularity.[101] The presumption was that Guelph was fundamentally a woman and that no amount of male attire, affect, or transing of gender would ever truly transform them into the "character" of a man.

Guelph hired a lawyer who quickly found two issues with the judge's ruling: the maximum charge for vagrancy was sixty days and there was actually no state law prohibiting "a person to dress in the attire of the opposite sex."[102] Mr. Murphy asserted that people misread the 1845 statute against disguise which targeted those whose "face was painted or otherwise disguised, or the person carried arms."[103] Guelph did not try to disguise or paint their face in anyway. The reporter covering the trial offered a clarifying explanation for its readers, "It seems that the statute originated in the anti-rent troubles, and was particularly designed for those cases."[104] This was in fact correct. The defense was brilliant because it earned Guelph's release and exposed the fact that transing gender was not in and of itself illegal.

This question of the legality or lawlessness of transing gender would soon be taken up more broadly. For now, it was important to note that the 1845 New York State Law against "Disguised and Armed Persons" specified that the target was people who covered their faces by having them "painted, discolored, covered or concealed, or being otherwise disguised, in a manner calculated to prevent him from being identified," subject to up to six months imprisonment.[105] An 1846 addition specifically targeted members of the militia, declaring it illegal for officers, musicians, or privates to "appear on parade wearing any personal disguise or other unusual or ludicrous article of dress," subject to a $5–$25 fine.[106] Such statewide legislation was a response to a broad and growing political dispute between large-scale landowners and renters. For twenty-five years, the tenants' rights movement grew. The more radical of the anti-rent activists numbered around 10,000 by 1845 and were known for their disguises, including "bulky, tall leather bag-shaped face masks" and calico dresses.[107] These laws sought to stifle political protest among a growing poor people's movement.

It is important to note the distinction between the intention of this law and the later application of it. It was never the intention of the New York legislature to target people for transing gender. Regardless of aim or intention, once the law was on the books, it legitimized the regulation of diverse gendered embodiments and expressions in a whole host of situations. It confirmed the idea that the state had the authority to police dress and opened the door to further punishment and stigmatization of this practice in the future. Regardless, it would be referenced many decades later as the legal basis for punishing people for a "gender expression" that differed from what was expected of someone assigned a certain sex.[108]

The case against Albert Guelph generated widespread awareness that there was no law against transing gender. This realization inspired some people to demand one. While the *Syracuse Daily Standard* reported near daily and largely factual updates on the case, the *Syracuse Daily Journal* editorialized harshly and profusely in its sporadic coverage. The lead sentence announcing Guelph's discharge from prison declared, "This silly and disgusting specimen of humanity is again at large."[109] Guelph continued to wear men's clothing, ignoring the counsel of the judge while raising eyebrows around town. The article concluded, "This shameless woman still persists in wearing her male apparel, thus rendering herself an object of general remark, and a disgrace to her sex and the community. Something could be done by the proper authorities, it seems to me, to meet her case."[110] The call for greater punishment by law enforcement officials would soon become a common refrain.

After all was said and done, Albert Guelph wanted to clear their name and that of their wife. They did not want people to see them as a fraud or imposter in any way. They asserted, "I am no enemy, no traitor, no spy or pretender."[111] They also sought to save their wife's reputation. Guelph declared that Miss Lewis was a woman of a "noble mind" who was drawn to helping others even though she could find success in moving with "circles of a fashionable world."[112] It is remarkable in some ways that Guelph was even given this platform in the press. While stories about female husbands were attention-getters, newspaper editors were more comfortable writing *about them* than letting husbands speak for themselves.

DRESSING IN PUBLIC

While debates swirled about the differences between men and women, more and more people assigned female at birth rejected the clothing they had been instructed to wear. This took several forms, from those who donned male attire temporarily for an outing to those who sought to live and pass as men for love or work. Much has already been said about these groups. A third group would become known as "bloomers" for the new style which combined a shortened skirt worn with pants underneath.

When someone assigned female at birth is described as having worn "male attire," it signals many different things. First, it is a literal description of clothing. Second, it points out that men and women each have their own approved type of clothing. The phrase "male attire" is seldom used to describe men wearing men's clothes. Rather, the whole notion of attire being sexed male is raised only when the clothing gender binary is violated and a woman puts on the clothes. The phrase "male attire" notes that someone without the proper authority to wear men's clothing decided to wear it anyway. When a woman, or someone assigned female at birth, assumes "male attire" they reject the social restrictions placed on women and try to assume social, economic, and sometimes political privileges that were reserved for men.

Donning "male attire" was principally a reference to clothing, first and foremost. This phrase dominates throughout the long nineteenth century. It grew out of a related phrase that was popular in the eighteenth century, that of "wearing the breeches." The claim that a woman "wore the breaches," however, was seldom a literal reference to pants. Rather its meaning was largely a metaphorical commentary about the balance of power within a heterosexual marriage. When a woman was said to "wear the breaches" it did not signal that she actually wore pants or moved in the world as a man or sought male authority in society. Rather, it meant that she was not submissive to her husband at home and might exert a significant degree of power in their household. "Breaches" jokes signaled eighteenth-century feminism's challenge to men's superior status in the home but seldom pointed to a threat beyond that.

References to "male attire" were another force entirely. Social change movements grew exponentially in antebellum America, marked principally by campaigns against slavery and in favor of temperance, women's rights, and general moral reform. These political activists now joined poor laborers, people who identified as men, and those with same-sex desires in donning "male attire" to get what they wanted. In this regard, references to such people in the newspaper might capture any number of social, political, economic, and cultural challenges to the social order. As such, they were both more numerous and more threatening. It was nearly impossible for a reader of newspapers to keep up with the varied usages and implications of the phrase.

Then came the "bloomers" (Figure 6.2). ~~Those who embraced bloomers were in some regards deemed a greater threat to social order than those who sought to live as men~~. Bloomers and those who associated with them were harassed in the press and in the streets for being masculine or manly. Perhaps most importantly, many of those who adopted bloomers were also known political activists who spoke in public trying to rally people to their causes, from abolition to peace to health reform to women's rights. They were educated women. They came from money. They expected people to listen to them. They wanted more rights, and they wanted them immediately. The combination of unconventional dress, assertiveness, and political advocacy marked them out.[113]

Elizabeth Smith Miller introduced the bloomer outfit in 1851. It was adopted by many leading advocates, including Elizabeth Cady Stanton, Lucy Stone, and Susan B. Anthony. Wearing bloomers, also known as "reform dress," became a visible demonstration of one's political views. If there was ever any doubt that appearance mattered, it was quickly put to rest by the public onslaught of criticism faced by those who gave public lectures in reform dress.[114] This was beyond distressing to those who believed women's physical health and well-being was at stake, as reform

Figure 6.2 John Leech, "Bloomerism – An American Custom," 1851. Bloomers drew a great deal of negative attention in the press both for their unconventional dress as well as the political claim to expanded rights that were associated with the bloomer dress.
Image courtesy of the Art and Picture Collection, the New York Public Library

dress liberated women from cumbersome hoops and unbearable corsets that actually restricted breathing.

Bloomer dress made a great splash but it did not last very long. The negative publicity generated made it harder for activists to win over audiences to their larger political aims. Many felt it had become a distraction. Amelia Bloomer, for whom the dress was named, said as much. "We all felt that the dress was drawing attention from what we thought of far greater importance – the question of women's right to better education, to a wider field of employment, to better remuneration for her labor, and to the ballot for the protection of her rights."[115] Elizabeth Cady Stanton gave in to pressure from family and friends. Even Lucy Stone abandoned the dress in her later years. But for many years, the stories in the press would refer to women activists as bloomers, regardless of whether they still wore reform dress. One anecdote read,

"And so do Fanny Wright and Lucy Stone. Such manly women as these bloomers are."[116] It became a shorthand way to signal the wearer's rejection of traditional gender roles.

These early gendered critiques of women for their activism remained part of the public discourse. Even sympathetic portrayals of luminaries Lucy Stone, Elizabeth Cady Stanton, Susan B. Anthony, and Ernestine Rose included assessments of their appearances. Sara A. Underwood was a writer for the "freethought" weekly newspaper, the *Boston Investigator*.[117] In her coverage of two major New York gatherings in 1868 – the anniversaries of "The Equal Rights Association" and "The Universal Peace Society" – Underwood offered the following insights about the key speakers. Susan B. Anthony was "tall, angular, and sallow, yet not unprepossessing in appearance" with a "self-reliant, trustworthy, and business-like air, combined with considerable severity of tone and manner." Lucy Stone surprised the author who couldn't believe the "round-faced, rosy-cheeked, brown-haired, house-wifely looking little dame, could be the indefatigable agitator and pioneer of the Women's Suffrage movement," further noting, "there is nothing unfeminine in her voice or gesture." Elizabeth Cady Stanton got a mixed review, "Every feature of the fair, plump face is thoroughly feminine; yet the firm mouth, clear cut features, and quiet, determined eyes, with the short rings of silver-grey hair over the wide, full brow, give a certain masculine character to her face." Ernestine Rose was seen as "more benignant and womanly" than Stanton, with her "sweet, calm, queen-like face, expressive of intelligence, dignity, and tenderness – the ideal type of face of intellectual womanhood."[118] Women's rights activists were constantly assessed in terms of gender norms and specifically measured against expectations and stereotypes that they were masculine.

Such references were continually thrown around by anti-suffrage politicians for decades. When Republican Senator William A. Buckingham of Connecticut introduced a petition that a group of women signed against their own suffrage before the forty-second congress, he used the assertion "They are not manly women" as a way to legitimize the effort. More than 10,000 women "of good sense" signed the petition in the hope that they may prevent "having imposed upon them more burdens and responsibilities unsuited to them."[119] One newspaper characterized this as a battle between the "womanly women" represented by Buckingham and the "gentler sex of manly women" who were fighting to save women's suffrage in Wyoming.[120]

A concerned defender of women's rights reminded readers there was no proof that women who vote or seek public attention as educators, advocates, etc. neglected their home lives or were less womanly than anyone else. "Now it would be doing these women great injustice to say that they are 'man-like,' or 'despise the duties of the home circle,' are not 'womanly women,' & c. This is not an argument – it is slang."[121] Slang, slur, or sensationalized headline grabber, such language was used to discredit women's activism and to draw negative attention to any woman whose decisions suggested she no longer saw her place as submissive to a man.

WERE FEMALE HUSBANDS FEMINISTS?

Where do female husbands fit into all of this? In some respects, they do not fit. The language used to attack women activists was entirely different than that used to mock female husbands. To call a female husband "masculine" or "manly" would have been affirming, not insulting. While husbands were marked by headlines as "extraordinary" or "singular" by way of soliciting curious readers for the mainstream press, feminists were less mysterious and more accessible. Few people got to meet a female husband in person or learn about their life or views in their own words but notable feminists were traveling, giving speeches, organizing meetings, and actively recruiting people to their cause. Though they lived contemporaneously and shared the pages of newspapers, the lives of female husbands and women's rights activists were worlds apart. Except when they weren't.

While there is no evidence that Albert Guelph or John Smith were interested in politics, abolition, public speaking, or women's rights activism, other people definitely viewed their lives in relation to these movements. Stories accompanied reports of John Smith's marriage suggesting that "a masculine turn of mind" could lead one to identify with manhood more than womanhood.[122] This involved a slippery slope that could lead people who identified as women to become men and marry women.

A writer for the *Pen and Scissors* could not resist the opportunity to link husbands to feminism when reporting on Guelph's arrest, writing, "Syracuse, N.Y., is a great place for Bloomerism and Women's Rights. This latter delusion has been carried to such a pitch, recently, that a woman not only assumed the garb of a man, but went so far as to *marry another woman*, claiming to *be* a man."[123] It was one thing to demand more rights for women as women but female husbands were seen as taking this issue to an absurd extreme. Why fight for more rights as a woman when you could simply become a man yourself? Why stop at becoming a man when you could also marry a woman, have your very own wife, and become a husband?

One reader wrote a letter to the editor that presented Guelph's case as part of the ongoing fight for women's rights, asserting that women should be allowed to wear whatever they want, including men's attire. She implied that attempts to punish women for wearing men's clothes was akin to some kind of slavery, stating, "Why, sir, have we not lately seen the unconstitutionality of *all kinds of slavery demonstrated*."[124] The author asserted that under no circumstances should a decision to trans gender concern legal authorities, regardless of motivation. Finally, this brief letter took up the question of motivation, settling on the idea that for some people, it was a "matter of choice" and for others, "a matter of necessity."[125] The idea that Guelph was arrested, detained, and criticized in the press for their gender expression during this period of tremendous social protest struck some as not right and even hypocritical.

The *Syracuse Standard* also perpetuated the link between the local celebrity female husband and the visible women walking around wearing bloomers instead of hoop skirts and corsets. The article states, "A couple of dashing Bloomers promenaded our streets yesterday afternoon. We thought we recognized the features of our former acquaintance, the 'Man Woman' under one of the bloomer hats, but perhaps we were mistaken."[126] This brief article – two short sentences – linked bloomers to those who lived fully as men. What was to keep someone who wore bloomers from turning to male attire and considering the possibility of life as a man? An out-of-town newspaper marked Syracuse as a place ripe for such experimentations. One catchy story states, "A gay young lady who has lately been getting around in male attire among the belles in

Syracuse, NY, has been arrested on the charge of palming herself off as a man."[127] Stories like these suggested a mutually reinforcing set of values between the two groups – husbands and bloomers. One group's challenge to gender norms encouraged that of the other.

~~Critics of women's political activities often raised the issue of marriage, claiming women's greater participation in public life threatened the institution.~~ This argument suggested that women would prioritize public life over domestic duties, and that these political activities would make women more masculine and therefore unattractive partners for sensible men. Associating political activism with undesirability and loneliness was an old trope previously attached to women's education. An association between women's rights advocacy and failure to marry was made in the local Syracuse press concurrently with news of Guelph, stating, "It is supposed that the reason why most of the women's rights women who are old maids don't marry, is that they consider themselves so far in advance of the age, that they are afraid their offspring would be grandchildren."[128] Such quips dismayed women activists and their defenders. Reverend Samuel May explicitly criticized newspapers, "fashionable novels," and poetry for making fun of strong, independent women and emphasizing marriage as "indispensable to the respectability and usefulness of females."[129] Some women took these warnings to heart and rushed into marriages that might not have been good for them. Others accepted such mockery as the price of their convictions and believed they were better off.

Arguments that politics made women into manly people who were undesirable for marriage never really went away. Newspapers printed glib truisms on a regular basis. For example, one states, "But we wish to marry with the feminine gender – that which is womanly, which we can cherish, love and feel our natures go out to in ever embracing sympathies...And a masculine woman is no companion of a true man. Intellectual women, they may be, and to be admired as such; yet they are no companions."[130] Refusing to enter into a traditional heterosexual relationship was a key source of critique levied against feminists: "A notable fact in this female rights movement is, that the agitators are either hopelessly unmarried, or else are cursed with husbands who have not the brains or the energy to support them."[131] ~~The suggestion that~~

feminists were undesirable partners for men persisted. But they were great partners for each other. This was more visible in England where noted female artists, writers, activists, and performers were known to have formed female marriages, which garnered social recognition if not full legal rights.[132]

For at least some women activists, heterosexual marriage was a barrier to their freedom and autonomy. Would marriage to a female husband have felt different to them, possibly less restraining? Surely that would depend on the attitude and personality of the individual female husband. Female husbands were not simply individual gender warriors but people who pursued intimate relationships and marriage to women. John Smith was accused of trying to get a hold of their wife's assets through the marriage in 1842, an issue that would become moot after New York State passed the Married Women's Property Act in 1848.[133] Women who married female husbands were expected to submit to the political and economic authority of their husbands, just like everyone else.

Anyone who challenged womanhood broadly defined could be associated with women's rights. People who were single by circumstance or choice, who worked at manual labor in masculine clothes, or who rejected the notion of woman's refinement were all suspect. A poor, elderly person assigned female at birth who ran a farm in rural Pennsylvania was suddenly characterized as being in cahoots with women's rights activists. Lize Schuler cared nothing for public speaking, convincing others of their political views, voting, or standing for office. Regardless, the reporter stated, "The "women's rights movement" should certainly know, as she is decidedly the champion...altogether the most manly woman I ever met with."[134] The physical description went as follows: "Imagine, if you can, a woman of medium size, dressed in men's clothes, with a soft hat, variously indented upon her head, no coat, barefooted, and you have this champion of 'women's rights' before you."[135] Schuler spoke of their two shepherd dogs and a bunch of chickens as their "children." There was nothing new about people like Schuler working hard to support themselves but now they too could be seen as advocating for political change simply by living their lives.

Female husband accounts always raised the question of sexual difference. Where was the line? The source of debate generally focused on one or more of three major themes: physical embodiment, sexual intimacy, and work. As we have seen, most prominent were concerns over secondary sex characteristics (voice, facial hair, stature) and how people assigned female at birth could possibly overcome these differences to live as men. They were judged in relation to manhood, not womanhood. This was even the case when female husbands had children from prior relationships, such as Guelph. I have yet to read an account that judges or criticizes a female husband for abandoning their child, not taking proper care of a child, or exposing their child to immoral behavior by virtue of their gender transition. Rather, the only significant reference to children was when a magistrate or judge made fun of the female husband and their wife for not being able to have children. Female husbands were principally judged by the standards and expectations of manhood.

When female husbands are juxtaposed against women activists from the antebellum period, an important distinction becomes visible: female husbands are never judged in relation to the norms or expectations of womanhood. As we have seen from the rigorous and contentious fights over women's activism, what it meant to be a woman was not exactly easy to pin down. When it came to discourses about dominant notions of white womanhood, it quickly became clear that distinctions between men and women varied by circumstance and sphere, be it in the home, family, church, statehouse, workplace, or school. Even those who embraced women's rights to a public voice in church or reform organizations might draw the line at political enfranchisement or advanced educational opportunities. The starting point of the debate for women activists was the social location of women and how much they should be permitted to depart from it. The starting point of the debate for female husbands was the social location of men and the ways in which they succeeded or failed in achieving manhood.

CHAPTER 7

THE CRIMINALIZED POOR

HROUGHOUT HISTORY, PARENTS HAVE HUMILIATED and disciplined their daughters who were too much like boys or sons who liked girly things. Nineteenth-century women's magazines and children's literature often recommended as much.[1] Ministers preached about women's proper role in the domestic sphere as wives and mothers, criticizing those who were outspoken about politics. Public institutions like almshouses, schools, and prisons established clearly defined spaces and policies for boys and men and a different set of spaces and rules for girls and women. Employers had clear visions for what constituted men's work and what kind of work was better suited to women. When people assigned female at birth expressed comfort or pleasure in doing things typically reserved for men – from play to work to politics to socializing – any number of people spoke up to challenge or discourage their behavior. In many instances, the disapproval and judgment of loved ones or the rejection and hostility of strangers deterred people from pursuing such a course repeatedly or for a sustained period of time. There was no single principle or law that maintained a gender binary and hierarchy; rather, it was redefined with each challenge and each attempt to suppress that challenge.

By the time someone determined that a man in their life, at their job, or on the streets was different – likely female – it signaled a failure of this surveillance. The warnings of a mother or the scolding of a father unheeded; the lessons from a young teacher or minister long forgotten; the pressure of peers dismissed. Local authorities – a constable, magistrate, or policeman – played a tremendous role in this reassertion of racial and gender hierarchies. People who were shocked, appalled, scared, or confused ran to local authorities and demanded the arrest of those who transed gender. They did not think twice about turning to the policing authorities, even if they were not sure if their targets had broken any law or what the police would do.

In the last few decades of the nineteenth century, numerous cities and states across the United States passed explicit laws against cross-dressing, generally making a transgender embodiment in and of itself a crime. Sixteen cities adopted laws against the practice between 1843 and 1866. With the exception of Wilmington, Delaware (1856) and Newark, New Jersey (1858) none of the oldest or most populated northeastern cities embraced such laws.[2] From 1873 to 1920, another thirty-five cities followed, chiefly in the west and throughout the South. In 1876, the New York State legislature updated the vagrancy statute to outlaw "assemblage in public houses or other places of three or more persons disguised" with punishment for up to one year imprisonment. The provision targeted sex workers but the widely expansive language allowed for the arrest of any gathering of people transing gender *anywhere*, except for rich people's "fancy dress ball[s]."[3] This intensified the focus of the policing authorities on a wide range of public spaces that supported the intermingling of people across race and class, provocative entertainment, sex work, gambling, illicit sexual intimacies, and expressions of gender nonconformity.[4]

The post-Civil War period ushered in the expansion of American policing with a laser beam target on low-level crimes of morals and social order. Immigrants streamed into American cities and those formerly enslaved migrated north. Major federal legislation was passed to restrict immigration, such as the 1882 Chinese Exclusion Act and the 1891 law denying entry to those "convicted of a crime of moral turpitude."[5] Interracial relationships threatened racial hierarchies, inspiring a wave of restrictions on interracial marriage.[6] In the UK the forces were different – wars between European nations and colonization – but the outcomes were similar: heightened policing of sexuality in the name of racial purity and national strength.[7]

Those who lived in the second half of the nineteenth century experienced a shift in popular attitudes about gender in ways that were not obviously positive or negative. Rather, these new beliefs were tightly bound up in political and scientific discourses of race and class, leading to various outcomes depending on the particulars of one's existence.

One female husband embodied and lived through all of these shifts. A focus on the life of Joseph Lobdell provides a window into the transformation in dominant ways of seeing gender transing from the mid to late nineteenth century.[8] Their actions were judged through the lens of their time, a lens that changed significantly between 1850 and 1880. In examining this life, no neat line can be drawn separating the identity of a woman who transed gender to get more lucrative employment as a man from that of a female assigned person who claimed a male identity and expression in an enduring way. There is no clear line separating homosexual from heterosexual, for this one person had intimacies with a man as a woman and with a woman as a man. Gender and sexuality were intertwined and changing, as we will see with the narrative they wrote of their own life around the age of twenty-five, privileging their self-reflection from these early years and contextualizing this perspective with the many varied newspaper accounts that followed. One person lived a long, rich life in which their gender and sexuality changed, as the world around them changed, too.

JOSEPH LOBDELL, PART ONE: *THE FEMALE HUNTER*

In rural southeastern New York, bordering northeastern Pennsylvania, a person assigned female at birth contemplated the limited options available to women and chose a different course. The person who would become widely known as Joseph Lobdell later in life published their memoir, *The Female Hunter of Delaware and Sullivan Counties, N.Y.* (1855), under the name Lucy Ann Lobdell while they were in the middle of a transformation (Figure 7.1).[9] Lobdell's memoir features someone assigned female at birth who lived as a woman and gradually came to embrace men's clothes in particular circumstances – to ride a horse or to hunt in the woods. Confident in their ability to engage in men's work and to be seen by others as a man, they decided that finding paid work as a man was the right course for them and their family who they supported. Lobdell shared these reflections in the memoir of their early years and young adulthood. But the memoir ends when Lobdell is on the cusp of a great change, presenting an account of gender that is incomplete at best. If this was all we knew of Lobdell, they might easily have

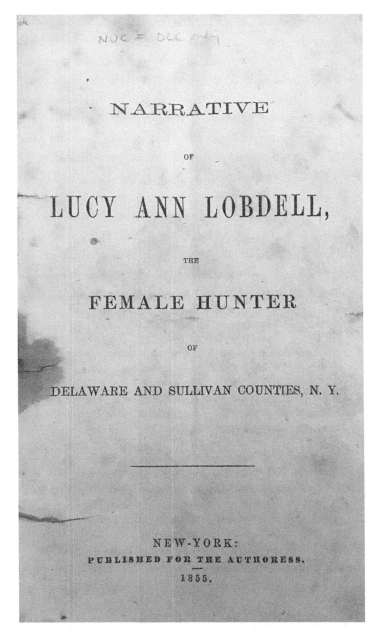

Figure 7.1 *Narrative of Lucy Ann Lobdell, the Female Hunter of Delaware and Sullivan Counties, N.Y.* (New York, 1855). Lobdell wrote an autobiography describing the first twenty-five years of their life.
Image courtesy of the Yale Collection of Western Americana, Beinecke Rare Book and Manuscript Library

been classified as simply an antebellum-era feminist and reform writer, one of dozens who complained of poor wages and limited prospects for financial stability and prosperity independent of men.

Lobdell's *The Female Hunter* was published *before* they embraced a male gender expression more fully, *before* they came to love and marry a woman, *before* they were declared a female husband in the press, and *before* they were institutionalized for their gender nonconformity and poverty. These developments will be discussed more fully later. First, we look at Lobdell's early life and writings where they explained the tremendous burden of responsibility they bore for their family, their courtship by various boys, and their skills in nearly everything from music, singing, and housework to farming, animal management, and hunting.

Lobdell was the oldest child of James and Sarah Lobdell, a couple that owned property in the remote town of Westerlo in the southwest part of Albany County, New York.[10] At the time of Lobdell's birth in 1829, the town of fifty-eight square miles had just over 3,000 inhabitants.[11] The couple remained married and had three other children: Mary, Sarah, and John. Lobdell had considerable responsibilities around the farm as a young child, raising birds and cows and tending to all of their needs before selling them or using them to feed the family. Lobdell learned to shoot a rifle in order to protect the birds from predators – "the hawk, the weasel, the mink and even down to the rat."[12] There are several explanations for why Lobdell was essentially self-taught in this area but all of them point to their father. Lobdell's father James remains a mystery in many of the writings about Lobdell, though he played a significant role in shaping Lobdell's sense of what was possible. We might assume that James didn't teach his oldest child – a daughter – to hunt because that was not something "girls" did. But Lobdell was granted a great deal of freedom as a young child, which they really enjoyed. They spoke of long walks in the woods alone, getting lost while chasing birds and following trails of wildflowers. In this respect, James treated his eldest much like boys were commonly treated.

Mother Sarah did not approve of these wanderings, accusing Lobdell of truancy and threatening to tie a bell on them so she could keep track of their movements. Lobdell seldom refers to their mother's thoughts or feelings in the memoir. One such reference appears in the recounting of

their teenage years when a variety of boys sought out a romantic relationship with them. Lobdell avoids any physical intimacies or verbal
commitment to two different boys and returns home to report the whole
thing to their mother. Their mother approved of the situation – Lobdell
reports "[I] told mother all the news, and she finally said I was a good
girl." Here is the first instance that Lobdell notes receiving their
mother's approval. What exactly earned this commendation remains
unclear. Was it that boys were showing interest or that Lobdell refused
these advances? Sarah was probably relieved by both: that boys were
showing interest in her eldest child *and* that their child refused these
advances – for now. Such was the delicate balance expected of young
women – to be desired by men and to encourage such interest but to stop
short of sexual intimacies. Lobdell got Sarah's message loud and clear –
mother was finally proud.

Some years passed with Lobdell showing minimal interest in men.
Lobdell was pursued by another suitor – a Mr. George Washington
Slater. Lobdell describes Slater as "an innocent sort of a boy" who was
"quite agreeable."[13] They began to spend time together. But this was no
simple love story. Lobdell repeatedly characterized Slater as a pitiful
character. For their part, Slater manipulated Lobdell's pity and drew
them closer. After one memorable incident when Lobdell declared their
relationship over because their father did not approve, Slater turned ill.
Lobdell reported of that moment, "I felt such pity for the poor fellow
that I arose from my seat, and walked to where he was standing."[14] Slater
grabbed Lobdell, held them close, kissed them, and declared his
undying love. Lobdell was principally a caretaker. The weakness and
neediness that Slater exhibited strengthened the emotional bond
between the two.

This event, relayed by Lobdell in their memoir, upends conventional
norms of nineteenth-century courtship. Though assigned female and
living socially as a woman at this time, it was Lobdell who embodied
strength, courage, and resolve. This heterosexual courtship did not draw
out Lobdell's vulnerability but rather required their strength. It was
Lobdell's concern for Slater's well-being that compelled them to put
on their brother's clothing, borrow their father's horse, and ride a few
miles to ensure Mr. Slater was safe.[15] Even in the midst of courtship by a

man, Lobdell assumed many of the freedoms and responsibilities reserved for men.

Lobdell feared their growing entanglement with Slater, who was known by others as both "industrious and cunning."[16] Lobdell was torn between their attraction to someone who needed them but might also not be good for them. Lobdell was also torn between a dominant cultural expectation that women marry men and their own ambivalence toward men. Their father disapproved of Slater at first, but eventually wanted Lobdell to marry.[17] Lobdell might have thought Slater was a manageable – though pathetic – choice. Lobdell sought to delay what seemed inevitable – marriage to Slater – and instead announced they would continue their schooling at the Coxsackie School, about twenty miles away.

Lobdell loved attending Coxsackie School. Their father James decided to sell the family home and buy property closer to the school upon the advice of his eldest child that land was plentiful and cheap. James and Sarah moved their family to be closer to their eldest child in school. But with the family move, Slater returned to the scene. At this point, Lobdell confided in their father that they were trying to get away from Slater – that this was in fact the main motivation in attending Coxsackie in the first place. Lobdell recalls this conversation with their father, "I told him my heart had no joy in him, for my early love was no more." It was not long before Lobdell gave in and married Slater. The pressure of women to marry was too great. Even though Lobdell was talented, hardworking, and educated enough to secure employment as a school teacher, there was a sense of coercion and inevitability. Lobdell felt trapped by Slater's persistence and saw no way to get away from him, blaming their father for making them receive Slater's visit in the first place.

Slater was a laborer who found work in a saw mill owned by Mr. Levally. Married, the couple moved into tenant housing provided by Levally near the mill, a few miles from Lobdell's family home.[18] Things quickly got out of control, as Slater turned their house into an afterhours party for the crew from the mill and expected Lobdell to serve and entertain the men who drank, swore, and played cards. Fights ensued.

Lobdell was pregnant and later gave birth to the couple's only child, Helen Slater, perhaps the one good thing to come from this short-lived, volatile relationship. James was right about Slater – he was prone to excessive smoking, drinking, gambling, and mistrust – but advised his eldest to stick it out.[19] When Slater agreed to a separation and moved Lobdell back into their parents' home, Lobdell's mother Sarah had little patience for his cruel words toward Lobdell and ordered Slater "to leave her house instantly, and not to darken her door again" until he changed his attitude and behavior toward his wife.[20]

Lobdell was free from Slater and now able to help their increasingly needy parents. James became disabled and unable to hunt, leaving Lobdell to set off into the expansive woods surrounding their property in Delaware County, New York to shoot a deer so that the family might have meat to eat (Figure 7.2). Lobdell later reflected that their father's injury necessitated their adoption of men's work: "My father was lame, and in consequence, I had worked in-doors and out." Lobdell did not ask for this duty but they managed to kill their first deer and replenish the family's meat supply. This hunting prowess made Lobdell into a local celebrity.

A man named Mr. Talmage who traveled as a peddler through the woods near the Lobdell family home ran into them. Everything about Lobdell's appearance and actions signaled they were a man. Talmage described being passed on the road by someone who he, "at first, supposed was a young man, with a rifle on his shoulder." He noted Lobdell wore a hood typical of that "worn by deer hunters" along with a rubber overcoat, "snug-fitting corduroy pants, and a pair of Indian moccasins." He celebrated their marksmanship, including an ability to hit the center of a target from at first thirty yards and then eighteen rods away. Only one thing made Talmage doubt whether this person was a man: their voice, which he described as "peculiar." Talmage was overwhelmingly impressed by how Lobdell excelled at men's work (sharpshooting) and women's work (housework and cooking), and all of the other work that needed to be done, such as tending to the farm animals and chopping firewood. Mr. Talmage wrote down their observations of Lobdell and had them published in the national press under a variety of

Figure 7.2 Lobdell portrait, *c.*1853. This picture was taken when Lobdell lived at home in upstate New York, prior to cutting off their hair, putting on men's clothes, and setting out into the world as a man.

Image courtesy of the Wayne County Historical Society, Honesdale, PA, Photo Archives headlines, from "Extraordinary Performances of a Young Lady," to "Good Girl," to "One of the Gals."[21] Lobdell included the text of this article in their own memoir, suggesting they enjoyed and did not dispute the account. The recognition gave them confidence – and an idea.

Later that same year, Mr. Slater sent a letter home suggesting he would like to come visit their child, but only if Lobdell wrote to him and made him feel welcome. Inspired by the encouragement of Mr. Talmage and threatened by the return of Slater, Lobdell decided to leave home completely and set off on their own. Lobdell reflected they wanted to get away before their husband returned: "I resolved to try, after hearing that Mr. Slater was coming, to get work away among strangers."[22] They noted that their family was struggling and that women were not well paid for their work, resolving to live as a man, "and as hard times were crowding upon us, I made up my mind to dress in men's attire to seek labor, as I was used to men's work. And as I might work harder at house-work, and get only a dollar per week, and I was capable of doing men's work, and getting men's wages."[23] Lobdell knew they could handle any kind of work and was ready to go out and try to make a better living.

In the mid-1850s, Lobdell was celebrated in newspaper accounts that treated their masculine gender expression as both curious and admirable. The headlines sought to draw attention to the idea of a contradiction, highlighting the fact that a "woman" who *seemed like a man* excelled at tasks reserved for men. The tone of the article about Lobdell was laudatory and unequivocally positive. Lobdell's talents and experiences would have stood out in nearly any other period, but in the 1850s the American press was brimming with accounts of exceptional feats by any number of female assigned people who donned male attire. Lobdell was not yet presenting fully as male and had not yet adopted the name Joseph – two factors that would contribute to the dramatically different treatment they received by relatives, authorities, and the press in the decades that followed. For now, Lobdell's masculinity was explained and contained with the well-established framework that some women must live and work as men to survive. Lobdell even described themself as someone who was driven by circumstance to wear men's clothes and take up the work traditionally reserved for men.

JOSEPH LOBDELL, PART TWO: MANHOOD AND MOBILITY

Evidence for the next fifteen-year period of their life was not available to the reading public until after the fact, when news stories resumed in the 1870s. And yet *everything* happened that would set Lobdell on a path to the heights of fulfillment and love as well as the depths of betrayal and tragedy. They would prove what they instinctively knew all along: they could survive anywhere and successfully handle any number of skilled and unskilled tasks. They pursued numerous romantic relationships with women, something they did not even hint at desiring in their autobiography published just a few years prior. Finally, away from their parents, their abusive husband, and their young daughter, Lobdell would have the opportunity to befriend, to charm, to impress, and to endear themselves to a new community as a man named Joseph Lobdell.

Once they set off on their own to make a living as a man, they did not pursue the factory work that would have been readily available throughout New England (Figure 7.3). Albany, the tenth largest city in the nation in 1850 with major industries in lumber, brewing, book production, and welding, did not appeal. Lobdell got off to a great start on their new life, settling in Bethany, Pennsylvania, about twenty-five miles from Long Eddy, New York. Lobdell was presenting as male and "started a singing school" that attracted predominantly female students from some of the town's most prominent families.[24] Lobdell had flirtations with two different students and was engaged to marry one of them. This all went on for three months, during which Lobdell was said to be "successfully carrying out the character she assumed."[25] They were accepted by the community. One the eve of Lobdell's marriage, however, someone "discovered by accident" that Lobdell was female.[26] Some said a person from Long Eddy was passing through and recognized Lobdell. Accounts from twenty years later were vague, stating, "the discovery was made in some way that the music teacher was not a man but a woman."[27] Locals threatened to tar and feather Lobdell, who was basically run out of town. A tip from their landlord, a Mr. Bode, may have spared their life. Further violence

Figure 7.3 Lobdell portrait, n.d. An undated photo of Lobdell with short hair.
Image courtesy of the Wayne County Historical Society, Honesdale, PA, Photo Archives

was intended: "some terrible outrage would be committed upon her in comparison to which the proposed tarring and feathering would be light," implying great physical and possibly sexual violence.[28] Such rage was provoked not simply by the fact of Lobdell's employment and gender but from the fact that a local family entrusted Lobdell with their daughter who would have become Lobdell's bride.

Since Lobdell's sex was once before discovered by the so-called "peculiarity" of their voice by the wandering Mr. Talmage in the woods earlier that year, one might wonder if Lobdell's voice again betrayed them in Bethany. This is a reasonable question, since presumably the music teacher's voice was an important instrument of their trade. Expecting this question from their readers, the story explained, "She was an excellent bass singer, and never attempted any other part, except to illustrate some point in a lesson."[29] This remark suggests Lobdell's talent included skillful command of their voice, something that in this instance may have helped them successfully live as a man.[30] Nevertheless, this incident scarred Lobdell and made them rethink their plan. It seemed obvious they needed to move farther from home. Rather than jump into the heart of a community, working as a teacher with young people, Lobdell decided to live and work on the margins where they would be under less scrutiny.

They headed west – all the way to the territory of Minnesota. Local newspapers in Lobdell's community promoted Minnesota as a frontier destination for those looking to start over and get rich quick.[31] Lobdell went by the name La-Roi Lobdell in Manannah, Minnesota.[32] Lobdell was hired to occupy some land "on the upper shore of Lake Minnetonka" in the absence of its owner. It is there Lobdell met a man named Edwin Gribble who had a claim on some land that happened to be next to that which Lobdell was looking after.[33] Lobdell and Gribble became quite friendly during this time. Histories characterized their relationship as one that was "pretty thick" as the two went "tramping together through the woods in pursuit of game, and sleeping together under the same blanket."[34] The original landowner disappeared, leaving Lobdell to sell the land to Gribble for a "$75 rifle." From there, Lobdell headed to Meeker County where they were again hired to hold land, this time with another person in the winter of 1856–7 on what became the future site of Kandiyohi County.[35]

The very fact that people were hired to "hold land" is a phrase that captures the violence of settler colonialism. This particular area had long been home to the powerful Dakota nation. The Dakota (Santee Sioux) nearly prevailed in retaining control of their land when the US Senate considered accepting a treaty in 1842 that would have preserved much of the region that became southern Minnesota for their people. Instead, something quite the opposite happened nearly a decade later. In 1851, then governor of the territory, Alexander Ramsey, and the commissioner of Indian Affairs offered the Dakota a treaty that took most of their land in return for 7.5 cents an acre.[36] Two other nations were nearby: the Ojibwa people who occupied the northern half of the territory, which they gradually lost most of by 1855, and the Winnebago (Ho-Chunk) people, who resettled in the southern corners after being forced from their land in Wisconsin and Iowa.[37]

We must not lose sight of the fact that Lobdell's livelihood was enabled by and contributed to the violence of settler colonialism. Like most poor people throughout history, Lobdell didn't have the luxury to exactly pick and choose work opportunities. Having grown up in the wilderness of New York State, Lobdell was well suited to the wild forests of the Midwest. They accepted the work that best suited their skills. Despite the fact that various constraints pushed Lobdell to such work, it is doubtful that they were principally opposed to the violence and treaties that drove the Dakota and Ojibwa from their homes. Lobdell grew up among loggers, laborers, hunters, and those who used the natural environment to sustain families and fuel economies. By the time Lobdell arrived in Minnesota in the mid-1850s, much of the land theft had already occurred.

It is somewhat ironic and even a little sad that Lobdell, a person who fought against the tyranny of the gender binary in their own life, was part of the colonizing project that imposed it on other people. Through land theft and municipal expansion, Native American communities – known for embracing a wider range of gender expressions and identities beyond the binary – were marginalized, and in some cases destroyed. There is no singular concept for a transgender, third-sex, or two-spirit person in native American culture.[38] Rather, each nation might have a special word for such a person, often one that did not neatly translate into any modern or Western concept and changed over time.[39]

The three nearby tribes each had names for someone assigned male at birth who lived as a woman in some way: Dakota called this person *winkta*, Ojibwa called this person *agokwa* (man-woman), and Winnebago used the term *shiange* (unmanly man). Only the Ojibwa of northern Minnesota also had a term for those assigned female at birth who lived as men: *okitcitakwe*, which translates to "warrior woman."[40] Anthropologists documented accounts of *okitcitakwe* people much later, in 1915, though we have no reason to believe this category was new. In this context, the salient feature of the *okitcitakwe* was of someone assigned female at birth who achieved some great feat in war and acquired the privileges of male soldiers in the process.[41] It is hard to know how prominent this role was and if it was legible in the community in the 1850s. When Lobdell was in Minnesota between 1855 and 1858, some things were settled and others were in turmoil. The Dakota people ceded much of their land and retreated to reservations – including a plot of land that cut through the southwestern corner of the state, not far from where Lobdell was.

Lobdell worked at odd jobs in Manannah in the summer of 1857, "chopping wood, hunting, washing dishes, etc. for her board."[42] Lobdell would have excelled in this work, getting paid wages to do tasks they had done to support the family their entire life. Observers who later learned that Lobdell was assigned female noted that their skill in the fields along with their pleasing personality deterred everyone from ever suspecting they were not who they claimed to be. They were described as "a splendid hunter," "good company," and "offensive to none."[43] It is hard to reconcile such positive endorsements of one's character generally with the hostile treatment they received when their gender became an issue.

We do not know what happened to raise suspicions about Lobdell's sex, but in the summer of 1858 they were the target of an investigation. They must have been terrified. Would they face threats of crowd violence again? Or would they be arrested and subject to the more orderly and restrained violence of the state? At the very least, they could assume their life would be torn upside down and they would not be allowed to continue living as they were. William Richards presented his charge to Justice of the Peace John Robson.[44] The charge was this: "One Lobdell, being a woman, falsely personates a man, to the great scandal of the community, and against the peace and dignity of the State of Minnesota."[45] The attorney asked that Lobdell be made an example of so as to not disrupt the norms of "this land of steady habits."[46] The defendant, Lobdell, pleaded not guilty. A.C. Smith served as counsel for the defendant alongside Virginian and attorney U.S. Willie.

The writer who brought this incident to life for a broader public thirty years later was Lobdell's own attorney, A.C. Smith. Smith used vivid language in describing what happened, portraying Lobdell as alternately evil, vulnerable, and respectable. Longstanding cultural norms, new legal codes, and centuries-old doctrines together informed Lobdell's fate in this case. Smith invoked Satan in explaining what happened, saying, "'Satan, with the aid of original sin,' discovered and exposed her sex." It was a loaded charge that is difficult to unpack because he later presents a somewhat sympathetic view of Lobdell. Furthermore, Smith recounted, "The blue code of Connecticut was consulted, and the law was invoked to purge the community of the scandal."[47] There is no denying that many people instinctively saw transing gender as a sin.

Perhaps this association with evil is what inspired the Minnesota authorities' unusual decision to consult a legal book from far away and 200 years prior: the blue codes of Connecticut, known for strict, devout adherence to scriptures. To this day, "blue laws" is a reference to the religious and social conservativism of Puritanism in early New England colonies and the seemingly quirky array of actions that were punished and/or frowned upon.[48] The phrase is neither factual nor neutral, but rather originated in the early 1700s as a slur by New Yorkers against their New Haven neighbors for going too far with their theocracy.[49] Episcopal missionaries criticized the New Haven colonists for their rigidity and the "abundance of *odd kinds of Laws* to prevent any dissenting from their church." This sentiment spread and the word "blue" was sometimes used as a stand in for "odd" when describing colonial laws that were, in the words of one nineteenth-century scholar, "over-strict, or queer, or 'puritanic.'"[50]

A widespread belief in a specific set of blue laws took off after the 1781 publication of a bizarre list by Samuel Peters. Peters was a known

Tory sympathizer who fled the wrath of the Sons of Liberty on the eve of revolution by sailing for England in 1774.[51] From there he penned his mocking critique of the colonies – Connecticut in particular – under the deceptively straightforward title, *A General History of Connecticut*.[52] The legitimacy of the blue laws published in Peter's book were hotly debated for the next century. Peters notes the blue laws of New Haven Colony were never explicitly documented (in his words, "never suffered to be printed") and credits (or blames) neighboring colonies with coining the name "blue laws."[53] Once this was established, he was free to make up the content of said laws. They were just as often reprinted whole cloth as the official law as they were denounced as total fabrications. It was easy for people in the 1780s to believe the list was true because in their post-revolutionary fervor, many people frowned on laws that restricted personal liberties – particularly in the name of religion.

In an 1889 political essay called "Let the Blue Laws Rest," Elizabeth Cady Stanton drew parallels between a campaign of the national reform party and "the old Puritan blue laws of Connecticut" which she characterized as an anti-democratic conflation of church and state.[54] Stanton deemed the laws absurd by then modern standards, as they violated the constitutional separation of church and state and disrupted work, commerce, and leisure on Sundays. Stanton invoked the great religious diversity of the nation and defended the value of public parks and newspaper reading on Sundays. To emphasize the absurdity of the reform party's campaign, she cited examples from Peters' 1781 volume, claiming, "a man could not kiss his wife nor a hen lay an egg on Sunday."[55]

There was no denying that the spirit of the blue laws described by Peters tapped into some truths about colonial New England in general and the colony of New Haven in particular, which was widely known for its severe laws.[56] In *The Fundamental Agreement*, at New Haven on June 4, 1639, planters agreed that "church members only shall be free burgesses, and that they only shall choose magistrates and officers among themselves, to have the power of transacting all the public civil affairs of this plantation."[57] Church and state were one.[58] The early codes of New Haven and Connecticut were largely based on those of nearby Massachusetts. Yes, they regulated church attendance, social activities on the Sabbath, sexual activities outside of marriage, idleness, and swearing (among many other things), but not to the particular or absurd extent characterized by Peters.[59] In the colony's early years, people (mostly servants) were punished for nearly everything: stealing, drinking, swearing, talking back, debt, property damage, breaking Sabbath, disorderly behavior, slander, corruption, and neglect of watch.[60] Men and women surely had distinct roles in Puritan families, but the rules were not as rigid as some expected. Women bore a tremendous burden of duties in farming households (including financial management) and did a wide range of physically demanding labor and travel *without* being criticized for challenging gender norms.[61] Women had standing before the courts and were able to testify on their own behalf.

There are several points of relevance here for adjudicating a case in the Midwest in the 1850s. First of all, colonial New Haven and Connecticut did not intensely subjugate women or necessarily have a harsh set of legal codes and social customs worthy of the legend of the "blue laws." More to the point, there was in fact no such thing as "blue laws" in Connecticut. It is unlikely that Minnesota lawyers at that time knew this. The controversy over "blue laws" gained steam in the 1880s, after the 1876 publication of a reputable and well-documented book that exposed this falsehood.[62] None of this mattered, because by the mid-nineteenth century the idea of the "blue laws" had taken on a life of their own, fueled by anecdotal yet persistent pop cultural references in newspapers, encyclopedias, and popular histories written by antiquarians.

Minnesota had quite literally just been ratified into statehood that summer of 1858. Minnesota joined Wisconsin to the east and Iowa to the south, which each achieved statehood a decade earlier. One of the things that distinguished states from territories was a penal code and a judicial infrastructure to enforce it. The Minnesota judicial system was brand new, so much so that Lobdell's case was explicitly referenced as one of the first. Smith recalled, "It was a little remarkable that among the first cases tried, was one of 'woman's right's'."[63] And so county attorney William Richards looked geographically to the east, where legal codes were old and exceptionally well established. At that time, Connecticut had no noteworthy ordinances or statutes against cross-dressing, lewd solicitation, obscene publications, or various forms of entertainment such as sports and theater. Neither did any other state in New England, the region associated with blue laws because of its puritanical origins.[64] Rather, it was Southern and Midwestern cities and states that were more likely to have such ordinances in place. Cities and states near Minnesota began adopting explicit anti-cross-dressing ordinances as early as 1843. Of the first sixteen such ordinances, half were in nearby places including St. Louis, Missouri (1843), Columbus, Ohio (1848), Chicago, Illinois (1851), Springfield, Illinois (1856), Louisiana, Missouri (1858), Jefferson City, Missouri (1859), Kansas City, Missouri (1860), and Toledo, Ohio (1862).[65]

There is no clear evidence that Lobdell was found "not guilty," but they were discharged on two interrelated points that suggest the judge fundamentally did not want to punish or detain them. The claims of the court were these. First, it was decided there was still reasonable doubt as to whether Lobdell was a woman impersonating a man. The story states that the court decided "the legal evidence to prove the necessary fact could not easily be obtained, and was left in doubt."[66] This explanation is vague and passive but leads to Lobdell's release. The second claim of the court presumed that Lobdell was female and had a legal right to wear men's clothes. This points to Smith's reference that the court viewed Lobdell's case as one of "women's rights."[67] The issue of their presentation or alleged false representation is put to the side. The court affirmed that Lobdell was to be released on the grounds "that the right of females to 'wear the pants' had been recognized from the time of Justinian, and that the doctrine was too well settled to be upset in the case at bar, and Mrs. Slater was therefore discharged."[68] In this brand new state in this still young nation, men of the law found comfort and clarity in fifth-century Roman laws – in this case, the Justinian code which granted significant legal rights to women.[69]

Smith provided a sympathetic account of the impact this ordeal had on Lobdell's life, emotions, and well-being. In short, it was absolutely devastating. Lobdell was discredited, the target of harassment, and treated as an outcast. Smith claims that people felt sympathy and commiseration for Lobdell, who soon became a public charge before saying they wanted to go home. The county itself covered the expense of Lobdell's trip. This is important because Lobdell became a pitied ward of the state and Smith was proud they supported Lobdell. But the state caused Lobdell's distress in the first place and made it impossible for them to make a living, something they had done successfully for many years.[70] We must not accept this outcome as inevitable. Lobdell had proven themself a more than capable laborer in any number of industries. When we think of the premium put on labor during this era of industrialization and expansion, we must consider the factors that denied some workers access to employment. In many situations during this era, racial discrimination served this function, as employers chose to uphold racist systems of segregation, for example, rather than hire African American workers who were skilled and/or talented. In the case of Lobdell, the social contract that prohibited people assigned female from doing certain kinds of work and living with freedoms reserved for men was of greater importance than labor needs. It was better to have a job unfilled – or handled by a less reliable or talented worker – than to allow said worker to exist outside the norms of the gender binary.

JOSEPH LOBDELL, PART THREE: A FEMALE HUSBAND

Even though the court ruled in their favor, the experience in Minnesota broke Lobdell's spirit. They were no longer confident in their ability to live and work as a man. Their greatest strength – the ability to learn nearly any skill or trade to earn money and support themself and their family – was challenged by those who determined Lobdell's gender was not proper or acceptable. No one found Lobdell in violation of any law but social conventions were far more powerful. Lobdell struggled from this point forward. They returned home to Hancock, New York, appearing in the 1860 census with their daughter Helen who was seven, their mother who was officially declared "insane," and their father who was long ill.[71] This stop home was brief, as Lobdell was soon off again, trying to find food and earn money for the family.

After Minnesota, poverty became the most profound constant in Lobdell's life. Lobdell was no longer heralded as resourceful and dutiful for their ability to provide for their family. Rather, they ended up in the poorhouse – a sign of failure and dependency. But even to get admitted to the poorhouse, they had to trans gender and present as a woman to ensure they would be met with sympathy. The *New York Tribune* tried to make meaning of this change, offering a theory of gender as part of one's temperament and easily mutable, somewhere in the realm of mind and heart. It states, "In 1860 her mood suddenly changed and she again assumed the garb of her sex and saddled herself upon the community, begging from door to door, and finally becoming an inmate of the Alms-House of Delaware County."[72] Lobdell's poverty and gender – and eventually their marriage – were all bound together, making Lobdell a source of mockery and embarrassment.

There was one clear upside to Lobdell's slide into poverty amid the scrutiny of family, neighbors, and even the national press: the love and companionship of a woman. Lobdell, at an all-time low in the poorhouse of Dehli, New York, met and joined lives with Marie Louise Perry some time around 1860 or 1861. The 1865 New York State census recorded Lobdell and Perry living together under the roof of Lobdell's parents in Hancock, Delaware County, New York.[73] Like many of the female husband and wife pairs in this book, they remained together for a very long time – about twenty years. Others thought they were an odd couple for many reasons, including a significant difference in age and class backgrounds. Lobdell was more educated and intelligent than observers gave them credit for but they were often presented as crass and stupid in juxtaposition with Marie's composed refinement. None could deny that the two had a "singular attachment" devotion to each other, though many questioned why Marie chose Lobdell instead of returning home to her wealthy family in Massachusetts.[74] Perry was said to have made Lobdell "full of life."[75] The couple moved around for years between Lobdell's family home, the surrounding woods, and neighboring towns. They were in and out of the poorhouse as well.

Lobdell was arrested in 1871 for numerous public disturbances. This put them back into the spotlight of the local, regional, and national press. Mr. E. Heller, an overseer of the poor in nearby Barret township, wrote an article titled, "Joe Lobdell and Wife – Their History, &c." The essay established Lobdell's sense of manhood by using the name Joe and male pronouns. It also acknowledged their marriage to Marie by designating her with the word "wife" in the title and throughout the account.[76] It recounts numerous arrests on charges of vagrancy and an attempt by the author to remove the pair from jail and return them to the Lobdell family home in Long Eddy. Upon finding James "pretty much broken down" and Sarah "insane," Heller delivered Lobdell and Perry back to the Delhi poorhouse instead. Heller's account and the various spin-off articles from this period offer two great juxtapositions, both of which feature Lobdell negatively: first, the great promise of Lobdell's youth vs. the tragedy their life had become; second, the appropriately gendered composure of Marie vs. Lobdell's uncontrollable gender-transing excesses.

As a young person in Long Eddy, Lobdell exhibited tremendous physical strength and prowess. They were described as "strong as a man, active as a deer, and as lithe as a serpent. She could hunt, fish, cut timber, raft, and do any of the labor that the men of the neighborhood did."[77] As a person who seemed like a masculine woman, Lobdell was impressive. The *New York Tribune* described Lobdell as one who was "handsome" and had "masculine" tastes in their youth and that even as a child, they "possessed few, if any, of the characteristics of her sex."[78] Lobdell's gender differences as a young person in the 1850s were admirable and allowed them to accomplish great feats. The intensification of their male identification in adulthood, however, was mocked and condemned. By the 1870s, Lobdell was characterized as tall, gaunt, and insane.[79] A *New York Times* story noted Lobdell's "beardless face" and "long hair," commenting on both the absence and presence of hair as cues that Lobdell was both unkempt and not a man. Lobdell was described as "rough and uncouth in manner and language, and evidently had always belonged to the lower order of humanity"[80] Lobdell's masculinity was attributed to their life experience, "the wild life she has led, and the hardships she has endured, have driven every feminine feature from her face."[81] In adulthood as a masculine person who lived as a man, Lobdell was deemed weak, unattractive, and insane. Such intense negative characterizations provided a cautionary tale: allowing a child to flout gender conventions – even in the name of supporting the family – could lead to irreversible gender identification and expression.

Marie Louise Perry of Plymouth County, Massachusetts, was portrayed favorably in the press in terms that primarily invoked her upper-class background. She was a sympathetic figure from the start, having been abandoned by her lover who she ran away from home to be with in the first place. Alone and penniless, she was "put off" a train at Basket Station, Pennsylvania for lack of funds.[82] This led her to the poorhouse where she met Lobdell. Perry was described as someone "good-looking even in her rags" who was probably "used to good society at some time in her life."[83] Articles portrayed Marie as sane, composed, and competent in contrast to Lobdell's childishness and dependency.[84] This fondness for Perry and disdain for Lobdell intensified over time. An 1877 *New York Times* story emphasized the incompatibility of the couple "inexplicable as it may seem, the two formed a mutual affection so strong that they refused to be separated, notwithstanding the great difference in their character, habit, and antecedents."[85] The article praised Perry's penmanship as "a really superior piece of composition" that affirmed she was "highly educated and capable of adorning the best circles," in contrast to Lobdell who was "insane, foul, and unsexed."[86] Regardless of these differing characterizations of the two and widespread disbelief at the pairing, nothing and no one came between them for nearly twenty years. And then someone did come between them, forcing their separation for life: Lobdell's brother John.

JOSEPH LOBDELL, PART FOUR: A BROTHER'S BETRAYAL

Lobdell dressed as a man, worked as a man, identified as a man, and was married to a woman. Sometimes they were forced into women's clothes by carceral authorities as a condition of receiving alms. From at least the 1870s onward, they were known as both Lucy and Joseph. Newspaper accounts made hiding knowledge of their past as a girl and wife impossible even as they persisted in going through the world as a man.[87] Both at the time and certainly later in the eyes of historians, Lobdell was held up as someone who challenged sexual and gender norms. They argued for women's rights, they rejected the constraints of womanhood, they married both a man and then later a woman. Few accounts from this later period in the 1870s and 1880s associated Lobdell with women's rights or feminism, but the fact that some did is significant. One blurb read: "Lucy Ann Lobdell, the female huntress and women's rights actress of the wild woods, after years of wanderings, has at last settled down to a peaceful life."[88] Much like the local press in Syracuse did of their famous female husband, so too this local press featured blurbs about Lobdell's mundane movements, reporting "Lucy Lobdell, the man-woman, as popularly known as the 'female hunter,' struck Honesdale last week."[89] Lobdell made an impact in their rejection of most constraints of womanhood for the era. This made them threatening and forced them to a life on the margins of society and into poverty.

News about Lobdell shared the pages with news about women's rights in New York. In one column in the *Port Jervis Evening Gazette*, a box stated, "Our exchanges are reproducing that hackneyed story about Lucy Ann Lobdell, the female huntress. The Gazette a short time ago published all the particulars relating to this unfortunate and strange being."[90] Two stories below, the headline titled "Progress of Women's Rights" noted the New York State law regarding women and contracts: "Contracts or obligations hereafter made or entered into by a married woman, except between herself and her husband, and except also contracts of suretyship for her husband in writing shall be as valid for all purposes as if she were unmarried, and may be enforced as if she were single." This was a huge victory for women, noted by the summary comment, "Woman is rapidly getting her rights."[91] Sadly, it was too late to have any meaning for Lobdell.

When word got out that Lobdell became a landowner in 1878, it was newsworthy, "Lucy Lobdell Again. The Man-Woman Becomes a Land Owner in Wayne County, PA."[92] They were said to have been employed picking whortleberries for shipment to New York and then gathering wintergreen leaves for sale to a local man who turned them into oil. This manufacturer of oil – Yeddo – sold the couple roughly three or four acres for sixty dollars.[93] In this act of legal record making – transferring the deed – Lobdell was said to be competent of mind and body, looking "fully competent to manage a farm" and appearing as required before the esquire with the requisite money. It was unlikely their desire, but the deed was rendered in the name of Lucy, something the newspaper found noteworthy, despite the fact that they were "dressed in her usual style" which meant men's clothes.

Just how did Lobdell come into the means to buy land after so many years of poverty? Lobdell's brother John helped them apply for a widow's pension including thousands of dollars of back pay because their husband George W. Slater was killed during the Civil War.[94] The pension was made official on February 6, 1879.[95] Slater had enlisted in 1862 at the age of thirty-two at Stuyvesant and died on February 4 1865 at Richmond, Virginia.[96] These funds enabled Lobdell to purchase land of their own for the first time.

This was a crucial turning point in their life that would protect them from being arrested or detained in the local poorhouse for want of a residence. Lobdell and Perry were finally home. This moment was followed by two inexplicable developments that remain a mystery but would have a devastating impact on their life forever. For some reason, Lobdell left the recently acquired land and their wife, Perry, to visit their brother John at his residence. Lobdell's daughter Helen was living with her uncle John, now with two children of her own. Perhaps Lobdell went to visit them? To pick something up or drop something off? Lobdell left their wife Marie and their newly acquired land one day to visit her brother John *and never returned.* John thought so little of Lobdell's relationship with Marie and Marie's basic humanity that he never bothered to reach out to her. Two years after Lobdell was deemed legally competent in securing a land deed, their brother swore they were insane and unable to govern themself.

Lobdell was institutionalized by their brother John. John delivered Lobdell to the authorities, subjecting Lobdell to a life of confinement indoors, isolation from their wife, and scrutiny by doctors. John Lobdell swore that he was providing for Lobdell and their descendants – a daughter named Helen and her two children – for nearly two years. He asserted that Lobdell was insane and had been for more than ten years. In addition to their "habit of dressing in men's clothes" John listed a range of disturbing behaviors, from tearing clothes and bedding to threatening to burn the building to imagining snakes and other animals inside the house. He claims Lobdell had spells that came and went and that they were not capable of self-care or government. John claimed Marie, who Lobdell "sometimes claims is her wife," was also insane.[97]

How can we ever know if Lobdell actually had a mental illness unrelated to their gender or sexuality? Were the signs and symptoms of insanity a result of the judgment, cruelty, and violence they experienced throughout the course of their life because of their gender? Or did they truly inherit some illness from their mother who was said to have been insane for decades? How did poverty and its related diseases factor into Lobdell's behavior and others' perceptions of them? Did forced institutionalization by their brother plunge them into madness? Was Lobdell in fact unable to care for themself? Did John believe these things were true and turn to the state out of desperation? Or did John tire of the nuisance his older sibling had become? Did he want Lobdell's land and pension for himself? We only have John's version of the events and the observations of neighbors gathered by John to verify his view before the court. But it is significant that he circulated a false obituary for Joseph Lobdell in 1879, which many people – including their wife Marie – believed for a while.[98]

John and nearly a dozen others offered testimony claiming Joseph Lobdell was insane before the court as part of the required process to authorize institutionalization. Many of the testimonies reference Lobdell's gender. A neighbor named Sidney Lobdell (no relation specified), who knew Lobdell for about six years, declared "That the habits, doings, language and actions of the said Lucy Ann Slater during the past two years have been those of an insane person. She frequently claims that she is a man and has a wife, sometimes dresses in men's clothes and uses such other language as to convince the deponent that she is a conferred lunatic and has been so called by those who knew her for many years last past."[99] Fifty-year-old William W. Main knew Lobdell for twenty years as a neighbor and assessed that Lobdell "talked quite sensibly" on other matters except for one issue – their gender. Main swore, "I know that she sometimes dresses in men's clothes and it is on that subject that I think her of unsound mind."[100] Harry Walsh reported some acquaintance with Lobdell for many years and each anecdote he offered to support his view that they were insane had something to do with gender, from the first time he saw Lobdell in men's clothes about twenty or twenty-five years previously to a later incident at the home of David Hallock in Wayne, Pennsylvania. Of this encounter, he explained, "I was satisfied then that she was crazy. She was dressed in men's clothes and had a gun and pretended to be a hunting."[101] Walsh also saw Lobdell with their wife and believed them both to be insane, in no small part due to their claim that they were in fact husband and wife. He swore, "After that I saw her in company with another woman traveling along the roads. That woman was crazy. They both claimed that they were man and wife and pretended to love each other so that they could not be separated. When they came to my brother's he said they frequently came there together in that way and wanted to be together and sleep together."[102] Walter Peak deposed, "the language and actions of the said Lucy Ann Slater during the last two years have been those of an insane person. That she very frequently dressed in men's attire. Sometimes says she is a hunter. Sometimes claims and acts as if she was in love with another woman and says that that husband is her husband or wife, is vulgar and incoherent in her conversations."[103] Lobdell may have spoken in tongues, tore at clothing, and yelled at passers-by, but the key thread that runs through the testimony is a claim that they rejected the gender restrictions of womanhood.

Lobdell's principal biographer, Bambi Lobdell, is convinced that John turned on Lobdell by circulating a false obituary and having them institutionalized.[104] Erroneous stories of Lobdell's death mixed up names, marital status, and salutations in confusing ways. One article referred to Lobdell by their husband's name, Slater, and Perry by the first name of the man who abandoned her, Wilson. Still, even in this mash-up of people, the press recognized the marriage between Lobdell and Perry, stating, "The two were living together as man and wife at Mrs. Slater's death."[105] The local *Port Jervis Gazette* ran a short announcement of their death while the more sensational *National Police Gazette* highlighted Lobdell's many roles in the subtitle, including "Hermit, Hunter, Music Teacher, Author, and 'Female-Husband.'"[106]

A year passed before Perry was able to get to the bottom of things. What a terrifying year it must have been for her! She got the word out that Lobdell was in fact still alive.[107] Shortly thereafter, news of Lobdell's institutionalization appeared. A cheeky writer who had great familiarity with Lobdell's public profile described them as having "recently varied her singular performances by going insane."[108] It was suggested that Lobdell disappeared and the discovery of remains near their home led to the belief they had perished. When Lobdell was later seen, however, some claimed they had become "hopelessly insane."[109] The fabricated obituary, however, undermines any claim to legitimacy and integrity on the part of John. For Lobdell and so many who came before them, their birth families were sources of pain, misunderstanding, and betrayal.

With Lobdell institutionalized, news of the couple trickled to a stop. Perry was said to be heartbroken and eventually moved away.[110] Occasional stories offered updates on Perry such as, "This wife of the 'female hunter' is now about forty-five years old and still lives near here. Her hair is as white as snow and since the death of her 'female husband' she has been in poor health."[111] Another story focused on Perry's family, emphasizing their wealth and the fact that she had an inheritance she never claimed despite living in poverty.[112] What a mysterious woman! While so much attention has been given to Lobdell, many more questions remain about Marie Louise Perry. What motivated her decision to stay with Lobdell? Did she ever contact her family again? Did they read about her in the news? How did Lobdell's absence affect her? Did she ever have another intimate relationship? If so, was it with another female husband?

JOSEPH LOBDELL, PART FIVE: DR. P.M. WISE'S "CASE OF SEXUAL PERVERSION"

Far from the pages of the daily press where female husbands were sources of intrigue for a reading public, doctors began studying gender nonconformity and same-sex attraction with fervor. Joseph Lobdell became a prominent subject of such work – and one of the first in the United States. This was done against their will and was only possible because their brother John had them forcibly committed to an asylum. Dr. P.M. Wise began his examinations of Lobdell at the Willard Asylum for the Insane. Wise published his assessment of Lobdell in 1883.[113] The issue of transing gender and female masculinity had long been popular headline-grabbers in the nineteenth-century press. Now, doctors and psychiatrists would have their say.

Wise knew he was contributing to a new and growing field of study on the subject of sexual perversion or perverted sexual instinct. Wise based his assessment of Lobdell on both interview and observation. Wise's factual report on Lobdell did not differ remarkably from newspaper accounts about Lobdell. But there was a shift in classification and terminology, with an emphasis on masculinity and sexuality. First, Wise emphasized the word "masculine" when describing Lobdell's life of hunting, for example, "Her voice was coarse and her features were masculine" and "she followed her inclination to indulge in masculine vocations most freely; donned male attire," "the unsexed woman assumed the name of Joseph Lobdell," and "following her masculine ovation of hunting and trapping." Everything that Lobdell had previously done was now deemed "masculine."

The second difference in characterizations of Lobdell by Wise compared to the newspaper accounts was an intense focus on sex. In Dr. Wise's account, Lobdell was driven principally by sexual desire. This is jarring for a reader who has become familiar with Lobdell's life from other sources where sexual intimacy was not a visible motivating force. But for Wise, their "masculine" tendencies were driven by their sexual desire. Lobdell's sexual desire for women drove their decision to live as a man. To fortify this claim, Wise cites a bizarre scene in which Lobdell is said to have initiated physical contact with numerous women shortly after their admission, "Her excitement was of an erotic nature and her sexual inclination was perverted. In passing to the ward, she embraced the female attendant in a lewd manner, and came near overpowering her before she received assistance. Her conduct on the ward was characterized by the same lascivious conduct, and she made efforts at various times to have sexual intercourse with her associates." Wise characterizes Lobdell's physical aggression toward all women as sexual. This description seems more aptly that of a predatory or drunken serial abuser than an older person who felt exhausted, disoriented, and misunderstood. Wise allows this odd description to stand without explanation, refusing to distinguish between the panic and anger typical of one forcibly institutionalized and expressions of sexual desire.

Wise allowed Lobdell to offer a characterization of themself in his report. Wise quotes Lobdell as saying, "I may be a woman in one sense, but I have peculiar organs that make me more of a man than a woman." Wise reports that he was "unable to discover any abnormality of the genitals." This suggests, not surprisingly, that Lobdell was subject to an intrusive physical exam against their wishes. Wise did point out that Lobdell's clitoris was enlarged and covered by "a large relaxed praeputium." Lobdell also insisted they had sexual function, including "the power to erect this organ in the same way a turtle protrudes its head." Wise remained skeptical of this. The fact that Lobdell offered a turtle's head as an analogy for their own sexuality and not a penis offers several important insights into Lobdell. Lobdell spent their life in the woods among animals. It seems Mr. Slater is the only man they had sexual intimacies with and probably not very often given the short duration of their marriage, which was soured even before it began. Turtles might spend countless hours with their heads tucked away, hidden beneath their shells for protection, much as Lobdell spent decades of their own life protecting their own vulnerabilities from a cruel and ignorant world. When given the chance to explain how they experienced sexual desire, Lobdell used a metaphor of a peaceful, cautious animal.

* * *

Historians of sexuality have long scoffed at the assertions of sexologists that same-sex desires were only enabled by a cross-sex identification. The importance of masculinity and aggression in female subjects was obvious. Of P.M Wise's report on Lobdell, George Chauncey noted, "The perversion described by Wise was not so much in the object of the woman's sexual desire as in the masculine, aggressive form it took: the woman had inverted her whole sexual character."[114] What made Lobdell perverted was not their object of choice but rather their aggression combined with their male identification. One longstanding explanation for this has been Victorian ideology, which deemed female sexual desire impossible. Within this context, even a mild expression of desire from someone perceived to be a "woman" could be deemed "aggressive," so we must not accept this particular characterization without skepticism.

Wise saw Lobdell's masculine aggression and declared them a lesbian. At least since the 1970s, there has been a movement among some lesbians to disassociate the category from masculinity. We must step back and consider two different but interrelated questions: What is served by minimizing gender nonconformity as a key component of lesbian identity for some? Could sexologists have been right in defining gender difference as a cornerstone of same-sex attraction? For those assigned female at birth who did in fact embrace manhood and/or masculinity, the concept of sexual inversion was simply descriptive. This conclusion, based on Wise's views of Lobdell, may well have applied to any number of female husbands in this book. Given the lives they chose, it is certainly a reasonable explanation that living as a man and desiring women did in fact signify a complete reversal of one's sex role. This concept of sexual inversion was not neutral, however, and it became the basis of a negative psychiatric diagnosis that was also criminalized.

For some lesbians looking back in time, however, sexology under-mined their claim to womanhood. As we have seen throughout this book, people assigned female at birth adopted a wide range of behaviors to access male privilege, freedom, mobility and/or the opportunity to be sexually intimate with and/or married to women. All of these people were linked by their rejection of the constraints of womanhood. Beyond that, some of them lived lives that were light years away from each other in substance. Even femme lesbians – those who visibly embraced what appeared to be dominant expressions of femininity in women – were never deemed actual lesbians in sexology.

Sexology claimed a one-size-fits-all reductive model for gender non-conformity. Doctors determined that women who inverted their gender role in one aspect of their life would inevitably invert it in every area.[115] They were wrong. Evidence of this error could be found everywhere, from boarding schools to factory floors to popular magazines to news-paper accounts of people transing gender in any number of ways. As the ideas of sexologists circulated, expanded spheres of same-sex sociality also emerged.[116] Doctors were out of step with broader public discourses in which many people displayed a wide range of gender expressions and partial inversions, in one way or another. The sheer abundance of people challenging limitations and transing gender explains why some of them – such as female husbands – were treated harshly during this period.

Studies of sexual inversion from this formative period focused dispro-portionately on men. In a scholarly overview of German research pub-lished for an American audience in 1883, only two of the nineteen cases concerned women or people who were assigned female at birth. Both of these people – Miss N., a thirty-five-year-old housekeeper and an unnamed twenty-eight-year-old Jewish servant girl – sought and experi-enced sexual pleasure with women. Miss N. also expressed strong feel-ings of identification as a man. The doctor reported that Miss N. reported, "In her voluptuous dreams she appeared to herself to be a man," and that many years later after release they "still had a great desire to be a man."[117] Dr. Allan McLane Hamilton researched the existence of facial hair on menstruating women, arguing that beards were a result of mental illness or sexual misconduct. In his words, "From time to time I have seen insane women who were the possessors of beards or growths of hair. Some of these cases, in fact most of them, presented some history of sexual trouble, and in nearly every instance the growth of hair was coincident with the development of mental diseases."[118] This study was one small but crucial step in establishing a correlation between women's facial hair, masculinity, and insanity. Together, these cases established correlations between masculinity, aggression, and same-sex attraction while also looking for biological bases, such as facial hair, on which to judge sexual disorders.

American sexologists have generally been overlooked in studies of early sexology, as scholars have assumed that they simply followed the views of their European counterparts.[119] But European and American sexologists were contemporaries in dialogue who read and cited each other, linking the ideas of racial ethnologists and sexologists. None of their findings were neutral, however. Rather, they were weaponized by a broader social and political movement to defend longstanding hierarchies of race, class, and gender that were challenged from seemingly every direction. Doctors, psychiatrists, and psychologists developed elaborate and official means by which to stigmatize, criminalize, isolate, and torture those assigned female at birth who stepped beyond the confines of appropriate gender and sexual behavior.

Lobdell would have had no way of predicting the shift in attitudes about gender transing that occurred from the mid to late nineteenth century. They received so much positive feedback about their masculine ways when they still presented as a woman. They learned the hard way over the decades that other factors shaped public attitudes about someone like them. Behavior that was charming and inspiring in a young person became condemnable in adulthood. It was one thing to trans gender, it was another thing entirely to pursue a romance with someone of the same sex while transing gender. Poverty made everything harder – and subjected one's embodiment to an unbearable level of scrutiny unknown by those of means. Love and commitment between two people that was not legally recognized or religiously sanctioned could only stand as a buffer against a harsh and unforgiving society for so long. Maybe we are wrong to mourn the fate of Lobdell and Perry as a tragedy – of a love disrupted and a life imprisoned. Perhaps it is more fitting to celebrate and marvel at their resilience and ability to remain together *for so long* in the face of such tremendous judgment, hostility, and rejection.

CHAPTER 8

THE END OF A CATEGORY

A GROWING NUMBER OF PEOPLE ASSIGNED FEMALE AT birth rejected the constraints of womanhood near the end of the nineteenth century. There were more ways to do this than ever before. Some embraced a male identity and were known by neighbors as men while others were known to be women. Gender expressions proliferated and varied. Female husband – once a clear category that signaled a particular life experience and gender expression – suddenly meant other things. In the late nineteenth century, the category was used in an expansive way to describe a variety of people. Broadway star Annie Hindle was thought of as a woman who dressed in men's clothing for their work on stage and sometimes off-stage as well. At the same time, homosocial environments in schools and workplaces nurtured same-sex friendships and intimacies, enabling more women to reject conventional heterosexual marriages. Many forces contributed to these shifts, including industrialization, urbanization, feminism, and progressive social movements.[1]

Female husband as a descriptive category lost its meaning in public discourse just as it proliferated in the US from roughly 1878 to 1906. It had already largely fallen out of use in the UK. Female husbands – once defined by manhood and masculinity – were quietly and subtly subsumed under a newly expansive category of woman. Same-sex relationships became more visible and included women who embraced a range of gender expressions. Those who refused the category of woman outright and insisted on claiming manhood for themselves – as Joseph Lobdell, Frank Dubois, and Alan Hart were known to do – were harshly stigmatized. Accounts continued to blur lines of gender and sexuality in reporting on female husband cases. This period marks a dramatic shift, however, away from gender toward sexuality. In other words, the fact of two "women" married to each other becomes the central drama, replacing the fact that someone assigned female could become and live as a man. This shift created some openings and foreclosed on others. A challenge to the stigma of sexual inversion also brought with it a critique of transing gender. The recognition of informal relationships between two women grew, whereas marriages between female husbands and wives had been formal legal contracts.

FRANK DUBOIS AND SAME-SEX MARRIAGE

As was the case with most female husband accounts, the 1883 story of Frank Dubois broke because their manhood was challenged by someone. In this case, a man named S.J. Hudson from Illinois tracked Dubois down in Waupun, Wisconsin and claimed that Dubois was his wife who abandoned him and their two children.[2] The Dubois case encapsulates a change in popular attitudes toward female husbands and their lovers from one of curiosity to one of overt hostility. The reporter was at odds with the subject of the story. They spoke of Dubois as a woman and downplayed evidence supporting Dubois' claim of manhood. Through the coverage of Dubois' life, a transformation took place in the popular understandings of and attitudes toward female husbands. The female husband category no longer signaled gendered transformation but rather indicated a new relationship form: that of two women.

On what basis was Dubois a man? Statements from Dubois, their wife, and acquaintances who knew the couple all asserted Dubois was a man. One reporter pushed Dubois, saying, "You insist that you are a man!" to which Dubois replied, "I do; I am. As long as my wife is satisfied it's nobody's business."[3] Dubois refused to entertain the idea that they would give up their life and male identity even though their former husband tracked them down. Dubois claimed, "I will not return to live with Hudson, and propose to wear pants and smoke and earn my living as a man."[4] Another story claimed that no one ever suspected Dubois was anything other than a man, stating, "To everyone, even to the intimate acquaintances of the couple, to all except, perhaps, to the "wife," the secret of Frank Dubois' sex was as unsuspected as it was unknown."[5]

The interesting claim here is the recognition that the wife knew what she was getting into when she married Frank. For over a century, wives were thought to have no idea their husbands were assigned female at birth. Indeed, they were often forced to take this position to protect their own personal safety and reputations.

On what basis was Dubois *not a man*? First, we must not underestimate the existence and claim of Hudson, their alleged husband. His appearance alone – along with the assertion that Dubois was the mother of his children – would carry tremendous weight in the eyes of the public. A newspaper reporter who tracked down Mr. and Mrs. Dubois offered their own assessment of Dubois' physical body and stature. In this rendering, the account combines male pronouns while emphasizing a female body, stating, "Dubois was in his shirt sleeves, a slightly built, effeminate-looking personage. He is four feet, eleven inches tall, slight figure, weighing about 100 pounds, hips broad, chest full, arms short, and hands and feet very small and slender. He has every appearance of a woman."[6] After the initial confrontation, Dubois allegedly openly discussed their sex with the reporter, who wrote, "Dubois finally acknowledged herself to be a woman and the wife of S.J. Hudson, the Belvidere man."[7] These accounts by a former husband and disinterested reporter supported the claim that Dubois was not a man by society's standards. But a sympathetic reader would note Dubois was a man to themself – and their wife – and that this fact was what mattered most.

Theories abound as to why Gertrude Fuller married Dubois in the first place. One is that Fuller was sympathetic to Dubois' "domestic troubles" with Mr. Hudson and determined that the marriage would provide Dubois with a layer of protection. In an essay called "The Fooled Girl," the theory is floated that Fuller "agreed the latter should assume the name of Dubois and play the part of a husband" by smoking, chewing tobacco, and swearing. Dubois, however, was said to contest this theory, asserting instead that Fuller "did not know she had married a woman until after the ceremony," and that it was "nobody's business" as to what motived Dubois in the first place.[8] More details about Fuller's family life provide further insights. A few years before the two met, Fuller at age fourteen was noted as living with her fifty-three-year-old mother and seventy-four-year-old stepfather.[9] Fuller may have been eager to get out of their home and move on with her life.

An explosion of references to female husbands in the US press, combined with the broad effects of the women's movement generally, led people to consider such accounts in a new way. This rise in visibility led more mainstream writers, thinkers, and politicians to weigh in on the role of the husband, the question of sexual difference, and the future of heterosexual marriage. The women's movement threatened all of these things. Stories about the Dubois marriage in Wisconsin in particular marked a turning point. Major coverage in the *New York Times* and in *Peck's Sun* out of Milwaukee used the story as an occasion to think about the broader social and political implications of marriages between two women. Even if done in jest, such reflections pointed to real truths that could no longer be denied. Such accounts fundamentally redefined the threat of female husbands from one of transing gender to one of same-sex marriage.

Consider the provocatively titled essay, "Evolution of the Man-Woman," which suggests female husbands were a different species than either men or women.[10] The scientific reference was not a literal one but rather mocked those broadly speaking who were committed to opening up education and professional opportunities for women by arguing against their inferiority. The "evolution" of a so-called "he-woman" in this case was an important development for "the guild of female scientists who for years have been struggling manfully to release women from the bonds of sex and lift her to the possession of the inalienable rights of masculinity."[11] This critique relied on the assumption that men and women were fundamentally distinct, though women were "struggling" to claim the abilities of men, too. It was true that numerous groups of women (and those assigned female who lived as men) were clamoring for the rights of men. While older essays emphasized women's physical differences and inferiority from men, this one accepted the fundamental premise that someone assigned female could learn to adopt mannerisms and attitudes commonly expected of men. Of Dubois, this essay claims,

> It was found that she could sharpen a lead pencil; that when a mouse was let loose in her room she did not pull up her trousers and jump upon the bureau; that she always shut the door after her when she got into a railroad car; that she carried her umbrella perpendicularly and not across her

breast, nursing fashion; and, finally, it was shown that she chewed tobacco and swore. But in spite of these irrefragable proofs of sex, Wisconsin, with inscrutable pertinacity, insists that she is a woman.[12]

The essay concedes that gender is flexible and different from sex before strongly asserting this distinction to support its claim: Dubois could not be a man. Even though a female husband could learn to walk like a man, talk like a man, and live like a man, they would no longer be recognized or tolerated as men.

More than any coverage of female husbands to date, these stories took up the serious question of same-sex marriage. Would people stand for it? Should society care? How did it differ from women's rights in other realms? As was often the case, husbands could avoid the wrath of the carceral state if they simply claimed what everyone wanted to hear: they were women. In making this claim to avoid intrusive physical exams, further interrogation, and jail, husbands of earlier times were generally freed and sent on their way. Never before considered a serious threat in the United States, the possibility of same-sex marriages between women seemed just on the horizon. To this threat, the *New York Times* declared in 1883, "public opinion will not tolerate the marriage of two women."[13] Why did they even need to say that? That is the important take away here. Female husbands, long ignored and dismissed as LGBTQ ancestors or political actors, opened the door to national and transatlantic debates over transing gender, same-sex marriage, and eventually, sex changes.

Dubois did not concede to being a woman and instead dug in their heels, defending themself and claiming their manhood. Despite this, they were spared "imprisonment and threatened tar and feathers."[14] It is a curious reference – the one to tarring and feathering – evoking the physically painful and humiliating punishments of a much earlier era, long since abandoned. Tarring and feathering, rooted in early modern Europe, became popular in Revolutionary America as a symbol of rebellion and independence from Britain. As a form of punishment, it retained its association with patriotism long after the war for independence was over.[15] Through brutal violence against their new-found "enemies," colonists worked through their sense of allegiance and identity, in part bonding themselves to each other.[16] This kind of ritualistic violence aimed at those who transed gender – or even its threat – united the perpetrators together, affirming and solidifying their own allegiance to the gender norms that had been violated.

Thankfully, this violence remained only a threat. Modernity prevailed. And the question of same-sex marriages between women was critically, seriously, and at times satirically explored. Under the headline "Female Husbands," *New York Times* writers noted the various things to consider, from the issue of kids, "Such a marriage concerns the general public less than the normal sort of marriage, since it does not involved the promise and potency of children," to one of preference, "There are many women who, if they had the opportunity, would select other women as husbands rather than marry men."[17] There were so many reasons given for this claim, including that women understood, supported, and enjoyed each other. It almost seemed as if this was in fact a widely held view. Women made good company – why bother with men?

This essay took particular aim at the prospect of marriage between women in the New England states. This is curious because New England is one of the few regions that did not feature as a hometown or location of a female husband to date. Female husbands could be found in every other region of the US and all throughout the UK. Why did New England matter so much now? The reference hints at the idea that the women of New England were "different" from other women, driven by their intellect, love of literature, and disdain of typical male behaviors of smoking, swearing, and door slamming. The solution proposed was both evocative and conservative: "If half of these neglected women were to put on trousers and marry the other half, the painful spectacle of a hundred thousand lonely spinsters would forever disappear." This exaggerated suggestion included some truth, which readers of female husband accounts were all too aware of. But the claim was also an erasure of the same-sex couples that could already be found all over New England, especially in educated circles and sometimes referred to as "Boston Marriages." This essay willfully refused the existence of such partnerships, instead reducing everyone to the category of "spinster."

In 1883, George W. Peck addressed these same concerns, reminding readers that there was no way a female husband could ever replace "the old-fashioned male article."[18] Peck was publisher of *The Sun*, later named

Peck's Sun. He went on to become mayor of Milwaukee in 1890 and governor of Wisconsin in 1891, signaling at the very least a degree of popularity for his viewpoints.[19] His turn of phrase, "the old-fashioned male article," dismissed female husbands as something contemporary, modern, and fleeting. They were no match for the tried and true men who were assigned male at birth.[20] His article echoes the themes previously addressed by defining manhood in relation to a series of instincts, such as bravery in the face of a burglary, confidence in the face of a confrontation, or a "can-do" spirit and ability to multitask amid a family emergency.[21] Neither female husbands nor female wives were up to these tasks in Peck's view. Peck asserted, "It is well that the female husband business in Wisconsin is thus early nipped in the bud, and it is hoped that an end has been put to it for all time." Even if he truly believed this, however, Peck – like so many other publishers – could not resist the fact that such headlines sold papers, and books. Peck included a chapter on female husbands in his popular book, ensuring that knowledge of such people would continue to spread far and wide.

THE LAST BRITISH FEMALE HUSBAND

Female husband as a category in the British press peaked from the 1820s through the 1850s. It persisted in light doses for a few more decades. Later cases, such as Josiah Charles Stephenson (1869) and the nameless farm servant of Mid Calder (1870) were important in marking the ongoing existence of female husbands and keeping this laboring tradition alive. With the death of Belfast laborer John Coulter in 1884, however, the British press finally put the category of "female husband" to rest. Unlike the contemporaneous account of Frank Dubois (1883) in the United States, which pointed to the future understanding of sex and gender in same-sex relationships, Coulter's life (and the telling of it) pointed to the past.

Coulter had much in common with James Allen, the London dockworker who died fifty-five years prior. Many papers reported the news of Coulter's deathbed revelation – that this well-established man who lived in the community as such for over twenty years was assigned female. Coulter was a drunk, and though estranged from their wife Martha for the last six years of their twenty-nine-year marriage, she showed up to collect the body that no one else wanted. The local community attended the inquest to have their curiosity satisfied, inflicting nothing short of cruelty upon Martha as they laughed and snickered at the questions of the coroner. The local paper printed the transcript of the inquest, which was common for prominent, scandalous, or unusual cases of death.[22] But the regional and national publications that ran the initial scandal with headlines such as "A Female Husband" or "A Woman Married to a Woman," had already moved on.[23] The British press no longer embraced the phrase "female husband" and reduced their coverage of the cases that occurred.

Sexologists used these accounts to illuminate their new theories about homosexuality. In volume one of *Studies in the Psychology of Sex*, for instance, Havelock Ellis mentioned John Coulter, the last UK female husband, in a footnote that was principally about Joseph Lobdell.[24] This chapter concerned "Sexual Inversion in Women," and grappled with the relationship between gender nonconformity and same-sex desire.[25] "The chief characteristic of the sexually inverted woman is a certain degree of masculinity. As I have already pointed out, a woman who is inclined to adopt the ways and garments of men is by no means necessarily inverted."[26] Ellis notes people drawn to men's clothing but who were not known to be involved sexually with women, such as Mary Frith (Moll Cutpurse) and Sir James Barry.[27] But sexual inverts are driven to wear men's clothes – and the reasoning given by Ellis is important. "In such cases male garments are not usually regarded as desirable chiefly on account of practical convenience, nor even in order to make an impression on other women, but because the wearer feels more at home in them."[28] Ellis placed Lobdell and Coulter in this category.[29]

The most generous coverage of Coulter was a story that focused on their work and did not mention their relationship to a woman. This account, "A Female Labourer in Male Attire," described Coulter's accidental death and the disclosure of their sex as "a singular and touching incident," without hint of mockery or cruelty. The tone was very matter of fact in declaring two seemingly contradictory points: the body was that of a woman, while the life lived was that of a man, who "for many years worked as a labourer on the quays."[30] In death, Coulter was not a threat but rather could be a target of humane sympathy, as someone who died long before their time and labored under grueling conditions.

Coulter was convincingly male in life, and their sex "had never been suspected."[31] This was affirmed in a variety of ways, partly because they "had always worn male attire" and labored "in work peculiar to men."[32] Their twenty-nine-year marriage to a woman was less central in their life and death, due to their six-year separation.[33] Their excessive drinking destroyed their marriage while reinforcing their manhood, as they were known for frequenting a variety of public houses with fellow male laborers. Such was the case on the night before their death – Coulter enjoyed two "half ones" also known as "glasses of whisky," with co-worker John Steele in one pub and then another whiskey in another pub.[34] The two returned to Steele's home for dinner after which Coulter went out drinking, again. Coulter shared Steele's bed that night due to excessive intoxication, causing Steele's wife to sleep in another room with the children. Coulter fell down the stairs in the Steele family home around two in the morning, receiving life-threatening injuries. The Steele's daughter was the first to see Coulter at the bottom of the stairs, head awkwardly bent backward, pressed against the front door.

Once cause of death was established, Dr. Dill, borough coroner at Royal Hospital, turned the discussion to a question of sex. He invited Dr. Barron to "volunteer any additional statement" about the deceased. Dr. Barron did indeed introduce the subject of Coulter's sex, to which the coroner formally asked, "Is this a man or a woman?" Dr. Barron replied, "It is a woman." The crowd assembled gasped while the coroner pressed on, asking, "Without doubt?" to which Dr. Barron confirmed, "Yes, without doubt." Still unsatisfied, the coroner persisted in asking if Coulter was a hermaphrodite, to which Dr. Barron answered "No." With the question of Coulter's sex settled to the satisfaction of the coroner, the jury foreman raised the issue of Coulter's wife, who was in attendance.

There was no reason for the coroner to allow the foreman to call another witness and question them. The cause of Coulter's death was settled, as was the question of their sex. But the coroner allowed Mr. Lemon to question Coulter's wife, Martha, even though it was immediately clear from the laughter of those in attendance that Mr. Lemon's motives were cruel. Martha took the stand and explained she was from

Dungannon, where she and John were married by Mr. Ewens.[35] Mr. Lemon took over, asking Martha, "Had you any family by him?" Her reply of "No, sir" was met with great laughter. Still, Lemon persisted while laughing, "Was your husband a man?" This time, much to her credit, Martha refused to answer. No authority figure – such as the coroner or the medical examiner – stopped Mr. Lemon's inappropriate and pointless mocking of this elderly woman. Rather, she put her foot down and said, "Thank you, Mr. Lemon; that is quite enough." Still, Lemon, fellow jurors, and the audience laughed as Lemon asserted, "There is a mistake in the identity." The coroner finally stepped in and asked Martha who would take responsibility for Coulter's body, to which she graciously offered herself.[36] The now deceased fifty-five-year-old John Coulter was buried in Belfast City Cemetery.[37]

Newspapers on both sides of the Atlantic had long celebrated female husbands who worked hard and provided for their wives throughout the nineteenth century. In this regard, female husband accounts in the news advanced a clear narrative of a model work ethic for a life well lived by white men of the lower sort.[38] This changed quite dramatically by the 1880s. The British press was no longer taken with female husbands and stopped covering stories with such headlines. The US papers experienced quite the opposite – a sudden burst of female husbands. But just who exactly these people where and what was meant by the reference quickly lost its meaning, as the following accounts demonstrate.

HUSBANDS OF A DIFFERENT KIND

The US press fully embraced the descriptor in its headlines in the final decades of the nineteenth century. From 1871 to 1886, US newspapers featured about ten different female husbands. In the year 1902 alone, four different female husband cases emerged across the country in New York, Maryland, Virginia, and California, followed by Missouri (1906) and Chicago (1907). Even these stories received fewer column inches than they once did. A short paragraph with minimal details contributed to some readers' sense that the accounts were flights of editorial fancy. This group of husbands – Samuel Pollard, Leroy Williams, Annie Hindle, and John Whittman – were different kinds of husbands. They represented a departure from the dominant trope that circulated for about 150 years. None of the relationships considered here were lasting and loving, built on a foundation of economic and social interdependence and/or desire. One comes close, but this featured two people socially known to be women, something unheard of in female husband relationships previously. Each of these husbands shattered the mold in one way or another, contributing to a loss of meaning and utility for the term at the turn of the century.

SAMUEL POLLARD

In 1878, the news of Samuel Pollard was introduced to a national readership as something nearly impossible to fathom (Figure 8.1). The opening line to the story claimed, "We were never so deeply impressed with the false adage that 'truth is stranger than fiction.'"[39] But many readers would know that this was a disingenuous adage at best. Anyone who read the news with some regularity would already be familiar with other people who seemed a lot like Pollard, making this "truth" more common than many cared to admit. News of Joseph Lobdell in particular was still popular in the years before and after Pollard's story broke. The account, reprinted nationally from the *Tuscarora Review*, introduced Samuel Pollard to the readers first as a feminine man, using male pronouns: "The bridegroom was a youthful and rather effeminate-looking person, a stranger here, and about whom but little was known, except that he came from Colorado, where he represented he had been engaged in business." Pollard was granted manhood via the pronoun "he" in relation to matters of work. The phrase "effeminate-looking" suggests something was different about Pollard without completely undoing their gender right away.

Samuel M. Pollard and Marancy Hughes were married in Tuscarora, Elko County, Nevada on September 29, 1877.[40] Pollard turned out to be a terrible husband who "abused, ill-treated, and at times severely beat" their wife.[41] When Marancy finally escaped and fled to her uncle's house for safety, she relayed the particulars of what happened between the two just after their marriage. Two different stories circulated. In the first, Pollard used the marriage as a further front to enhance their newly

Figure 8.1 *National Police Gazette,* Saturday, June 8, 1878. Samuel Pollard was featured on the cover in a series of pictures and an extensive story that continues inside.
Image courtesy of the Library of Congress, Chronicling America

adopted male disguise. They fled the authorities in Colorado after some unspecified business-related wrongdoing.[42] In the second story, a familial dispute resulted in Pollard's loss of property and need to find a new way to earn money. Marancy – seemingly the source of both accounts – later denied her husband was involved in any criminal activity.[43] But all of this made Pollard one of the only female husbands to claim purely financial motivations for their decision. Pollard claimed they became a man to take advantage of "avenues for making money" that were not available to women.[44] Marancy reported believing Pollard pursued marriage to her under the assumption that "the concealment of her sex would be better maintained" if married to a woman.

Most coverage of Pollard emphasized in every way imaginable the assertion that they were a woman – from leading stories featuring their birth name, "a young woman named Sarah. M. Pollard," to use of predominantly female pronouns. "Samuel Pollard is a Woman" was the title of a brief blurb that assured its readers, "there is no doubt whatever of the sex of Pollard."[45] A certainty of sex and a conflation between sex and gender was asserted by such accounts.

The issue of Pollard's sex was left somewhat unresolved in the press, as different neighbors were quoted as swearing with certainty that Pollard was and wasn't a man. The court case initiated to "settle the question" charged Pollard with perjury for "having sworn falsely when the marriage license was obtained."[46] But this case went nowhere, offering little satisfaction to a curious public. Marancy protected her husband in this matter, reconciling (if briefly) in a very public fashion before the court, as they "walked off arm in arm without a word of explanation to the wondering officers."[47] This action confirmed what had long been true: the wife of a female husband had tremendous social and political authority in asserting their husband's manhood.

Pollard leveraged this lingering ambiguity about their sex into a speaking tour for an interested public.[48] As part of the publicity for this tour, reporters used three pronouns simultaneously in reference to Pollard: he, she, and it. The objectifying and inhuman introduction of "it" was not unprecedented.[49] The reviewer of the performance in which Pollard begins in male attire and ends in women's clothing declares, "Pollard, whether a man or a woman or an it, actually lives and moves and has being." This was meant to be a humanizing compliment but from a contemporary perspective is anything but.[50] The writer declared the excitement and uniqueness of Pollard's life, stating, "Why Pollard married a woman, and why he, she or it did other remarkable things, is fully explained in the forthcoming biography."[51] No biography emerged.

Pollard remained in the county and continued living as a man. The 1880 Federal Census counted a twenty-four-year-old married white male S.M. Pollard who worked as a farm laborer in Independence Valley, Elko, Nevada.[52] Marancy Hughes dropped Pollard and must have been granted an annulment because under her maiden name she married a local man, John R. Linebargar of Elko, Nevada on December 28, 1880, three years after her first marriage.[53] Pollard's decision to continue living as a man certainly raises questions about their initial claim that they did not really want to be a man or marry a woman. But we know that time influences our gender, that living as a man for a period of time generally made one into more of a man, and some people enjoyed this feeling. Pollard was apparently one of those people. We don't know if Pollard's new friends, neighbors, or employer knew of their past scandalous marriage or knew them to be someone who had transed gender a few years prior. But the fact that Pollard remained living and working as a man not far from where the incident blew up in the press suggests it is possible that Pollard was accepted as a trans man in the community rather than as a man unknown by others to have transed genders.

Pollard's account instantly reminded readers that gender was different from sex – even someone assigned female could live and pass as a man. Furthermore, it pointed to marriage as a social and legal vehicle that stabilized gender. Pollard plotted their marriage based on the assumption that it would further stabilize their expression of manhood. Marancy herself even testified to this fact. As we have seen over and over again in female husband accounts, being married to a woman was the most obvious and socially recognized way to achieve certainty and legitimacy in one's manhood. Whether or not Pollard read about female husbands in newspapers prior to this move, there is no denying the history and tradition of female husbands and others who transed genders and pursued what looked like conventional heterosexual marriages, which helped make this course of action possible.

ANNIE HINDLE

Just a few days after it happened, news of this particular wedding hit the papers, "'Annie Hindle,' a variety actress, who, fifteen years ago, married Charles Vivian, the comedian, and lived with him as a wife, was again wedded at Grand Rapids Sunday evening, but gave the name of 'Charles Hindle,' his (or her) bride being Annie Ryan, of Cleveland, Ohio" (Figure 8.2).[54] This was an accurate description of the situation, as Michigan state marriage records confirm the marriage between the pair on June 5, 1886 Grand Rapids, Kent County, Michigan.[55] Hindle was known as a woman though they presented as a man for their ceremony. Same-sex marriage between two women was not legal. How on earth did this legal marriage even occur? And how did the press come to know about it?

Reverend E.H. Brooks presided over the small private ceremony. A friend and co-worker of the couple – another male impersonator – was the best man. The bride wore "her traveling costume" while the groom wore "a dress suit."[56] The minister swore he believed not only that Hindle was a man but perhaps just as importantly that the pair belonged together. He claimed, "I believe they love each other and that they will be happy."[57] Still, he was harassed when news of the marriage broke. Hindle was a theatrical star at the time, not an unknown laborer. Brooks swore that nothing gave him any reason to wonder or doubt if Hindle was in fact "a full-fledged man."[58] Despite uproar from some quarters, there is no evidence that the authorities punished either Brooks or Hindle.

The couple lived together for five years in a Jersey City home that Hindle purchased with their savings.[59] They made the headlines again in 1891 when Annie Ryan died. One story of Ryan's death declared Hindle a "widower" and acknowledged Ryan's role as "the wife." Specifically, the essay described Ryan as the wife of a woman, stating "the wife of the woman who now shed tears over the coffin." Immediately, the accuracy of this claim is identified for its absurdity but also verified in its truth. Recounting the old adage "truth indeed is stranger than fiction," this reporter declared, "The wife of a woman? The expression sounds absurd, yet it is absolutely, literally correct. Annie Ryan, the wife, was dead, and Annie Hindle, the female husband, was burying her."[60] This passage was powerful and

Figure 8.2 "Annie Hindle," n.d. Hindle was known as a woman who was also masculine, married to a woman, and performed men's parts onstage.
Image courtesy of the Miriam and Ira Wallach Division of Art, Prints, and Photographs: Print Collection, the New York Public Library

achieved several things: it verified the existence of the relationship and it asserted the legitimacy of marriage between two women.

Furthermore, this was an account of respectability and acceptance that sought to make both the couple and the community look good. Not only did the pair behave nobly (they caused "no scandal" and were held in great "esteem" by friends and neighbors), just as importantly the neighbors responded in kind by respecting them – it "did not disturb them with gossip." It was an arrangement of mutual respect. One key to this mutual admiration was the fact that Hindle, the female husband, did not scandalize the pair by wearing men's clothes – or so the essayist claimed. This passage states, "That they could live together openly as husband and wife, the husband in female attire always, and yet cause no scandal, is the best proof of the esteem in which those around them held them."[61] This passage is a cautionary tale. It captures what we know was true of the era: an increase in scrutiny of nonconforming gender expressions and a growing acceptance of the idea that two women could marry each other.

While a popular account made much of the fact that the couple was respectable and both wore women's clothes, there is little to support that claim given Hindle's documented practice of wearing men's attire while *off the stage*. For instance, in Kanas City, Missouri in 1870, Hindle "occasionally appeared on main street in a semi-masculine costume, with an immaculate shirt front decorated with a gorgeous diamond, she astonished the natives."[62] This was long before their marriage to Ryan. It mattered little that Kansas City passed an anti-cross-dressing ordinance in 1860. One essay even suggests that after their marriage, Hindle embraced men's clothing full time. "Hindle soon afterward began wearing men's clothes and retired from the stage, having amassed a small fortune."[63] Even if friends and neighbors knew Hindle wore men's clothes most of the time, the press sought to minimize this claim.

Female husband was no longer a designation reserved for those who were assigned female at birth and embraced the opportunity to live as both men and husbands. Now it was also used in reference to those known to have lived all of their lives as women while embracing various expressions of masculinity. The "female husband" moniker in the media no longer clearly established the subject as one who had transed gender. Instead, it created a bridge, helping to legitimize the idea of same-sex marriage between women.

LEROY WILLIAMS

A brief marriage between fifty-five-year-old Civil War veteran Leroy S. Williams and forty-eight-year-old Matilda D. Smith ended in a public dispute that made headlines. Williams had been living a simple, modest life in Sawetelle, Los Angeles, including a few years in the Sawetelle Veterans Home.[64] For many years, Williams sold fruits, vegetables, and cigars from their little shop.[65] The $12 a month pension Williams received in 1890 helped them to make ends meet.[66] Both Williams and Smith were lonely, which made them open to a risky but direct way of meeting a future spouse: a matrimonial paper.[67] We do not know of Williams' prior relationships but it certainly required a clarity of purpose to run such an ad, follow through on the correspondence, and meet up in person. Williams stated, "I had an advertisement in the paper for a wife and she wrote me in reply to it."[68] In addition to being lonely, Smith was physically tired from working at the needle to earn her keep and emotionally tired of living with her in-laws in Portland, Oregon in the wake of her husband's death.[69] After a period of time together in each other's company (which is highly disputed – she says a matter of hours, Williams says two weeks) they were legally wed on January 10, 1902.[70] After about three days of marriage (or four weeks, depending on who you believe), Matilda Smith wanted her marriage to be annulled and gave this as the reason: "He was no man, but a woman."[71] We have heard of similar stories in the past, but there were three key differences in this case: Smith did not give one piece of evidence to substantiate this claim, Williams denied it, and no third-party doctor or policeman corroborated the claim.[72]

As Smith told it to her lawyer and before the court, Williams was deceptive, if not an outright liar. The key matters of this claim concerned wealth and ability. Smith pictured a comfortable cottage in which they would build their lives together, only to discover Williams lived in a shack, no larger than eight by ten feet. Smith expected the cottage to sit comfortably on twelve acres of rolling hills, but Williams did not in fact own this land. Finally, Smith pictured a fully able man and was dismayed upon learning that Williams had lost a foot and part of a leg. Or at least this is her version. Before the court, she told of all this and more. If Williams was in fact assigned female, this seemed beside the point. The headlines read, "Mrs. Williams Swears She Married a Woman," but her chief complaints concerned Williams' failure to be the particular *kind of man* whom she hoped to attract: financially well off and able-bodied.

Williams was having none of this. Far from an apologetic, obfuscating, or confessional posture, Williams struck back not only against the facts of the case but also against Smith's gender, asserting, "I'm as much a man as she is a woman and a good deal more, for that matter."[73] Williams contends they spent "plenty of time" together before they were married in which it was easy for her to "find out all about" their finances and physical abilities. Williams was proud to be "a very lively invalid" who "came by it defending my country."[74] Williams claimed the couple lived together for about a week after the wedding before Smith took off for two weeks, returning and demanding money from Williams. After this, Smith applied for a divorce.

The judge threw out the case when neither Smith nor Williams showed up in court. It shed little light on the question of sex or the validity of the marriage. Rather, the only insight it offered to a curious public was a claim that Williams lied about the cause of the injury that cost them their foot. It was not in the war but rather an accident in 1889/ 90 in which the foot was "chewed up in a threshing machine."[75] This incident compelled Williams to a few years in the Veterans Home and also explains why they ran "a little candy store" rather than engaging in more lucrative but physically arduous work.[76]

The case might have been put to bed but the fact remained that female husband stories still caught readers' eyes and sold papers. Eight months after the initial hearing, it was rumored that Williams came into a small inheritance from a half-brother Peter.[77] This gave the old story new life, as a writer speculated that Matilda might want to remain married to Williams after all, stating, "In fact it was rumored at the Courthouse yesterday that Mrs. Williams lawyer was preparing a motion to dismiss the complaint." This baseless speculation, however, fueled the subtitle for the piece, "Wife May Withdraw Complaint for Annulment of Marriage When She Hears That Fortune is Smiling on 'Hubby' Whom She Says is Not a Man." Williams confirmed this was preposterous and that there would be no reconciliation, seeming more irked than fearful. The framing of this entire story, however, assumes Smith was disappointed that Williams had neither money nor the means to earn significantly more.

Williams never really addressed this aspect of the situation head-on but felt the need to fight back against the claim they were not a man.

Williams was said to have "vigorously denied that he was not of the masculine gender," and there are many different ways for one to do this, as we have seen.[78] Williams staked their claim to manhood on the assertion that two military doctors examined them and could confirm as much, stating, "How could I have passed a medical examination to get into the army, and again, to get a pension, if I was not a man? It seems to me that ought to settle the question of my sex if nothing else."[79] Nothing in this case seemed to challenge this assertion or raise doubt in the eyes of the Veterans Home or the pension administrators.[80]

This leads us to grapple with a singular question: Was Williams in fact assigned male? I believe the answer is yes, for three reasons: this story is unusual and different from other female husband accounts, Matilda Smith is the only source for the claim that Williams was a woman, and there was in fact someone named Leroy S. Williams of the right age who grew up in Illinois in a large family with a half-brother named Pete.[81] This story presents us with yet another twist, an entirely new meaning behind the term female husband. Now, even those assigned male at birth who lived and presented as men could be accused of not really being men. This did not come out of nowhere. Rather, for Smith to invoke such a charge points to a fascinating development. Smith believed that claiming her husband was not really a man was likely to win her sympathy and an annulment because it had been done before by female wives of female husbands.

JOHN A. WHITTMAN

Finances also played a major role in the story of John A. Whittman. On January 19, 1906, Whittman was married to co-worker Etta Jelley in Independence, Missouri. Jelley worked as a cashier in the same restaurant as Whittman, who worked as a cook.[82] Both lived lives of hardship and supported themselves in laboring occupations from young ages. The owner of the restaurant, a Mr. Cornell, had long looked out for Jelley who was described as disabled, with paralysis on her right side.[83] Jelley worked as a cashier for years – and then later as a binder.[84] Cornell also held Jelley's savings as a personal favor. Jelley was mad that Cornell refused to turn it over to her on the occasion of her wedding, but Cornell was afraid that Whittman would take it.[85] His suspicion that Whittman was after Jelley for her modest money was seemingly confirmed when it became apparent that Whittman had made no provisions for housing and caring for their young wife. Suspicious about this seeming indifference to taking care of Jelley, Cornell went to the authorities and accused Whittman of vagrancy.

Under the close inspection of the carceral authorities, Whittman was determined to be a liar on several accounts, including those of finances and sex. Accounts circulated that presented the news from two dramatically different perspectives. In Whittman's words, the marriage was Jelley's idea – a cover to get her boss to give her the money she saved to open a restaurant. "I have worked as a man and lived as one. I married this girl as a matter of accommodation; she said she couldn't live without me. My real name is Pauline Webster."[86] It was quite unusual for Whittman to offer their legal name at this point. This suggests one of two things: they believed they were in serious trouble and this admission alone would get them out of it, or they believed they had done nothing wrong and were not entirely wedded to their manhood and male identity.

Whittman offered a sympathetic account of their life to date: familial hardship and a need to work. They had always worked, mostly in hotels and restaurants until three years prior when they adopted male attire and an expression of manhood to secure a job that paid $60 a month to cook (far more than women were paid).[87] They did admit to lying about things to Jelley, especially money. In this regard, Whittman's betrayal of Jelley was real.[88] But Whittman also saved themself from the policing authorities by quickly telling the officials what they wanted to hear. Whittman did not defend their gender nor their identity, asserting instead, "I am a woman" and "My real name is Pauline Webster."[89] Whittman was said to be "prosecuted for perjury committed in obtaining the marriage license," but the case did not materialize when Whittman declared themself a woman and Jelley expressed disdain for Whittman and no desire to continue as a wife.[90] Whitman's willingness to be known as a woman and Jelley's desire to separate probably warded off a perjury trial and diffused the controversy.[91]

Despite Whittman's confession of womanhood, there was still ambiguity about their gender expressed in a variety of ways. One, Jelley referred to them using both pronouns. Two, stories combined female pronouns with masculine physical descriptions. Three, many versions of the story featured a special guide on how to be a man. Jelley's testimony was heartbreaking, "I loved him and thought that, with his money and my little savings we could buy a restaurant and make a good living."[92] In another version, Jelley expressed dismay, stating, "I cannot believe he-she-is a woman. It is too awful. I thank God, though I didn't leave Kansas City with him, or her, or – Oh, I don't know what to say. He wanted my money, little that it was."[93] If physical descriptions of Whittman are even remotely accurate, it easy to see why Jelley and everyone thought they were a man. This writer described someone masculine and unattractive, using female pronouns: "Her hair is cut short and it is stringy and neglected," and "Her voice is unpleasant, being soft and feminine one moment and breaking coarsely the next. Her teeth are worn and broken, and yellow from the use of tobacco."[94]

The best part of the coverage of the Whittman/Jelley marriage was the circulation of a special inserted box offering a guide to instruct those assigned female on how to live as men.[95] The inlay was titled, "What Pauline did to Appear like a Man," and offered the following unnumbered list: "Learned to smoke and chew tobacco; Practiced walking with long steps; Used a razor to induce a beard to come; Kept her hair clipped close; Enunciated slowly to avoid talking in high tones."[96] This list was amazing, combing recognition of the social and physical dimensions of gender-making. These instructions were reinforced by the images that accompanied the text in many of the stories. One commonly reprinted article included four different sketches of Whittman in a variety of situations: working, getting married, getting arrested, and staring straight at the camera (Figure 8.3). The carceral state played an expanded and visible role in this case. It was noted that "The woman prisoner was measured and photographed for the rogues' gallery this morning."[97] This image circulated far beyond the rogues' gallery, making its way across the country and into the hands of the reading public.

This story made it all the way to China, written principally with male pronouns in quotation marks, such as "This morning 'his' wife found 'him' at police headquarters, after she had searched all night." This account uses several different terms to reference a disjuncture between

PAULINE WEBSTER, "FEMALE HUSBAND."

Figure 8.3 "Eventful Career of a Woman Who Became 'Female Husband,'" *Spokane Press,* February 9, 1906. John Whittman was portrayed in series of photos capturing several moments in their life.
Image courtesy of the Library of Congress, Chronicling America

sex and gender, from the title, "Bridegroom is a Woman," to the line "her husband is a woman."[98] It also uses the somewhat new phrase indicating that sex is something fixed and visibly identifiable, stating "when 'his' true sex was revealed."[99] The rise of this notion that people had a "true sex" that was fixed, knowable, and binary was also accompanied by an explicit view that gender was distinct from sex and could be manipulated if one followed the right steps.

THE NATIONAL POLICE GAZETTE

Pictorial newspapers played an important role in American public life from the antebellum period onward. Mainstream staples such as *Frank Leslie's Illustrated News* catered to and cultivated a respectable middle-class readership. Others were less reputable, with a penchant for scandal and exaggeration. The *National Police Gazette* was one such publication, often characterized as a "men's" paper and known for mocking women in one way or another.[100] These sources present a challenge to historians aspiring to write histories of working-class and other marginalized people with nuance and respect, because they were often stereotyped and carica-tured.[101] *Frank Leslie's Illustrated News* portrayed laboring poor women and well-dressed socialites, indoors and out, in rural and urban settings. Despite this range, however, the paper seldom deviated from its celebration of a respectable womanhood palatable to a mainstream middling audience.[102]

More extreme renderings of a wider variety of experiences seem to have been reserved for men's papers. In this respect, the *National Police Gazette* is often described as less reputable, more debasing, and filled with "cruder titillations."[103] Their editorial policy embraced shock, scandal, and behaviors deemed eccentric and/or antisocial. This was often seen as sexist or demeaning of women. Perhaps women at the time felt that way. But the *National Police Gazette* also ensured that the lives of those people, including many who transed gender, would not go unremarked. In this way, the publication made a wide variety of gender nonconformity visible to a mass audience.

The *National Police Gazette* helped shape how readers encountered gender-transing subjects in an era of tremendous change. For gener-ations, readers of the daily, weekly, and monthly press, from newspapers to story papers, expected to encounter stories of people assigned female who put on men's clothes and lived as men. This was a great tradition, marked by tropes and justifications honed in the press over the years. By the 1870s, however, papers also reported on those who were assigned male at birth and transed gender to live as women. In these cases, a quite different set of terms and explanations were used. The *National Police Gazette* ran stories of all kinds of gender transing during this formative era. In this respect, wittingly or not, the editors sensationalized transgender expressions and helped to define what would later become known as a transgender subject. Although we discussed the life of Joseph Lobdell in Chapter 7, it is important to note that a major story about Lobdell and their life and romance with Marie Perry was featured in the *Gazette* in October 1879.[104]

The marriage between Samuel Pollard and Marancy Hughes was a featured cover story in the *Gazette* with a full-size image of the two. In this bedroom scene, Pollard is partly undressed, enabling their young wife to see their embodied difference. They are wearing a traditional men's dark suit and light-colored dress shirt. They are standing with their legs quite far apart, staring intently at their wife. Their hair is unmistakably a man's cut, parted to the side and a little long on the top. The only thing that signals to the viewer that Pollard was assigned female is the trace of breasts, as the shirt is halfway unbuttoned. They are wearing no under-shirt or binding of any kind. This is affirmed by the subtitle of the story, which declares, "The Supposed Bride Avers That the Ostensible Husband is a Well-Developed Woman."[105] This image is strikingly different from many that presented Pollard as mostly masculine. It is unrealistic in its portrayal of no binding or undershirt. It was potentially humiliating and sexist for Pollard and viewers who respected the rights of someone to trans gender without having their bodies subject to such a voyeuristic, demeaning gaze. The tension between what the trans subject wanted and what the reader craved was broken by favoring the reader, presumed to be male and heterosexual. But the *Gazette*'s representations in these cases were not simply harmful – they also gave life and light to stories that were uncommon and helped to establish transing gender as a thing that people did and would continue to do.

Frank Dubois was featured in the *Gazette* over a two-week period at the end of 1883. The picture of Frank Dubois which accompanied the first story in November was very masculine.[106] The headline that accompanied that story was charged with violence, however, noting that Dubois was "Threatened with Tar and Feathers."[107] Furthermore, objectifying lan-guage was used to dehumanize Dubois, as their wife's mother was said to refer to Dubois as a "thing."[108] While their mother-in-law cast them beyond humanity with this charge, Dubois' step-mother offered a different view, claiming that even in childhood they were "more like a boy than a girl." By consulting the various mothers of the parties involved, this account revealed an extensive network of family and friends who were all party to the lives of those who transed genders, each person making meaning of it in their own way. The *Gazette* also used a range of language in this piece about Dubois, from "man-woman" to "female in man's clothing." This suggests the terms were thought to be interchangeable – that Dubois and others like them might be viewed alternately as occupying a third gender category or simply as wearing clothes they were not supposed to.[109]

The *Gazette* was not all violence and slurs. Readers still wanted to know more about Dubois. The question of sex and gender was still up for debate. For much of the period under study in this book, a variety of people might be authorized to physically inspect the body of someone who transed gender, including a group of women, a policeman, a coroner, a judge, or a doctor. By the late nineteenth century, the authority of the medical profession was well established. In matters of determining sex, none but a doctor could say for sure. In this case, a doctor from Belvidere, Illinois where Dubois was said to have lived was invited to weigh in. The doctor claimed "that there can be little doubt as to the sex of Frank Dubois, as he attended her during confinement, when she was known as Mrs. Sam Hudson."[110] The weight of the doctor's opinion, combined with his use of their name from a previous marriage, served to undo Dubois' gender in the press.

The *National Police Gazette* specialized in sensational, scandalous, and violent crimes. One reason their coverage of gender transing has been overlooked is because their coverage of other things – terrible violence, major crimes, and competitive boxing – overshadowed the importance of any one person's gender. The fact that their coverage principally concerned crime, however, certainly marked gender transing as criminal and bolstered policing practices, both formal and informal. Informal systems of judgment, scorn, and ostracisms were still the most powerful forces in establishing a gender binary and hierarchy, but the explicit force of law was also invoked to deal with those rebellious, destitute, and disposable people who were beyond reach of other forces. Anti-cross-dressing laws both reacted against and helped to enable social and cultural norms that were increasingly supportive of expansive gender expressions.

* * *

Female husbands attracted unprecedented levels of visibility in the United States during the final decades of the nineteenth century, inspiring a wide range of debates and dilemmas. Transing gender faded in significance as the defining feature of the identity of a female husband as the category expanded to encapsulate same-sex relationships between women of any gender expression. Older concerns about how someone assigned female could live as a man, or particular descriptions about physical embodiment, were replaced with reflections on the existence and meaning of marriages between women. While female husbands and their wives already demonstrated that two people assigned female at birth were perfectly suited to partnerships, same-sex marriages offered the threat (or promise) of marriage without men or masculinity. Growing tolerance and recognition of same-sex relationships, such as that between Annie Hindle and Annie Ryan, may have intensified stigma against and hastened rejection of female husbands and other trans figures.[111]

Increasingly, not all who presented in masculine attire were socially stigmatized outliers. As long as those who embraced expansive genders conformed to dominant social values in other ways, they were generally tolerated, and sometimes celebrated. Civil War hero Dr. Mary Walker presented in men's clothing for decades. Walker was occasionally mocked in the press but nationally lauded, receiving the highest honor bestowed by the US military, the Medal of Honor. Walker was part of a movement of countless women who embraced more educational, occupational, and political rights along with new styles of dress. Clothing often involved modified versions of conventional men's clothing made specifically for women. There was no doubt that such people were assigned female, but they pushed the boundaries of gendered expression without raising too much ire. They were more tolerable if they did not partner with women, as male husbands minimized the social threat of their gender nonconformity.

Conclusion: Sex Trumps Gender

FEMALE HUSBAND WAS NEVER A SELF-DECLARED GENDER identification. The subjects of this book simply assumed the identity of "man" and the role of "husband." Few others ever would have known they lived a portion of their lives as girls before becoming men. It was a designation reserved for those who lived their lives fully as men – often beginning in their teenage years – until some accident or incident led to a revelation of their complicated pasts. Female husbands left home and recreated their lives among strangers. Most were alone when they decided to trans gender, facing the daunting prospect of becoming a new person in a new place all at once, alone. For some, separation from family and friends was devastating. For others, this change and forced relocation meant freedom. Despite all of its attendant hardships, this path was not without privilege. Within the British Empire, settler colonialism, slavery, and war determined the conditions for and parameters of most peoples' lives. Female husband narratives demonstrate a freedom, self-determination, and mobility that were hard to come by. In a way, they represent what Lisa Lowe describes as "the liberal affirmation of individualism, civility, mobility, and free enterprise" at the heart of modern liberalism.[1] Female husbands were not simply disruptors of heteronormativity and sexual difference; they were empowered by and helped to stabilize liberalism, including the white supremacy that was embedded in the gender binary.

It is no small matter that accounts of female husbands seldom raised the issue of children. In the eighteenth century, women were less likely to be seen as sexually powerful or threatening and more likely to be seen as domesticated and respectable wives and mothers. British imperialism helped bolster the centrality of motherhood, while maternity – especially that of white women – was a marker of civilization. Motherhood became much more central to the understanding of women's character than sexuality.[2] On a few occasions, wives of female husbands had children from prior relationships that female husbands helped raise after their marriage. When female husbands had children from prior marriages, the children were sometimes invoked as evidence of their sex and used to delegitimize their manhood. Shockingly, such accounts seldom reflect extensively on the husband's neglect of their maternal duty. There are several explanations for this. First, it presumes that their children are better off wherever they were left – with parents, ex-husbands, or siblings – than they would be with the female husband and their wife. Second, it suggests that the centrality of motherhood did not extend to the poor and laboring classes from which most husbands emerged. Third, it affirms their gender in that they were assessed by how good they were at being men, not women.

There are some timeless elements to the stories written about female husbands in the Anglo-American press from 1746 to 1910. When it came to reporting the news that someone assigned female at birth decided to live as a man and marry a woman, certain questions were nearly always raised, whether in Europe's greatest city or America's tiniest town. Why did they do it? How did they do it? Did their wives know?

When female husbands were given the chance to explain what motivated them, it was often under duress. The stated reason may have been the whole truth, a partial truth, or a complete fabrication intended to appease hostile neighbors or state officials. This book concedes the futility of trying to parse individual feelings and motivation. Instead, it focuses on the perceptions and views of others. This decision was informed by gender theories which claim the gender of any one person is constituted most fully and powerfully by those around them. If you wanted to be a man, you needed to be seen by others as a man.[3] This relational dimension of gender was demonstrated repeatedly throughout the female husband narratives – in ways that are both affirming and negating – revealing the power of recognition and relationships in establishing identity.

There are several plausible arguments as to why female husbands lived the lives they lived. One explanation is that people transed gender so that they might get to love, have sex with, and marry a woman because they weren't allowed to do so as a woman. This explanation posits female husbands as historic antecedents to modern-day lesbians, bisexuals, pansexuals, or queer women. Another explanation is that people wanted to live as men – or to not live as women – regardless of the romantic or sexual implications. Financial security, geographic mobility, and/or gender identity were all motivating factors. Gender, not sexuality, was the saliant category. A third explanation is that they intentionally wanted both a romantic partnership with a woman and the experience of manhood. For them, masculinity was given weight and meaning by the recognition of their female lover. This group bares resemblance to some who identify as transmen, transbutches, and butches in the present.

How did they do it? The means by which someone assigned female transed genders remained remarkably constant for over 150 years. Before medical advances made it possible for people to change their sex, transitions involved presenting oneself as a man of one's race, rank, and region presented himself. The key practice, then, involved acquiring a set of men's clothes, including men's undergarments. Some accounts mention chest binding. While some also cut their hair, short hair was not necessarily a common or universal code of manhood. People often ask if menstruation was an issue in outing people as assigned female, but I have never seen the issue referenced even once in the thousands of accounts I have read.[4] There are a few reasons why people may not have menstruated regularly, chiefly diet and exercise. Other characteristics with strong correlations to sex, such as facial hair or the pitch of one's voice, were generally noted only in hindsight. In other words, no one was outed solely because of one of these factors but when they were outed, neighbors and co-workers often pointed to these areas to find clues and affirmation. While many people transed genders for short periods of time, most female husbands featured here did so for decades undetected. This suggests they were exceptional in their ability to pass as men, which would have been easier for some than others.

Did their wives know? When asked if they knew, most female wives were in situations of great distress. Their husbands had died or were being detained by the police. Most wives, as well as husbands, engaged in selective truth telling and strategic cooperation in order to minimize any persecution, violence, or harassment. Sometimes they were met with sympathy, compassion, and/or pity. Other times they were attacked and had their own gender interrogated. Taken at its most literal, the question asks if the wives knew their husbands were assigned female. But they were not just any relative, friend, or co-worker; rather, as a wife, sexual intimacies were expected to be a fundamental constitutive dimension of the relationship. In asking if the wives "knew," then, authorities and reporters were asking a more profound question about sexual intimacy.[5] To "know" someone in this context is to really know them – to have had sex.

Wives in long-term relationships certainly knew the truth of their husbands. The suggestion that they did not – and the desire of reporters and the public to believe it – is absurd. But this denial was a crucial part of the reporting of female husbands and their wives. First, it established distance between the two. Second, it allowed readers to imagine their relationship as a sexless one. Third, it encouraged readers to believe that two people assigned female probably couldn't have pleasurable sex together. This framing advanced the idea that female husbands and wives were probably friends, not lovers. The alternative – that they experienced great sexual satisfaction together – was too dangerous. In most cases, however, the question of sexual intimacy was not explicitly denied. Newspaper editors knew such unresolved issues might lure readers in and motivate them to buy the next week's paper. All of that said, I do believe the claims made in some of the cases that the wives really did not know. In these cases, the wives generally told someone within weeks of marriage and sought an annulment.

* * *

Perceptions of female husbands changed gradually for numerous reasons. Attitudes about sex and sexuality changed throughout the eighteenth century. General ambiguity about the nature of sexual difference itself explains the somewhat unpredictable and wide-ranging responses to female husbands in the eighteenth century – from brutal public whippings to a certain amount of public respect.[6] The early nineteenth century marked the heyday of female husbands in the UK. These accounts came to embody the hardships of married life, defined by hard work, excessive drinking, and fighting between husbands and wives. These accounts increasingly emphasized the goodness of women and the weaknesses of men. They demonstrated the wide variety of responses to husbands and wives by the state, from support and respect to hostility and derision. They advanced the view that living as a man *made one into more of a man*, and that anyone could do it. Just because anyone *could*, however, does not mean that everyone or even significant numbers of people *did*. They revealed competing ways of defining sex, when a marriage certificate said one thing and a doctor declared another. Relatives and neighbors took matters into their own hands, looking for a pattern of social relations, scrutinizing a person's embodiment, and largely looking to the wife for an explanation.

By the mid-nineteenth century, female husbands were viewed in relation to the women's rights movement. Though not known to organize politically, they were seen as a symptom of the movement to expand what was possible for women. While accounts of people transing gender to secure work as men were treated relatively sympathetically, those who claimed other male privileges – such as the right to marry a woman or have sex with a woman – were viewed differently. They crossed a line. By the late nineteenth century, popular attitudes in the press toward female husbands reflected a different view of gender and became generally more hostile. This can be seen in subtle shifts in the retelling of older accounts. This was principally marked by a shift toward gendered names, pronouns, categories, and groupings that were female in reference to female husbands. Stories that were once complex and murky accounts that left it to the reader to grapple with and interpret the limits of gender were replaced by more simplistic, reductive, and sometimes hostile stories.

The phrase "woman husband" was used more frequently later in the nineteenth century. The old phrase "female husband" connoted two kinds of things – sex and gender – whereas "woman husband" connoted one kind of thing – gender. If we recognize "woman" as a socially constructed gender category, we can see that this shift from female husband to woman husband is a meaningful one. This usage aims to naturalize the category of woman, conflate it with biological sex, and disguise all of the learned norms and behaviors that go into making one a "woman." Its message is truly a contradiction because to be a woman was fundamentally at odds with being a husband. Observers might strategically use the term "woman husband" to reduce, erase, or minimize the threat of female manhood or female masculinity that female hus-band connoted. In the late nineteenth century, when the two were used interchangeably, this paved the way for the erasure of the manhood and masculinity that was the defining characteristic of earlier husbands. In the twentieth century, individuals might be called "woman husbands" or couples referred to as "woman marriages."[7] This elevated recognition and visibility of same-sex relationships and intimacies. It naturalized the category of woman. It removed gender transing from the equation.

In the eighteenth century, female husbands were less threatening because the prospects for widespread gains in women's education, eco-nomic opportunities, and political rights seemed dim. But advances in women's advocacy, autonomy, and mobility made the prospect of a world without men more imaginable. Heterosexuality was fragile. Articles warned women not to be lured into thinking a female husband was better than a male husband. New concerns about female homosexuality motivated doctors and psychiatrists to protect white women who ascribed to conventional gender norms from the threat of those who transed gender, especially if they were African American. Medicine threatened potential female husbands with a diagnosis of "abnormal" and forced institutionalization. But such policing and stigmatizing efforts themselves never fully deterred people from transing gender.[8]

The turn of the twentieth century marked an increased stigmatization of certain kinds of gender expressions. Doctors associated those who transed gender with mental illness and sexual deviance. At the same time, there was a great expansion in the range of ways people assigned female were able to relate to the category of woman. Female strength was celebrated. Writers turned to those who transed gender in the past and celebrated them again despite growing stigma from other quarters. Female masculinity retained its place in popular discourse as something that *could* be positive. Advances in women's access to education, physical activity, political rights, and employment opportunities were significant and supported this claim.

Female husband waned as a descriptor in the British and US press after 1910. Sexologists characterized those with trans gender identifica-tion as pathological and abnormal. The carceral state wielded its author-ity in service of ridding society of those who threatened its order. These two forces created tremendous incentives for people who were transing gender to make themselves as undetectable as possible, to find other routes to express and experience their gender, or to reframe their masculinity as a tool for realizing same-sex desire. Though largely the reserve of middling and upper-class women, there was a longstanding tolerance of "female marriages." Such relationships were between women who were known by others as women, living together "in part-nerships visibly modeled on marriage."[9] This was widespread in Victorian England but also evident in antebellum America.[10] Certainly some found refuge in such relationships.

With the rise of the LGBTQ rights movement in the 1970s, research-ers began looking for evidence of sexual and gender minorities in every imaginable place, period, and field of study. Historian Jonathan Ned Katz brought to life long-lost archival sources in his pathbreaking *Gay American History* and the follow-up *Gay/Lesbian Almanac.*[11] These volumes included primary source materials on several husbands featured in this book, including Joseph Lobdell and James Howe. The framing of these subjects reflected the needs and concerns of its time. For Katz, it was imperative to put out a book on gay history that was not male-centric. Highlighting records of women who could in some way or another be described as "gay" led to the grouping of a variety of people who transed gender under the title "passing women."[12] This intellectual and political decision had merits: it raised the visibility of women in the queer past. But at what cost? As we have seen throughout this book, these so-called "passing women" *seemingly* did everything they could to escape the category of woman.

We don't know – and likely never will – precisely what motivated each individual person. In that respect, the subjects of this study confound our contemporary notions of gender identity. That should not, however, undermine the power they offer us as a window into our collective past – and future. In requiring us to learn about them as they were perceived by others, female husbands refuse us a simple self-determined assertion of gender identity. This was, of course, not their doing. Who knows how many diaries and letters were burned in which female husbands wrote to wives, friends, and future generations about love, desire, betrayal, or joy? Given the class status of most, however, this was unlikely. But what of the wives – a few of whom were noted as educated and middle class? Did they commit their feelings to paper, explaining how they understood their attraction to and relationship with their husbands? If so, these records are also lost to us – or written in code.

Absent such self-declarations, I have aspired to write about them in a way that is both expansive and clear. I wanted to allow for a trans reading of their lives without foreclosing on the idea that some may have identified with the category of woman. I also wanted to hold gender and sexuality as a web of desires and experiences that might develop, conflict, and change over time. To allow for both of these things, I only used gender neutral pronouns in reference to female husbands and others who transed genders. I chose "they/them/theirs." I did this because most female husbands lived trans lives but also because their lives reveal in a significant and ongoing way the overlap between categories of gender and sexuality, refusing a simple reductive reading as one or the other as a driving force.

Why didn't I use "he/him/his" to fully embrace their manhood, when most clearly lived as men? There are three reasons. First, to embrace "he/him/his" in reference to a female husband's life would have forced an undesirable compromise: either only refer to them using masculine pronouns, even prior to their transition (which erases their childhood in advancing a unified narrative of manhood); or refer to them with feminine pronouns for part of their life and masculine pronouns after their transition (which would serve to stabilize girlhood/womanhood in a false way). To embrace "he/him/his" would stabilize manhood in a way that does not capture the experience of all female husbands across their lifespan, as several embraced a nonbinary gender, moving back and forth between male and female gender expressions at least once. To embrace "he/him/his" would undermine the possibility that some husbands were in fact driven by same-sex attraction and only occupied manhood as a means to that end. For all of these reasons, reading and writing trans histories offers us an opportunity to move past some of our very particular identity borders in search of a more expansive and collective understanding.

Such was the call of the "antiracist white, working-class, secular Jewish, transgender, lesbian, female revolutionary communist," writer Leslie

Feinberg.[13] Feinberg's writings addressed sexuality and gender in an overlapping way that was anchored in the experience and needs of workers.[14] They embraced a variety of identities and expressions in their life, including butch, trans, and lesbian. They refused attempts to resolve the contradictions between their assigned sex and gender expression. For instance, Feinberg did not want to be referred to by "he/him/his" pronouns in non-trans settings because they argued it would serve to erase their transgender expression.[15] This is not to say, however, that Feinberg didn't enjoy having their manhood seen and acknowledged with masculine pronouns within the trans community – they did. For Feinberg, their gender was situational. Different forms of recognition and expression felt validating for them, depending on the context.

I hope that I have been true to the lives and legacies of female husbands and their wives in this telling. Their stories offer us a fresh perspective on the past. This radical and longstanding tradition of resistance to gender norms was well documented. These accounts – like our lives – are marked not only by resilience, love, and joy but also vulnerability, loneliness, and conflict. This piece of LGBTQ history has been written and cannot be erased. It is true and it belongs to us.

Epilogue: The First Female-to-Male Transsexual

Each of us must take into account the raw material which heredity dealt us at birth and the opportunities we have had along the way, and then work out for ourselves a sensible evaluation of our personalities and accomplishments.

Dr. Alan L. Hart[1]

As long as gender was changed socially and informally – by the cut of one's hair and the style of one's clothes – it could mean any number of things. This allowed for alignment, conflation, or common cause between any number of people transing gender, from those who momentarily challenged the constraints of women's lives to those who lived fully as men in the world. In all of these cases, one key united them: such a change could be undone. For hundreds of years, we have seen parents, employers, and carceral authorities order such people to surrender their men's clothing and put on a dress or other attire deemed appropriate for women. In their eyes, since men's clothing facilitated the transformation of one's gender, women's clothing could undo the transformation – at least for the most part.

In the twentieth century, new avenues opened up for those who wanted to permanently change their bodies to reflect their gender. Many forces converged to enable this development, including changes in medicine that led doctors increasingly to use invasive surgeries to treat women for a variety of conditions. This trend was not universally celebrated. Some believed doctors were too quick to operate, citing women's loss of childbearing capacity and hormones which would "unsex" women in the process. Others noted the potential for abuse, as racist eugenicist sterilization projects targeted African American, American Indian, and poor immigrant women.[2] The eugenics movement also called for the sterilization of sexual deviants.[3]

While the charge of being "unsexed" was used as a slur and meant to point to something undesirable for women, this view was not universally held. For those assigned female at birth who wanted to live fully as men, the opportunity to be "unsexed" through a medical procedure was a dream. Hysterectomies were also a source of liberation for those who could convince doctors to administer them. This and other procedures that *could* facilitate a sex change were developed at the same time some doctors became obsessed with the psychology of sex.

Still, it was a challenge for any patient to convince a doctor to pursue a series of invasive medical procedures on what appeared to be healthy tissue. An early recipient of such treatment who wanted to deliberately "unsex" themself was an exception, not the norm. This person had access to the latest scientific theories of gender and was able to use this information to persuade their doctor to remove their uterus. Eugenicist arguments for the sterilization of sexual deviants surely played a part as well. Dr. Alan L. Hart, often celebrated as the first woman to graduate from the University of Oregon medical school, pursued a medical transition shortly thereafter.[4] In 1917, they underwent a hysterectomy and sterilization so their body was more aligned with what their doctor called their "natural male instincts" and "aggressive male characteristics."[5] This was not celebrated in the press or widely known at the time. They did, however, begin living full time as a man and secured an internship at a San Francisco Hospital under the name Dr. Alan L. Hart (Figure E.1). They legally married a woman – Inez Stark – as a man.[6]

The only obvious difference between Hart and the so-called female husbands in this book was Hart's access to a gender affirming surgery. Maybe Hart knew of female husbands and drew on their lives for inspiration while charting the course of their own life. We will never know for certain if any or all of the female husbands would have chosen this procedure if it was available to them. And if they did, what would have compelled this choice: To lessen the effects of estrogen? To not menstruate? To remove one's capacity for childbirth? To be less of a woman? To be more of a man? Does the *motivation* really matter if the result is the same?

Figure E.1 "Alan L. Hart," 1943. Dr. Alan L. Hart was a medical doctor, an expert in tuberculosis, and a writer.
Author photo, *These Mysterious Rays* by Alan L. Hart (Harper & Brothers, 1943)

It is impossible to isolate the role of medical knowledge in shaping Hart's sense of themself. Highly intelligent, motivated, and a leader, Hart's unease about their sex may have motivated their decision to attend medical school in the first place, where they would have access to the latest studies and information about sexual difference. Here they could learn the medical diagnoses and terms that allowed them to believe they had a "condition" as someone who was "not like other girls." Hart's so-called condition was highly social and subjective. In the words of Dr. Gilbert, "her condition seemed so natural to herself and she was so strong and healthy that she gave the matter but little thought." While there was no denying that Hart's difference was a problem, even Gilbert's assessment points to the idea that social norms and judgment were the true source of Hart's troubles. He continued: "However, her mode of dressing – men's coats, collars, ties, tailored hats, English shoes, etc. – made her conspicuous and the object of so much criticism and conjecture as to make her very uncomfortable."[7]

Hart was creative, ambitious, and resourceful. They were a leader who received recognition and won awards their entire life. They led their debate team in high school and received fourth place for their essay on "The Treason of Benedict Arnold" in the Sons of American Revolution essay contest.[8] They were awarded the prestigious Saylor medal from the University of Oregon "offered to the graduate in highest standing in all departments."[9] The women's movement made space for their ambitions and talent.

As an educated person with a professional degree, Hart stands apart from many of those visibly noted for transing gender in the nineteenth century. In this regard, Hart had everything to lose professionally by their transition.[10] By 1917, women physicians were carving out a place for themselves in the profession and Hart could have joined them with all of the respect and accolades they racked up during their college and medical school years. Instead, Hart became a "nobody" and was taunted by former friends and classmates who recognized them as the person previously known by the name Lucille.

A series of stories ran in early 1918 when a former male classmate from Stanford University encountered Hart while working as an intern at San Francisco Hospital. One story that was reprinted under numerous headlines including "Girl Shaves and Smokes" and "Safety Razor and Cigarets Do Not Always Mean Male" signaled how gender was defined largely through social gestures and consumer goods. It warned readers that such gestures, however, were no longer foolproof indicators of sex, stating, "Just because a hospital interne smokes cigaretes and owns a safety razor, it is no reason to be sure that the interne isn't a woman."[11] The story offered a brief attempt to explain why Hart would pursue this course, stating that Hart "was afraid she would fall as a doctor in skirts and curls – so she cast them aside."[12] The explanation, then, mocked women for being clumsy and irrational and framed Hart as sign of the women's movement's failures.

This incident was also confirmed by Dr. Gilbert. In his 1920 article he wrote, "Having an 'M.D.' degree she applied for and was appointed to a position in a hospital where she 'made good' in every way until she was recognized by a former associate under the operation of that fanciful law of chance which threw one of her former intimate associates across her track."[13] Gilbert felt badly for Hart and attributed this harassment to a flawed set of social values and norms, never once suggesting or implying that Hart was the problem or deserved abuse or exposure. "Sensible to the extreme, she accepted her condition as one of abnormal inversion and was ready to face the affair on its merits."[14] For Gilbert, Hart made a reasonable and rational decision in embracing life as a man.

A follow-up story verified the identity of the doctor and the truth of the claim. A reporter interviewed Hart's family in Albany, Oregon. The "relatives" confirmed not only that Hart had taken to wearing "male attire" but they had done so for "several months" at this point. Hart's family's knowledge and endorsement of this practice surely took the wind out of any sails that might have made the story become a national scandal. They defended Hart by drawing on the long legacy of those assigned female who lived and passed as common laboring men, stating that Hart "has as much right to dress in convenient attire as any woman engaged in factory or shop work."[15] Another follow-up account editorialized as to Hart's personality, stating, "Dr. Hart has been noted for independence in thought and action particularly in the discarding of feminine frills and substitution of more simple and mannish modes."[16] These assessments are devoid of the stigma associated with sexuality or sexual inversion. They belong to the past – the long nineteenth century's obsession with women and work – rather than the future – sexology's obsession with female masculinity and sexual inversion. This suggests the transition between the two occurred later and less completely than historians generally claim.

For Hart, there was really no question that this was the right course for them – despite all of the risk and hardship involved. Four months after this dreaded publicity appeared, Hart explained themself to the press, stating, "For years I had been unhappy. With all the inclinations and desires of the boy I had to restrain myself to the more conventional ways of the other sex. I have been happier since I made this change than I ever have in my life, and I will continue this way as long as I live."[17] While we might try to parse Hart's words in search of the most singular or compelling factor that drove them to seek manhood (heteronormativity? male privilege?) that is beside the point. For Hart, there was one binary: happiness vs. unhappiness. They chose happiness.

Once gay historians determined that Dr. Alan Hart was assigned female at birth, many celebrated Hart as an early "lesbian" or "passing woman" who used gender as a vehicle to pursue relationships with women.[18] Though Hart only attended Stanford University very briefly, the school claimed them as their own, granting them the first entry on a 1984 list celebrating "Gay Men and Lesbians at Stanford University: A Chronology" for their 1984 GALA Week.[19] Hart was celebrated in 1991 in Oregon by gay and lesbian activists who characterized them as someone who "was run out of Albany, Oregon for living as a lesbian on her own terms."[20] Transgender scholars and activists challenged this assessment for situating gender as secondary rather than as the principle defining factor of Hart's life. Of this struggle, one scholar noted, "Hart's biography is manipulated by others in order to contribute to various 'origin stories' that validate epistemological categories of 'lesbian' or 'transsexual.'"[21] The fact of this struggle points to the ideological anxiety over the category of woman that has fractured some lesbian and trans-gender communities. But more importantly, it confirms the ambiguity surrounding those who challenged dominant norms of gender and sexuality. Despite the best medical minds of the era constantly trying to categorize and define people, Hart and others like them persisted in evading neat classification.[22]

As a college student, Hart felt nostalgic about the freedom reserved for those understood to be tomboys and wrote about it in their 1911 college yearbook, stating,

> Perhaps you were called a Tom-boy; probably you deserved the name. You liked to ride the horses at a wild gallop over the big pasture. You were

entranced when grandfather made you a little wooden gun, and began straightaway, in the back-yard, to enact the Civil War and other dreadful scenes of carnage. You passed whole hours of delight in the toolroom making all sorts of things that never would go.

But time did not stand still, and now Hart and their college-aged peers were expected to adhere to a different code of conduct, one which Hart bemoaned, stating, "when you are strictly honest, don't you wish you hadn't grown up and come to the day when you must look in the glass to see if your nose shines, and, if it does, powder it accordingly." Furthermore, Hart mocked the rituals and amusements that were typically enjoyed by girls. "You sneered at the mild games of the girls; you scorned playing house and were altogether superior to dolls."[23] Instead, even at this age, Hart embraced bold activities such as "dressing up in boy's clothes and scandalizing the whole neighborhood," or saving up their money so they could buy "a straw hat like the one Johnny Brown wore" once their mother refused the purchase.[24]

Hart continued writing in defense of women's liberation, and dress reform in particular. In 1913 they penned an editorial against efforts to restrict women's dress, either by custom or by law. Hart wrote, "It would be much more to the point if men would pay more attention to their own morals and less to criticism of women's clothing."[25] Furthermore, Hart tried to elevate the focus away from clothing in particular to a broader engagement with society, stating, "The remedy will be found not in a swathing, formless, all-concealing garment for women, but in stronger backbones for our whole body social."[26] The issue of dress restrictions at this time was fought from both sides: a wave of new anti-cross-dressing laws aimed at stigmatizing gender nonconformity, removing such people and expressions from the public sphere, and reinforcing clear binary gender roles for men and women, often anchored in whiteness. In the western part of the country, they took root in San Francisco, California (1866; 1903), Oakland, California (1879), San Jose, California (1882), Tucson, Arizona (1883), Butte, Montana (1885), Denver, Colorado (1886), and Cheyenne, Wyoming (1892).[27] These laws did not appear in a vacuum, however, but rather reacted to the visible and growing movement to expand women's access to public life, education, viable employment, and political rights. This included freedom to dress as they pleased, sometimes in men's clothes or in a close approximation. Hart saw themself as part of the women's movement, fighting for an expansion in women's rights and freedoms. But the push from the other side – to stigmatize, criminalize, and make life untenable for those who fully crossed genders – would damage Hart's career and threaten their safety for their entire life.

Born to a financially secure white family, Hart had the resources and support to pursue their education. This status of access and respectability, along with Hart's talent and drive, shaped the way everyone saw them, including their psychologist. Joshua Allen Gilbert was born in Ohio in 1867. He received his BA from Otterbein University in 1889 and PhD in psychology from Yale in 1894. His dissertation was titled "Researches on the Mental and Physical Development of School Children." Gilbert worked as a physician and assistant professor of clinical medicine at the University of Oregon, Eugene.[28] His wife Florence died in 1917. In 1920, when he published his case study of Hart, he was a fifty-two-year-old widower with a fourteen-year-old girl named Dorthea and a live-in housekeeper.[29] There was nothing remarkable in Gilbert's career to signal that he would treat Hart with empathy, but his report of their sessions and Hart's very personal reflections reveal that he viewed Hart with curiosity and humanity, not disgust and pity.

Gilbert's assessment of Hart was wide ranging and fascinating. It linked Hart to the distant past through references to "tribadism," which was long used to describe sexual intimacies between women, to nineteenth-century signifiers of manhood such as "smoking, drinking, and going to fast cafes" and to modern transgender/butch sexual practices of male identification: "Mrs. D. would call H 'Dear boy'" and "I.C. often said going about with her was exactly like going with a man."[30] In these brief excerpts alone, it is evident that any attempt to separate sex, gender, and sexuality is a fool's errand. All of these dimensions of experience were bound together in Gilbert's notes. Hart blurred time, transcended the limitations of physical embodiment, and experienced great sexual pleasure with women. It is true that Gilbert, like many sexologists of the era, wrote a great deal about the sexual encounters

274

that Hart described. Sex, it seemed, was at the heart of their relationships – or at least was the most intriguing dimension for Gilbert.

In Gilbert's rendering, Hart became a man not simply by donning men's clothes, as was the common account of the nineteenth century. Rather, after extensive reflection and consultation with both a psychologist and a medical doctor, Hart's commitment to manhood was signaled by the hysterectomy. As Gilbert recalled, "Hysterectomy was performed, her hair was cut, a complete male outfit was secured and having previously identified herself with red cross, she made her exit as a female and started as a male with a new hold on life and ambitions worthy of her high degree of intellectuality."[31] There are many ways to assess whether this was the right decision for Hart – personally, or in the eyes of Gilbert and others. As was long the case with female husbands, the ability to attract the interest and love of a woman was granted significant weight. Gilbert wrote, "Her natural male instincts carried her into associations with the female sex and positive attractions were unavoidable. Women of normal sex life felt themselves attracted by her because of her aggressive male characteristics. One, to whom she is now married, fell in love with her because of her psychological characteristics."[32] Hart's manhood was thus sealed, not with the surgery that "unsexed" them, nor by their dress, but once again by the affirmation of another person: a woman who became Hart's wife.

Hart was married twice: the first marriage to Inez Stark 1918 could not weather the tumult caused by Hart's outing in San Francisco. Hart found love again and married Edna Ruddick in Manhattan, New York on May 15, 1925.[33] Faced with a series of professional setbacks due to threats of outings about their gender as well as broader economic downturns, Hart put their professional medical training aside for a time and picked up a pen instead. They authored three works of fiction and one nonfiction, all published by major houses and many reviewed widely in the national press, including *Doctor Mallory* (1935), *In the Lives of Men* (1937), *Doctor Finlay Sees it Through* (1942), and *These Mysterious Rays* (1943).[34] Rumors and threats that plagued Hart professionally in the Pacific Northwest in the 1920s did not emerge in the national media coverage they received as an author. They settled in West Hartford, Connecticut. Hart passed the Connecticut State Medical Board in 1945 and was licensed to practice in the state.[35] Hart worked as X-ray director of the Connecticut State Health Department Office of Tuberculosis Control. Hart was even pictured in the paper with the mayor's wife and a technician showing off a new X-ray machine and was frequently featured in the local press educating the public on a wide variety of subjects.[36] They became active members of the First Unitarian Congregational Society of Hartford.[37] Hart served as vice president of the society in 1953.[38] When Hart died in 1962 the obituary was straightforward, with no hint that Hart was different from other men. Rather, Hart was simply described as husband of Edna (Ruddick) Hart of West Hartford, Connecticut.[39] Edna lived for decades after Hart's death.

* * *

Historians of sexuality once had to rely significantly on medical journals and court records to find enough discussion of gender and sexual nonconformity to craft a narrative of the past. These records are still invaluable but are now considered within a much broader context and a wider array of sources, from diaries and memoirs to novels, newspapers, and organizational papers. Digital technologies enable historians to bring together a dazzling array of source material on one person that previously may have taken a team of people decades to piece together. This is certainly the case here in regards to our discussion of Hart, which cites just a few of the dozens of news stories in which they appeared as a fierce and talented youngster, scandalized medical resident, accomplished novelist, and respected community leader. Dr. Gilbert's obsessive detailing of Hart's sexual experiences shrinks in significance when we are able to see Hart's life over time in a more holistic fashion – even without significant personal writings in Hart's own voice.

Hart's life provides a powerful bridge across time. Their early writings anchor them within quintessential nineteenth-century demands for women's equality. Their decision as a young person to have a hysterectomy so that they would no longer menstruate or have childbearing capacity makes them an early pioneer of practices that would become routine for trans people by the late twentieth century. Only a handful of people assigned female at birth – mostly accomplished athletes from

Europe – sought to have their sex medically changed in the 1930s and 1940s. News reports on this group were framed as celebrations of extreme athleticism that distinguished these people from others. Mark Weston, noted British shot-put and javelin thrower, was one of the first, allegedly saying, "I began to realize that I was abnormal and [had] no business competing in women's games." Weston reported a quick and easy process of medical transition, citing just several weeks between their first consultation with a specialist and two ensuing surgeries at Charing Cross Hospital that enabled them to return home "as a man."[40] One year later in 1937, headlines rang out touting "Another Sportswoman Changes Sex, Fourth in Recent Months," recounting numerous similar cases, including a Belgian cyclist named Debruyne, a "champion girl athlete" from Czechoslovakia named Koubek, and an unnamed "Polish girl athlete" in addition to the previously mentioned Weston.[41] Before the summer came to an end, another female athlete followed suit, this time a twenty-four-year-old tennis player from Wellington, New Zealand.[42]

Sex change surgeries were still rare. Despite this early wave of stories about female-to-male sex changes in the period between the wars, it wasn't until after World War II that such procedures became more common. The first prominent case in the United States involved Christina Jorgensen in the early 1950s, who went to Europe for a series of surgeries, returning to the United States a celebrity drawing headlines such as "Ex-GI Turned Blonde Beauty."[43] In this era, people assigned male at birth who sought to change their sex that they might live as women became more visible. Most doctors and psychiatrists worked with those assigned male at birth who wanted to live as women.

Female husbands charted a course that made way for a variety of people who came after them seeking liberation from the category of woman, the gender norms expected of women, and/or heterosexual relationships with men. Their impact transcends any one simple reading of their gender or sexuality. Those who followed in their wake lived lives that were lesbian, bisexual, gay, pansexual, queer, femme, butch, aggressive/AG, stud, transgender, transsexual, and nonbinary. Some of them entered into respectable same-sex partnerships with women as women. Some embraced the opportunity to transition or live in-between genders. Others embraced the masculinity associated with categories such as butch, stud, or AG. Some embraced their own femininity and chose partners who were masculine, trans, androgynous, or feminine. All of these paths were made possible, wider, and more acceptable in the twentieth century because of the courage, visibility, and suffering of the female husbands and female wives who came before them. If only each successive generation had not been denied access to these powerful stories – the history of their ancestors. If only they had known they were not alone but rather part of a movement against the conflation of sex with gender. If only we had known sooner what female husbands knew in their hearts all along: that gender was theirs for the making and that what makes a man is not the sex they are assigned at birth but the life they live, day in and day out, whether in 1746, 1906, or today.

NOTES

INTRODUCTION: EXTRAORDINARY LIVES

1. Valerie Traub defines queer historicism as "one that seeks to explain such categories' constitutive, pervasive, and persistent force." Valerie Traub, *Thinking Sex with the Early Moderns* (Philadelphia: University of Pennsylvania Press, 2015), 81.

2. Most saw those transing genders as seeking economic, social, or political power. Daniel A. Cohen, ed., *The Female Marine and Related Works: Narratives of Cross-Dressing and Urban Vice in America's Early Republic* (Amherst: University of Massachusetts Press, 1998); Fraser Easton, "Gender's Two Bodies: Women Warriors, Female Husbands and Plebian Life," *Past and Present*, no. 180 (August 2003): 131–74; Alfred F. Young, *Masquerade: The Life and Times of Deborah Sampson, Continental Soldier* (New York: Vintage, 2005); Michael McKeon, "Symposium: Before Sex – The Seventeenth- and Eighteenth-Century Sexuality Hypothesis," *Signs: Journal of Women in Culture and Society* 37, no. 4 (2012): 791–801, 793.

3. Judith Butler, *Gender Trouble: Feminism and the Subversion of Identity* (New York: Routledge, 1990); Jay Prosser, "Judith Butler: Queer Feminism, Transgender, and the Transubstantiation of Sex," in Susan Stryker and Stephen Whittle, eds., *The Transgender Studies Reader* (New York: Routledge, 2006), 257–80.

4. Joan Scott describes gender as "not the assignment of roles to physically different bodies, but the attribution of meaning to something that always eludes definition." Joan W. Scott, *The Fantasy of Feminist History* (Durham, NC: Duke University Press, 2011), 6; also see "Gender: A Useful Category of Historical Analysis," *The American Historical Review* 91, no. 5 (December 1986): 1053–75 and "Some More Reflections on Gender and Politics," in *Gender and the Politics of History*, 2nd edition (New York: Columbia University, 1999), 199–222; Jeanne Boydston, "Gender as a Question of Historical Analysis," *Gender and History* 20, no. 3 (November 2008): 558–83.

5. Richard D. Brown, *Knowledge Is Power: The Diffusion of Information in Early America, 1700–1865* (New York: Oxford University Press, 1991); Jeffrey L. Pasley, *The Tyranny of Printers: Newspaper Politics in the Early American Republic* (Charlottesville: University of Virginia Press, 2001); Joshua Brown, *Beyond the Lines: Pictorial Reporting, Everyday Life, and the Crisis of Gilded Age America* (Berkeley: University of California Press, 2002); Andrew Pettegree, *The Invention of News: How the World Came to Know About Itself* (New Haven: Yale University Press, 2014).

6. Kevin Williams, *Read All About It! A History of the British Newspaper* (Routledge: New York, 2010), 68, 85, 127; Guy Reel, *The National Police Gazette and the Making of the Modern American Man, 1879–1906* (New York: Palgrave, 2006), 44; Lisa Duggan described a "continuum of publication" about the "lesbian love narrative" at the turn of the twentieth century, a concept which applies to female husbands for quite an extended period of time. Lisa Duggan, *Sapphic Slashers: Sex, Violence, and American Modernity* (Durham, NC: Duke University Press, 2001): 180–1.

7. Cathy N. Davidson, *Revolution and the Word: The Rise of the Novel in America* (New York: Oxford University Press, 1987); Diane Dugaw, *Warrior Women and Popular Balladry, 1650–1850* (New York: Cambridge University Press, 1989); Robert A. Gross and Mary Kelley, eds., *A History of the Book in America, Volume 2, An Extensive Republic: Print, Culture, and Society in the New Nation, 1790–1840* (Chapel Hill: University of North Carolina Press, with the American Antiquarian Society, 2010).

8. Randolph Trumbach, "Review Essay: The Origin and Development of the Modern Lesbian Role in the Western Gender System: Northwestern Europe and the United States, 1750–1990," *Historical Reflections* 20, no. 2, Lesbian Histories (Summer 1994): 287–320; Anna Clark, "Anne Lister's Construction of Lesbian Identity," *Journal of the History of Sexuality* 7, no. 1 (1996): 23–50; Emma Donohue, *Passions Between Women, British Lesbian Culture 1668–1801* (New York: Harper Perennial, 1996); Valerie Traub, *The Renaissance of Lesbianism in Early Modern England* (Cambridge: Cambridge University Press, 2002); Susan S. Lanser, "'Queer to Queer': The Sapphic Body as Transgressive Text," in Katharine Kittredge, ed., *Lewd and Notorious: Female Transgression in the Eighteenth Century* (Ann Arbor: University of Michigan Press, 2003), 21–46; Susan Lanser, *The Sexuality of History* (Chicago: University of Chicago Press, 2014); Rachel Hope Cleves, *Charity and Sylvia* (New York: Oxford University Press, 2014).

9. Carroll Smith-Rosenberg, "The Female World of Love and Ritual: Relations Between Women in Nineteenth-Century America," *Signs: Journal of Women in Culture and Society* 1, no. 1 (Autumn, 1975): 1–29; Lilian Faderman, *Surpassing the Love of Men: Romantic Friendship and Love Between Women from the Renaissance to the Present* (New York: Morrow, 1981); John D'Emilio and Estelle Freedman, *Intimate Matters: A History of Sexuality in America* (Harper and Row, 1988); Martha Vicinus, "Lesbian History: All Theory and No Facts or All Facts and No Theory?" *Radical History Review* 60 (1994): 57–75; Karen V. Hanson, "'No *Kisses* is Like Youres': An Erotic Friendship between Two African-American Women during the Mid-Nineteenth Century," *Gender and History* 7, no. 2 (1995): 153–82; Leila J. Rupp, *A Desired Past: A Short History of Same-Sex Love in America* (Chicago: University of Chicago Press, 1999); Martha Vicinus, *Intimate Friends: Women Who Loved Women, 1778–1928* (Chicago: University of Chicago Press, 2004); Sharon Marcus, *Between Women: Friendship, Desire, and Marriage in Victorian England* (Princeton: Princeton University Press, 2007); Leila J. Rupp, *Sapphistries: A Global History of Love Between Women* (New York: New York University Press, 2009).

10. Important scholarship on female husbands includes Terry Castle, "Matters Not Fit to Be Mentioned: Fielding's *The Female Husband*," *ELH* 49, no. 3 (Autumn 1982): 602–22; Faderman, *Surpassing the Love of Men*; Donohue, *Passions Between Women*; Susan Clayton,

"Can Two and a Half Centuries of Female Husbands Inform (Trans)Gender History," *Journal of Lesbian Studies* 13 (2009): 289; Traub, *The Renaissance of Lesbianism*; Vicinus, *Intimate Friends*; Leila J. Rupp, *Sapphistries*; Rachel Hope Cleves, "'What, Another Female Husband?': The Prehistory of Same-Sex Marriage," *Journal of American History* 101, no. 4 (March 2015): 1055–81; Emily Skidmore, *True Sex: The Lives of Trans Men at the turn of the Twentieth Century* (New York: New York University Press, 2017).

11. Jack Halberstam, "Transgender Butch: Butch/FTM Border Wars and the Masculine Continuum," *GLQ: A Journal of Lesbian and Gay Studies* 4, no 2 (1998): 287–310, 293.

12. A 2012 comprehensive overview of women's and gender history featured only two monographs that fundamentally challenge this binary: Joanne Meyerowitz's *How Sex Changed: A History of Transsexuality in the U.S.* (Cambridge, MA: Harvard University Press, 2002) and Elizabeth Reis, *Bodies in Doubt: An American History of Intersex* (Baltimore: Johns Hopkins University Press, 2009). See Cornelia H. Dayton and Lisa Levenstein, "The Big Tent of U.S. Women's and Gender History: A State of the Field," *Journal of American History* (December 2012): 793–817. An important series of articles and chapters about the seventeenth-century intersex/transgender person Thomas/ine Hall also explore this issue. See Kathleen Brown, "'Changed...into the Fashion of Man': The Politics of Sexual Difference in a Seventeenth Century Anglo-American Settlement," *Journal of the History of Sexuality* 6, no. 2 (October 1995): 171–93; Mary Beth Norton, *Founding Mothers and Fathers: Gendered Power and the Forming of American Society* (New York: Alfred A. Knopf, 1996); Elizabeth Reis, "Impossible Hermaphrodites: Intersex in America, 1620–1960," *The Journal of American History* 92, no. 2 (September 2005): 411–41; Kathryn Wichelns, "From the Scarlet Letter to Stonewall: Reading the 1629 Thomas(ine) Hall Case, 1978–2009," *Early American Studies* 12, no. 3 (Fall 2014): 500–23; Alice Dreger, *Hermaphrodites and the Medical Invention of Sex* (Cambridge, MA: Harvard University Press, 1998).

13. Transgender studies is at a crossroads between two seemingly contradictory views: one that gender is a social construct, the other that gender identity is innate. Paisley Currah, "Transgender Rights without a Theory of Gender?" *Tulsa Law Review* 52, no. 3 (Spring 2017): 441–51. Important overviews of transgender history include Genny Beemyn, "A Presence in the Past: A Transgender Historiography," *Journal of Women's History* 25, no. 4 (Winter 2013): 113–22 and Genny Beemyn, "U.S. History," in Laura Erickson-Schroth, ed., *Trans Bodies, Trans Selves: A Resource for the Transgender Community* (New York: Oxford University Press, 2014).

14. Foundational books in the field include Susan Stryker and Stephen Whittle, *The Transgender Studies Reader* (New York: Routledge, 2006); David Valentine, *Imagining Transgender: An Ethnography of a Category* (Durham, NC: Duke University Press, 2007); Meyerowitz, *How Sex Changed*; Susan Stryker, *Transgender History* (Berkeley: Seal Press, 2008); Trystan Cotton, *Transgender Migrations: The Bodies, Borders, and Politics of Transition* (New York: Routledge, 2011); Peter Boag, *Re-Dressing America's Frontier Past* (Berkeley: University of California Press, 2011); Dean Spade, *Normal Life: Administrative Violence, Critical Trans Politics, and the Limits of Law* (Boston: South End Press, 2011); A. Finn Enke, ed. *Transfeminist Perspectives in and beyond Transgender and Gender Studies* (Philadelphia: Temple University Press, 2012); Susan Stryker and Aren Aizura, *The Transgender Studies*

Reader 2 (New York: Routledge, 2013); Clare Sears, *Arresting Dress: Cross-Dressing, Law, and Fascination in Nineteenth-Century San Francisco* (Durham, NC: Duke University Press, 2014); Emily Skidmore, *True Sex*; C. Riley Snorton, *Black on Both Sides: A Racial History of Trans Identity* (Minneapolis: University of Minnesota Press, 2017).

15. Susan Stryker, *Transgender History*, 1.

16. Susan Stryker, Paisley Currah, and Lisa Jean Moore, "Introduction: Trans-, Trans, or Transgender?" *WSQ: Women's Studies Quarterly* 36, no. 3/4 (2008): 11–22; Sears, *Arresting Dress*, 9. For a critique of the limits of "transing" as a verb in transgender studies, see Andrea Long Chu and Emmett Harsin Drager, "After Trans Studies," *TSQ* 6, no. 1 (2019): 103–16

17. Meyerowitz, *How Sex Changed*, 12–13.

18. The category was later picked up on scholarship on gender relations in Africa. See Denise O'Brien, "Female Husbands in Southern Bantu Societies," in A. Schlegel, ed., *Sexual Stratification: A Cross-Cultural View* (New York: Columbia University Press, 1977), 109–26; Regine Smith Oboler, "Is the Female Husband a Man? Woman/Woman Marriage among the Nandi of Kenya," *Ethnology* 19, no. 1 (January 1980): 69–88; Will Roscoe and Stephen O. Murray, eds., *Boy-Wives and Female-Husbands: Studies of African Homosexualities* (London: Palgrave, 1998).

19. See Ann Bodine, "Androcentrism in Prescriptive Grammar: Singular 'They', Sex-indefinite 'He', and 'He or She,'" *Language in Society* 4 (1975): 129–46; Linda D. Wayne, "Neutral Pronouns: A Modest Proposal Whose Time Has Come," *Canadian Woman Studies* 24, no. 2 (2005); On avoiding pronouns when one's identity is unclear, see C. Jacob Hale, "Consuming the Living, Dis(Re)membering the Dead in the Butch/FTM Borderlands," *GLQ* 4, no. 2 (1998): 311–48.

20. In recent years, singular "they/them/theirs" has become widely used in conversation. In 1900, the gender neutral pronoun "thon" was described as "an epicene term approved by eminent philologists" (*Oxford English Dictionary*). "Epicene" meaning people who had "characteristics of both sexes, or of neither," a term used sporadically throughout history.

21. Stryker, Currah, and Moore, "Introduction," 14.

1 THE FIRST FEMALE HUSBAND

1. Certification of marriage. Charles Hamilton and Mary Price of St. Cuthbert were married by banns at Wells St. Cuthbert, July 16, 1746. Q/SR/314/159. Quarter Sessions, Somerset Archives, Taunton, England.

2. Examination. Evidence given by Mary Hamilton, September 13, 1746. Q/SR/314/172. Quarter Sessions, Somerset Archives, Taunton, England.

3. Examination. Evidence given by Mary Hamilton, September 13, 1746. Q/SR/314/172. Quarter Sessions, Somerset Archives, Taunton, England.

4. It was alleged quacks made compounds by mixing animal feces with sugar and flour. "Confessions of a Quack Doctor," *The British Medical Journal* 2, no. 760 (July 24, 1875): 111–12.

5. A. Fessler, "A Medical Contract from the Eighteenth Century," *The British Medical Journal* 2, no. 4688 (1950): 1112–13.

6. *Oxford English Dictionary*, mountebank, n. 1. A.; Also see Leslie G. Matthews, "Licensed Mountebanks in Britain," *Journal of the History of Medicine and Allied Sciences* 19, no. 1 (January 1964): 30–45 and M.A. Katritzky, "Marketing Medicine: The Image of the Early Modern Mountebank," *Renaissance Studies* 15, no. 2 (June 2001): 121–53.

7. Roy Porter, "Dr. Doubledose: A Taste of One's Own Medicine," *BMJ: British Medical Journal* 309, no. 6970 (December 24–31, 1994): 1714–18. "The faculty warned the public against imposters. But the common retort was that the profession itself was quackery in camouflage, cashing in whenever it could," 1715.

8. Green was quickly overshadowed on the international stage by Chevalier John Taylor who was more skilled at both medicine and self-promotion. James Kelly, "Health for Sale: Mountebanks, Doctors, Printers and the Supply of Medication in Eighteenth-century Ireland," *Proceedings of the Royal Irish Academy. Section C: Archaeology, Celtic Studies, History, Linguistics, Literature* 108C (2008): 75–113, 91.

9. Kathleen M. Brown, *Foul Bodies: Cleanliness in Early America* (New Haven: Yale University Press, 2009), 31.

10. Caroline Derry has identified Mary Creed as the same woman who was then married to Richard Creed, a rag-man, when she appeared in court, alleging that one of her boarders stole from her. See Examination of Mary Creed, May 20, 1732, SRO Q/SR/300/86 in Caroline Derry, "Sexuality and Locality in the Trial of Mary Hamilton, 'Female Husband'," *King's Law Journal* 19, no. 3 (2008): 595–616, 600.

11. It is possible that Creed was hired by the landlord to manage the property, a common practice in Bath during the period. See Karen Harvey, *The Little Republic: Masculinity and Domestic Authority in Eighteenth-Century Britain* (Oxford: Oxford University Press, 2012), 174–5.

12. "Tuesday Last a Woman," *Bath Journal*, September 22, 1746.

13. Ruthann Robson, *Dressing Constitutionally: Hierarchy, Sexuality, and Democracy from Our Hairstyles to Our Shoes* (Cambridge: Cambridge University Press, 2013), 19.

14. "Tuesday Last a Woman," *Bath Journal*, September 22, 1746.

15. Such was the widely held view of previously mentioned Chevalier John Taylor. See A. Dickson Wright, "Quacks Through the Ages," *Journal of the Royal Society of Arts* 105, no. 4995 (1957): 161–78.

16. "Wrigley and Schofield identified a similar pattern in England where 10 per cent of women born in 1700 never married, dipping to a low of 5 per cent about 1740, rising again towards 10 per cent by 1800," in Deborah Simonton, *A History of European Women's Work: 1700 to the Present* (New York: Routledge, 1998), 57.

17. Examination. Evidence given by Mary Price of Glastonbury concerning her marriage to a person she believed to be Charles Hamilton, and who afterwards she discovered to be a woman. Justices of the Peace: J. Masters, mayor of Glastonbury, Thomas White, October 7, 1746. Q/SR/314/173. Quarter Sessions, Somerset Archives, Taunton, England.

18. Letter to the Clerk of the Peace, October 9, 1746, Q/SR/314/170a. Quarter Sessions, Somerset Archives, Taunton, England.

19. Tim Hitchcock, "The Reformulation of Sexual Knowledge in Eighteenth-Century England," *Signs: Journal of Women in Culture and Society* 37, no 4, Sex: A Thematic Issue (Summer 2012): 823–32, 826.

20. Tim Hitchcock, *English Sexualities, 1700–1800* (New York: St. Martin's Press, 1997), 79.

21. Nancy Cott, *Public Vows: A History of Marriage and the Nation* (Cambridge, MA: Harvard University Press, 2001), 11.

22. Examination. Evidence given by Mary Price of Glastonbury, October 7, 1746. Q/SR/314/173. Quarter Sessions, Somerset Archives, Taunton, England.

23. Hitchcock, *English Sexualities*, 80–1.

24. Not talking about or naming illicit sex – especially sodomy or buggery – was an important eighteenth-century tradition. This is one reason why sex between women was not more explicitly condemned by the law. See Donohue, *Passions Between Women*; Traub, *The Renaissance of Lesbianism*.

25. Derry, "Sexuality and Locality," 599–601.

26. Brown, "Changed into the fashion of a man," 174.

27. "Report and Estimate Concerning Repairs to Shepton Mallet Gaol," 14 September 1745. Q/SR/313/104–5. Quarter Sessions, Somerset Archives, Taunton, England.

28. John Howard, *The State of the Prisons in England and Wales* (London, 1777); Frank McLynn, *Crime and Punishment in Eighteenth-century England* (New York: Routledge, 1989), 295.

29. Letter to the Clerk of the Peace, October 9, 1746. Q/SR/314/170a. Quarter Sessions, Somerset Archives, Taunton, England.

30. Anna Clark, "Twilight Moments," *Journal of the History of Sexuality* 14, no. 1/2 (January–April 2005): 139–60, 153.

31. Sarah Nicolazzo, "Henry Fielding's 'The Female Husband' and the Sexuality of Vagrancy," *The Eighteenth Century* 55, no. 4 (Winter 2014): 335–53.

32. Two exceptions were John Harris, who owed surety for "good behaviour" towards Captain James Gredy, and Edward Lampert, an admitted deserter from the military. Calendar of Prisoners, April 28, 1747. Q/SR/315/12–13. Quarter Sessions, Somerset Archives, Taunton, England.

33. Calendar of Prisoners, October 7, 1746. Q/SR/314/165; Hamilton continued in jail, appearing on the next Calendar of Prisoners, October 13, 1746. Q/SR/314/199. Quarter Sessions, Somerset Archives, Taunton, England.

34. "Friday, Nov. 28," *Boston Weekly Post Boy*, February 6, 1747; "London, Nov. 21," *NY Gazette or Weekly Post Boy*, March 2, 1747.

35. *The Boston Weekly Post Boy*, February 6, 1747; slightly different language is used in earlier British reports, "We Hear from Taunton," *Bath Journal*, November 3, 1746; "Bath, Nov. 4," *London Evening Post*, November 6, 1746; "News," *Penny London Post or The Morning Advertiser*, November 7, 1746.

36. This is not referenced in the surviving court documents. The claim may have been discussed or substantiated in court, or it may have simply been a salacious rumor. The *Bath Journal* reported it as a fact established by the court. "We Hear from Taunton," *Bath Journal*, November 3, 1746.

37. Faramerz Dabhoiwala, *The Origins of Sex: A History of the First Sexual Revolution* (New York: Oxford University Press, 2012), 73.

38. *The Male and Female Husband; or, A Strange and Wonderful Relation how a Midwife living in St. Albans, being brought to Bed of an hermaphrodite, brought it up in Woman's Apparel, and carried it with her as her Deputy to be assisting at the Labours of several Women, going under the name of Mary Jewit* (Printed for P. Brooksby, at the Golden-ball in West-smithfield, 1682).

39. *The Male and Female Husband* (West-smithfield, 1682).

40. Patricia Crawford and Sara Mendelson, "Sexual Identities in Early Modern England: The Marriage of Two Women in 1680," *Gender and History* 7, no. 3 (November 1995): 362–77.

41. Sheridan Baker established the archival link between the real Charles Hamilton and Fielding's Hamilton in a path-breaking interdisciplinary work. See Sheridan Baker, "Henry Fielding's the Female Husband: Fact and Fiction," *PMLA* 74, no. 3 (June 1959): 213–24.

42. Susan Catto, Henry Fielding, 1707–1754, *Literature Online Biography*.

43. For instance, *The Female Fop: or, the False One Fitted. A Comedy* (London, 1724); *The Female Fortune-Teller. A Comedy* (London, 1726); *The Female Faction: or, the Gay Subscribers, A Poem* (London, 1729); *The Female Parson: or, Beau in the Sudds* (London, 1730); *The Female Rake: or, Modern Fine Lady* (London, 1736); *The Female Rebels: Being Some Remarkable Incidents of the Characters, and Families of the Titular Duke and Dutchess of Perth* (London, 1747); *Female Revenge: or, the British Amazon: Exemplified in the Life of Boadicia* (London, 1753); *The Female Parliament. A Seri-Tragi-Comi-Farcical Entertainment* (London, 1754).

44. Karen O'Brien, *Women and Enlightenment in Eighteenth-Century Britain* (New York: Cambridge University Press, 2009), 1, 27.

45. Tiffany Potter, "Introduction: Life in Excess: Eliza Haywood and Popular Culture in *The Masqueraders* and *The Surprize*," in Tiffany Potter, ed., *Eliza Haywood The Masqueraders, or Fatal Curiosity and The Surprize, or Constancy Rewarded* (Toronto: University of Toronto Press, 2015), 17–19.

46. See Peter Lake and Steve Pincus, "Rethinking the Public Sphere in Early Modern England," *Journal of British Studies* 45, no. 2 (April 2006): 270–92.

47. Trans'vest, v. sources from 1652 and 1654, *Oxford English Dictionary*.

48. R. Valerie Lucas, "'Hic Mulier': The Female Transvestite in Early Modern England," *Renaissance and Reformation* 12, no. 1, Sexuality in the Renaissance (Winter 1988): 65–84, 80.

49. Potter, "Introduction: Life in Excess," 23.

50. This is a matter of debate. Lucas, "Hic Mulier," 80. Cressy argues, "The degree to which this creative or polemical literature was grounded in social practice is never convincingly shown." David Cressy, "Gender Trouble and Cross-Dressing in Early Modern England," *Journal of British Studies* 35, no. 4 (October 1996): 438–65, 441; Original claim by Linda Woodbridge, *Women and the English Renaissance, 1540–1620* (Champaign, IL: University of Illinois Press, 1984).

51. Historians attribute this change to the "decline of humoural or Galenic medicine." Broadly conceptualized, this period runs from 1670 to 1820. Hitchcock, *English Sexualities*, 5. Anna Clark, *Desire: A History of European Sexuality* (New York: Routledge, 2008).

52. Hitchcock, *English Sexualities*, 2. Also see Greta LaFleur, "Sex and 'Unsex': Histories of Gender Trouble in Eighteenth-Century North America," *Early American Studies: An Interdisciplinary Journal* 12, no. 3 (Fall 2014): 469–99.

53. "Books and Pamphlets Published this Month," *Gentleman's Magazine*, November 1, 1746.

54. *London Evening Post*, November 11, 1746; ditto except "&c." is omitted from this one, *General Advertiser*, November 12, 1746.

55. "Advertisements and Notices," *General Advertiser*, November 29, 1746, December 1, 1746; "Advertisements and Notices," *London Evening Post*, December 2, 1746, March 5, 1747.

56. "Extract of a Pamphlet, entitled, The Female Husband; or Surprising History of Mrs. Mary alias Mr. George Hamilton," *British Magazine*, December 1746, 377–82.

57. Donohue, *Passions Between Women*, 73.

58. On a distinction between the sexed body and the sexual body, see Fraser Easton, "Gender's Two Bodies: Women Warriors, Female Husbands and Plebian Life," *Past & Present* 180 (August 2003): 131–74.

59. Fielding, *The Female Husband* (1746), 4.

60. Catherine Craft-Fairchild, "Sexual and Textual Indeterminacy: Eighteenth-Century English Representations of Sapphism," *Journal of the History of Sexuality* 15, no. 3 (2006): 408–31.

61. Fielding, *The Female Husband* (1746), 5.

62. Fielding, *The Female Husband* (1746), 14.

63. Thomas Lacquer, *Making Sex: Body and Gender from the Greeks to Freud* (Cambridge, MA: Harvard University Press, 1992).

64. Angela J. Smallwood, *Fielding and the Woman Question: The Novels of Henry Fielding and Feminist Debate 1700–1750* (New York: St. Martin's Press, 1989); Jill Campbell, *Natural Masques: Gender and Identity in Fielding's Plays and Novels* (Stanford: Stanford University Press, 1995); on Fielding's feminism, see Guyonne Leduc, "Was Fielding a Prefeminist?" in Claude Rawson, ed., *Henry Fielding (1707–1754) Novelist, Playwright, Journalist, Magistrate: A Double Anniversary Tribute* (Newark: University of Delaware Press), 271–92.

65. Campbell, *Natural Masques*, 56.

66. Donohue sees triumph in Fielding's account of Hamilton, stating, "A lesbian reader of *The Female Husband* would learn that she was not monstrous, only immoral, at times distinctly heroic – and, most importantly, that there were 'others' out there whom nothing could deter," 80; See Donohue, *Passions Between Women*, 73–80.

67. "Philadelphia, July 16," *Pennsylvania Gazette*, July 16, 1752; Mr. Robinson worked as a mariner out of Topsham and owed the king twenty pounds in taxes as of April 30, 1750. QS/4/1750/Midsummer/RE/11. Devon Archives and Local Studies, Devon, England.

68. James T. Lemon and Gary B. Nash, "The Distribution of Wealth in Eighteenth-Century America: A Century of Change in Chester County, Pennsylvania, 1693–1802," *Journal of Social History* 2, no. 1 (1968): 1–24, 14.

69. The Connecticut Code of 1784 viewed mountebanks as frauds who undermined order, setting punishment at twenty pounds for those found performing in public. Lawrence

Henry Gibson, "The Criminal Codes of Connecticut," *Journal of the American Institute of Criminal Law and Criminology*, 6, no. 2 (July 1915): 177–89, 187.

70. William H. Williams, "The 'Industrious Poor' and the Founding of the Pennsylvania Hospital," *The Pennsylvania Magazine of History and Biography* 97, no. 4 (1973): 431–43.

71. *Bath Journal*, September 22, 1746.

72. "Virginia, Lancaster County, September 22, 1752," *Pennsylvania Gazette*, February 20, 1753; February 27, 1753.

73. "Virginia, Lancaster County, September 22, 1752," *Pennsylvania Gazette*, February 20, 1753; February 27, 1753.

74. "Taken from the Plantation," *the Pennsylvania Gazette*, January 12, 1764.

75. Charges for horse stealing in Virginia in 1751 and 1752 were all of men: John Hill and Edward Stoakes in 1751; George Smith, John Shockley, Moses Thomson, and Thomas Aubery in 1752, "Extract from Virginia Gazette 1752 and 1755," *The Virginia Magazine of History and Biography* 24, no. 4 (October 1916): 404–16.

76. "Taken from the Plantation," *The Pennsylvania Gazette*, January 12, 1764.

77. "Ludicrous Crime," *The Carlisle Republican*, Carlisle Pennsylvania, February 22, 1820.

78. There were many books and editions published under this title. Hamilton only featured in the series published by Knapp and Baldwin in London in 1809, 1824, 1825, and later volumes that took excerpts.

79. In the annulment case of Arabella Hunt against her husband James Howard, see P. Crawford and S. Mendelson, "Sexual Identities in Early Modern England: The Marriage of Two Women in 1680," *Gender and History* 7, no. 3 (1995): 362–77.

80. "We Hear from Taunton," *Bath Journal*, November 3, 1746.

81. "Mary Hamilton," *Criminal Chronology; or, The New Newgate Calendar*, vol. 2 (London: Knapp and Baldwin, 1809); "Mary Hamilton," *The Newgate Calendar*, vol. 2 (London: Knapp and Baldwin, 1824); "Mary Hamilton," *The Newgate Calendar*, vol. 2 (London: Knapp and Baldwin, 1825); "Mary Hamilton," *The Newgate Calendar and the Divorce Court Chronicle*, 1872; "More About Marriage – Marrying with Her Own Sex," *Hampshire/Portsmouth Telegraph*, March 25, 1893; "Mary Hamilton," *The Complete Newgate Calendar*, vol. 3 (T.G. Crook: 1926).

82. "Mary Hamilton," *Criminal Chronology; or, The New Newgate Calendar*, vol. 2 (London: Knapp and Baldwin, 1809); "Mary Hamilton," *The Newgate Calendar*, vol. 2 (London: Knapp and Baldwin, 1824); "Mary Hamilton," *The Newgate Calendar*, vol. 2 (London: Knapp and Baldwin, 1825); "Mary Hamilton," *The Newgate Calendar and the Divorce Court Chronicle*, 1872; "More About Marriage – Marrying with Her Own Sex," *Hampshire/Portsmouth Telegraph*, March 25, 1893; "Mary Hamilton," *The Complete Newgate Calendar*, vol. 3 (T.G. Crook: 1926).

2 THE PILLAR OF THE COMMUNITY

1. Mary East, Probate Date June 15, 1780, Stepney, Middlesex, England, England and Wales, Prerogative Court of Canterbury Wills, 1384–1858.

2. "The Female Husband; or, A circumstantial account of an extraordinary affair, which lately happened at Poplar, as mentioned in our last Magazine," *The British Magazine*, England (August 1766), 389; "The Female Husband," *The Royal Magazine*, England (August 1766), 53; "The Female Husband," *The Universal Magazine*, England (August 1, 1766); "The Female Husband," *Gazetteer and New Daily Advertiser*, England (August 11, 1766); "The Female Husband," *Public Advertiser*, London (August 11, 1766); "The Female Husband," *The London Evening Post*, London, England (August 12, 1766); "The Female Husband," *The Manchester Mercury and Harrops General Advertiser* (August 26, 1766); "The Female Husband," *The Scots Magazine*, Edinburgh (September 1, 1766).

3. "Mary East, Sworn in Court, True Bill," Indictment, no. 200; "Mary East, John Williams, Sarah Smith, Sworn in Court, True Bill," Indictment no. 201; Sessions Rolls, September 1766, London Metropolitan Archives.

4. "The Female Husband; or a Circumstantial account of the extraordinary Affair which lately happened at Poplar," *British Magazine*, August 1766.

5. Jas, Jams, and James Howe, Stepney, Middlesex, England, Land Tax Records, 1741, 1743, 1744, 1745, 1747, 1749, 1750, 1751, 1752, 1753, 1754, 1755, 1756, 1758, 1759, 1760, 1761, 1762, 1763, 1774.

6. For analysis of this issue in a twenty-first century context, see Center for American Progress and Movement Advancement Project, *Paying an Unfair Price: The Financial Penalty for Being LGBT in America*, September 2014.

7. "The Female Husband; or, A circumstantial account of an extraordinary affair, which lately happened at Poplar, as mentioned in our last Magazine," *The British Magazine*, England (August 1766), 389; "The Female Husband," *The Royal Magazine*, England (August 1766), 53; "The Female Husband," *The Universal Magazine*, England (August 1, 1766); "The Female Husband," *Gazetteer and New Daily Advertiser*, England (August 11, 1766); "The Female Husband," *Public Advertiser*, London (August 11, 1766); "The Female Husband," *The London Evening Post*, London, England (August 12, 1766); "The Female Husband," *The Manchester Mercury and Harrops General Advertiser* (August 26, 1766); "The Female Husband," *The Scots Magazine*, Edinburgh (September 1, 1766).

8. An article recounted a common version of the story of Howe's life titled, "Remarkable Connection of Two Women," *The New Lady's Magazine*, 1788.

9. Richard S. Dunn, *Sugar and Slaves: The Rise of the Planter Class in the English West Indies, 1624–1713* (Chapel Hill: University of North Carolina Press, 1972); Roderick A. McDonald, *The Economy and Material Culture of Slaves: Goods and Chattels on the Sugar Plantations of Jamaica and Louisiana* (Baton Rouge: Louisiana State University Press, 1994); Frederick H. Smith, *Caribbean Rum: A Social and Economic History* (Gainesville: University Press of Florida, 2006).

10. "The Female Husband; or, A circumstantial account of an extraordinary affair, which lately happened at Poplar, as mentioned in our last Magazine," *The British Magazine*, England (August 1766), 389; "The Female Husband," *The Royal Magazine*, England (August 1766), 53; "The Female Husband," *The Universal Magazine*, England (August 1, 1766); "The Female Husband," *Gazetteer and New Daily Advertiser*, England (August 11, 1766); "The Female Husband," *Public Advertiser*, London (August 11, 1766); "The

Female Husband," *The London Evening Post*, London, England (August 12, 1766); "The Female Husband," *The Manchester Mercury and Harrops General Advertiser* (August 26, 1766); "The Female Husband," *The Scots Magazine*, Edinburgh (September 1, 1766).

11. "London. Oct 23," *Leeds Intelligencer*, October, 28, 1766.

12. "London, Nov. 3," *The Scots Magazine*, November 1, 1766; "Came on at Hicks's-hall," *The annual register, or, a view of the history, politicks, and literature for the year 1766*, J. Dodlsey (1767), 144.

13. "Mary East, Sworn in Court, True Bill," Indictment, no. 200; "Mary East, John Williams, Sarah Smith, Sworn in Court, True Bill," Indictment no. 201; Mary East, John Williams, Sarah Smith, Sworn in Court, True Bill," Indictment no. 202; Sessions Rolls, September 1766; London Metropolitan Archives.

14. Birbeck, bail piece; Bentley, bail piece by Richard Arnold, farrier, and Thomas White-head, stable keeper, both of Whitechapel, December 1770, Old Bailey Associated Records, 1740–1834, London Metropolitan Archives.

15. Mary East could be considered a dead name, not to be used after transitioning out of respect. This situation is a little different because Howe voluntarily began using the name Mary East – at least in court and legal records – after 1766. Personally and socially, they may have gone by James or Mary – we simply do not know. See Amanda Armstrong, "Certificates of Live Birth and Dead Names: On the Subject of Recent Anti-Trans Legislation," *The South Atlantic Quarterly* 116, no. 3 (July 2017): 621–31; Jamison Green, Dallas Denny, and Jason Cromwell, "'What Do You Want Us to Call You?': Respectful Language," *TSQ: Transgender Studies Quarterly* 5, no. 1 (February 2018): 100–10.

16. "The Female Husband; or, A circumstantial account of an extraordinary affair, which lately happened at Poplar, as mentioned in our last Magazine," *The British Magazine*, England (August 1766), 389; "The Female Husband," *The Royal Magazine*, England (August 1766), 53; "The Female Husband," *The Universal Magazine*, England (August 1, 1766); "The Female Husband," *Gazetteer and New Daily Advertiser*, England (August 11, 1766); "The Female Husband," *Public Advertiser*, London (August 11, 1766); "The Female Husband," *The London Evening Post London*, England (August 12, 1766); "The Female Husband," *The Manchester Mercury and Harrops General Advertiser* (August 26, 1766); "The Female Husband," *The Scots Magazine*, Edinburgh (September 1, 1766).

17. "Mary East, Sworn in Court, True Bill," Indictment, no. 200, Sessions Rolls, September 1766, London Metropolitan Archives.

18. Middling families were ideally "harmonious, monogamous, well-ordered, and virtuous." Margaret R. Hunt, *The Middling Sort: Commerce, Gender, and the Family in England, 1680–1780* (Berkeley: University of California Press, 1996), 149.

19. Harvey, *The Little Republic*, 22–3.

20. Hannah Barker, "England, 1760–1815," in Hannah Barker and Simon Burrows, eds., *Press, Politics, and the Public Sphere in Europe and North America, 1760–1820* (Cambridge. Cambridge University Press, 2002), 93–112, 93.

21. Nancy Cott, *Public Vows: A History of Marriage and the Nation* (Cambridge, MA: Harvard University Press, 2001), 18.

22. Simonton, *A History of European Women's Work*, 19.
23. Simonton, *A History of European Women's Work*, 62.
24. "A Curious Married Couple," *Fincher's Trades' Review* (July 25, 1863) in Jonathan Ned Katz, *Gay American History* (New York: Avon Books, 1978).
25. Dabhoiwala, *The Origins of Sex*, 67.
26. "The Female Husband," *New London Gazette*, December 5, 1766. Similar wording in most accounts pre-1790.
27. Hunt, *The Middling Sort*, 1–21.
28. This fact was integrated into subsequent versions, merging this later development into their life story regardless of time. "They had a servant, but each performed the duties belonging to their station." "Georgetown," *Pennsylvania Gazette*, October 18, 1790; This excerpt was repeated in "The Female Husband," *The Republican Watchman*, 1875–7; "A Female Husband," *Wilmington Commercial*, Wilmington, DE, May 26, 1876; A Female Husband, *American Citizen*, Canton, MS, June 10, 1876; "A Female Husband," *Port Royal Standard and Commercial Beaufort*, South Carolina, July 1876; "A Female Husband," *Middletown Daily Argus*, Middletown, New York, June 16, 1876.
29. "Entertainment," *New York Gazette*, October 20, 1766; "From the London Chronicle," *Boston Post-Boy and Advertiser*, November 17, 1766; "Article 9 – No Title," *The American Magazine of Wonders and Marvelous Chronicle*, 1809; "Mary East," *Cincinnati Mirror, and Western Gazette of Literature, Science, and the Arts*, May 23, 1835.
30. "The Female Husband," *The American Magazine of Wonders and Marvelous Chronicle*, 1809.
31. James How, Marriage, December 1732 to Mary Snapes, London, England. London, England, Clandestine Marriage and Baptism Registers, 1667–1754; Mary Snapes, Marriage, December 24, 1732 to James Howe, London, England. Fleet Notebooks. London, England, Clandestine Marriage and Baptism Registers, 1667–1754.
32. Randolph Trumbach, *Sex and the Gender Revolution, Volume 1: Heterosexuality and the Third Gender in Enlightenment London* (Chicago: University of Chicago Press, 1998).
33. Jack Halberstam, *Female Masculinity* (Durham, NC: Duke University Press, 1998), 9.
34. "The Female Husband; or, A circumstantial account of an extraordinary affair, which lately happened at Poplar, as mentioned in our last Magazine," *The British Magazine*, England (August 1766), 389; "The Female Husband," *The Royal Magazine*, England (August 1766), 53; "The Female Husband," *The Universal Magazine*, England (August 1, 1766); "The Female Husband," *Gazetteer and New Daily Advertiser*, England (August 11, 1766); "The Female Husband," *Public Advertiser*, London (August 11, 1766); "The Female Husband," *The London Evening Post*, London, England (August 12, 1766); "The Female Husband," *The Manchester Mercury and Harrops General Advertiser* (August 26, 1766); "The Female Husband," *The Scots Magazine*, Edinburgh (September 1, 1766).
35. "The Female Husband; or, A circumstantial account of an extraordinary affair, which lately happened at Poplar, as mentioned in our last Magazine," *The British Magazine*, England (August 1766), 389; "The Female Husband," *The Royal Magazine*, England (August 1766), 53; "The Female Husband," *The Universal Magazine*, England (August 1, 1766); "The Female Husband," *Gazetteer and New Daily Advertiser*, England (August 11, 1766); "The Female Husband," *Public Advertiser*, London (August 11, 1766); "The

Female Husband," *The London Evening Post*, London, England (August 12, 1766); "The Female Husband," *The Manchester Mercury and Harrops General Advertiser* (August 26, 1766); "The Female Husband," *The Scots Magazine*, Edinburgh (September 1, 1766); "Mary East, The Female Husband," *The Life and Sketches of Curious and Odd Characters* (Boston, 1840), 134.

36. The only exception to this is when Howe was paid a small settlement from a quarrel with another man that resulted in damages of £500 being "paid him" suggesting that some financial matters were also reserved for men. "Entertainment," *New York Gazette*, October 20, 1766; "From the London Chronicle," *Boston Post-Boy and Advertiser*, November 17, 1766; "Article 9 – No Title," *The American Magazine of Wonders and Marvellous Chronicle*, 1809.

37. "Entertainment," *New York Gazette*, October 20, 1766; "From the London Chronicle," *Boston Post-Boy and Advertiser*, November 17, 1766.

38. The October 1766 issue edited out the repetitions of "his supposed wife" using it only once while the November 1766 issue dropped the "he" and stated "which not doing" instead of "he not doing." "From the London Chronicle," *Boston Post-Boy and Advertiser*, November 17, 1766.

39. Mary East, June 3, 1780, Greater London, England, Buried at St. Matthias' Churchyard, Poplar, London Borough of Tower Hamlets, Greater London, England.

40. "Mr. Urban," *Gentleman's Magazine*, January 1, 1781.

41. "Death Notice," *Norwich Packet*, January 12, 1786; "Death Notice," *Pennsylvania Evening Post*, May 25, 1781.

42. This version added the idea that they had a servant, which was not the case until after Mrs. Howe died. "Georgetown, September 18," *Pennsylvania Packet*, Philadelphia, PA, October 18, 1790.

43. Dabhoiwala, *The Origins of Sex*, 85.

44. For an overview of the notion of "separate spheres," see Mary Kelly, "Beyond the Boundaries," *Journal of the Early Republic* 21, no. 1 (Spring, 2001): 73–8.

45. Catherine Allgor, *Parlor Politics: In Which the Ladies of Washington Help Build a City and a Government* (Charlottesville: University of Virginia Press, 2000); Mary Kelly, "'A More Glorious Revolution': Women's Antebellum Reading Circles and the Pursuit of Public Influence," *The New England Quarterly* 76, no. 2 (June, 2003): 163–96; Mary Kelley, *Learning to Stand and Speak: Women, Education, and Public Life in America's Republic* (Chapel Hill: University of North Carolina Press, 2006); Rosemarie Zaggari, *Revolutionary Backlash: Women and Politics in the Early American Republic* (Philadelphia: University of Pennsylvania Press, 2007).

46. "The sharp emphasis of the antebellum era on difference came to dominate after women had attempted to live merely – and then more fully – as the equals of man." Lucia McMahon, *Mere Equals: The Paradox of Educated Women in the Early American Republic* (Ithaca, NY: Cornell University Press, 2012), 169; Also see Carolyn Eastman, *A Nation of Speechifiers: Making an American Public after the Revolution* (Chicago: University of Chicago Press, 2009); April Haynes, *Riotous Flesh: Women, Physiology, and the Solitary Vice in Nineteenth-Century America* (Chicago: University of Chicago Press, 2015).

47. Margaret R. Hunt, *Women in Eighteenth-Century Europe* (New York: Pearson Longman, 2010), 295.

48. *The Ladies' Companion: Containing First, Politeness of Manners and Behaviour from the French of the Abbe De Bellegarde. Second, Fenelon on education – Third, Miss More's essays – Fourth, Dean Swift's Letter to a Young Lady Newly married – Fifth, Moore's Fables for the Female Sex* (Worcester: Printed [by Samuel B. Manning] at the Spy Office, 1824), 57.

49. O'Brien, *Women and Enlightenment*, 232.

50. O'Brien, *Women and Enlightenment*, 232.

51. Priscilla Wakefield, *Variety; or, Selections and Essays: Consisting of Anecdotes, Curious Facts, Interesting Narratives, with Occasional Reflections* (Philadelphia: Brown & Merritt, 1809), 156.

52. Wakefield, *Variety; or, Selections*, 146–51.

53. Wakefield, *Variety; or, Selections*, 57–8.

54. Wakefield, *Variety; or, Selections*, 60.

55. Meyerowitz, *How Sex Changed*. Specifically, see theories of Robert J. Stoller, 115–17.

56. Mary Kelley, "Designing a Past for the Present: Women Writing Women's History in Nineteenth-Century America," *Proceedings of the American Antiquarian Society* 105, no. 2 (October 1995): 315–46; O'Brien, *Women and Enlightenment*, 204.

57. Dabhoiwala, *The Origins of Sex*, 334.

58. "Stepney," *The Environs of London, Vol 2 Part 2 County of Middlesex*, 2nd edition (London, 1811), 701. Records suggest Mary Howe was buried on August 31, 1766 at Ingatestone, Essex, England. Select Church of England Parish Registers, 1518–1960.

59. For example, when describing the blackmail attempt by Mrs. B, the story says Mrs. B knew what good circumstances "she lived" in and continued that Mrs. B was acquainted "with James in her younger days." The robbers "inquired for Mr. Howe, who answered to the name; they told her that they came." "The Female Husband; or, a Circumstantial Account of an Extraordinary Affair Which Happened at Poplar in England," *American Magazine of Wonders and Marvelous Chronicle*, July 1, 1809.

60. "The Female Husband; or, a Circumstantial Account of an Extraordinary Affair Which Happened at Poplar in England," *American Magazine of Wonders and Marvelous Chronicle*, July 1, 1809.

61. "The Female Husband," *The Female's Encyclopedia of Useful and Entertaining Knowledge* (Warwick Square, England, 1830), 258–60. On the popularity of women's reading circles, see Kelly, "A More Glorious Revolution."

62. "Mary East, the Female Husband," *The Life and Sketches of Curious and Odd Characters* (Boston, 1840); also see Joshua Watts, *The Museum of History* (Mansfield, 1841–99), 218–21.

63. "Mary East," *Cincinnati Mirror, and Chronicle: Devoted to Literature and Science*, May 23, 1835.

64. Female husband held strong as the "go to" term in the 1820s. See "Singular Account of James How, the female Husband," *Kirby's Wonderful and Eccentric Museum* (R.S. Kirby, 1820); "The Female Husband," *Remarkable Events in the History of Man* (Judah Dobson,

J. Harding, 1826); "Mary East, the Female Husband," *The Wonders of the Universe* (Jones and co, 1827).

65. "Disguised Females," *New York Organ*, New York, June 25, 1853.

66. "Disguised Females," *New York Organ*, New York, June 25, 1853.

67. "Stepney," *The Environs of London, Vol 2 Part 2 County of Middlesex*, 2nd edition, London, 1811.

68. "Disguised Females," *The New York Organ*, June 25, 1853. A later account claims she was with her brother in Essex, "The Woman Husband," November 19, 1881, *Leicester Chronicle*, Leicester, England.

69. Sharon Marcus, "The State's Oversight: From Sexual Bodies to Erotic Selves," *Social Research* 78, no. 2, The Body and the State: How the State Controls and Protects the Body, Part 1 (Summer 2011): 509–32, 512.

70. The tax rate that Howe paid to the city the following year plummeted dramatically. One possible cause of this is that they gave their wife's brother a good chunk of the estate.

71. "The Woman-Husband," *Recollections of the Court Room* (H. Dayton, 1860); "The Woman Husband," November 19, 1881, *Leicester Chronicle*, Leicester, England.

72. "The Romance of the 'White Horse'," *East London Antiquities* (London, 1902), 67.

73. "Romantic Tales and Historic Sketches, 'The Woman Husband'," *Chronicle & Mercury*, November 19, 1881; similar version reprinted as "The Woman Husband," *Tit-Bits from all the most interesting books, periodicals and newspapers in the world England*, November 18, 1882; *Daily Gazette for Middleborough*, July 2, 1891.

74. On the concept of "true sex" see Skidmore, *True Sex*.

75. Anna Clark, "Twilight Moments," *Journal of the History of Sexuality* 14, no. 1/2 (January–April 2005): 139–60, 155.

3 THE SAILORS AND SOLDIERS

1. Dugaw, *Warrior Women*; Lotte C. van de Pol and Rudolf M. Dekker, *The Tradition of Female Transvestism in Early Modern Europe* (London: MacMillan Press, 1989); Julie Wheelwright, *Amazons and Military Maids: Women Who Dressed as Men in the Pursuit of Life, Liberty, and Happiness* (London: Pandora Press, 1989); Suzanne J. Stark, *Female Tars: Women Aboard Ship in the Age of Sail* (Annapolis, MD: Naval Institute Press, 1996); Joan Druett, *She Captains: Heroines and Hellions of the Sea* (New York: Simon & Schuster, 2000).

2. Van de Pol and Dekker, *Tradition of Female Transvestism*, 32.

3. Anna Clark, *Women's Silence, Men's Violence: Sexual Assault in England 1770–1845* (New York: Pandora Press, 1987), 3.

4. "Cultural strictures are very strong; not many women in any society take the drastic step of acquiring a male identity in order to gain release from the prohibitions imposed on them," Stark, *Female Tars*, 95.

5. Maintaining a consistent methodology throughout the book, this chapter continues the practice of referring to those who transed gender by the names they chose for

themselves during this crucial moment of their lives. When this differs from the name more commonly used in scholarship, that name will be cited parenthetically for reference.

6. Hannah Snell, *The Female Soldier; Or, The Surprising Life and Adventures of Hannah Snell, Born in the City of Worcester, Who Took upon herself the Name of James Gray; and, being deserted by her Husband, put on Mens Apparel and travelled to Coventry in quest of him, where she enlisted in Col. Guise's Regiment of Foot, and marched with that Regiment to Carlisle, in the Time of the Rebellion in Scotland; shewing what happened to her in that City, and her Desertion from that Regiment* (London: R. Walker, 1750); Hannah Snell, *The Widow in Masquerade, or, The Female Warrior Containing a Concise Narrative of the Life and Adventures of Hannah Snell Who Served with Credit for Several Years in the British Army and Navy* (Northampton, [MA: s.n.], 1809).

7. Mary Slade, *The History of the Female Shipwright; To Whom the Government has granted a Superannuated Pension of Twenty Pounds per Annum, during her Life, Written by Herself* (London: M. Lewis, 1773); Mary Lacy, *The Female Shipwright, or, Life and Extraordinary Adventures of Mary Lacy Giving an Account of Her Leaving Her Parents Disguised as a Man* (New-York: Printed for Georg Sinclair by J.C. Totten, 1807); John Paul Jones, *The Life, Travels, Voyages, and Daring Engagements, of the Celebrated Paul Jones: To Which Is Added, The Life and Extraordinary Adventures of Mary Lacy; Giving an Account of Her Leaving Her Parents Disguised as a Man; Serving Four Years at Sea, and Seven Years Apprenticeship in Portsmouth Dock-yard., Life, Travels, Voyages, and Daring Engagements of Paul Jones* (New-York: Printed for E. Duyckinck, 1809).

8. Herman Mann, *The Female Review: Or, Memoirs of an American Young Lady: Whose Life and Character Are Peculiarly Distinguished–being a Continental Soldier, for Nearly Three Years, in the Late American War* (Dedham, [MA]: Nathaniel and Benjamin Heaton, 1797).

9. Interracial sex involving a white woman, same-sex sex, and rape of a man, child, or white person, are examples where state authority would be more likely to intervene. Kathleen M. Brown, *Good Wives, Nasty Wenches, Anxious Patriarchs 1830* (Chapel Hill: University of North Carolina Press, 1996); Richard Godbeer, *Sexual Revolution in Early America* (Johns Hopkins University Press, 2002); Thomas Foster, *Sex and the Eighteenth-Century Man: Massachusetts and the History of Sexuality in America* (Boston: Beacon Press, 2007); Sharon Block, *Rape and Sexual Power in Early America* (Chapel Hill: University of North Carolina Press, 2006); Clare Lyons, *Sex Among the Rabble: An Intimate History of Gender and Power in the Age of Revolution, Philadelphia, 1730–1830* (Chapel Hill: University of North Carolina Press, 2006).

10. For a critique of this stereotype, see Jesse Lemisch, "Jack Tar in the Streets: Merchant Seamen in the Politics of Revolutionary America," *The William and Mary Quarterly* 25, no. 3 (July 1968): 371–407; Margaret S. Creighton and Lisa Norling, *Iron Men, Wooden Women: Gender and Seafaring in the Atlantic World, 1700–1920* (Baltimore: Johns Hopkins University Press, 1996); Jesse Lemisch, *Jack Tar vs. John Bull: The Role of New York's Seamen in Precipitating the Revolution* (New York: Routledge, 1997); Myra C. Glenn, *Jack Tar's Story: The Autobiographies and Memories of Sailors in Antebellum America* (New York: Cambridge University Press, 2010).

11. *Onania; or, the Heinous Sin of Self-Pollution, and all its Frightful Consequences, in Both Sexes, Considered*, 8th edition (London, 1723) and (Boston, 1724). A later version published in

London in 1756 is widely accessible via internet archive. Thomas W. Laqueur, *Solitary Sex: A Cultural History of Masturbation* (New York: Zone Books, 2003). Also see Haynes, *Riotous Flesh*.

12. Godbeer, *Sexual Revolution*, 66–7; William Gibson and Joanne Begiato, *Sex and the Church in the Long Eighteenth Century* (London: I.B. Tauris, 2017), 195–231.

13. Arthur N. Gilbert, "Buggery and the British Navy, 1700–1861," *Journal of Social History* 10, no. 1 (1976): 72–98; Robert F. Oaks, "Things Fearful to Name: Sodomy and Buggery in Seventeenth-Century New England," *Journal of Social History* 12, no. 2 (1978): 268–81.

14. B.R. Burg, *Sodomy and the Pirate Tradition: English Sea Rovers in the Seventeenth-Century Caribbean* (New York: New York University Press, Revised Edition, 1995); Hans Turley, *Rum, Sodomy, and the Lash: Piracy, Sexuality, and Masculine Identity* (New York: New York University Press, Revised Edition, 2001); B.R. Burg, *Boys at Sea: Sodomy, Indecency, and Courts Martial in Nelson's Navy* (New York: Palgrave Macmillan, 2007).

15. Godbeer, *Sexual Revolution*; Clare Lyons, "Mapping an Atlantic Sexual Culture: Homo-eroticism in Eighteenth-Century Philadelphia," *The William and Mary Quarterly* 60, no. 1, Sexuality in Early America (January 2003): 119–54; Lyons, *Sex Among the Rabble*; Foster, *Sex and the Eighteenth-Century Man*.

16. Judith R. Walkowitz, *City of Dreadful Delight: Narratives of Sexual Danger in Late-Victorian London* (Chicago: University of Chicago Press, 1992); Hitchcock, *English Sexualities*; Seth Koven, *Slumming: Sexual and Social Politics in Victorian London* (Princeton: Princeton University Press, 2004); Tim Hitchcock, *Down and Out in Eighteenth-Century London* (New York: Hambledon and London, 2004); Dabhoiwala, *The Origins of Sex*; Heather Shore, *London's Criminal Underworlds, c. 1720–c. 1930: A Social and Cultural History* (New York, Palgrave Macmillan, 2015).

17. "Some account of Hannah Snell, the Female Soldier," *Moral and Entertaining Magazine*, March 1, 1779.

18. Stark, *Female Tars*, 104.

19. "Some account of Hannah Snell, the Female Soldier," *Moral and Entertaining Magazine*, March 1, 1779.

20. Stark, *Female Tars*, 105–6.

21. "News," *London Evening Post*, June 26, 1750; "London, June 26," *New York Gazette or Weekly Post Boy*, September 17, 1750.

22. "London, May 17," *Boston Post-Boy*, Boston, MA, August 6, 1753.

23. Courts only pursued explicit charges (beyond vagrancy) when an attempt at legal marriage to a woman was involved. See Lynne Friedli, "Passing Women: A Study of Gender Boundaries in the Eighteenth Century," in G.S. Rousseau and Roy Porter, eds., *Sexual Underworlds of the Enlightenment* (Manchester: Manchester University Press, 1987), 234–60.

24. "Some account of Hannah Snell, the Female Soldier," *Moral and Entertaining Magazine*, March 1, 1779.

25. "Some account of Hannah Snell, the Female Soldier," *Moral and Entertaining Magazine*, March 1, 1779.

26. *The Female Soldier; or, the surprising Life and Adventures of Hannah Snell, born in the city of Worcester, etc.* (London: R. Walker, 1750), 179.

27. "Some account of Hannah Snell, the Female Soldier," *The Gentleman's Magazine*, July 1750.

28. "Some account of Hannah Snell, the Female Soldier," *The Gentleman's Magazine*, July 1750.

29. *The Female Soldier* (London: R. Walker, 1750), 1.

30. "Some account of Hannah Snell, the Female Soldier," *The Gentleman's Magazine*, July 1750 and *The Boston Weekly News Letter*, Boston, MA, December 6, 1750; "Some account of Hannah Snell, the Female Soldier," *Moral and Entertaining Magazine*, March 1, 1779 and *Hibernian Magazine*, May 1, 1779; "Biography of Hannah Snell: Selected," *The Lady's Miscellany; or, Weekly Visitor, and Entertaining Companion for the Use and Amusement*, October 3, 1812, 376–80; Oct 10, 1812, 392–4; Oct 17, 1812, 406–8.

31. "Some Account of Hannah Snell, the Famous Female Soldier, to be Lately Went to the East-Indies," *The Boston Weekly News-Letter*, Boston, MA, December 6, 1750; "Some Account of Hannah Snell, the Female Soldier," *Moral and Entertaining Magazine*, March 1, 1779; "Some account of Hannah Snell, the Female Soldier," *Hibernian Magazine*, May 1, 1779; This one is cut off after the first page but seems to follow suit: "Some account of Hannah Snell, the Female Soldier," *The Gentleman's Magazine*, July 1750.

32. Hannah Snell, *The Widow in Masquerade, or, The Female Warrior Containing a Concise Narrative of the Life and Adventures of Hannah Snell Who Served with Credit for Several Years in the British Army and Navy* (Northampton [Mass: s.n.], 1809), 4, 10.

33. *The Widow in Masquerade* (Northampton [Mass: s.n.], 1809), 14–15.

34. *The Female Soldier* (London: R. Walker, 1750), 19.

35. *The Female Soldier* (London: R. Walker, 1750), 17.

36. *The Widow in Masquerade* (Northampton [Mass: s.n.], 1809), 14.

37. *The Widow in Masquerade* (Northampton [Mass: s.n.], 1809), 15.

38. *The Female Soldier* (London: R. Walker, 1750), 141–2.

39. *The Female Soldier* (London: R. Walker, 1750), 142.

40. "Some account of Hannah Snell, the Female Soldier," *The Boston Weekly News Letter*, Boston MA, December 6, 1750.

41. My assessment of the text as well as that offered by Suzanne Stark in *Female Tars*.

42. *The Female Soldier* (London: R. Walker, 1750), 142.

43. Elissa Gurman, "'Never yet did any Woman/more for Love and Glory do': Gender, Heroism, and the Reading Public in The Female Soldier; Or, the Surprising Life and Adventures of Hannah Snell," *Women's Studies* 44, no. 3 (2015): 321–41, 322; Gurman argues for the relevance of the text beyond that of capturing plebian masculinity.

44. "Chatham, Oct. 30," *Boston Evening Post*, Boston, MA, March 15, 1756.

45. "News," *Gazetteer and New Daily Advertiser*, December 22, 1779. A shorter notice also appeared, "Norwich, Dec. 18.," *London Chronicle*, December 18, 1779.

46. "The Female Husband," *Whitehall Evening Post*, London, England, March 25, 1760; "The Female Husband," *Sussex Advertiser*, Lewes, England, March 31, 1760.

47. "This Day the Female Husband," *Whitehall Evening Post*, London, England, April 1, 1760.

48. Samuel Bundy and Mary Parlour, Parish Register, London Metropolitan Archives, London, England; Reference Number: p92/sav/3014, Church of England Marriages and Banns, 1754–1932 and Samuel Bundy, England, Select Marriages, 1538–1973.

49. "This Day the Female Husband," *Whitehall Evening Post*, London, England, April 1, 1760.

50. "The Female Husband; or, The Life and Imaginations of Sally Paul. Hooper, 2s," in *A Catalogue of Books, Imperial Magazine or Complete Monthly Intelligencer*, London, England, December 2, 1760; "This Day is Published," *Public Advertiser*, London, England, December 5, 1760.

51. "Life and Imaginations of Sally Paul," *Monthly Review*, December 2, 1760.

52. *The Life and Imaginations of Sally Paul* (London: S. Hooper, 1760), 3.

53. *The Life and Imaginations of Sally Paul* (London: S. Hooper, 1760), 153.

54. Lisa Forman Cody, *Birthing the Nation: Sex, Science, and the Conception of Eighteenth-Century Britons* (New York: Oxford University Press, 2005), 12.

55. "They helped shape a new gender system that actually viewed the sexes as akin in fundamental emotional and human ways." Cody, *Birthing the Nation*, 15.

56. *The Life and Imaginations of Sally Paul* (London: S. Hooper, 1760), 159; Lanser argues that this text and this passage are evidence of "noncommittal portrayal of same-sex habits." Susan Lanser, *The Sexuality of History*, 164–5.

57. *The Life and Imaginations of Sally Paul* (London: S. Hooper, 1760), 140.

58. *The Life and Imaginations of Sally Paul* (London: S. Hooper, 1760), 159.

59. *The Life and Imaginations of Sally Paul* (London: S. Hooper, 1760), 159.

60. *The Life and Imaginations of Sally Paul* (London: S. Hooper, 1760), 58.

61. *The Life and Imaginations of Sally Paul* (London: S. Hooper, 1760), 80.

62. *The Life and Imaginations of Sally Paul* (London: S. Hooper, 1760), 141.

63. *The Life and Imaginations of Sally Paul* (London: S. Hooper, 1760), 35.

64. *The Life and Imaginations of Sally Paul* (London: S. Hooper, 1760), 36.

65. *The Life and Imaginations of Sally Paul* (London: S. Hooper, 1760), 143.

66. *The Life and Imaginations of Sally Paul* (London: S. Hooper, 1760), 143.

67. *The Life and Imaginations of Sally Paul* (London: S. Hooper, 1760), 161.

68. "News," *London Evening Post*, London, England, December 30, 1760.

69. *The Life and Imaginations of Sally Paul* (London: S. Hooper, 1760), 160.

70. Sarah Paul and William Kitchen, DL/A/D/005/MS10091/104, London and Surrey, England, Marriage Bonds and Allegations, 1597–1921.

71. Birth name Sarah Paul, St. Sepulchre, London, July 1, 1739 to Christopher and Mary Paul, England, Select Births and Christenings, 1538–1975.

72. Slade, *The History of the Female Shipwright*, 1.

73. Slade, *The History of the Female Shipwright*, 3–4.

74. Slade, *The History of the Female Shipwright*, 7.

75. Slade, *The History of the Female Shipwright*, 10.

76. Slade, *The History of the Female Shipwright*, 11.

77. Slade, *The History of the Female Shipwright*, 11.

78. Slade, *The History of the Female Shipwright*, 13.

79. Slade, *The History of the Female Shipwright*, 16.

80. Stark, *Female Tars*, 1996.

81. *Public Advertiser*, London, England, October 12, 1773. Note here it was printed and sold by three different people, M. Lewis, M. Hawes, and "the Author, King-Street, Deptford."

82. Slade, *The History of the Female Shipwright*, 10.

83. Slade, *The History of the Female Shipwright*, 22.

84. John Paul Jones, *The Life, Travels, Voyages, and Daring Engagements, of the Celebrated Paul Jones, To Which Is Added, The Life and Extraordinary Adventures of Mary Lacy* (1809), 76–8.

85. Jones, *Life, Travels, Voyages*, 85.

86. Slade, *The History of the Female Shipwright*, 129.

87. Jones, *Life, Travels, Voyages*, 76.

88. Peter Guillery, "The Further Adventures of Mary Lacy: 'Seaman', Shipwright, Builder," *History Workshop Journal*, 49, no. 1 (March 2000): 212–9.

89. Daniel Vickers, "Beyond Jack Tar." *The William and Mary Quarterly* 50, no. 2 (1993): 422; Daniel Vickers *Farmers and Fishermen: Two Centuries of Work in Essex County, Massachusetts, 1630–1859* (Chapel Hill: University of North Carolina Press, 1994).

90. Druett, *She Captains*.

91. Slade, *The History of the Female Shipwright*, 190; the 1809 edition adds minor embellishments "having heard much talk of" the metamorphosis and enquired "very kindly" about health.

92. Jones, *Life, Travels, Voyages*, 99.

93. Slade, *The History of the Female Shipwright*, 191; in the 1809 edition, 100.

94. Stark, *Female Tars*, 167; Guillery, "The Further Adventures of Mary Lacy".

95. Guillery argued that Chandler never married and that their female roommate, Elizabeth Slade, was a likely lover. Guillery, "The Further Adventures of Mary Lacy."

96. Mary Lacy and Josias Slade, October 19, 1772, Allegation MS 10091/128, London and Surrey, England, Marriage Bonds and Allegations, 1597–1921. Slade was noted as a shipwright in the bond, Mary Lacy and Josias Slade, October 19, 1772, Bond, DL/A/D/24/MS10091E/85/4 London and Surrey, England, Marriage Bonds and Allegations, 1597–1921, London Metropolitan Archives.

97. Josias Slade, Baptism, May 14, 1775, St. Nicolas, Deptford, Greenwich, Kent, England, Parish Register, London, England, Church of England Baptisms, Marriages, and Burials, 1538–1812, P78/NIC/005. Josiah Slade, Baptism, March 29, 1778, St. Nicolas, Deptford, Greenwich, Kent, England, Parish Register, London, England, Church of England Baptisms, Marriages, and Burials, 1538–1812, P78/NIC/005, London Metropolitan Archives.

98. Josias son of Josias Slade, Ship't King Street, Burials 1781, September, p. 301, Josias Slade, September 3, 1781, St. Paul, Deptford, Lewisham, Kent, London, England, Church of England Baptisms, Marriages, and Burials, 1538–1812, P75/PAU/001, London Metropolitan Archives.

99. Mary Slade, St. Paul, Deptford, Lewisham, England, May 3, 1801. London, England, Church of England Baptisms, Marriages and Burials, 1538–1812. Also verified by correspondence with Felicity Croydon, Archivist, London Borough of Lewisham, Lewisham Library and Information Services, who noted "Mary Slade wife of Josias

from St. Nicholas, Deptford buried at St. Paul's Deptford 3 May 1801 aged 54. Described as 'Female Shipwright' – 'Served time at Portsmouth'."

100. "An American Joan of Arc – A Heroine of the Revolution," *Chicago Daily Herald*, Chicago, IL, April 12, 1860; Also see Scott Larson, "'Indescribable Being': Theological Performances of Genderlessness in the Society of the Publick Universal Friend, 1776–1819," *Early American Studies* 12, no. 3 (2014), 576–600.

101. "New-York, January 10," *Connecticut Courant*, Hartford, CT, February 17, 1784; "The Female Soldier," *Boston Weekly Magazine: Devoted to Morality, Literature, Biography, History, the Fine Arts, Agriculture, & c.*, December 29, 1804; "Entertaining," *Concord Gazette*, Concord, NH, February 4, 1812; also see *The Independent Gazette; of the New-York Journal Revived*, January 10, 1784 in Curtis Carroll Davis, "A 'Gallantress' Gets Her Due: The Earliest Published Notice of Deborah Sampson," *Proceedings of the American Antiquarian Society at the Annual Meeting Held at Worcester* 91, part 2, October 21, 1981 (Worcester, MA, 1982), 319–23.

102. Judith Hiltner, "'She Bled in Secret': Deborah Sampson, Herman Mann, and The Female Review," *Early American Literature* 34, no. 2 (1999): 190–220; 199; Karen Weyler, "An Actor in the Drama of Revolution: Deborah Sampson, Print and Performance in the Creation of Celebrity," in Mary Carruth, ed., *Feminist Interventions in Early American Literature* (Tuscaloosa: University of Alabama Press, 2006), 183–93.

103. Young, *Masquerade*, 10–11.

104. This work of historical fiction offers a compelling transgender reading. See Alex Myers, *Revolutionary* (Simon and Schuster, 2014).

105. Hiltner, "She Bled in Secret," 202–8.

106. Hiltner, "She Bled in Secret," 204.

107. Mann, *The Female Review*, 113.

108. Mann, *The Female Review*, 232.

109. Mann, *The Female Review*, 248.

110. Mann, *The Female Review*, 235.

111. Mann, *The Female Review*, 236.

112. Excerpt as "The Female Soldier," *National Aegis*, Worcester, MA, May 7, 1828.

113. "Entertaining," *Concord Gazette*, Concord, NH, February 4, 1812.

114. "Deborah Sampson," *Graham's American Monthly Magazine of Literature & Art*, September 1, 1851.

115. "Deborah Sampson," *Historical Magazine*, November 1, 1858.

116. "Deborah Sampson, the Woman Soldier," *Working Farmer and United States Journal*, May 1, 1862.

117. Elizabeth F. Ellet, *The Women of the American Revolution*, vol. 2 (New York: Baker and Scribner, 1848), 122; "Heroic Women of the Revolution," *Godey's Lady's Book*, July 1, 1848, 6.

118. Ellet, *The Women of the American Revolution*, 126; "Heroic Women of the Revolution," 7.

119. Ellet, *The Women of the American Revolution*, 127; "Heroic Women of the Revolution," 7.

120. Ellet, *The Women of the American Revolution*, 135 says "robust and masculine." Together without the word "strength." "Heroic Women of the Revolution," 7–8.

121. Ellet, *The Women of the American Revolution*, 135; "Heroic Women of the Revolution," 9.

122. Mann as quoted in Greta L. LaFleur, "Precipitous Sensations: Herman Mann's *The Female Review* (1797), Botanical Sexuality, and the Challenge of Queer Historiography," *Early American Literature* 48, no. 1 (2013): 93–123, 103. Such passages suggest Sampson's gender transing in response to new sensations was "an expression of interiority."

123. *The Widow in Masquerade* (Northampton [Mass: s.n.], 1809), 14.

124. "Heroic Women of the Revolution," *Godey's Lady's Book*, July 1, 1848, 8.

125. *The Life and Imaginations of Sally Paul* (London: S. Hooper, 1760), 80–1.

126. *Oxford English Dictionary* – Miss Molly, n.; Also noted in Weyler, "An Actor in the Drama of Revolution," 185.

127. Trumbach, *Sex and the Gender Revolution*; Charles Upchurch, *Before Wilde: Sex Between Men in Britain's Age of Reform* (Berkeley: University of California Press, 2009).

128. Susan Gane, "Common Soldiers, Same-Sex Love and Religion in the Early Eighteenth Century British Army," *Gender and History* 25, no. 3 (November 2013), 637–51; Alan Bray, *Homosexuality in Renaissance England* (London: Gay Men's Press, 1982), 86, 102.

129. Lanser, "Queer to Queer," 34.

4 THE WIVES

1. Mr. Wood lived at 6 Camberwell Terrace, "The Female Husband," *The Standard*, London, January 17, 1829. Another article says Mr. Ward, "The Female Husband," *Morning Post*, London, January 19, 1829.

2. *An Authentic Narrative of the Extraordinary Career of James Allen, the Female Husband, who was married for the space of twenty-one years, without her real sex being discovered, even by her wedded associate: containing, also the particulars of her singular death; and the "post-mortem" examination of the body; with a variety of other interesting and exclusive facts* (London: I.S. Thomas, 1829), 7.

3. James Allen to Abigail Naylor, St. Giles, Camberwell Parish, Southwark Borough, December 13, 1807. London Metropolitan Archives, Saint Giles, Camberwell, Register of Marriages, P73/GIS, Item 014. *London, England, Church of England Marriages and Banns, 1754–1921.*

4. *The Female Husband. The History of an Extraordinary Individual, Named James Allen, Whose Sex remained undiscovered, although married to a woman, upwards of twenty-one years* (London: G. Smeeton, n.d), 3; "A Female Husband," *Bury and Norwich Post*, London, January 21, 1829.

5. Abigail is sometimes named "Mary" in the early news reports. One says she began going by Mary Allen after her marriage. I use Abigail because it is the name she uses for herself and the name in her legal documents.

6. Elisabeth Cawthon, "New Life for the Deodand: Coroners' Inquests and Occupational Deaths in England, 1830–46," *The American Journal of Legal History* 33, no. 2 (April 1989): 137–47, 138.

7. Cawthon, "New Life for the Deodand," 137.

8. "The Female Husband," *London St. James Chronicle*, London, January 17, 1829; reprinted as "The Female Husband," *The Standard*, London, January 19, 1829.

9. Mary Beth Emmerichs, "Getting Away with Murder? Homicide and the Coroners in Nineteenth-Century London," *Social Science History* 25, no. 1, Special Issue: Bloody Murder (Spring 2001): 93–100.

10. Rogers Forbes, "Crowner's Quest," *Transactions of the American Philosophical Society* 68, no. 1 (1978): 1–52, 5.

11. Wakely argued that cause of death was often declared as "visitation of God" instead of serious scientific examination utilizing the latest medical knowledge. Emmerichs, "Getting Away with Murder?" 95.

12. Forbes, "Crowner's Quest," 8. Also describes Shelton as a wealthy bachelor who "conducted more than six thousand inquests" and "had several Corporation appointments," 8.

13. "Most Singular Affair – A Female Husband," *Trewman's Exeter Flying Post*, January 22, 1829.

14. Forbes, "Crowner's Quest," 44.

15. "Inquisition," on Death of James Allen, January 14, 1829, Coroner's Inquests: London and Southwark, 1788–1837. London Metropolitan Archives.

16. "A Female Husband – Most Extraordinary Fact," *Leeds Intelligencer*, January 22, 1829. One article identifies the surgeon as a Mr. Green, "Most Singular Affair – A Female Husband," *Trewman's Exeter Flying Post*, January 22, 1829.

17. This study did not include London. Thomas R. Forbes, "Coroners' Inquests in the County of Middlesex, England 1819–42," *Journal of the History of Medicine and Allied Sciences* 32, no. 4 (October 1977): 375–94, 382. Of the 6,741 deaths from the eastern county of Middlesex, 6,654 included sex and cause, of which 105 men and six women died from falling objects (378).

18. "A Female Husband – Most Extraordinary Fact," *Leeds Intelligencer*, January 22, 1829; a different article identifies the surgeon as a Mr. Green. "Most Singular Affair – A Female Husband," *Trewman's Exeter Flying Post*, January 22, 1829.

19. "Inquisition," on Death of James Allen, January 14, 1829, Coroner's Inquests: London and Southwark, 1788–1837. London Metropolitan Archives.

20. "A Female Husband – Most Extraordinary Fact," *Leeds Intelligencer*, January 22, 1829.

21. "The Students of St. Thomas's Hospital," *The British Medical Journal* 2, no. 657 (December 6, 1873): 680.

22. *The Female Husband. The History of an Extraordinary Individual*, 3. The same quotes appeared in a short account of the story that seems to be a factual reporting. "A Female Husband – Most Extraordinary Fact," *Leeds Intelligencer*, January 22, 1829 and "A Woman Husband," *The Albion*, New York, March 14, 1829.

23. The account states 1808 as the year of marriage but the marriage certificate is dated 1807. James Allen to Abigail Naylor, St. Giles, Camberwell Parish, Southwark Borough, December 13, 1807. London Metropolitan Archives, Saint Giles, Camberwell, Register of Marriages, P73/GIS, Item 014. *London, England, Church of England Marriages and Banns, 1754–1921*.

24. "Most Singular Affair – A Female Husband," *Trewman's Exeter Flying Post*, January 22, 1829.

25. "The Female Husband," *London St. James Chronicle*, London, January 17, 1829; reprinted as "The Female Husband," *The Standard*, London, January 19, 1829.

26. "Inquisition," on Death of James Allen, January 14, 1829, Coroner's Inquests: London and Southwark, 1788–1837. London Metropolitan Archives.

27. "The Female Husband," *London St. James Chronicle*, London, January 17, 1829; reprinted as "The Female Husband," *The Standard*, London, January 19, 1829.

28. In contrast to treatment of James Carey in Philadelphia in 1830. See Reis, *Bodies in Doubt*, 24–8.

29. "The Female Husband," *Morning Post*, London, January 19, 1829; William Shrive was co-worker named in this piece, "Most Singular Affair – A Female Husband," *Trewman's Exeter Flying Post*, January 22, 1829; and John Shrive in this piece, "Extraordinary Investigation," *Leicester Journal*, January 23, 1829.

30. "A Female Husband," *Bury and Norwich Post*, London, January 21, 1829.

31. *The Female Husband. The History of an Extraordinary Individual, Named James Allen, Whose Sex remained undiscovered, although married to a woman, upwards of twenty-one years* (London: G. Smeeton, n.d), 6.

32. "The Female Husband," *The Standard*, London, January 17, 1829.

33. "The Female Husband," *Caledonian Mercury*, January 22, 1829.

34. "The Female Husband," *Caledonian Mercury*, January 22, 1829.

35. "A Female Husband," *Bury and Norwich Post*, January 21, 1829; "A Female Husband," *Devizes and Wiltshire Gazette*, January 22, 1829; "Female Husband," *Stamford Mercury, British*, January 23, 1829.

36. "The Female Husband," *Morning Post*, January 19, 1829.

37. "Extraordinary Investigation; or, the Female Husband," *Newcastle Courant*, January 24, 1829; Mary Daly is referred to as Jane Daley in the pamphlet, which also asserts that Abigail told Jane that James was not a proper man.

38. "The Female Husband," *The Standard*, London, January 17, 1829.

39. Simonton, *A History of European Women's Work*, 61.

40. "They were virtually unaccountable, because they moved in and out of work, because statisticians did not always consider them as workers, and because they were 'hidden' at home." Simonton, *A History of European Women's Work*, 149.

41. *The Female Husband. The History of an Extraordinary Individual, Named James Allen, Whose Sex remained undiscovered, although married to a woman, upwards of twenty-one years* (London: G. Smeeton, n.d), 7.

42. "The Female Husband," *London St. James Chronicle*, London, January 17, 1829; Reprinted as "The Female Husband," *The Standard*, London, January 19, 1829.

43. Lynn Hollen Lees, *The Solidarities of Strangers: The British Poor Law and the People, 1700–1948* (New York: Cambridge University Press, 1998), 177–229.

44. Anna Clark, "The New Poor Law and the Breadwinner Wage: Contrasting Assumptions," *Journal of Social History* 34, no. 2 (Winter 2000): 261–81.

45. "The Female Husband," *Morning Post*, London, January 19, 1829.

46. "The Female Husband," *Morning Post*, London, January 19, 1829.

47. "The Female Husband," *London St. James Chronicle*, London, January 17, 1829; reprinted as "The Female Husband," *The Standard*, London, January 19, 1829.

48. *The Female Husband. The History of an Extraordinary Individual, Named James Allen, Whose Sex remained undiscovered, although married to a woman, upwards of twenty-one years* (London: G. Smeeton, n.d), 8.

49. *The Female Husband. The History of an Extraordinary Individual, Named James Allen, Whose Sex remained undiscovered, although married to a woman, upwards of twenty-one years* (London: G. Smeeton, n.d), 7.

50. "The Female Husband," *Standard*, January 22, 1829; "The Female Husband," *Morning Post*, January 23, 1829.

51. "The Female Husband," *Sussex Advertiser*, Britain, January 26, 1829 and *Lancaster Gazetteer*, Britain, January 31, 1829 and *Leicester Journal*, Britain, January 30, 1829. This story was reported but without the verbatim of the affidavit itself in other publications. See "The Female Husband," *The Standard*, Britain, January 22, 1829 and *Morning Post*, Britain, January 23, 1829 and *Hampshire Chronicle*, Britain, January 26, 1829.

52. "The Female Husband," *The Standard*, London, January 17, 1829.

53. "The Female Husband," *The Standard*, London, January 17, 1829.

54. "Female Husband," *Leicester Journal*, January 30, 1829.

55. "The Female Husband," *Sussex Advertiser*, January 26, 1829.

56. "A Correct Portrait of James Allen, the Female Husband; and also Abigail his wife," *The Examiner*, January 25, 1829.

57. "The Female Husband," *The Examiner*, February 8, 1829.

58. "A correct portrait of James Allen," *The Examiner*, January 25, 1829; *Lancaster Gazetteer*, January 31, 1829; *Sussex Advertiser*, January 26, 1829. Weeks later, Thomas offered the public the compilation of news stories, promising, "A true narrative of the whole affair" for 1s. or 1s. 6d. for the edition that included portraits in the February 8, 1829 edition of *The Examiner*. This version was of a high quality, featuring full-color pictures and significant spacing around the margins. "Advertisements and Notices," *The Examiner*, February 8, 1829.

59. "James Allen was an habitual smoker of tobacco when at his own fireside, and while at labour he chewed it. These habits conferred on his features a course and anti-feminine tinge; yet his general abstinence, particularly from ardent spirits, enabled him to preserve a countenance ruddy and healthful." *An Authentic Narrative of the Extraordinary Career of James Allen, the Female Husband, who was married for the space of twenty-one years, without her real sex being discovered, even by her wedded associate: containing, also the particulars of her singular death; and the "post-mortem" examination of the body; with a variety of other interesting and exclusive facts* (London: I.S. Thomas, 1829).

60. *The Female Husband*. J. Catnach, Printer, 2, Monmouth-Court, 7 Dials. Sold by Bennett, Brighton; Pierce, South Borough, and Marshall, Bristol. n.d.; A short take on the case was *The Female Husband Who Had Been Married to Another Female Twenty-One Years*. Printed by T. Birt, No. 10, Great St. Andrew-Street, Seven Dials, n.d.

61. "The Female Husband," *Morning Post*, January 19, 1829.

62. For early scholarship on domesticity and passionlessness, see Barbara Welter, "The Cult of True Womanhood," *American Quarterly* 18, no. 2 (Summer 1966): 151–74; Kathryn

Kish Sklar, *Catharine Beecher: A Study in American Domesticity* (New Haven: Yale University Press, 1973); Smith-Rosenberg, "The Female World of Love and Ritual"; Nancy F. Cott, "Passionlessness, An Interpretation of Victorian Sexual Ideology, 1790–1850," *Signs* 4, no. 2 (Winter 1978): 219–36. For a complication and critique, see Haynes, *Riotous Flesh.*

63. Halberstam, *Female Masculinity,* 9.

64. "An Extraordinary Occurrence," *Hereford Journal,* London, January 21, 1829.

65. "A Female Husband," *Republican Advocate,* Batavia Genessee, NY, April 10, 1829.

66. Most news stories refer to Henry Stoakes (and later Stoke) but the marriage license clearly states Henry Stoake, Parish Church of Sheffield St. Peter and St. Paul, Sheffield Archives, 1817.

67. From Chart, "Building Trades, Wages and Hours of Work Per Week, 1839–59 by Trade, Specifically Bricklayers Labourers in 1839" in "On the Rate of Wages in Manchester and Salford, and the Manufacturing Districts of Lancashire, 1839–59," *Journal of the Statistical Society of London* 23, no. 1 (March 1860): 1–36, 12.

68. "A Female Husband," *Manchester Guardian,* April 11, 2018.

69. They settled in Manchester in 1829. "A Female Husband," *Manchester Guardian,* April 11, 1838.

70. "The Female Husband," *Westmorland Gazette,* April 28, 1838.

71. "A Female Husband," *Manchester Guardian,* April 11, 1838.

72. "A Female Husband," *Long Island Farmer,* Jamaica, NY, June 6, 1838.

73. In 1751, the term "Town's Husband" was coined in reference to a new position established for someone whose job was "to go about and examine what wants Repairing." Also see Town Husband, 1784, "a trustee of a charity responsible for providing relief and assistance to the poor and needy." *Oxford English Dictionary.*

74. "Communications," Laurel Thatcher Ulrich, *William and Mary Quarterly* 41, no. 1 (January 1984): 177–8.

75. Jeanne Boydston, "The Woman Who Wasn't There: Women's Market Labor and the Transition to Capitalism in the United States," *Journal of the Early Republic* 16, no. 2, Special Issue on Capitalism in the Early Republic (Summer 1996): 183–206, 192.

76. Karen Robbins, "Power among the Powerlessness: Domestic Resistance by Free and Slave Women in McHenry Family of the New Republic," *Journal of the Early Republic* 23, no. 1 (Spring 2003): 47–68, 48.

77. Long versions include: "A Woman Husband," *Rhode Island Republican,* June 23, 1838; "A Female Husband," *Plattsburg Republican,* Plattsburg, NY, June 2, 1838; "A Female Husband," *Long Island Farmer,* Jamaica, NY, June 6, 1838; untitled, *Olive Branch,* Boston, MA, June 16, 1838; "Another Female Husband," *Barre Weekly Gazette,* Barre, MA, June 8, 1838; "A Female Husband," *Evening Post,* NY, May 26, 1838; "The Woman's Husband in Manchester," *Alexandria Gazette,* Alexandria, VA, June 9, 1838. Short versions include Untitled, *Republican Watchman,* Monticello, NY, n.d.; "A Female Husband," *The Daily Atlas,* Boston MA, May 22, 1838.

78. Long versions include: "A Woman Husband," *Rhode Island Republican,* June 23, 1838; "A Female Husband," *Plattsburg Republican,* Plattsburg, NY, June 2, 1838; "A Female

Husband," *Long Island Farmer*, Jamaica, NY, June 6, 1838; untitled, *Olive Branch*, Boston, MA, June 16, 1838; "Another Female Husband," *Barre Weekly Gazette*, Barre, MA, June 8, 1838; "A Female Husband," *Evening Post*, NY, May 26, 1838; "The Woman's Husband in Manchester," *Alexandria Gazette*, Alexandria, VA, June 9, 1838. Short versions include Untitled, *Republican Watchman*, Monticello, NY, [undated]; "A Female Husband," *The Daily Atlas*, Boston, MA, May 22, 1838.

79. Henry Stoake and Ann Hants, St. Peter and St. Paul's Parish Church of Sheffield England, on January 14, 1817 (Ref: PR138/114), Sheffield Archives.

80. "The Female Husband," *Westmorland Gazette*, April 28, 1838. Also see stories such as "A Female Husband in Manchester," *The Morning Chronicle*, April 13, 1838; "A Female Husband," *Morning Post*, April 13, 1838. This edition cut the final paragraph, "A Female Husband in Manchester," *Standard*, April 13, 1838.

81. "An Extraordinary Case is Now Pending Before the Civil Tribunal of Castelsarrazin, Near Toulouse," *Cheltenham Chronicle*, August 31, 1858; "The Wife Has Sued for Divorce," *Sheffield Independent*, October 22, 1869.

82. "A Female Husband," *Belfast News-Letter*, April 20, 1838; *Bristol Mercury*, April 21, 1838.

83. Long versions include: "A Woman Husband," *Rhode Island Republican*, June 23, 1838; "A Female Husband," *Plattsburg Republican*, Plattsburg, NY, June 2, 1838; "A Female Husband," *Long Island Farmer*, Jamaica, NY, June 6, 1838; untitled, *Olive Branch*, Boston, MA, June 16, 1838; "Another Female Husband," *Barre Weekly Gazette*, Barre, MA, June 8, 1838; "A Female Husband," *Evening Post*, NY, May 26, 1838; "The Woman's Husband in Manchester," *Alexandria Gazette*, Alexandria, VA, June 9, 1838. Short versions include Untitled, *Republican Watchman*, Monticello, NY, [undated]; "A Female Husband," *The Daily Atlas*, Boston, MA, May 22, 1838.

84. Untitled, *Spirit of the Times*, New York, May 19, 1838.

85. "Items," *Daily Commercial Bulletin and Missouri Literary Register*, St. Louis, MO, May 31, 1838; an otherwise typical version of the story ended "Altogether, this is one of the most singular cases that ever come to our knowledge," in "An Odd Connexion," *Pawtucket Chronicle*, Pawtucket, RI, June 1, 1838.

86. The only birth certificate under the name Harriet around the right time. Harriet Stoakes, July 22, 1798, St. Thomas, Portsmouth, Hampshire, England to Thomas and Sarah Stoakes. England, Select Births and Christenings, 1538–1975.

87. "Another Female Husband," *Leicestershire Mercury*, April 21, 1838.

88. The wife was seventeen years old at marriage, "The Woman's Husband in Manchester," *Alexandria Gazette*, Alexandria, VA, June 9, 1838. Henry Stoake and Ann Hants married on January 14, 1817 at St. Peter and St. Paul's Parish Church of Sheffield (Ref: PR138/114), Sheffield Archives.

89. "The Female Husband," *Westmorland Gazette*, April 28, 1838; similar accounts appeared as "The Woman Husband," *Western Times*, April 21, 1838.

90. "A Woman Husband," *Rhode Island Republication*, Newport Rhode Island, May 23, 1838.

91. "A Female Husband in Manchester," *The Morning Chronicle*, April 13, 1838; "A Female Husband," *Morning Post*, April 13, 1838; "A Female Husband in Manchester," *Freeman's Journal*, April 16, 1838; "A Female Husband," *Brighton Patriot*, April 17, 1838; "Female

Husband," *Stamford Mercury*, April 20, 1838; This edition was identical except for cutting the final paragraph, "A Female Husband in Manchester," *Standard*, April 13, 1838 and "A Female Husband," *Preston Chronicle*, April 14, 1838 and "A Female Husband in Manchester," *Newcastle Courant*, April 20, 1838; this edition was identical except for cutting the second to last paragraph, "A Female Husband," *Worcestershire Chronicle*, April 19, 1838; this edition was identical but eliminated the last two paragraphs, "A Female Husband in Manchester," *Sherborne Mercury*, April 23, 1838; shorter excerpts of the account often lead with the line "A silly report." A short summary of the news referred to it as "a singular circumstance." "A Female Husband," *Hereford Journal*, April 18, 1838.

92. Other accounts focused directly on the facts of the case, deleting the opening that emphasized the sensational impossibility of the story as well as references to other gender crossers. "A Female Husband," *Belfast News-Letter*, April 20, 1838; *Bristol Mercury*, April 21, 1838; "A Female Husband in Manchester," *Bath Chronicle and Weekly Gazette*, April 19, 1838; this edition was identical but also deleted the previous paragraph about the wife's belongings, "A Female Husband," *Reading Mercury*, April 14, 1838 and "A Female Husband," *Bristol Mercury*, April 21, 1838.

93. Judith Butler, "Doing Justice to Someone: Sex Reassignment and Allegories of Transsexuality," in Susan Stryker and Stephen Whittle, eds., *The Transgender Studies Reader* (New York: Routledge, 2006), 183–93.

94. Lanser, "Queer to Queer," 24.

95. Lanser, "Queer to Queer," 29–30, 34.

96. Reis, *Bodies in Doubt*, 24.

97. Reis, *Bodies in Doubt*, 30.

98. Reis, *Bodies in Doubt*, 43.

99. James Akin, *Facts Connected with the Life of James Carey, Whose Eccentrick Habits Caused a Post Mortem Examination by Gentlemen of the Faculty; to Determine Whether he was Hermaphroditic: With Lithographed Drawings, made at their request* (Philadelphia, 1839), 5.

100. Akin, *Facts Connected with the Life of James Carey*, 5, 8.

101. Akin, *Facts Connected with the Life of James Carey*, 6.

102. Akin, *Facts Connected with the Life of James Carey*, 5.

103. Akin, *Facts Connected with the Life of James Carey*, 6.

104. Akin, *Facts Connected with the Life of James Carey*, 8.

105. Akin, *Facts Connected with the Life of James Carey*, 3.

106. Reis, *Bodies in Doubt*.

107. Akin, *Facts Connected with the Life of James Carey*, 7.

108. Akin, *Facts Connected with the Life of James Carey*, 7.

109. "Extraordinary Discovery – A Female Husband," *Wollmer's Exeter and Plymouth Gazette*, December 20, 1834.

110. "A Female Husband," *The Bury and Norwich Post*, January 21, 1829.

111. "Most Singular Affair – A Female Husband," *Trewman's Exeter Flying Post*, January 22, 1829.

112. "A Female Husband – Most Extraordinary Fact," *Leeds Intelligencer*, January 22, 1829.

113. "Another Female Husband," *Bury and Norwich Post*, April 18, 1838.

114. Also see Susan Stryker, "My Words to Victor Frankenstein Above the Village of Chamounix: Performing Transgender Rage," in Susan Stryker and Stephen Whittle, eds., *The Transgender Studies Reader* (New York: Routledge, 2006), 244–56.

115. "A Real Romance of Life. Remarkable Case of Concealment of Sex by a Woman," *The Manchester Courier and Lancashire General Advertiser*, October 22, 1859.

116. "Extraordinary Case: A Woman Passing as a Man for Forty Years," *The Hampshire Advertiser*, October 22, 1859; "A Woman Passing as a Man for Forty Years," *Salisbury and Winchester Journal*, October 22, 1859; "A Woman Passing as a Man for Forty Years," *Falkirk Herald*, October 27, 1859;

117. Marcus, "The State's Oversight," 513.

5 THE WORKERS

1. Joan Scott writes, "We need to attend to the historical processes that, through discourse, position subjects and produce their experiences. It is not individuals who have experience, but subjects who are constituted through experience." See Joan Scott, "The Evidence of Experience," *Critical Inquiry* 17, no. 4 (Summer 1991): 773–97, 779.

2. For more on the science of sexual difference, see Anne Fausto-Sterling, "The Five-Sexes: Why Male and Female are Not Enough," *The Sciences* (March/April 1993), 20–5; Anne Fausto-Sterling, "The Five Sexes, Revisited," *The Sciences* (July/August 2000), 19–23; Anne Fausto-Sterling, *Sexing the Body: Gender Politics and the Construction of Sexuality* (New York: Basic Books, 2002); Anne Fausto-Sterling, *Sex/Gender: Biology in a Social World* (New York: Routledge, 2012); Veronica Sanz, "No Way Out of the Binary: A Critical History of the Scientific Production of Sex," *Signs: Journal of Women in Culture and Society* 43, no. 1 (2017): 1–27.

3. "Items," *Circular*, March 20, 1856. The *Circular* was published by the utopian Oneida Community in New York.

4. Jen Manion, *Liberty's Prisoners: Carceral Culture in Early America* (Philadelphia: University of Pennsylvania Press, 2015); Adam Malka, *The Men of Mobtown: Policing Baltimore in the Age of Slavery and Emancipation* (Durham, NC: University of North Carolina Press, 2018); Carolyn Strange, *Discretionary Justice: Pardon and Parole in New York from the Revolution to the Depression* (New York: New York University Press, 2016); Amy Wood and Natalie Ring, eds. *Crime and Punishment in the Jim Crow South* (Champaign: University of Illinois Press, 2019).

5. On the many shared experiences of vagrants, runaways, and wanderers in life and under the law, see Kristin O'Brassill-Kulfan, "Vagabonds and Paupers: Race and Illicit Mobility in the Early Republic," *Pennsylvania History: A Journal of Mid-Atlantic Studies* 83, no. 4 (Autumn 2016): 443–69 and *Vagrants and Vagabonds: Poverty and Mobility in the Early American Republic* (New York: New York University Press, 2019).

6. Amy Dru Stanley, *From Bondage to Contract: Wage Labor, Marriage, and the Market in the Age of Slave Emancipation* (New York: Cambridge University Press, 1998).

7. The address of this incident was reported in the following accounts: "Singular Case," *Commercial Advertiser*, New York, August 13, 1836; "Singular Case," *American and Commercial Daily Advertiser*, Baltimore, MD, August 16, 1836; "Singular Case," *Spectator*, New York, August 18, 1836; "Singular Case," *Daily Globe*, Washington, DC, August 19, 1836; "Singular Case," *Daily Globe*, Washington, DC, August 20, 1836.

8. Charles R. Foy, "Seeking Freedom in the Atlantic World, 1713–1783," *Early American Studies: An Interdisciplinary Journal* 4, no. 1 (Spring 2006): 46–77, 50. "By 1850, there were 43,340 people in manufacturing and 11,360 in commerce. New York's port may have been the catalyst for the city's rise, but New Yorkers were far more likely to be involved in producing manufactured goods than in working on the ships themselves." Edward L. Glaeser, "Urban Colossus: Why is New York America's Largest City?" *Federal Reserve Bank of New York Economic Policy Review* (December 2005), 7–24, 14.

9. Manion, *Liberty's Prisoners*, 97–102.

10. "New York City from July 1st to October 15th 1845," in *Report of persons apprehended, as made to the Chief of Police, from the 1st of July, to the 15th of October, 1845.*

11. Federal Census Data 1840, 1850; New York Police establishment, 1845, *New York Police 1844* – text of law outlining police force – originally 650 officers; based on 1840 population, ratio of 1:481; 1850 population ratio of 1:793; *New York Police 1864* – detailed; includes number of patrolmen (1,800) and population (900,000).

12. Of those arrested by police in New York City from July 1 to October 15, 1845, a whopping 1,343 were charged with disorderly conduct, 2,945 with illegal lodging, and 3,205 with intoxication. Vagrancy was fifth on the list at 692, after assault and battery, 834. These five categories represented most arrests. Arrests explicitly for cross-dressing totaled a scant five and were designated "Persons dressed in disguise," stated "2 males in female dress; 3 females in male dress," one of the least significant categories calculated. *Report of persons apprehended, as made to the Chief of Police, from the 1st of July, to the 15th of October, 1845.*

13. Officer Collins is identified in the following accounts: "Singular Case," *Commercial Advertiser*, New York, August 13, 1836; "Singular Case," *American and Commercial Daily Advertiser*, Baltimore, MD, August 16, 1836; "Singular Case," *Spectator*, New York, August 18, 1836; "Singular Case," *Daily Globe*, Washington, DC, August 19, 1836; "Singular Case," *Daily Globe*, Washington, DC, August 20, 1836. One article mentions the drunk cart that was commonly used for this purpose, "A Man Turned Out to Be a Woman," *Rhode Island Republican*, Newport, RI, August 17, 1836.

14. "A Discovery," *Evening Star*, New York, August 13, 1836; *Public Ledger*, August 15, 1836; *Alexandria Gazette*, Alexandria, VA, August 16, 1836.

15. "Singular Case," *Commercial Advertiser*, New York, August 13, 1836; *American and Commercial Daily Advertiser*, Baltimore, MD, August 16, 1836; *Spectator*, New York, August 18, 1836; *Daily Globe*, Washington, DC, August 19, 1836.

16. "From the Journal of Commerce," *Commercial Advertiser*, New York, August 15, 1836; I have thirty-nine records of publication of this account in other places; it was probably reprinted nearly one hundred times.

17. "From the Journal of Commerce. Police Office – August 13," *Commercial Advertiser*, New York, August 15, 1836. The same version of the article was reprinted at least thirty-nine

times. By 1850, however, the paper developed a reputation among some abolitionists as the strongest "apologist of slavery" in the north National Anti-Slavery Standard, in Eric Foner, *Gateway to Freedom: The Hidden History of the Underground Railroad* (Norton: New York, 2015), 127.

18. Will Slauter, *Who Owns the News: A History of Copyright* (Stanford University Press, 2019), 75–6.

19. Slauter, *Who Owns the News*, 108. Quoted in *North American* (Philadelphia) June 17, 1841.

20. Slauter, *Who Owns the News*, 147–9.

21. Slauter, *Who Owns the News*, 163–4.

22. Slauter, *Who Owns the News*, 207.

23. For references to their work as a hatter, see "More Romance," *Atkinson's Saturday Evening Post*, August 27, 1836 and "From the New York Sun," *Springfield Republican*, August 27, 1836.

24. Listed at 160 Broadway in 1829 in *Longworth's American Almanac, New-York Register, and City Directory* (New York: Thomas Longworth) for 1829.

25. Roland was the carpenter Paltiall S. Rowland. *Longworth's American Almanac, New York Register, and City Directory* (New York: Thomas Longworth) for 1832.

26. *Longworth's American Almanac, New-York Register, and City Directory* (New York: Thomas Longworth) for 1835, 1836. He's not listed in the 1841 directory.

27. Alison Matthews David, *Fashion Victims: The Dangers of Dress Past and Present* (Bloomsbury Visual Arts, 2015), chapter 2.

28. "Singular Case," *Daily Pennsylvanian*, Philadelphia, PA, August 16, 1825.

29. "A Discovery," *Evening Star*, New York, August 13, 1836; "A Singular Case," *Commercial Advertiser*, New York, August 13, 1836.

30. Glenn, *Jack Tar's Story*, 3.

31. "Singular Case," *Daily Pennsylvanian*, Philadelphia, PA, August 16, 1825; "New York Police," *Mississippian*, September 16, 1836.

32. "James Cummin and Margt Ogilvie had their 4th child born the 1st bapt 21st named Elisabeth. James Ogilvie and John McFarlane wit." Cummin, Elisabeth, Old Parish Registers Births, June 21, 1804, Barony, National Records of Scotland, 348.

33. "From the New York Sun," *Springfield Republican*, Springfield MA, August 27, 1836.

34. "George Wilson cotton spinner [bardgeton?] and Elisabeth Cummin residency there married 6th April by the Rev.d John McFarlane." Wilson, George, Old Paris Registers Marriages, April 6, 1821, Barony, National Records of Scotland.

35. "More Romance," *Atkinson's Saturday Evening Post*, August 27, 1836.

36. "From the New York Sun," *Springfield Republican*, Springfield, MA, August 27, 1836.

37. "Singular Case," *Daily Pennsylvanian*, Philadelphia, PA, August 16, 1836; "New York Police," *Mississippian*, September 16, 1836; "Female Husband," *The Corrector*, Sag Harbor, August 24, 1836.

38. Monica E. Hawley, Historic American Engineering Record, The Ivanhoe Mill Wheelhouse, Spruce and Market Streets, Paterson, NJ, www.patersonhistory.com/industry/ivanhoe.html.

39. *Report of persons apprehended, as made to the Chief of Police, from the 1st of July, to the 15th of October, 1845.*

40. Olive Decker, furcutter at 51 Forsyth Street; Hatters – Daniel Gillis, 54 Forsyth; Edward B. Hobby, 86 Forsyth; Frederick Keeler, 143 Forsyth; Lewis Rich, 25 Forsyth. *Longworth's American Almanac, New-York Register, and City Directory* (New York: Thomas Longworth, 1836).

41. Billy Smith, *The "Lower Sort": Philadelphia's Laboring People, 1750–1800* (Ithaca, NY: Cornell University Press, 1994).

42. This line was used in the original story which I have traced in thirty-nine different publications in a six-week period from August 15, 1836 to September 30, 1836. The first I have is "From the Journal of Commerce," *Commercial Advertiser*, New York, August 15, 1836.

43. "Singular Case," *Daily Pennsylvanian*, Philadelphia, PA August 16, 15; New York Police," *Mississippian*, September 16, 1836.

44. "Singular Case," *Daily Pennsylvanian*, Philadelphia, PA, August 16, 1836; "New York Police," *Mississippian*, September 16, 1836; "Female Husband," *The Corrector*, Sag Harbor, August 24, 1836.

45. "From the New York Sun," *Springfield Republican*, Springfield, MA, August 27, 1836.

46. "From the Journal of Commerce. Police Office – August 13," *Commercial Advertiser*, New York, August 15, 1836.

47. "More Romance," *Atkinson's Saturday Evening Post*, August 27, 1836.

48. "More Romance," *Atkinson's Saturday Evening Post*, August 27, 1836.

49. "From the New York Sun," *Springfield Republican*, Springfield, MA, August 27, 1836.

50. "A Man Turned Out to Be a Woman," *Rhode Island Republican*, August 17, 1836.

51. "Singular Case," *Daily Pennsylvanian*, Philadelphia, PA, August 16, 1836 and "New York Police," *Mississippian*, September 16, 1836 and "Female Husband," *The Corrector*, Sag Harbor, August 24, 1836.

52. "A Female Husband," *Columbian Register*, New Haven, CT, August 20, 1836; a unique claim to this article.

53. "Municipal Police. Chapter XVII. An Ordinance To establish a Municipal Police, or Night and Day watch. Passed November 27, 1844." *By-Laws and Ordinances of the Mayor, Alderman, and Commonality of the City of New York*, 1845, 209.

54. "A Female Husband," *Columbian Register*, New Haven, CT, August 20, 1836; a unique claim to this article.

55. This dates back to the colonial era in the decision to have a local woman examine the body of Thomas/ine Hall. See Kathleen Brown, "Changed . . . into the Fashion of Man": The Politics of Sexual Difference in a Seventeenth Century Anglo-American Settlement," *Journal of the History of Sexuality* 6, no. 2 (October, 1995): 171–93.

56. "Singular Case," *Daily Pennsylvanian*, Philadelphia, PA, August 16, 1836 and "New York Police," *Mississippian*, September 16, 1836.

57. "New York Police," *Mississippian*, September 16, 1836.

58. "A Man Turned Out to Be a Woman," *Rhode Island Republican*, Newport, RI, August 17, 1836.

59. "Awful Disclosure," *New York Herald*, New York, August 15, 1836.

60. "Leap Year," *Delaware Gazette*, Delhi, NY, October 7, 1835.

61. Marcus Rediker, *Between the Devil and the Deep Blue Sea: Merchant Seamen, Pirates and the Anglo-American Maritime World, 1700–1750* (New York: Cambridge University Press, 1987); Glenn, *Jack Tar's Story*; Daniel Vickers, *Farmers and Fishermen: Two Centuries of work in Essex County, Massachusetts, 1630–1850* (Chapel Hill: University of North Carolina Press, 1994); Lisa Norling, *Captain Ahab Had a Wife: New England Women and the Whalefishery, 1720–1870* (Chapel Hill: University of North Carolina Press, 2000); Creighton and Norling, *Iron Men, Wooden Women*.

62. Stark, *Female Tars*, 122.

63. W. Jeffrey Bolster, *Black Jacks: African American Seamen in the Age of Sail* (Cambridge, MA: Harvard University, 1997); Julius S. Scott, *The Common Wind: Afro-American Currents in the Age of the Haitian Revolution* (New York: Verso, 2018).

64. Cohen, ed., *The Female Marine and Related Works*, 2–3.

65. *The Female Marine, or the Adventures of Miss Lucy Brewer* (10th edition, 1816) in Cohen, *The Female Marine*, 75.

66. *The Female Marine* (Boston: N. Coverly, 1816); *The Surprising Adventures of Almira Paul* (Boston: N. Coverly, 1816).

67. "Female Sailor," *Commercial Advertiser*, New York, January 30, 1834.

68. "A colored person," *Boston Daily Advertiser*, Boston, MA, February 3, 1834.

69. "On Monday Last," *Evening Post*, New York, January 30, 1834; one newspaper omitted William's racial designation entirely, referring to them simply as a person, "A Curious Circumstance," *Newburyport Herald*, Newburyport, MA, February 4, 1834.

70. Allyson Hobbs, *A Chosen Exile: A History of Racial Passing in American Life* (Cambridge, MA: Harvard University Press, 2014).

71. *Alexandria Gazette*, February 4, 1834; *Baltimore Patriot*, February 3, 1834; *Commercial Advertiser*, New York, January 30, 1834; *National Gazette*, Philadelphia, PA, February 1, 1834; *New York Spectator*, February 10, 1834; *Essex Gazette*, Haverhill, MA, February 8, 1834; *Norfolk Advertiser and Independent Politician*, February 8, 1834; *Salem Gazette*, February 4, 1834; *Workingmen's Advocate*, February 27, 1834; *New-York Spectator*, New York, February 10, 1834.

72. "Female Sailor," *Commercial Advertiser*, New York, January 30, 1834.

73. "Yet having heard of my metamorphosis," was used as a phrase by female sailor William Chandler describing their shift from life as man to live as a woman. Slade, *The History of the Female Shipwright*, 190.

74. Metamorphosis, n. *Oxford English Dictionary*. Nos. 1, 2, and 3; also see Greta LaFleur, *The Natural History of Sexuality in Early America* (Baltimore: Johns Hopkins University Press, 2018).

75. Talitha LaFlouria, *Chained in Silence* (Chapel Hill: University of North Carolina Press, 2015).

76. Jen Manion, "Gendered Ideologies of Violence, Authority, and Racial Difference in New York State Penitentiaries, 1796–1848," *Radical History Review, Reconsidering Gender, Violence and the State*, 126 (October 2016): 11–29.

77. "Female Sailor," *Commercial Advertiser*, New York, January 30, 1834.

78. See discussion of Samuel Johnson in Manion, *Liberty's Prisoners*, 164–5.

79. Stark, *Female Tars*, 86–8.

80. "Female Sailor," *Morning Post*, London, England, September 2, 1815.

81. Snorton argues that in these situations, "the dichotomized and collapsed designations of male-man-masculine and female-woman-feminine remained open – that is fungible – and the black's figurative capacity to change form as a commoditized being engendered flow." Snorton, *Black on Both Sides*, 59.

82. Anthony J. Sebok, "Judging the Fugitive Slave Acts," *The Yale Law Journal* 100, no. 6 (April 1991): 1835–1854, 1835.

83. Estimates on the number vary widely from about fifteen to 40,000. Sharon A. Roger Hepburn, "Following the North Star: Canada as a Haven for Nineteenth-Century American Blacks," *Michigan Historical Review* 25, no. 2 (Fall 1999): 91–126; Michael Wayne's research has defined prevailing wisdom of around 20,000. Michael Wayne, "The Black Population of Canada West on the Eve of the American Civil War: A Reassessment Based on the Manuscript Census of 1861," *Social History* 28 (1995): 465–85. Early studies put the number around 15,000–20,000, such as in the work of Fred Landon, "The Negro Migration to Canada after the Passing of the Fugitive Slave Act," *The Journal of Negro History* 5, no. 1 (January 1920): 22–36.

84. "A Romance of the Ocean," *National Aegis*, Worcester, MA, December 19, 1849; nearly identical language in, "A Romance of the Ocean," *Plain Dealer*, Cleveland, OH, December 21, 1849; "A Romance of the Ocean," *New Bedford Mercury*, New Bedford, MA, December 21, 1849; "A Romance of the Ocean," *Charleston Courier*, Charleston, SC, December 21, 1849; "A Romance of the Ocean," *Boston Daily Bee*, Boston, MA, December 31, 1849; "A South Sea Adventure," *North American*, January 26, 1850; "A South Sea Adventure," *Emancipator and Republican*, Boston, MA, January 31, 1850.

85. "A Romance of the Ocean," *National Aegis*, Worcester, MA, December 19, 1849; nearly identical language in, "A Romance of the Ocean," *Plain Dealer*, Cleveland, OH, December 21, 1849; "A Romance of the Ocean," *New Bedford Mercury*, New Bedford, MA, December 21, 1849; "A Romance of the Ocean," *Charleston Courier*, Charleston, SC, December 21, 1849; "A Romance of the Ocean," *Boston Daily Bee*, Boston, MA, December 31, 1849; "A South Sea Adventure," *North American*, January 26, 1850; "A South Sea Adventure," *Emancipator and Republican*, Boston, MA, January 31, 1850.

86. "Female Sailor," *Republican Farmer*, Bridgeport, CT, August 21, 1849.

87. "A South Sea Adventure," *Emancipator and Republican*, Boston, MA, January 31, 1850.

88. "A South Sea Adventure," *Emancipator and Republican*, Boston, MA, January 31, 1850.

89. "A Female Sailor," *Boston Evening Transcript*, August 18, 1849.

90. Stanton Garner, ed., *The Captain's Best Mate: The Journal of Mary Chipman Lawrence on the Whaler Addison, 1856–1860* (Hanover, NH: University of New England Press, 1966), xix.

91. "A Curious Freak of a Young Woman," *Philadelphia Inquirer*, Philadelphia, PA, August 20, 1849; also in *Bridgeton Chronicle*, Bridgeton, NJ, August 25, 1849.

92. "Female Sailor," *Republican Farmer*, Bridgeport, CT, August 21, 1849. This account includes a street address for the father which I could not verify, 22 Oak Street, Rochester, NY.

93. Garner, *The Captain's Best Mate*; Anne MacKay, ed., *She Went A-Whaling: The Journal of Martha Smith Brewer Brown from Orient, Long Island, New York, Around the World on the Whaling Ship Lucy Ann, 1847–1849* (Orient, NY: Oysterponds Historical Society, 1993); Annette Brock Davis, *My Year Before the Mast* (Toronto: Hounslow Press, 1999); Jim Coogan, *Sail Away Ladies: Stories of Cape Cod Women in the Age of Sail* (East Dennis: Harvest Home Books, 2008).

94. Estelle Freedman, *Their Sister's Keepers: Women's Prison Reform in America, 1830–1930* (Minnesota: University of Michigan Press, 1981).

95. A Romance of the Ocean," *National Aegis*, Worcester, MA, December 19, 1849; nearly identical language in, "A Romance of the Ocean," *Plain Dealer*, Cleveland, OH, December 21, 1849; "A Romance of the Ocean," *New Bedford Mercury*, New Bedford, MA, December 21, 1849; "A Romance of the Ocean," *Charleston Courier*, Charleston, SC, December 21, 1849; "A Romance of the Ocean," *Boston Daily Bee*, Boston, MA, December 31, 1849; "A South Sea Adventure," *North American*, January 26, 1850; "A South Sea Adventure," *Emancipator and Republican*, Boston, MA, January 31, 1850.

96. "A South Sea Adventure," *Emancipator and Republican*, Boston, MA, January 31, 1850.

97. "A Female Sailor," *The Baltimore Sun*, Baltimore, MD, January 18, 1850.

98. "A Woman in Man's Clothes," *Raftsman Journal*, Clearfield, July 2, 1856.

99. "A Male Girl," *Brother Jonathan*, June 14, 1856.

100. One year, in "A Woman Disguised as a Man," *New York Herald*, New York, June 25, 1856; two years, in "A Woman in Man's Clothes," *Raftsman Journal*, Clearfield, July 2, 1856.

101. "A Woman Disguised as a Man," *New York Herald*, New York, June 25, 1856.

102. "A Male Girl," *Brother Jonathan*, June 14, 1856; "Singular Case," *Daily Pennsylvanian*, Philadelphia, PA, August 16, 1836.

103. "Transpositions," *Nantucket Inquirer*, Nantucket, MA, August 20, 1836.

6 THE ACTIVISTS

1. Nancy A. Hewitt, *Women's Activism and Social Change: Rochester, New York, 1822–1872* (Ithaca, NY: Cornell University Press, 1984); Nancy Isenberg, *Sex and Citizenship in Antebellum America* (Chapel Hill: University of North Carolina, 1998); Kathi Kern, *Mrs. Stanton's Bible* (Ithaca, NY: Cornell University Press, 2001); Bruce Dorsey, *Reforming Men and Women: Gender in the Antebellum City* (Ithaca, NY: Cornell University Press, 2002); Anne M. Boylan, *The Origins of Women's Activism: New York and Boston, 1797–1840* (Chapel Hill: University of North Carolina Press, 2002); Judith Wellman, *The Road to Seneca Falls: Elizabeth Cady Stanton and the First Women's Rights Convention* (Champaign: University of Illinois Press, 2004); Lori D. Ginzberg, *Untidy Origins: A Story of Woman's Rights in Antebellum New York* (Chapel Hill: University of North Carolina Press, 2005);

Sally McMillen, *Seneca Falls and the Origins of the Women's Rights Movement* (New York: Oxford University Press, 2008); Lori Ginzberg, *Elizabeth Cady Stanton: An American Life* (New York: Hill and Wang, 2010); Carol Faulkner, *Lucretia Mott's Heresy: Abolition and Women's Rights in Nineteenth-Century America* (Philadelphia: University of Pennsylvania, 2011); Lisa Tetrault, *The Myth of Seneca Falls: Memory and the Women's Suffrage Movement, 1848–1898* (Chapel Hill: University of North Carolina Press, 2014); Nancy Hewitt, *Radical Friend: Amy Kirby Post and Her Activist Worlds* (Chapel Hill: University of North Carolina Press, 2018).

2. Kristan Poirot, *A Question of Sex: Feminism, Rhetoric, and Differences that Matter* (Amherst: University of Massachusetts Press, 2014).

3. Jen Manion, "Gender Expression in Antebellum America: Accessing the Privileges and Freedoms of White Men," in Leslie Brown, Jacqueline Castledine, and Anne Valk, eds., *U.S. Women's History: Untangling the Threads of Sisterhood* (New Brunswick: Rutgers University Press, 2017), 151–70.

4. "A Curious Case of Female Deception," *Cabinet*, Schenectady, NY, November 15, 1842; "Albany Police – A Curious Case of Female Deception," *Spectator*, New York, November 16, 1842; "Albany Police – A Curious Case of Female Deception," *Evening Post*, New York, November 17, 1842.

5. "The Woman Who Married the Woman," *Kendall's Expositor*, November 29, 1842.

6. "A Curious Case of Female Deception," *Cabinet*, Schenectady, NY, November 15, 1842.

7. Mrs. Donnelly, Albany Ward 5, Albany, New York, 1840 Federal Census.

8. "The Woman Who Married the Woman," *Kendall's Expositor*, November 29, 1842.

9. Articles says Rev. Mr. Stillwell instead of Stillman. Stephen Lewis Stillman was born in Burlington, CT on April 15, 1795. *Old Sands Street Methodist Episcopal Church, of Brooklyn, N.Y. : an illustrated centennial record, historical and biographical*, Warriner, Edwin, 1839–1898, 1885; he was pastor of the Washington Street Methodist Church, 188 Washington St. Albany in 1844 and the North Second Street Methodist Episcopal Church in 1845. "Stillman," in *Hoffman's Albany directory and city register for the years 1844–5*, 311; Joel Munsell, *Collections on the History of Albany: From Its Discovery to the Present Time; with Notices of Its Public Institutions, and Biographical Sketches of Citizens Deceased*, Vol. 4 (Albany, NY 1871), 55.

10. "A Curious Case of Female Deception," *Cabinet*, Schenectady, NY, November 15, 1842; "Strange," *Milwaukee Sentinel*, Milwaukee, WI, December 7, 1842.

11. "The Woman Who Married the Woman," *Kendall's Expositor*, November 29, 1842.

12. These cases described the husband's name as McGarahan but later reports claim they entered into the marriage as John Smith. See, McGarahan, "A Female Husband," *Public Ledger*, Philadelphia, PA, November 16, 1842; McGarshan, "An Odd Character," *The Sun*, Baltimore, November 17, 1842; M'Garahan, "A Female Husband," *New Bedford Register*, New Bedford, MA, November 23, 1842.

13. "A Curious Case of Female Deception," *Cabinet*, Schenectady, NY, November 15, 1842.

14. "A Curious Case of Female Deception," *Cabinet*, Schenectady, NY, November 15, 1842; "Albany Police – A Curious Case of Female Deception," *Spectator*, New York, November 16, 1842; "Albany Police – A Curious Case of Female Deception," *Evening Post*, New York, November 17, 1842.

15. "An Awkward Mistake," *Philadelphia Inquirer*, Philadelphia, PA, November 17, 1842.

16. "A Female Husband," *Hingham Patriot*, Hingham, MA, December 3, 1842.

17. "Singular Marriage," *Times-Picayune*, New Orleans, LA, November 30, 1842.

18. "Untitled," *Maine Farmer and Journal of the Arts*, October 2, 1841.

19. "Did You Ever Hear the Like!" *Arkansas Times and Advocate*, December 12, 1842.

20. Dorsey, *Reforming Men and Women*.

21. Lucia McMahon, *The Paradox of Educated Women in the Early American Republic* (Ithaca, NY: Cornell University Press, 2012), 169.

22. McMahon, *The Paradox of Educated Women*, 167–9.

23. Martha S. Jones, *All Bound Up Together: The Woman Question in African American Public Culture, 1830–1900* (Chapel Hill: University of North Carolina Press, 2007), 23–30.

24. Phillip Lapansky, "Graphic Discord: Abolitionist and Antiabolitionist Images," in Jean Fagan Yellin and John C. Van Horne, eds., *The Abolitionist Sisterhood: Women's Political Culture in Antebellum America* (Ithaca, NY: Cornell University Press, 1994), 201–30, 222–3.

25. Stephen Howard Browne, *Angelina Grimke: Rhetoric, Identity, and the Radical Imagination* (Michigan State University Press, 1999), 115.

26. Browne, *Angelina Grimke*, 116.

27. Hubbard Winslow, "The Appropriate Sphere of Woman? A Discourse Delivered in the Bowdoin Street Church, July 9, 1837" (Boston: Weeks, Jordan & Co., 1837), 5.

28. Winslow, "The Appropriate Sphere of Woman?" 7.

29. Winslow, "The Appropriate Sphere of Woman?" 8.

30. Winslow, "The Appropriate Sphere of Woman?" 13.

31. Winslow, "The Appropriate Sphere of Woman?" 15–16.

32. Winslow, "The Appropriate Sphere of Woman?" 4–5

33. Winslow, "The Appropriate Sphere of Woman?" 5.

34. Winslow, "The Appropriate Sphere of Woman?" 14.

35. "Gender was never peripheral to the meaning of representation; it was vital in explaining the masculine marks of presence and speech that remained crucial to a nineteenth-century understanding of the public forum." Nancy Isenberg, "'Pillars in the Same Temple and Priests of the Same Worship': Women's Rights and the Politics of Church and State in Antebellum America," *The Journal of American History* 85, no. 1 (June 1998): 98–128, 100.

36. Jones, *All Bound Up Together*, 46.

37. Susan Zaeske, "'The South Arose as One Man': Gender and Sectionalism in Antislavery Petition Debates, 1835–1845," *Rhetoric and Public Affairs* 12, no. 3 (Fall 2009): 341–68, 353.

38. Zaeske, "The South Arose as One Man," 353.

39. Zaeske, "The South Arose as One Man," 353.

40. Len Gougeon, "Emerson and the Woman Question: The Evolution of His Thought," *The New England Quarterly* 71, no. 4 (December 1998): 570–92.

41. Gougeon, "Emerson and the Woman Question," 575.

42. Gougeon, "Emerson and the Woman Question," 585–6, fn. 39.

43. "Woman and Her Work," *Sibyl*, May 1, 1858.

44. "Female Disturbers," *Portland Transcript*, September 17, 1853.

45. Patricia Cline Cohen, "Nichols: A Radical Critique of Monogamy in the 1850s," *Journal of the Early Republic* 34, no. 1 (Spring, 2014): 1–20.

46. Mary S. Grove Nichols, "Dress Reform," *Water-Cure Journal,* January 1, 1853.

47. Catherine E. Beecher, *Letters on the Difficulties of Religion* (Hartford, CT, 1836), 23.

48. Nancy Hewitt, "From Seneca Falls to Suffrage? Reimagining a 'Master' Narrative in U.S. Women's History," in Nancy Hewitt, ed., *No Permanent Waves: Recasting Histories of U.S. Feminism* (Chicago: Rutgers University Press, 2010), 15–38.

49. New York Anti-Slavery Convention, Utica, NY, 1835; Anti-Slavery Convention of American Women, New York City, 1837; New York State Convention of Colored Citizens, Troy, NY, 1841; Women's Rights Convention, Seneca Falls, NY, 1848; Rochester Women's Rights Convention, Rochester, NY, 1848.

50. Nancy Isenberg, "Pillars in the Same Temple and Priests of the Same Worship," 12; Matilda Joslyn Gage was the star speaker who inspired a call to women's suffrage. She was only twenty-six and had her five-year-old daughter on stage with her. Susan Grodier and Karen Pastorello, *Women Will Vote: Winning Suffrage in New York State* (Ithaca, NY: Cornell University Press, 2017), 7.

51. The pamphlet was printed in 1853 and circulated by the movement. See Grodier and Pastorello, *Women Will Vote*, p. 8.

52. Samuel J. May, *The Rights and Condition of Women: A Sermon Preached in Syracuse, Nov. 1845, Third Edition* (Lathrop's, 1853?), 3.

53. Herbert Winslow wrote: "The abject condition of the female sex in all but Christian countries is universally known and admitted. In all savage and pagan tribes the severest burdens of physical toil are laid upon their shoulders; they are chiefly valued for the same reason that men value their more useful animals, or as objects of their sensual and selfish desires." Hubbard Winslow, *Woman as She Should Be* (Boston: T.H. Carter, 1838), 34.

54. May, *The Rights and Condition of Women*, 3–4.

55. W.W. Gardner, "Graduation of Women," *Worcester Journal of Medicine,* June 1, 1853, 188–89.

56. Gardner, "Graduation of Women," 190.

57. "Dr. Bushnell's New Work: A Broadside Against Woman Suffrage," *Hartford Daily Courant,* June 11, 1869; "A Blast at Sorosis," *Cleveland Daily Herald,* June 16, 1869.

58. Sharon Marcus, *Between Women: Friendship, Desire, and Marriage in Victorian England* (Princeton, NJ: Princeton University Press, 2007), 207.

59. Mary Ann Robins, 1851 England Census, piece 1481, folio 296, 16.

60. All three children were baptized in 1839 at St. John the Evangelical, Lambeth, London. London, England, Church of England Births and Baptisms, 1813–1916. First characterized as Mrs. Robins and later Mrs. Reubens. See, for example, "A Female Husband," *London Atlas,* and "A Female Husband," *The Norfolk News*, October 15, 1853.

61. "Westminster," *London Daily News,* October 12, 1853; later reports beginning with "A Female Husband," *Alexandria Gazette,* Alexandria, VA, December 22, 1853, which reported the marriage year as 1853.

62. "A Female Husband," *The Concordia Intelligencier*, Vidalia, LA, December 17, 1853.

63. "Westminster," *London Standard*, October 13, 1853.

64. One exception was John Smith (not the John Smith in the previous chapter) who was raised by a "gypsy" and presented as a boy from the age of three. Smith, who worked as a knife grinder and spoon maker, was married to the same woman for fourteen years, and also raised their seven stepchildren until their death in 1848. "A Female Husband," *Sherborne Mercury*, November 4, 1848; *Bath Chronicle and Weekly Gazette*, October 26, 1848.

65. John Murphy was born in Sligo, Ireland. When their parents died, at the age of thirteen they decided to present themselves as a boy so as to better take care of themselves. They moved to England where they found work as a day laborer. "Multiple News Items," *Berrows Worcester Journal*, July 14, 1825; "Singular Circumstance," *Stamford Mercury*, July 8, 1825.

66. Rubens in "Westminster," *London Daily News*, October 12, 1853; Robins in "Westminster," *London Standard*, October 12, 1853. While the series of articles varied this spelling, there was consistency between mother and daughter within each story.

67. "Westminster," *London Daily News*, October 12, 1853.

68. "Westminster," *London Daily News*, October 12, 1853.

69. Mary Robins' parents, Bruton Robins and Mary Ann Brooks were married at St. John's in Hackney, England on July 6, 1834; London, England, Church of England Marriages and Banns, 1754–1931.

70. Mary Ann, April 21, 1835; a son named Bruton for the father in April 7, 1837 and a girl named Louisa, May 12, 1839. London, England, Church of England Births and Baptisms, 1813–1916. All three children were baptized together in 1839 at St. John the Evangelical Church in Lambeth, London.

71. Norton, *Founding Mothers and Fathers*, 139.

72. "A Female Husband," *Norfolk News*, October 15, 1853; "A Female Husband," *Bury and Norwich Post*, October 19, 1853.

73. Just like Mary Ann's first husband Bruton, Blewett also followed in his father's occupational footsteps. Records show the couple was already living together at 9 Duke Street at the time of the marriage, on February 13, 1854 at St. Giles in the Fields, Holborn, Camden, England. Mary Ann Brooks, Marriage, London, England, Church of England Marriages and Banns, 1754–1931.

74. The two were wed at Christ Church, Southwark, on January 11, 1855. The two were living together at 42 Stanford Street at the time of their wedding. James's dad John was also an artist.

75. I have sixteen different publications with the story in it, suggesting it ran in dozens, if not hundreds of papers.

76. "A Female Husband," *Miners Journal*, Pottsville, PA, January 28, 1854.

77. "The Man Woman," *Syracuse Daily Standard*, April 22, 1856.

78. "The Man Woman," *Syracuse Daily Standard*, April 22, 1856.

79. "Human Frailty," *Warren Mail*, May 3, 1856.

80. "The Man Woman!" *Syracuse Daily Standard*, April 22, 1856.

81. "It seems that the case of the 'Man Woman'," *Syracuse Daily Standard*, April 25, 1856.

82. "The Female in Disguise Discharged on a Writ of Habeas Corpus," *Syracuse Daily Standard*, April 26, 1856.

83. "The Man Woman," *Syracuse Daily Standard*, April 22, 1856.

84. "Human Frailty," *Warren Mail*, May 3, 1856.

85. "The Man Woman," *Syracuse Daily Standard*, April 22, 1856.

86. "The Question," *Syracuse Daily Journal*, April 22, 1856.

87. "The Female in Disguise," *Syracuse Daily Standard*, April 24, 1856.

88. "The Female in Disguise," *Syracuse Daily Standard*, April 24, 1856.

89. "The Female in Disguise," *Syracuse Daily Standard*, April 24, 1856.

90. An 1851 England census noted thirty-seven-year-old Sarah, dressmaker, Kensington, England with five children and two guests, teenagers Henry and Sarah Pamlo; Sarah Edgar, 1851 England Census.

91. "The Female in Disguise," *Syracuse Daily Standard*, April 23, 1856.

92. Thomas Joseph Edgar was born December 27, 1813 to John and Elizabeth Edgar; John worked as a coachmaker's laborer. Thomas Joseph Edgar, St. Giles in the Fields, Holborn, Camden, England, London, England, Church of England Births and Baptisms, 1813–1916.

93. Stours or Stoure or Stoun, "The 'Man Woman' Arrested Again," *Syracuse Daily Standard*, June 3, 1856.

94. Diana Jackson, New York State Census, 1855.

95. Eleanor (15), Lewis (13), Maryann (11), Maria (9), Louisa (7), Thomas Edgar (43), Sarah (42), Syracuse City, Ward 7, Onondaga, New York, United States, New York State Census, 1855.

96. "The Man Woman," *Syracuse Daily Standard*, April 22, 1856; "All Sorts of Paragraphs," *Boston Post*, April 28, 1856; "The Female in Disguise," *Syracuse Daily Standard*, April 23, 1856.

97. The widely circulating explanations for what motivated Guelph to pursue Miss Lewis are extreme: that Guelph was hired by Miss Lewis' prior jilted lover to win her affection and exact revenge or that Guelph stood to receive an inheritance that required they be married "What Motive Induced," *Syracuse Daily Standard*, April 24, 1856.

98. "The Man Woman," *Syracuse Daily Standard*, April 22, 1856.

99. "Developments Extraordinary," *Syracuse Daily Journal*, April 22, 1856.

100. "Hard Up," *Syracuse Daily Standard*, April 23, 1856; "It Appears," *The Brooklyn Daily Eagle*, April 26, 1856; "The Female Husband at Syracuse," *The Buffalo Courier*, April 27, 1856.

101. "The women must be very hard up for husbands when they take to marrying one another. This is leap year." *The Brooklyn Daily Eagle*, April 26, 1856.

102. "It Seems That," *Syracuse Daily Standard*, April 25, 1856; "The Female in Disguise Discharged on a Writ of Habeas Corpus," *Syracuse Daily Standard*, April 26, 1856.

103. "The Female in Disguise Discharged on a Writ of Habeas Corpus," *Syracuse Daily Standard*, April 26, 1856.

104. "The Female in Disguise Discharged on a Writ of Habeas Corpus," *Syracuse Daily Standard*, April 26, 1856.

105. John Duer et al., "Beggars and Vagrants," Chapter XX, Number 5, *The Revised Statutes of the State of New-York, as Altered by Subsequent Enactments: together with Statutory Provisions of a General Nature, Passed Between the Years 1828 and 1845* (New York: Weare C. Little and Co.), 1846, 803.

106. Duer et al., "Beggars and Vagrants," Chapter X, Title 7, *The Revised Statues of the State of New-York*, 354.

107. Eric Kades, "The End of the Hudson Valley's Peculiar Institution: The Anti-Rent Movement's Politics, Social Relations, and Economics," *Law and Social Inquiry* (2002): 941–65, 945.

108. Jennifer Levi and Daniel Redman, "The Cross-Dressing Case for Bathroom Equality," *Seattle University Law Review* 34, no. 1 (2010): 133–71, 152; People v. Archibald, 296 N.Y.S.2d 864 (N.Y. App. Term 1968).

109. "The Male-Attired Female Discharged," *Syracuse Daily Journal*, April 26, 1856.

110. "The Male-Attired Female Discharged," *Syracuse Daily Journal*, April 26, 1856.

111. "Communication from 'Nancy'," *Syracuse Daily Standard*, May 8, 1856.

112. "Communication from 'Nancy'," *Syracuse Daily Standard*, May 8, 1856.

113. Gayle V. Fisher, *Pantaloons and Power: A Nineteenth-Century Dress Reform in the United States* (Kent, OH: Kent State University Press, 2001); Carol Mattingly, *Appropriate[ing] Dress: Women's Rhetorical Style in Nineteenth Century America* (Carbondale: Southern Illinois University Press, 2002).

114. Fisher, *Pantaloons and Power*, 101.

115. Dexter C. Bloomer, *Life and Writings of Amelia Bloomer* (Boston, 1895), 70.

116. "Women's Rights. Dialogue," *The Dover Gazette and Strafford Advertiser*, July 7, 1860.

117. Underwood was married to B.F. Underwood who worked as a lecturer and writer for the free-thought movement. See Bonnie S. Anderson, *The Rabbi's Atheist Daughter: Ernestine Rose International Feminist Pioneer* (New York: Oxford University Press, 2017), 204, note 29.

118. Sara A. Underwood, "New York Anniversaries," *Boston Investigator*, May 27, 1868.

119. "Forty-Second Congress, Second Session. Washington, Dec. 12." *The North American*, December 15, 1871.

120. "Woman Suffrage," *Independent Statesman*, January 4, 1872.

121. "Friendly Remarks," *Boston Investigator*, October 22, 1879.

122. "This of course will serve as a warning to all ladies of a masculine turn of mind, not to carry the joke too far. If they get intimate with one of their sex, they will be sure to be found out." "Did you Ever Hear the Like!" *Arkansas Times and Advocate*, December 12, 1842.

123. "Going the Whole Figure," *Pen and Scissors*, Portland, ME, May 10, 1856.

124. "Man-Woman," *Syracuse Daily Standard*, April 24, 1856.

125. "Man-Woman," *Syracuse Daily Standard*, April 24, 1856.

126. "A Couple of," *Syracuse Daily Standard*, May 28, 1856.

127. "A Woman Married to a Woman – Interesting Developments," *Gettysburg Adams Sentinel*, May 5, 1856.

128. "It is Supposed," *Syracuse Daily Standard*, Syracuse, NY, April 25, 1856.

129. May, *The Rights and Condition of Women*, 12.

130. "Does Woman Desire to Reconstruct Society?" *Vermont Watchman and State Journal*, March 2, 1870.

131. "A Notable Fact," from the *Chicago Tribune*, in *Macon Weekly Telegraph*, Macon, Georgia, January 24, 1871.

132. Marcus, *Between Women*.

133. New York's Married Women's Property Act April 7, 1848, https://memory.loc.gov/ammem/awhhtml/awlaw3/property_law.html.

134. "A Man-Woman," *Morning Republican*, November 20, 1873.

135. "A Man-Woman," *Morning Republican*, November 20, 1873.

7 THE CRIMINALIZED POOR

1. Jen Manion, "Transgender Children in Antebellum America," http://outhistory.org/exhibits/show/transgenderchildrenantebellum. Books on the queerness of childhood include Steven Bruhm and Natasha Hurley, eds., *Curiouser: On the Queerness of Children* (Minneapolis: University of Minnesota Press, 2004); Kathryn Bond Stockton, *The Queer Child, or Growing Sideways in the Twentieth Century* (Durham, NC: Duke University Press, 2009).

2. Missouri led the way with four cities passing laws against cross-dressing (St. Louis 1843, Louisiana 1858, Jefferson City 1859, Kansas City 1860) while three other states each had two cities that passed such laws: Ohio (Columbus 1848, Toledo 1862), Illinois (Chicago 1851, Springfield 1856), and Tennessee (Nashville 1850, Memphis 1863). Southern cities included Charleston 1858, New Orleans 1856, and Houston 1861. The authority on this subject is William N Eskridge, Jr. *Gaylaw: Challenging the Apartheid of the Closet* (Cambridge, MA: Harvard University Press, 1999), appendix A2. I found additional municipalities with early anti-cross-dressing laws in Nashville and Jefferson City; the St. Louis date is updated from 1864 in *Gaylaw* to 1843, as seen in *The Revised Ordinances of the City of Saint Louis* (St. Louis, MO) 1843; Also see *The Revised Laws of the City of Nashville* (Watterson, Nashville, TN) 1850; *Revised Ordinances of the City of Louisiana* (B.F. Hesser, Louisiana, MA) 1858; *The Revised Ordinances of the City of Jefferson* (Jefferson, MO) 1859.

3. "Beggars and Vagrants: In Public Houses. Masquerades," (1876) *Text from 1881 edition of NY Statutes*.

4. Clare Sears has shown this play out in San Francisco. See Sears, *Arresting Dress*.

5. Mae M. Ngai, *Impossible Subjects: Illegal Aliens and the Making of Modern America* (Princeton, NJ: Princeton University Press, 2003); Margot Canaday, *The Straight State: Sexuality and Citizenship in Twentieth Century America* (Princeton, NJ: Princeton University Press, 2009), 24.

6. Peggy Pascoe, *What Comes Naturally: Miscegenation Law and the Making of Race in America* (Oxford: Oxford University Press, 2009).

7. Clark, *Desire*, 142–61.

8. For a similar argument of how understandings of one's gender might shift over the course of the long nineteenth century, see Rachel Hope Cleves, "Six Ways of Looking at a Trans Man? The Life of Frank Shimer (1826–1901)," *Journal of the History of Sexuality*, 27, no. 1 (January 2018): 32–62.

9. Their legal name at the time was Lucy Ann Slater. *The Narrative of Lucy Ann Lobdell, the Female Hunter of Delaware and Sullivan Counties* (1855).

10. James Lobdell, 50; Sarah Lobdell, 24; Lucy Lobdell, 20; John Lobdell, 18; Mary Lobdell, 14; Sarah Lobell, 12, in Westerlo, Albany, NY. Sarah was probably really 44. *1850 United States Federal Census.*

11. Federal Census, 1820: 3,458; 1830: 3,321.

12. Lucy Ann Lobdell, *Narrative of Lucy Ann Lobdell, the Female Hunter of Delaware and Sullivan Counties, N.Y.* (New York: Published for the Authoress, 1855), 30.

13. Lobdell, *Narrative of Lucy Ann Lobdell*, 8.

14. Lobdell, *Narrative of Lucy Ann Lobdell*, 8.

15. Lobdell, *Narrative of Lucy Ann Lobdell*, 9.

16. Lobdell, *Narrative of Lucy Ann Lobdell*, 11.

17. Bambi Lobdell thinks James made Lobdell marry Slater. Bambi L. Lobdell, *"A Strange Sort of Being": The Transgender Life of Lucy Ann/Joseph Israel Lobdell, 1829–1912* (Jefferson, NC: McFarland & Company, 2012), 34.

18. George Washington Slater married Lucy Ann Lobdell, Delaware, NY in 1851. They had one child – Helen Slater in 1852. Lobdell Family Tree.

19. Lobdell, *Narrative of Lucy Ann Lobdell*, 24.

20. Lobdell, *Narrative of Lucy Ann Lobdell*, 25.

21. "Extraordinary Performances of a Young Lady," *Washington Sentinel*, Washington, DC, February 4, 1854; "A Young Lady of Varied Accomplishments," *Zion's Advocate*, Portland, ME, March 24, 1854; "Extraordinary Performances of a Lady," *Vermont Watchman and State Journal*, Montpellier, VT, March 24 1854; "Good Girl," *The Pittsfield Sun*, Pittsfield, MA, March 30, 1854; "Miscellaneous," *Christian Register*, Boston, MA, April 1, 1854; "Extraordinary Performances of a Young Lady," *Newport Mercury*, Newport, RI, April 22, 1854; "Extraordinary Performances of a Lady," *New York Observer*, New York, June 15, 1854; "One of the Gals," *Daily True American*, Trenton, NJ, September 30, 1854.

22. Lobdell, *Narrative of Lucy Ann Lobdell*, 41.

23. Lobdell, *Narrative of Lucy Ann Lobdell*, 41.

24. "The Man-Woman," *Port Jervis Evening Gazette*, Port Jervis, NY, August 10, 1876.

25. "The Man-Woman," *Port Jervis Evening Gazette*, Port Jervis, NY, August 10, 1876.

26. "The Man-Woman," *Port Jervis Evening Gazette*, Port Jervis, NY, August 10, 1876.

27. "The Man-Woman," *Port Jervis Evening Gazette*, Port Jervis, NY, August 10, 1876.

28. "The Man-Woman," *Port Jervis Evening Gazette*, Port Jervis, NY, August 10, 1876.

29. "The Man-Woman," *Port Jervis Evening Gazette*, Port Jervis, NY, August 10, 1876.

30. This article is advertised elsewhere in the same edition of the same paper emphasizing the drama of the story, "Her life affords material for an excellent romance. "Another incident," *Port Jervis Evening Gazette*, Port Jervis, NY, August 10, 1876.

31. Lobdell, "*A Strange Sort of Being*," 70.

32. This is the main primary source with the Minnesota material in it. A. C. Smith, "A Wild Woman's History – The Slayer of Hundreds of Bears and Wild-Cats," *A Random Historical Sketch of Meeker County, Minnesota* (Litchfield, MN: Belfoy & Joubert, 1887), 98–111. The story became public amid Lobdell's arrest and may have been printed in local papers and/or in the court record.

33. Smith, *A Random Historical Sketch of Meeker County*, 102.

34. Smith, *A Random Historical Sketch of Meeker County*, 102.

35. Smith, *A Random Historical Sketch of Meeker County*, 103.

36. Rhoda R. Gilman, "Territorial Imperative: How Minnesota Became the 32nd State," *Minnesota History*, vol. 56, no. 4, Making Minnesota Territory, 1849–1858 (Winter, 1998/1999): 154–71, 156 and 160.

37. Gilman, "Territorial Imperative," 158.

38. For work on "third sex" concepts, see William Roscoe, *Changing Ones: Third and Fourth Genders in Native North America* (New York: St. Martin's Press, 1998); for a critique of queer appropriation of native genders, see Mark Rifkin, *When Did Indians Become Straight? Kinship, the History of Sexuality, and Native Sovereignty* (Oxford: Oxford University Press, 2011); for more on the emergence of "two-spirit" as a salient category among Native Americans, see Jenny L. Davis, "More Than Just 'Gay Indians': Intersecting Articulations of Two-Spirit Gender, Sexuality, and Indigenousness," in Lal Zimman, Jenny L. Davis, and Joshua Racla, eds., *Queer Excursions: Retheorizing Binaries in Language, Gender, and Sexuality* (Oxford: Oxford University Press, 2014).

39. For a powerful argument against advocating a fixed notion of a third gender in native communities, especially in scholarship predominantly by or about people of European descent, see Evan B. Towle and Lynn Marie Morgan, "Romancing the Transgender Native: Rethinking the Use of the 'Third Gender' Concept," *GLQ* 8, no. 4 (2002): 469–97.

40. Harlan Pruden and Se-ah-dom Edmo, "Two-Spirit People: Sex, Gender and Sexuality in Historic and Contemporary Native America," Northeast Two-Spirit Society. National Congress of American Indians.

41. Alanson Skinner, "Political Organization, Cults, and Ceremonies of the Plains-Ojibway and Plains-Cree Indians," *Anthropological Papers American Museum of Natural history*, vol. 11, part 6 (New York: Order of the Trustees, 1914), 475–511, 485–6.

42. Smith, *A Random Historical Sketch of Meeker County*, 104.

43. Smith, *A Random Historical Sketch of Meeker County*, 105.

44. Smith, *A Random Historical Sketch of Meeker County*, 105.

45. Smith, *A Random Historical Sketch of Meeker County*, 105.

46. Smith, *A Random Historical Sketch of Meeker County*, 106.

47. Smith, *A Random Historical Sketch of Meeker County*, 105.

48. Henry G. Newton, "Blue Laws of New Haven," *The Yale Law Journal* 7, no. 2 (November 1897): 75–85.

49. J. Hammond Trumbull, *The True-Blue Laws of Connecticut and New Haven and the False Blue Laws Invented by the Rev. Samuel Peters* (Hartford, 1876), 29.

50. Trumbull, *The True-Blue Laws of Connecticut*, 27.

51. Trumbull, *The True-Blue Laws of Connecticut*, 33; Newton, "Blue Laws of New Haven."

52. Samuel Peters, *A General History of Connecticut, from its first settlement under George Fenwick, Esq. to its Latest Period of Amity with Great Britain; including a description of the country, and many curious and interesting Anecdotes. By a Gentleman of the Province*, 2nd edition (London: Printed for the Author, 1782).

53. Peters, *A General History of Connecticut*, 63.

54. Elizabeth Cady Stanton, "Let the Blue Laws Rest," *Omaha Bee*, March 17, 1889, in Ann D. Gordon, et. al, *The Selected Papers of Elizabeth Cady Stanton and Susan B. Anthony: Their Place Inside the Body-Politic, 1887–1895* (Chicago: Rutgers University Press, 2009), 191–4.

55. Elizabeth Cady Stanton, "Let the Blue Laws Rest," in *The Selected Papers of Elizabeth Cady Stanton*, 191.

56. Leon Goodman, "Blue Laws, Old and New," *The Virginia Law Register*, 12, no. 11 (March 1927): 663–73, 663.

57. "The Fundamental Agreement at New Haven June 4, 1639," in Trumbull, *The True-Blue Laws of Connecticut*, 166; Dayton, *Women Before the Bar*, 22–4.

58. "The New Haven Code of Laws from 1655," created by Eaton, was printed in 1656 in London by M.S. for Livewell Chapman and in 1838 under the title *The Blue Laws of New Haven Colony, usually called Blue Laws of Connecticut* and again in 1858 by Mr. Hoadley in volume two of New Haven Colonial Records, in Trumbull, *The True-Blue Laws of Connecticut*, 40–1.

59. "The First code of Laws, Established by the General Court of Connecticut May 1650," in Trumbull, *The True-Blue Laws of Connecticut*. "Honor the Lord's day, public fast days and days of Thanksgiving" (84). Those who do not attend services to hear the minister will be fined five shillings "after due means of conviction used" (84). Fornication between man and single woman punished by "enjoining to marriage, or fine, or corporal punishment" (87). The only provision against gaming banned shuffle board in public houses because they encouraged "much waste of wine and beer" and the punishment was twenty shillings for the keeper, five shillings for each participant (87–8). The law against idleness was vague and broad, encapsulating "common coasters, unprofitable fowlers, and tobacco takers," for whom punishment was left open to the court to determine (89–90). Fine of ten shillings for swearing; in the absence of money, stocks between one and three hours (118). No one under twenty years old could use tobacco (134).

60. Newton, "Blue Laws of New Haven," 79–81.

61. Dayton, *Women Before the Bar*, 58.

62. Trumbull, *The True-Blue Laws of Connecticut*. Trumbull knew what he was talking about as co-editor of *The Public Records of the Colony of Connecticut, 1636–1776*, fifteen volumes (Hartford, 1850–90).

63. Smith, *A Random Historical Sketch of Meeker County*, 132.

64. Massachusetts, which restricted "obscene" plays, films, and publications in 1915. Eskeridge, *Gaylaw*, appendix 2: municipal sex offense ordinances, 1850–1950, 339.

65. The remaining eight are Nashville, TN (1850), Wilmington, DE (1856), New Orleans, LA (1856), Newark, NJ (1858), Charleston, SC (1858), Houston, TX (1861), Memphis, TN (1863), and San Francisco, CA (1866). The authority on this subject is Eskridge, *Gaylaw*, appendix A2. I found additional municipalities with early anti-cross dressing laws in Nashville, Louisiana, and Jefferson City; the St. Louis date is updated from 1864 in *Gaylaw* to 1843, as seen in *The Revised Ordinances of the City of Saint Louis* (St. Louis, MO) 1843; also see *The Revised Laws of the City of Nashville* (Watterson, Nashville, TN) 1850; *Revised Ordinances of the City of Louisiana* (B.F. Hesser, Louisiana, MA) 1858; *The Revised Ordinances of the City of Jefferson* (Jefferson, MO) 1859.

66. Smith, *A Random Historical Sketch of Meeker County*, 106.

67. Smith, *A Random Historical Sketch of Meeker County*, 132

68. Smith, *A Random Historical Sketch of Meeker County*, 106.

69. Jeanette M. Fregulia, "Widows, Legal Rights, and the Mercantile Economy of Early Modern Milan," *Early Modern Women* 3 (Fall 2008): 233–8.

70. Smith, *A Random Historical Sketch of Meeker County*, 106.

71. *1860 United States Federal Census*, Lucy A. Lobdell, 30; James Lobdell, 60; Sally Lobdell, 54; Helen Lobdell, 7 in Hancock, Delaware, NY, 1860 "housekeeper." Sally listed as "insane"; James "farmer," *1860 United States Federal Census*. *1865 New York State Census*, Family: James Lobdell, 55; Sally Lobdell, 55; Lucy Lobdell, 30; John Lobdell, 25; Maryann Lobdell, 22 in Hancock, Delaware, NY, 1865 "daughter." Mary Ann is "wife" probably of John.

72. "Romantic Paupers," *New York Tribune*, New York, August 25, 1871.

73. *1865 New York State Census*, Family: James Lobdell, 65; Sarah Lobdell, 57; Mariah Perry, 32; Lucy Ann Lobdell, 32 in Hancock, Delaware, NY, 1865.

74. "Extraordinary Narrative," *New York Times*, New York, August 25, 1871.

75. "Extraordinary Narrative," *New York Times*, New York, August 25, 1871.

76. The account is generally accurate with minor discrepancies common for the time, such as misidentifying Lobdell's daughter as "Mary" when Lobdell's memoir and the census records call her Helen; "Joe Lobdell and Wife – Their History, &c.," *The Jeffersonian*, Stroudsburg, PA, August 17, 1871; *1860 United States Federal Census*, Lucy A. Lobdell, 30; James Lobdell, 60; Sally Lobdell, 54; Helen Lobdell, 7 in Hancock, Delaware, NY, 1860 "housekeeper." Sally listed as "insane"; James "farmer."

77. "A Romance in Real Life," *Port Jervis Gazette*, August 22, 1871.

78. "Romantic Paupers," *New York Tribune*, New York, August 25, 1871. This story was reprinted numerous places including the *Albany Evening Journal*, August 26, 1871, *Albany Argus*, August 28, 1871, *Schenectady Evening Star*, August 28, 1871, *Lehigh Register*, September 6, 1871, and *Schenectady Reflector*, September 7, 1871.

79. "Romantic Paupers," *New York Tribune*, New York, August 25, 1871. This story was reprinted numerous places including the *Albany Evening Journal*, August 26, 1871, *Albany Argus*, August 28, 1871, *Schenectady Evening Star*, August 28, 1871, *Lehigh Register*, September 6, 1871, and *Schenectady Reflector*, September 7, 1871.

80. "Extraordinary Narrative," *New York Times*, New York, August 25, 1871.

81. "Extraordinary Narrative," *New York Times*, New York, August 25, 1871.

82. "Romantic Paupers," *New York Tribune*, New York, August 25, 1871.

83. "Extraordinary Narrative," *New York Times*, New York, August 25, 1871.

84. "Romantic Lunatics," *Port Jervis Evening Gazette*, Port Jervis, NY, September 21, 1876.

85. "A Mountain Romance," *The New York Times*, April 8, 1877; *Watertown Reunion*, April 19, 1877.

86. "A Mountain Romance," *The New York Times*, April 8, 1877; *Watertown Reunion*, April 19, 1877.

87. "Lucy Lobdell Again. The Man-Woman Becomes a Land Owner in Wayne County, PA," *The Evening Gazette*, Port Jervis, NY, February 26, 1878; "On Saturday Lucy Lobdell," *The Catskill Recorder*, March 8, 1878.

88. "Lucy Ann Lobdell," *Tri-States Union*, April 2, 1878.

89. "Lucy Lobdell," *Tri-States Union*, September 10, 1878.

90. "Our Exchanges" and "Progress of Women's Rights," *The Evening Gazette*, April 12, 1877.

91. "Our Exchanges" and "Progress of Women's Rights," *The Evening Gazette*, April 12, 1877.

92. "Lucy Lobdell Again. The Man-Woman Becomes a Land Owner in Wayne County, PA," *The Evening Gazette*, Port Jervis, NY, February 26, 1878; "On Saturday Lucy Lobdell," *The Catskill Recorder*, March 8, 1878.

93. "Lucy Lobdell Again. The Man-Woman Becomes a Land Owner in Wayne County, PA," *The Evening Gazette*, Port Jervis, NY, February 26, 1878; "On Saturday Lucy Lobdell," *The Catskill Recorder*, March 8, 1878.

94. Lobdell, "*A Strange Sort of Being*," 121.

95. Name of Soldier, Slater, George W. Name of Dependent, Widow, Slater, Lucy A.L. Service G128 NY. Inf. Date 1879 Feb 6, Class Widow, Application No. 241479 Certificate No. 259 782. *Civil War Widow filing Feb 6, 1879. U.S., Civil War Pension Index: General Index to Pension Files, 1861–1934.*

96. *In the New York, Civil War Muster Roll Abstracts, 1861–1900. In the New York, Civil War Muster Roll Abstracts, 1861–1900.*

97. John F. Lobdell, Subscribed and sworn to before Arthur More, Commissioner, June 16, 1880, Delaware County Court; In the Matter of the Lunacy of Lucy Ann Slater; Inquisition Ken J. Marble, Attorney, in Lobdell, "*A Strange Sort of Being*," 195.

98. "Death of a Modern Diana," *New York Times*, October 7, 1879; "A Strange History," *Tri-States Union*, October 10, 1879.

99. Sidney K. Lobdell, In the County Court in and for the County of Delaware; in the Matter of Lucy Ann Slater, a Supposed Lunatic, State of New York, County of Delaware, in Lobdell, "*A Strange Sort of Being*," 185.

100. William W. Maine, Subscribed and sworn to before Arthur More, Commissioner, June 16, 1880, Delaware County Court; In the Matter of the Lunacy of Lucy Ann Slater; Inquisition Ken J. Marble, Attorney, in Lobdell, "*A Strange Sort of Being*," 196.

101. Harry Walsh, Subscribed and sworn to before Arthur More, Commissioner, June 16, 1880, Delaware County Court; In the Matter of the Lunacy of Lucy Ann Slater; Inquisition Ken J. Marble, Attorney, in Lobdell, "*A Strange Sort of Being*," 197.

102. Harry Walsh, Subscribed and sworn to before Arthur More, Commissioner, June 16, 1880, Delaware County Court; In the Matter of the Lunacy of Lucy Ann Slater; Inquisition Ken J. Marble, Attorney, in Lobdell, "*A Strange Sort of Being*," 198.

103. Walter Peak, In the County Court in and for the County of Delaware; In the Matter of Lucy Ann Slater, a Supposed Lunatic, State of New York, County of Delaware, in Lobdell, "*A Strange Sort of Being*," 186.

104. Bambi Lobdell critiques a generation of scholars for presenting Lobdell as a lesbian and denying their manhood. Lobdell, *"A Strange Sort of Being."*

105. "A Curious Life Drama," *Daily Morning*, October 12, 1879 and *The Plattsburgh Sentinel*, November 21, 1879; "The Hunter of Long Eddy," *Sullivan County Recorder*, October 17, 1879.

106. "It Is Reported," *The Evening Gazette*, October 21, 1879; "A Curious Career," *The National Police Gazette*, October 25, 1879.

107. "The 'Wife' of the 'Female Hunter'," *Tri-States Union*, August 10, 1880.

108. "Lucy Ann Lobdell," *Tri-States Union*, October 22, 1880.

109. "A Woman's Strange Career," *The Sun*, New York, October 18, 1880; *Omaha Daily Bee*, February 21, 1882.

110. "Marie Louise Perry is said to be married, keeping house, and living alone in dwelling 35, family 36, Damascus Wayne County." *1880 United States Federal Census*.

111. "The Hunters of Long Eddy," *Rochester Democrat and Chronicle*, February 19, 1882.

112. "An Heiress' Strange Life. Legally married to a Woman Several Years her Senior," *Patriot*, Harrisburg, PA, November 15, 1883.

113. P.M. Wise, "Case of Sexual Perversion," *Alienist and Neurologist* 4, no. 1 (1883): 87–91. For many original transcripts concerning Lobdell, see "Lucy Ann Lobdell: P.M. Wise, 'Case of Sexual Perversion,' January 1883" at http://outhistory.org/exhibits/show/gender-crossing-women-1782–192/lucy-ann-lobdell-p-m-wise.

114. George Chauncey, "From Sexual Inversion to Homosexuality: Medicine and the Changing Conceptualization of Female Deviance," *Salmagundi*, no. 58/9 (Fall 1982–Winter 1983): 114–46, 119.

115. Chauncey, "From Sexual Inversion to Homosexuality", 119–21.

116. Skidmore, *True Sex*; Carolyn Dinshaw, "Born Too Soon, Born Too Late: The Female Hunter of Long Eddy, *Circa 1855*," in David A. Powell, ed., *21st Century Gay Culture* (Newcastle: Cambridge Scholars Publishing, 2008), 1–12.

117. A summary discussion of the issue of "Sexual Perversion" in the *Journal of Nervous and Mental Disease* in 1883 states that there were to date four such cases reported in the United States. This list included the findings of Dr. Allan McLane Hamilton (1881),

Dr. G. Alder Blumer (1883), Dr. P.M. Wise (1883), and Dr. J.C. Shaw and Dr. G.N. Ferris (1883). Dr. J.C. Shaw and Dr. G.N. Ferris, "Perverted Sexual Instinct," *The Journal of Nervous and Mental Disease* 10, no. 2 (April 1883): 185–204, 187–8.

118. Hamilton offered a few case studies of women held at the Hudson River State Hospital for the Insane, including that of a forty-year-old German woman Johanna G. on whom "Quite a beard has grown on chin since her admission," a forty-five year old black woman named Nancy S. described with "irregular tufts of hair upon her chin," a forty-five year old prostitute Sarah H. with "marked tufts of hair upon upper lip, chin, and sides of face" a thirty-two year old Sarah Ann S. with an "abundant beard and moustache of light color." Allan McLane Hamilton, "Upon the Significance of Facial Hairy Growths Among Insane Women," *Medical Record* 19, no. 11 (March 12, 1881): 281.

119. Melissa Stein, *Measuring Manhood: Race and the Science of Masculinity, 1830–1934* (Minneapolis: University of Minnesota Press, 2015). Also see Jennifer Terry, *An American Obsession: Science, Medicine, and Homosexuality in Modern Society* (Chicago: University of Chicago Press, 1999) and Siobhan Somerville, *Queering the Color Line: Race and the Invention of Homosexuality in American Culture* (Durham, NC: Duke University Press, 2000).

8 THE END OF A CATEGORY

1. Joanne J. Meyerowitz, *Women Adrift: Independent Wage Earners in Chicago, 1880–1930* (Chicago: University of Chicago Press, 1988); Joanne Meyerowitz, "Sexual Geography and Gender Economy: The Furnished Room Districts of Chicago, 1890–1930," *Gender and History* 2, no. 3 (Autumn 1990): 274–96; John D'Emilio, "Capitalism and Gay Identity," in Henry Abelove, Michele Aina Barale, and David M. Halperin, eds., *The Lesbian and Gay Studies Reader* (New York: Routledge, 1993), 467–76; Nan Enstad, *Ladies of Labor, Girls of Adventure* (Ithaca, NY: Columbia University Press, 1999); Sharon E. Wood, *The Freedom of the Streets: Work, Citizenship, and Sexuality in a Gilded Age City* (Durham, NC: University of North Carolina Press, 2005); Marcus, *Between Women.*

2. "A Female Husband," *Bismarck Tribune*, November 2, 1883.

3. "Frank Dubois A Woman," *The New York Times*, November 2, 1883.

4. "The Female Husband Confesses," *Wisconsin State Journal*, November 6, 1883; similar account "For a Novelist," *New York Daily Times*, Glen Falls, NY, November 3, 1883.

5. "A Female Husband," *Little Falls Transcript*, Little Falls, MN, November 2, 1883.

6. "The Female Husband Confesses," *Wisconsin State Journal*, November 6, 1883; similar account "For a Novelist," *New York Daily Times*, Glen Falls, NY, November 3, 1883.

7. "Frank Dubois A Woman," *The New York Times*, November 2, 1883.

8. "The Fooled Girl," *The Ogdensburg Journal*, New York, November 3, 1883.

9. Gertrude Fuller, Waupun, Dodge, Wisconsin. 14 years old born in NY in 1866, white female stepdaughter to head of house. Mother Emily Hewett aged 53, Russell Hewett aged 74. 1880 Federal Census.

10. "Evolution of the Man-Woman," *New York World*, New York, November 3, 1883.

11. "Evolution of the Man-Woman," *New York World*, New York, November 3, 1883.

12. "Evolution of the Man-Woman," *New York World*, New York, November 3, 1883.

13. "Female Husbands," *The New York Times*, November 4, 1883.

14. "Female Husbands," *The New York Times*, November 4, 1883.

15. Benjamin H. Irvin, "Tar, Feathers, and the Enemies of American Liberties, 1768–1776," *The New England Quarterly* 76, no. 2 (June 2003): 197–238, 227.

16. Irvin, "Tar, Feathers, and the Enemies of American Liberties," 228–9.

17. "Female Husbands," *The New York Times*, November 4, 1883.

18. "Female Husbands. Professor G. Washington Peck Demonstrates That They Will Never be Popular," *Boston Sunday Globe*, Boston, MA, December 30, 1883; "The Female Husband," *Jackson Daily Citizen*, Jackson, MI, January 26, 1884. Some reprints attributed the essay to George Washington Peck rather than the source: George Wilber Peck. George Washington Peck was a lawyer, politician, and publisher. He held a variety of political offices in his life including Michigan state house of representatives from 1846 to 1847, congressman from 1855 to 1857, and mayor of Lansing Michigan in 1864. He principally worked as a lawyer but also engaged with publishing as editor of the *Lansing Journal* and printer for the state of Michigan. He lived much of his adult life in Michigan. See George Washington Peck, 1818–1905, Biographical Directory of the United States Congress.

19. George Wilbur Peck, 1840–1916, writer, mayor of Milwaukee, governor of Wisconsin.

20. "Female Husbands. Professor G. Washington Peck Demonstrates That They Will Never be Popular," *Boston Sunday Globe*, Boston, MA, December 30, 1883; "The Female Husband" *Jackson Daily Citizen*, Jackson, MI, January 26, 1884.

21. "The Female Husband," George W. Peck, *Peck's Boss Book* (Belford, Clarke & Co., 1884), 138–40.

22. "The Extraordinary Male Impersonation Case: Inquest on the Body," *Belfast News-Letter*, January 22, 1884.

23. "A Woman Married to a Woman," *Daily Gazette for Middlesborough*, January 23, 1884, and "A Female Husband," *York Herald*, January 23, 1884 and "A Female Husband," *York Herald*, January 26, 1884.

24. Havelock Ellis, *Studies in the Psychology of Sex vol. 1 Sexual Inversion* (London: The University Press, Watford, 1897), 96.

25. Ellis, *Studies in the Psychology of Sex*, p. 77–103.

26. Ellis, *Studies in the Psychology of Sex*, p. 94.

27. Ellis, *Studies in the Psychology of Sex*, p. 95, note 1.

28. Ellis, *Studies in the Psychology of Sex*, p. 95.

29. Ellis, *Studies in the Psychology of Sex*, p. 95, note 2.

30. "A Female Labourer in Male Attire," *Derby Daily Telegraph*, January 22, 1884 and "A Female Labourer in Male Attire," *Grantham Journal*, January 26, 1884.

31. "A Female Labourer in Male Attire," *Derby Daily Telegraph*, January 22, 1884 and "A Female Labourer in Male Attire," *Grantham Journal*, January 26, 1884.

32. "A Woman Married to a Woman," *Daily Gazette for Middlesborough*, January 23, 1884, "A Female Husband," *York Herald*, January 23, 1884, and "A Female Husband," *York Herald*, January 26, 1884.

33. Martha testified they were married for twenty-nine years, which would have put their ceremony around 1855. I am unable to verify this.

34. "The Extraordinary Male Impersonation Case: Inquest on the Body," *Belfast News-Letter*, January 22, 1884.

35. The only John Coulter married in Dungannon in the period appears in the Civil Registration Marriages Index for 1859 without specific details of spouse, parish, or minister. Of the eight household members listed, one is named Martha A. Dailey. John Coulter, 1859, Dungannon, Ireland, in the Ireland, Civil Registration Marriages Index, 1845–1958.

36. "The Extraordinary Male Impersonation Case: Inquest on the Body," *Belfast News-Letter*, January 22, 1884.

37. John Coulter, UK and Ireland, Find a Grave Index, 1300s–current, buried in Belfast City Cemetery, death date January 20, 1884; aged 55 years. It is possible that wife Martha is the Martha Coulter who died on December 13, 1896 and was also buried in Belfast City cemetery at age eighty. This would have made her about thirteen years older than John, but it was noted in 1884 during the inquest that Martha was elderly.

38. For a similar argument about Fielding's *Female Husband*, see Sarah Nicolazzo, "Henry Fielding's *The Female Husband* and the Sexuality of Vagrancy," *The Eighteenth Century* 55, no. 4 (Winter 2014): 335–53.

39. "An Awful Sell," *The Pioche Weekly Record*, May 18, 1878; "A Female Husband," *The Inter Ocean*, Chicago, IL, May 25, 1878; *Oil City Derrick*, Derrick, PA, May 23, 1878; *Rochester Evening Express*, Rochester, NY, May 27, 1878; *Jackson Daily Citizen*, Jackson, MS, May 29, 1878; *Pomeroy's Illustrated Democrat*, Chicago, IL, June 8, 1878; *Tiffin Tribune*, June 13, 1878; *Brookfield Gazette*, Missouri, June 13, 1878.

40. Samuel M. Pollard, "This record can be found in the marriage book at the County Courthouse located in Elko Co., NV in Volume 1 on Page 140." Nevada Marriage Index, 1860–1987.

41. "An Awful Sell," *The Pioche Weekly Record*, May 18, 1878; "A Female Husband," *The Inter Ocean*, Chicago, IL, May 25, 1878; *Oil City Derrick*, Derrick, PA, May 23, 1878; *Rochester Evening Express*, Rochester, NY, May 27, 1878; *Jackson Daily Citizen*, Jackson, MS, May 29, 1878; *Pomeroy's Illustrated Democrat*, Chicago, IL, June 8, 1878; *Tiffin Tribune*, June 13, 1878; *Brookfield Gazette*, Missouri, June 13, 1878; wife's name is listed in these accounts, "Interesting Miscellany," *Washington Standard*, Olympia, WA, June 15, 1878; "A Female Husband. A Nevada Bride Marries One of Her Own Sex," *San Francisco Chronicle*, May 19, 1878.

42. "An Awful Sell," *The Pioche Weekly Record*, May 18, 1878; "A Female Husband," *The Inter Ocean*, Chicago, IL, May 25, 1878; *Oil City Derrick*, Derrick, PA, May 23, 1878; *Rochester Evening Express*, Rochester, NY, May 27, 1878; *Jackson Daily Citizen*, Jackson, MS, May 29, 1878; *Pomeroy's Illustrated Democrat*, Chicago, IL, June 8, 1878; *Tiffin Tribune*, June 13, 1878; *Brookfield Gazette*, Missouri, June 13, 1878.

43. "Interesting Miscellany," *The Washington Standard*, Olympia, WA, June 15, 1878; "A Female Husband," *Idaho Tri-Weekly Statesman*, Boise, ID, May 18, 1878.

44. "A Female Husband," *Idaho Tri-Weekly Statesman*, May 15, 1878; Pollard was outed by their wife, who related the story to her uncle shortly after Pollard left the area to escape being implicated in a business partner's misdeeds. Their wife says that Pollard confided in them about their gender on their wedding night and threatened the wife to secrecy.

45. "Samuel Pollard is a Woman," *Morning Appeal*, May 24, 1878.

46. "A Female Husband," *The New Orleans Daily Democrat*, June 16, 1878.

47. "A Female Husband," *The New Orleans Daily Democrat*, June 16, 1878; similar telling in "A Nevada Sensation," *Daily Alta California*, May 31, 1878.

48. "The Pollard 'female husband'," *The Salt Lake Weekly Tribune*, June 7, 1879.

49. "It" was also used in this article, "A Female Husband. A Nevada Bride Marries One of Her Own Sex," *San Francisco Chronicle*, May 19, 1878.

50. "Pollardana," *Morning Appeal*, April 26, 1879.

51. "Pollardana," *Morning Appeal*, April 26, 1879.

52. S.M. Pollard, 1880 Federal Census.

53. Marancy Hughes, Nevada Marriage Index, 1860–1987, "This record can be found in the marriage book at the County Courthouse located in Elko Co., NV in Volume 1 on Page 263."

54. "Domestic," *Daily Inter Ocean*, Chicago, IL, June 8, 1886.

55. Charles E. Hindle, white man 31 years old, born in London, married to Anna Ryan, 22 years old, born 1864 in Canada; Michigan, Marriage Records, 1867–1952.

56. "A Strange Case. A Widow and a Widower at the Same Time," *Tacoma Daily News*, Tacoma, WA, January 26, 1892. Story cites the *San Francisco Examiner*.

57. "A Strange Case. A Widow and a Widower at the Same Time," *Tacoma Daily News*, Tacoma, WA, January 26, 1892. Story cites the *San Francisco Examiner*.

58. "Her Maid Became Her Wife. The Remarkable Story of Actress Annie Hindle's Strange Love," *Kansas City Times*, Kansas City, MO, March 9, 1892.

59. Annie Hindle, Actress, Terrace av n Reserve av, Jersey City, NJ, Annie Hindle, Jersey City, New Jersey City Directory, 1875 and 1879, City Directories, 1822–1995; "A Woman's Wife," *The Buffalo Illustrated Express*, Buffalo, NY, December 27, 1891.

60. "A Woman's Wife," *The Buffalo Illustrated Express*, Buffalo, NY, December 27, 1891.

61. "A Woman's Wife," *The Buffalo Illustrated Express*, Buffalo, NY, December 27, 1891.

62. "Her Maid Became Her Wife. The Remarkable Story of Actress Annie Hindle's Strange Love," *Kansas City Times*, Kansas City, MO, March 9, 1892.

63. "Her Maid Became Her Wife. The Remarkable Story of Actress Annie Hindle's Strange Love," *Kansas City Times*, Kansas City, MO, March 9, 1892.

64. In 1896, Williams was admitted to Sawetelle, a Home for Disabled Soldiers; "Leroy S. Williams," born about 1847 Illinois; admitted 1896 age 49 Sawtelle, LA. Discharged March 23, 1899 – probably to move into own cottage on land. Height 5' 6" and complexion dark; Leroy S. Williams, National Homes for Disabled Volunteer Soldiers, 1866–1938.

65. "Leroy S. Williams, fruits 234 S. Main," Los Angeles, CA, City Directory, 1893; "Leroy S. Williams, fruits and cigars 234 S. Main, r. The Colton 204 E Fourth" Los Angeles, CA, City Directory, 1895; "Leroy S. Williams, Santa Monica, LA, CA, #59; White male, single household head; occupation: Fruit Pedler." 1900 Federal Census; "Leroy S. Williams, merchant of fruits and veggies. Rents house." 1910 Federal Census.

66. Leroy S. Williams (listed with no dependents) Service: A100 Ill, Inf. Date of filing Oct 24, 1890. Class. Invalid Application No. 960,030 Certificate No. 892,201. State from which filed. Ca. Civil War Pension Index: General Index to Pension Files, 1861–1934.

67. "Alleged 'Female' Husband Heir to An Estate," *Los Angeles Times*, November 5, 1903.

68. "Alleged 'Female' Husband Heir to An Estate," *Los Angeles Times*, November 5, 1903.

69. In 1890, Matilda D. Smith was listed as widow of Simeon Smith at 4th and Monroe, Portland, OR; Matilda D. Smith, Portland, OR, City Directories, City Directories, 1822–1995; in 1900, Smith was a thirty-three-year-old widow living with her mother-in-law in Portland's Ward 6, Oregon at 568 Fourth Street. White woman, German born with one child, Mathilda Smith, 1900 U.S Federal Census.

70. Married to Mathilda A. Smith January 10, 1902 in Los Angeles, CA. Williams was fifty-five at the time, born in Illinois 1847. Smith was a forty-eight-year-old, German-born, from Portland Oregon; Leroy S. Smith, California, County Birth, Marriage, and Death Records, 1849–1980.

71. "As to Williams' Sex: Superior Court Wrestles With Knotty Case," *Los Angeles Herald*, March 11, 1903.

72. "As to Williams' Sex: Superior Court Wrestles With Knotty Case," *Los Angeles Herald*, March 11, 1903.

73. "Williams Comes Back," *Los Angeles Herald*, March 11, 1903.

74. "Williams Comes Back," *Los Angeles Herald*, March 11, 1903.

75. "Williams' Sex Not Decided: The Court Orders Curious Case to be Stricken From Calender," *Los Angeles Herald*, March 22, 1903.

76. "Williams' Sex Not Decided: The Court Orders Curious Case to be Stricken From Calender," *Los Angeles Herald*, March 22, 1903.

77. Leroy S. Williams born about 1844, 16 in 1860, lived 1420 Wesley, Will, Illinois with parents John and Susan and many siblings; half-brother James W. Williams later mentioned is about 4 years younger. Leroy S. Williams, 1860 Federal Census.

78. "Alleged 'Female' Husband Heir to An Estate," *Los Angeles Times*, November 5, 1903.

79. "Alleged 'Female' Husband Heir to An Estate," *Los Angeles Times*, November 5, 1903.

80. Pvt. Leroy S. Williams, Died Feb 21, 1917, Los Angeles, CA, buried LA National Cemetery, Plot 31, 7 RW A.

81. Leroy S. Williams born about 1844, 16 in 1860, lived 1420 Wesley, Will, Illinois with parents John and Susan and many siblings; half-brother James W. Williams later mentioned is about 4 years younger. Leroy S. Williams, 1860 Federal Census.

82. John A. Whittman, married January 19, 1906 to Etta Jelley, Independence, Missouri; John A. Whittman, Missouri, Jackson County Marriage Records, 1840–1985, and Missouri, Marriage Records, 1805–2002.

83. "Matrimony Notice," *Kansas City Star*, Kansas City, Missouri, January 22, 1906.

84. Etta Jelley, 3938 Kenwood, Kansas City, Missouri, Occupation: Clerk, 1904; Etta Jelley, 133 Oakley, Kansas City, Missouri, Occupation: Clerk, 1906; Etta Jelley, 325 Roberts, Kansas City, Missouri, Occupation: Binder, 1907; Kansas City, Missouri City Directory, 1904, 1906, 1907, City Directories, 1822–1995.

85. "'Female Husband' Found in Missouri," *DeMoins Daily News*, February 4, 1906.

86. "Matrimony Notice," *Kansas City Star*, Kansas City, MO, January 22, 1906.

87. "Bridegroom Turns Out to Be a Woman," *Tucson Daily Citizen*, Tucson, AZ, January 25, 1906.

88. "The Bridegroom a Woman Married to a Restaurant Cashier by a Justice of the Peace," *Olympia Daily Recorder*, Olympia, WA, February 3, 1906. Similar essay to "Matrimony Notice," *Kansas City Star*, Kansas City, MO, January 22, 1906.

89. "The Bridegroom a Woman Married to a Restaurant Cashier by a Justice of the Peace," *Olympia Daily Recorder*, Olympia, WA, February 3, 1906. Similar essay to "Matrimony Notice," *Kansas City Star*, Kansas City, MO, January 22, 1906.

90. "Matrimony Notice," *Kansas City Star*, Kansas City, MO, January 22, 1906.

91. "The Bridegroom a Woman Married to a Restaurant Cashier by a Justice of the Peace," *Olympia Daily Recorder*, Olympia, WA, February 3, 1906. Similar essay to "Matrimony Notice," *Kansas City Star*, Kansas City, MO, January 22, 1906.

92. "Bridegroom Turns out to be a Woman," *Tucson Daily Citizen*, Tucson, AZ, January 25, 1906.

93. "Matrimony Notice," *Kansas City Star*, Kansas City, MO, January 22, 1906.

94. "Matrimony Notice," *Kansas City Star*, Kansas City, MO, January 22, 1906.

95. "Eventful Career of a Woman Who Became 'Female Husband'," *Indianapolis Sun*, February 6, 1906; *Spokane Press*, Spokane, WA, February 9, 1906; *Seattle Star*, Seattle, WA, February 15, 1906.

96. "Eventful Career of a Woman Who Became 'Female Husband'," *Indianapolis Sun*, February 6, 1906; *Spokane Press*, Spokane, WA, February 9, 1906; *Seattle Star*, Seattle, WA, February 15, 1906.

97. "Matrimony Notice," *Kansas City Star*, Kansas City, MO, January 22, 1906.

98. "Bridegroom is a Woman," *South China Morning Post*, March 30, 1906.

99. "Bridegroom is a Woman," *South China Morning Post*, March 30, 1906; see Skidmore, *True Sex*.

100. Brown, *Beyond the Lines*; Helen Lefkowitz Horowitz, *Rereading Sex: Battles over Sexual Knowledge and Suppression in Nineteenth-Century America* (New York: Knopf, 2002); Patricia Cline Cohen, Timothy J. Gilfoyle, and Helen Lofkowitz Horowitz, *The Flash Press: Sporting Male Weeklies in 1840s New York* (Chicago, University of Chicago Press 2008).

101. Brown, *Beyond the Lines*, 2.

102. Brown, *Beyond the Lines*, 222.

103. Brown, *Beyond the Lines*, 222.

104. "A Curious Career," *The National Police Gazette*, October 25, 1879.

105. "Such a Dilemma. Story of the Loves of Miss Marancy Hughes and Mr. Samuel M. alias Miss Sarah M. Pollard. A Red Hot Sensation," *The National Police Gazette*, June 8, 1878.

106. "Frank Dubois' Trial," *The National Police Gazette*, November 24, 1883.

107. "Frank Dubois' Trial," *The National Police Gazette*, November 24, 1883.

108. "Frank Dubois' Trial," *The National Police Gazette*, November 24, 1883.

109. "Frank Dubois' Trial," *The National Police Gazette*, November 24, 1883.

110. "The Female Husband," *The National Police Gazette*, December 8, 1883.

111. Also see Carroll Smith-Rosenberg, "The New Woman as Androgyne," in Carroll Smith-Rosenberg, ed., *Disorderly Conduct: Visions of Gender in Victorian America* (New York: Oxford University Press, 1985), 245–96; Emily Skidmore, "Ralph Kerwineo's Queer Body; Narrating the Scales of Social Membership in the Early Twentieth Century," *GLQ* 20, nos.1–2 (2014): 141–66.

CONCLUSION: SEX TRUMPS GENDER

1. Lisa Lowe, *The Intimacies of Four Continents* (Durham, NC: Duke University Press, 2015), 3.

2. Mary E. Fissell, "Hairy Women and Naked Truths: Gender and the Politics of Knowledge in 'Aristotle's Masterpiece'," *The William and Mary Quarterly* 60, no. 1, Sexuality in Early America (January 2003): 43–74, 72.

3. Gayle Salamon writes, "Interpellation explains the ways in which my identity has a social life that exceeds my own, that even my 'own' identity, in all its particularity, depends on the names I am called, the ways I am recognized, by others." Gayle Salamon, *Assuming a Body: Transgender and Rhetorics of Materiality* (Ithaca, NY: Columbia University Press, 2010), 123; also see Henry Rubin's call for transgender studies to embrace "a version of identity that is always unfolding and embodied" and "neither reifiable nor internally stable," Henry S. Rubin, "Phenomenology as Method in Trans Studies," *GLQ: A Journal of Lesbian and Gay Studies* 4, no. 2 (1998): 263–81, 279.

4. Joan C. Chrisler, Jennifer A. Gorman, Jen Manion, et. al., "Queer Periods: Attitudes Toward and Experiences with Menstruation in the Masculine of Centre and Transgender Community," *Culture, Health, and Sexuality* 18, no. 11 (2016): 1238–50.

5. I came to this argument after reading Sharon Marcus' similar claim about the question of sexual intimacies within female marriages. See Marcus, *Between Women*.

6. Hitchcock, *English Sexualities*, 45.

7. This was evident in both the popular press and sexology literature. See "Marriages Between Women," *Alienist and Neurologist*, 23, no. 4 (1902): 497–99, in Katz, *Gay American History*, 604, note 59.

8. On the carceral state at the intersection of race, gender, and sexuality in this period and later, see Regina Kunzel, *Criminal Intimacy: Prison and the Uneven History of Modern American Sexuality* (Chicago, 2008); Sarah Haley, *No Mercy Here: Gender, Punishment, and the Making of Jim Crow Modernity* (April 2016).

9. Marcus, "The State's Oversight," 526.

10. Marcus, *Between Women*.

11. Katz, *Gay American History* and *Gay/Lesbian Almanac: A New Documentary* (New York: Carroll and Graf, 1994).

12. Jen Manion "Language, Acts, and Identity in LGBTQ Histories," in Don Romesburg, ed., *The Routledge History of Queer America* (New York: Routledge, 2018), 213–23.

13. Feinberg's self-identification as communicated by their spouse Minnie Bruce Pratt in Bruce Weber, "Leslie Feinberg, Writer and Transgender Activist, Dies at 65," *New York Times*, November 2014.

14. Leslie Feinberg, *Stone Butch Blues* (Ithaca, NY: Firebrand, 1993); *Transgender Warriors: Making History from Joan of Arc to RuPaul* (Boston, MA: Beacon Press, 1996); *Transgender Liberation: Beyond Pink or Blue* (Boston, MA: Beacon Press, 1998).

15. Weber, "Leslie Feinberg, Writer and Transgender Activist, Dies at 65."

EPILOGUE: THE FIRST FEMALE-TO-MALE TRANSSEXUAL

1. Brian Booth, *The Life and Career of Alberta Lucille/Dr. Alan L. Hart with Collected Early Writings* (Portland, OR: Lewis & Clark College, 2003), 8.

2. Regina Moran Sanchez, *Conduct Unbecoming a Woman: Medicine on Trial in Turn-of-the-Century Brooklyn* (Oxford: Oxford University Press, 1999).

3. Skidmore, *True Sex*, 144.

4. "11 Doctors Graduated University Medical School Exercises Held Here," *Oregonian*, Portland, OR, June 10, 1917.

5. J. Allen Gilbert, "Homo-Sexuality and its Treatment," *Journal of Nervous and Mental Disease* 52, no. 4 (1920): 297–322, 321.

6. Married Inez Stark in February 1918 as Robert Allen Bamford, Jr. in California. Booth, *The Life and Career of Alberta Lucille/Dr. Alan L. Hart*.

7. Gilbert, "Homo-Sexuality and its Treatment," 317.

8. "Girls the Better Debaters. All Four Linn County Teams Led by Young Women," *Oregonian*, December 14, 1907; "Committee Gives Prizes," *Oregonian*, May 19, 1908.

9. "11 Doctors Graduated University Medical School Exercises Held Here," *Oregonian*, Portland, OR, June 10, 1917.

10. Peter Boag, "Go West Young Man, Go East Young Woman: Searching for the *Trans* in Western Gender History," *Western Historical Quarterly* 36 (Winter 2005): 477–97. Boag argues that Hart's professional life suffered dramatically, offering a powerful challenge to the "progress narrative" defined by Marjorie Garber as a way to explain how society justified and normalized female to male cross-dressing.

11. "Girl Shaves and Smokes," *San Bernardino News*, February 5, 1918; "Safety Razor and Cigarets Do Not Always Mean Male," *The Seattle Star*, February 5, 1918; "Stanford Girl Tries to Pose as Man Doctor," *Riverside Daily Press*, February 5, 1918.

12. "Girl Shaves and Smokes," *San Bernardino News*, February 5, 1918; "Stanford Girl Tries to Pose as Man Doctor," *Riverside Daily Press*, February 5, 1918; the Seattle paper omitted this line.

13. Gilbert, "Homo-Sexuality and its Treatment," 321.

14. Gilbert, "Homo-Sexuality and its Treatment," 321.

15. "Woman Doctor Attired as Male in Hospital," *Riverside Daily Press*, February 7, 1918; "Dr. A. Lucille Hart Wore Male Attire," *Daily Capital Journal*, February 6, 1918.

16. "Dr. Alan Hart Said to Be Oregon Girl," *Daily Capital Journal*, Salem, OR, February 5, 1918.

17. *Albany (Oregon) Daily Democrat,* March 26, 1918 in Boag, "Go West Young Man, Go East Young Woman," 481.

18. Jonathan Ned Katz connected the dots between Dr. Gilbert's patient "H" from the 1920 study and the person assigned female at birth named Lucille who went by Alan Hart for much of their adult life. Katz, *Gay American History.*

19. The text reads: "1911–12. Alberta Lucille Hart attends classes at Stanford, lives in Roble Hall; she returns for the 1916 Summer Session at the Stanford Medical School. Hart later becomes a 'passing woman' under the name 'Dr. Alan L. Hart.' She establishes a career as a radiologist and author. In 1936, Hart publishes *The Undaunted,* one of the earlier American novels to portray a gay male character sympathetically." In "GALA Week 1984," Stanford University, September 10, 1977–96, MS Lesbian Herstory Archives: Subject Files: Part 2: Breasts-Fem Folder No. 03670. Archives of Sexuality and Gender.

20. "The 10th Anniversary Lucille Hart Dinner," Program at Oregon Convention Center 1991, National Gay and Lesbian Taskforce Records, 1973–2000: Series I: Internal Files Box 13 Folder 36, Cornell University Libraries. Archives of Sexuality and Gender.

21. Emile Devereaux, "Doctor Alan Hart: X-ray Vision in the Archive," *Australian Feminist Studies* 25, no. 64 (June 2010): 175–87, 178.

22. For more on the limits of sexologists on categorizing female masculinity, see Halberstam, *Female Masculinity,* 75–110.

23. A.L. Hart, "An Idyll of a Country Childhood" from the Takenah, Albany College Yearbook, 1911. Booth, *The Life and Career of Alberta Lucille/Dr. Alan L. Hart,* 36.

24. A.L. Hart, "An Idyll of a Country Childhood," 37.

25. "Woman's Idea of 'Dress Reform',' *Oregonian,* Portland, OR, April 1, 1913.

26. "Woman's Idea of 'Dress Reform',' *Oregonian,* Portland, OR, April 1, 1913.

27. Eskridge, *Gaylaw,* appendix 2, municipal sex offence ordinances, 1850–1950, 338–41.

28. Joshua Allen Gilbert, Yale University, Connecticut, 1915, School Catalogs, 1765–1935.

29. J. Allen Gilbert, 1920 Federal Census, Portland, Multnomah, OR. By the 1930 census, he was living alone, J. Allen Gilbert, 1930 Federal Census, Portland, Multnomah, OR.

30. Gilbert, "Homo-Sexuality and its Treatment," see tribadism on p. 310, 312; smoking reference on p. 311; male sexual identifications pp. 314, 316.

31. Gilbert, "Homo-Sexuality and its Treatment," 321.

32. Gilbert, "Homo-Sexuality and its Treatment," 321.

33. Alan L. Hart, Edna Ruddick, Manhattan, NY, May 15, 1925, New York, Extracted Marriage Index, 1866–1937.

34. "Doctor and Idealist: Dr. Mallory," reviewed by Rose C. Feld, *New York Times,* March 31, 1935; "A Modern Crusade: The Undaunted by Alan Hart," reviewed by Louise Maunsell Field, *New York Times,* April 12, 1936; "Books Published Today," *The New York Times,* May 5, 1943; Booth, *The Life and Career of Alberta Lucille/Dr. Alan L. Hart.*

35. "23 Pass State Board Medical Examinations," *The Hartford Courant,* August 10, 1945.

36. "PTA Council Plans Series of Lectures," *The Hartford Courant,* February 24, 1947; "X-Ray Units in East Hartford," *The Hartford Courant,* May 3, 1957; "Medical Specialists Discuss Diseases at Barbour School," *The Hartford Courant,* January 18, 1960; "Dr. Hart to Give

Talk on Radiation at Senior Center," *The Hartford Courant*, June 20, 1960; "Felician Sisters Sponsor 2-Day Health Institute," *The Hartford Courant*, December 20, 1961; "Dr. Hart to Discuss 'Middle Age'," *The Hartford Courant*, March 6, 1962.

37. "Fellowship Dinner Launches Unitarian Fund Campaign," *The Hartford Courant*, April 18, 1961.

38. "First Unitarian Society Elects Mason President," *The Hartford Courant*, April 26, 1953.

39. "Obituary I – No Title," *The Hartford Courant*, July 8, 1962.

40. "British Girl Athlete Changes Sex; 2 Operations Turn Mary to Mark," *New York Herald Tribune (International)* May 29, 1936.

41. "Another Sportswoman Changes Sex, Fourth in Recent Months," *Evening Telegraph (British)* April 21, 1937.

42. "Girl Changes Sex," *New York Herald Tribune*, Paris, August 25, 1937.

43. Meyerowitz, *How Sex Changed.*

INDEX